CW00405518

Cuckoo in the Chocolate

By Chris L Longden

The prequel to 'Cuckoo in the Chocolate,' is 'Mind Games and Ministers' by Chris L Longden.

Chris' blog can be found at http://funnylass.com/

Text copyright © 2017 Chris L Longden

All Rights Reserved

No part of this book may be used or reproduced without written permission of the author except for brief permissions in relation to promotional material. This is a work of fiction; all names, characters, places or incidents are used in a fictitious manner. Any resemblance to actual persons living or dead, business establishments, organisations, locales or events is entirely coincidental.

First Edition, 2017

ISBN - 978-0-9928792-3-5

Acknowledgements:

For the good people of The North

Thanks to: Ian, Ruby and Gregory. My parents for going the extra mile in everything they do.

Leonora Rustamova for the editing and Graham Brown for the proof-reading.

Flora Rustamova - for the cover design and map.

Ian A and Tim T who suffered the early drafts. And everyone who read 'Mind Games and Ministers' and who badgered me to carry on with the story.

LEEDS

be "hippies"
designer
clothes)

HEBDEN
BRIDGE

...kshire

HUDDERSFIELD

HOLME
VILLAGE
(Rachael's Home)

♪ ♪ hills ♫
of the North
rejoice ♪

...rict
National
Park

about 200 miles to...

The Land
according to
Rachael
Russell

THAT LONDON.
Westminster, pigeons, grumpy folk
in black, etc.

THE SOUTH

CHAPTER 1

"Where's Lydia?"

"She's dead. I killed her."

I clutched the steering wheel with both hands, nails arcing indents onto cheap plastic. A seagull - perched on the brick wall next to the car - stabbed at the remnants of someone's Bargain Breakfast Burger. It hesitated, jerking a pin pricked eye at another black-headed chum who was threatening a dive-bomb attack. Threat over, it continued with another greasy beakful. Radio Four jabbered away in the background. Ofsted, Ofwat, Ofcom, if only you'd all Eff-Off, I thought. Then Lardarse Gull's buddy shat on my windscreen, so I flicked the wipers on; a smeary, grey, streaky mess.

I exhaled and tried again. Patience personified.

"Matthew. I've told you before. Making jokes about killing people - about people being dead - isn't funny. At all. Now. Where's your sister?"

"Dunno. Talking to a banana, I fink."

"Right. Stay in the car. I'll be one minute."

I slammed the car door shut, galloped up the steps, into the service station and yes, there was Lydia. Engaged in deep dialogue with a woman who looked to be a good few years older than my own mother. And who - at the unearthly hour of seven-thirty in the morning - also happened to be dressed as a banana.

"Lydia Russell!" I boomed. "Get your arse over here - right now!"

Banana woman ruffled her campaign leaflets, shedding a couple of them onto the gleaming service station floor. All nervy, like.

Lydia scowled at me, then stomped over.

"You just said 'arse', Mum!"

"And I'll be saying a lot more than that if you don't shove your backside into the car, this instant - I thought that you had followed us back outside! And what the hell were you doing with that lady in the banana thing?"

Lydia was braving it out. Arms folded, brown curls bobbing with defiance.

"You should be glad! I was telling her about why the chocolate - what you and the beated-up ladies make - is better than all the other kinds. But she was a bit thick. She reckons that the big bad chocolate companies are all okay now - 'cause they shove a nice-tradey stamp on things."

Here I allowed a small pause; acknowledgment for her efforts.

"Nice try. Glad you've been trying to preach to the masses, Lydia. But you still acted like a total twonk. There's all kinds of nutters hanging around at motorway service stations. And not just elderly people dressed as fruit."

It was going to be a long day.

*****

Normally I'd do anything to avoid travel with two under eight year olds. But this time I had no choice. Pull of the groin? Or tug of the heart? Either way, London was calling.

Now, they do say that travel with small children can be a marvellous way to build the family bond. To foster a greater sense of genetic solidarity. Yeah, well the people who come out with that kind of claptrap should take a wee peek at road traffic accident statistics caused by familial animosity. Stressed-out adults, trapped in a small tin can on wheels with squabbling siblings in tow, is all too often a tragedy waiting to happen.

And my family are a little bit more accident-prone than most.

Hence the absence of Daddy. And me being a little bit prickly about jokes in relation to death and dying. So, although I might be whirlwind woman in all other respects of my life, on the vehicle front, thanks to the loss of Adam, I've ended up with the label of 'Dull Driving Lady,' - "No, Liddy. I'm just cautious."

We set off at Stupid O'clock in the morning and, whilst Lydia's travel sickness had been thwarted by a little pink pill, Matthew had opted for the dodgy tummy handicap, resulting in unplanned stops at various bland service stations down the M1. When the first gleam of the sun began to snake across the carriageway, the kid was already on his third Pull-Up, despite his protestations of "Oi! I don't need no nappies! I'm a big boy!"

Tell that to your sphincter, our Matt.

The banana lady incident had occurred at our third motorway stop. As I frog-marched Lydia away from the fair and fruity brigade, we passed yet another one of those displays featuring plastic tosh, cunningly placed by the evil corporations who own service stations to line the pathways of families en route to toilet. Subsequently, Lydia began to dawdle, ogling at some purple squidgy ball claiming to be 'The Toy that Every Kid is Going Crazy For!'

I snapped at her;

"And don't even think about asking for one!"

"Meany old moo-face," came the response.

So, by the time we were back on the M1, I was already mid-rant;

"Lydia Russell, you're turning out to be an ungrateful little brat! The kind of kid who's obsessed with totally unethically produced products! I don't know why I bother making all this effort to do nice things – like spending time with you. It's not like I want to go to London – I hate London! I would do anything to stay

2

away from London…"

I caught myself just in time. The lady doth protest; just a tad bit too much. Pathetic really. So, I managed to swallow my words. It was the stress, of course; those sixth-former flutters. The anticipation of being in Michael's company again. And not just because he happened to be my parents' local MP, as well as being the UK's Minister for Local Government. Nah.

Rather, it was all down to the fact that a rather steamy encounter had taken place between us at his cottage, some three weeks ago. The sexual shenanigans had been quick off the mark; taking place just a few hours after Michael had ended up spending an Indian summer afternoon with me; a bizarre incident - the watery rescue of one Miss Mary Simpson, an elderly neighbour and constituent of his – whom we managed to remove from her flooded and flea-bitten home. This had all taken place in Stalybridge - a constituency that I didn't happen to be a resident of - but which my parents had been gerrymandered into under the 2013 boundary review.

But despite my initial reaction, that East Mancunian born n' bred default to cynicism, Michael – a man whom my dad had previously described as "a right bloody woofter," and "born with a silver spoon up his arse, never mind in his gob," - seemed very keen to pursue the connection with me; with a person whom I had presumed he would simply view as a one-off weekend-shag. No, he didn't even bugger off into the Parliamentary sunset when the 'News Of The Nation' - the UK's trashiest tabloid - printed photos of him on an uninsured motorbike on Brindleford council estate where we had relocated Miss Simpson into one of Manchester's shabbier hostels. Neither did he seem to be particularly perturbed when pictures were produced of him and 'New Mystery Lady', on that fateful day. We were somewhat semi-naked. And were looking all hot and bothered (although the less sordid truth was that I was investigating his flea bites).

We hadn't been in regular contact so much over the last week, though. The party conference in Brighton had been taking up a lot of his time, and there had been fewer phone calls and emails pinging between us. Resulting in a slight wobble of paranoia on my side of things. So, call me drippy; call me insecure; call me The Town Bike (as my best friend, Kate, does) but the very same week, a blast from the past had very nearly knocked me off balance and back into a certain big bugger's arms.

Shaun Elliot always came with a push-pull effect. This time, the push side of things had been his announcement that Shaun's municipal empire - Medlock Council - was going to yank the funding plug from my own meagre corner of his realm. Heralding disaster. Sisters' Space was more than just my job - more than just your bog-standard women's domestic violence centre up north - it represented a belief system. For all of us, it offered a sanctuary of sanity. Even if we did spend rather too much time bickering about unsavoury sandwich fillings and whose eldest son was back on the Category A Wing of Strangeways this week.

Shaun's pull-effect turned out to be double-edged. The offer of a new job; one that would have involved working directly for the Mighty One. Accompanied by an impressive salary; a rather attractive lure for a lady facing deep financial distress, thanks to a lack of insurance pay-out after Adam's death. And I would be a bare-faced liar if I denied that there were other tantalising Terms and Conditions on offer; a return to those addictive and secretive encounters of the past that had always comprised the Shaun and Rachael Show. And that's Shaun Elliot, you see. A maverick and a maestro at manipulative charm. But he didn't stop there. Shaun also ladled a bit of extra helpings into the bargain; informing me that he was the only person who had twigged that I was the mysterious lady parading in the photos with the Minister. Jealousy? Peevishness? I still wasn't sure of his exact motivation. But all of this added up to nudging me towards a big wobble - or 'relapse' if you had asked know-it-all Kate's opinions on the matter.

But just as I was about to cave in, a lifeline had presented itself. It came in the form of a Jehovah's Witness Miracle Cure. Or rather, Martyn Pointer. Martyn was Shaun's arch-enemy of old – now head of the local housing association and a bit of a religious fanatic - but not a bad egg. He offered to bail out Sisters' Space with a social enterprise loan. So, things had finally begun to look a bit more chipper. Meanwhile, Michael was badgering me about visiting him in London;

"Come on; parcel the kids off to someone. Book the kennels, or whatever. I'll treat you. Vast swathes of Michelin-starred restaurants to choose from here, you know. Surely, you've worn out your season ticket for Compo's Chippy in Holmfirth by now? Don't you fancy a bit of haute cuisine…?"

And Michael could be horribly upbeat; powerfully persuasive. Even after I had reminded him that no-one in their right minds – not even their grandparents – wanted to put up with both Lydia and Matthew overnight, he carried on with;

"Oh, for Christ's sake, Rachael! We can do The Ivy. We can do some God-awful musical that you'll no doubt want to see! I mean - I'll even pay for you to ride on the top deck of a London bus if it tickles your fancy…I know you like your buses. Or was it trams? Or was it those traction engine contraptions that you – or is it your father - has always possessed a bit of an infatuation for?"

At that point, I yielded. Because this throwaway comment meant that he had listened, had actually absorbed some of the prattle that I had subjected him to in relation to my background, which was more than Shaun had ever done, by the way. So, I had replied;

"Well at least I'm not a motorbike freak, like you are. Like … like Adam was. So. Right. Go on then. I'll do my best. Kennels, borstal, Freddy Kruger's Kiddy Care Centre - whatever. I'll try and find somewhere to park them."

The answer to the child-minding dilemma turned out to be a combination of Adam's parents in Reading and my sister - our Vicky, who had defected to

London a couple of years back.

But despite my eager acquiescence and the appearance of a laissez-faire approach to parenting, this northern broad was all strung-out. Not just because Shaun Elliot was trying his hand at puppet-mastery. Not just because the Prime Minister himself knew who I happened to be screwing. And not just because Lydia was still chunnering 'Mum's such a spanner-head' to Matthew under her breath. No. Much of my crabbiness was entirely due to the fact that, very shortly, we were going to be seeing Adam's parents. Guilt parading the same old performance in the production. What would Julia and Malcolm think if they knew the truth? If they realised why I wanted them to look after Matthew for me - whilst I dumped Lydia at my sister's place, leaving me free for a shag-athon or two.

Thoughts sludged their way around my head like an overloaded washing machine, causing me to nearly miss the exit for Reading. I skated my tiny car dangerously over the chevrons, receiving the one-fingered salute from a bald bloke in a Land Rover. And then, as always, the natural course of guilt-induced thinking skittered towards Shaun. Thank God, that Adam's parents had never known anything about Shaun; about Shaun and Rachael Round Two, occurring just a few days after their son's funeral.

I gave my head a good hard shake. Reminding myself that after I had waltzed out of Shaun's swanky office only yesterday – telling him where to stuff his job offer – I had promised myself not to waste any more brain synapses on the man that my closest pals referred to as 'Shaun the Shithead'.

Still, obsessive-compulsive sexual activities and accompanying shame is a tough habit to break in just a couple of decades.

We only had to face one more Pampers 'Pull-Up' pit-stop before we arrived safely at Julia and Malcolm's home on the outskirts of Reading. My in-laws were sitting by the living room window; all set for our arrival. All grins and matching leisure wear (Adam would have ridiculed them for the duplicate tracksuits, but then - his parents – his prerogative).

Julia looked older, frailer than when I saw her last, but she couldn't contain her elation as both children cannon-balled into her arms, with the obligatory cutting remark from Lydia;

"Watch out, Nanna. Matthew stinks like a poopy-pants!"

Lydia and I scoffed our elevenses before we dashed off for the train station, and I reminded Julia that "even when Matthew's got a dodgy tummy, he still eats anything. Other than pizza or pasta, mind. Not sure why he's taken against the Italians, but there you go."

"Dagos, we used to call them." Malcolm interrupted, all booming bass tones just as Adam had been. "But you can't say 'Filthy Wop Dagos' anymore these days, can you? Political correctness gone mad, it is!"

I ignored him.

"So, Julia. If Matthew starts being a total pain in the bum, I've packed his Power Ranger DVDs. Give him a good hour to come down after watching them, though. Oh, and if you take him to your church on Sunday - don't let him near those prayer cushion things."

My mother-in-law chuckled;

"Oh yes. The last time he went with me, he bit a hole in one of them…"

A few minutes later, we were whisked off to Reading station. As he pulled the car into the station forecourt, Malcolm shot me a wan smile.

"It's great to see the kids again, Rachael. This depression thing of Julia's, since we lost Adam…Well. It's the grandchildren that she lives for now, you know. I keep thinking… if only we'd never moved down south. But you never dream that something like this would happen, do you?"

No, Malcolm. Not even in my worst nightmares could I have ever imagined that my husband would have driven his bike off the edge of Cape Point in South Africa. A freak motorcycle accident. Not something that you could ever prepare for. And if only Adam hadn't been as laid back, as flippant about such grown-up matters as forking out for travel insurance policies that included cover for 'dangerous sports'.

I shook my head, batting the black clouds away as I manhandled my little suitcase and Lydia's overnight bag out of the back seat of the car.

"Nope, you don't," I replied. "But, as Adam would always say – life has to go on. Still, I just hope that Matthew doesn't exhaust you both. I realise it's a bit of an ask to be swapping him with Lydia, when we get back on Sunday. I know that you want to spend time with her too, but I feel a bit guilty … hope you don't think that I'm taking advantage…"

"Don't be daft, Rachael," he dismissed me with a shake of his head. "You never get a minute to yourself. Just have a bit of fun with your sister. Let your hair down. And give her our love, won't you?"

I smiled woodenly. Lying Toe-Rag Rachael. I thanked him for the umpteenth time.

"Bye, Gramps!" yelled Lydia, her corkscrew curls twirling in the draught of the station forecourt. "If Matthew is naughty, you're allowed to slap him - hard. Until his teeth rattle, okay?"

Two saffron be-robed Buddhists sandal-shuffled past us. They eyeballed us strangely. Lydia gawped back and hissed at me;

"You don't get folk like that in Yorkshire, do you Mum?"

"No. They've generally got enough sense to stay down south and away from the likes of us. Now, come on you," I propelled her forward. "Got a train to catch."

We boarded for London.

CHAPTER 2

Lydia hadn't been on a train;

"Since Grandma took us to Manchester Art Gallery and had a massive row with Grandad because she made us look at all the boring paintings, when all he wanted to do was go to the Football Museum."

The kid was itching with excitement. I tried to urge her to read a comic book and to listen to 'Jesus Christ Superstar' on her headphones, but Andrew Lloyd-Webber was no match for the First Great Western. Next, she badgered me to let her visit the loo at the end of the corridor by herself, but this turned out to be a mistake as it took her only five minutes to unearth her latest victims. I then had a bit of a battle on my hands; trying to dissuade her from extracting money from tipsy Scottish football fans, who were heading for the big England versus Scotland match at Wembley. But Lydia seemed to think that being paid a pound a time to shriek '*Scoooootland!*' every time a bloke shouted at her "Tell Es whoose goonna win todaay lessie?" was easy money.

As Liddy was being taught the words to 'Scotland The Brave', my phone began to ring. I had taken a day's leave in order to manage a long weekend away, but when I saw that it was Martyn, I took the call. This could be too important to get all prissy about the no work today rule.

I had known Martyn for donkey's years; from way back when we worked together with Shaun and Jake. We had all been based at Whalley Range housing office, overseeing Manchester's council estates. Even then, Martyn and Shaun had been career rivals and today they were still pitched up against each other, with Shaun heading up the Communities and Leisure Directorate at Medlock Council and Martyn the Chief Executive of New Banks – the housing association which had taken over the council's housing stock. So, whether the issue happened to centre on homelessness statistics, food banks, disabled adaptations or photo opportunities with young lacklustre apprentices – the two men were forever trying to shaft each other. But these days, thanks to Martyn's offer of the interest-free loan, he was on my Very Best Mates list.

Martyn originally hailed from Blackburn but he had lost a lot of the burr after twenty-odd years of living in leafy west Didsbury ("they castrate your accent, when you move to that side of Manchester, they do," my dad had always said). In fact, his clipped tones on the phone perfectly reflected his straight as a die approach, or his 'poker up the arse attitude' as Shaun had always referred to it as.

"Rachael. How are … But what on earth's going on at Sisters' Space today? Sounds like you're having a bit of a sing-song over there…"

I stuck a finger in my ear, trying to drown out Liddy and her gang and moved into the corridor.

"Well, Martyn, I'm not sure whether I should feel insulted that you've mistaken a bunch of drunken Scottish football fans for the women at Sisters' Space…I mean, I know that we can all get a bit lairy at times, but we're not that hard-arsed…"

Martyn laughed. "Ah yes, I thought I recognised the strains of 'Loch Lomond' there. Oh dear. Living up to their testosterone-induced stereotypes, eh?"

"Nah, Martyn. Let's not sound like regionalist bigots. Three of them are drinking herbal tea from the buffet car and two of the fellas are snogging the faces off each other."

"Gosh. But ... anyway. Sorry, Rachael. I forgot. You said that you were having the day off today. I shouldn't have—"

"No. No problem. My daughter is entertaining our new pals here. I'd rather speak to you anyway. What's up?"

"Well. Two things really. Dawn Hibbert – now that we've sorted her out with a house, I'll need assurance that she'll keep it all schtum about the location of her new place. We don't want that idiot turning up and trashing the property."

I had met Dawn and her young family during the mercy mission to rescue Mary Simpson. Dawn and co had been fleeing yet another beating at the hands of her thug of a partner, Vinnie. We had managed to get them into the safety of Brindleford's hostel, with Michael surprising – and impressing - me as he managed to calm Vinnie down; making the most of what little that they did have in common. The two loves of their lives turning out to be? Motorbikes and The Military.

I tried to give Martyn my utmost assurances. I had already impressed the importance of this onto Dawn. But at the end of the day you can't always keep this kind of thing quiet. Kids in particular - have a habit of blabbing stuff out to others. Martyn knew that. But he was a bit of a worrier, a bit of an old woman, was Martyn.

"But, Rachael, the main reason that I'm calling you, is this. Something that I should have foreseen, I suppose. Shaun Elliot seems to be refusing to sign the paperwork. The referee section in the final application for the social enterprise loan, I mean."

"Refusing? Why?"

"Can't rightly say. Can't get him to return my phone calls in order to discuss it. His PA is being all very evasive about it…"

"Yeah. The Rottweiler can be a total bitch…sorry. Not very PC of me to say so - I know, but…yeah. That doesn't surprise me."

"Indeed. Indeed. But what's really bothering me is that we've only got until next Thursday to complete. Otherwise we'll miss the boat. And I can't understand why he wouldn't want to agree to … I mean - it gets the whole issue off his back, doesn't it? Of his department being responsible for closing Sisters' Space. He'd be crazy not to go for it. He'd get shot of all the negative publicity that your closure would be bound to generate for him. The redundancies of your staff alone - never mind pulling the plug on victims of violence! It would look dreadful for Medlock council, so I really can't see why…"

I clicked my tongue.

"Yes – but you're forgetting that Shaun doesn't mind the odd bit of 'negative publicity'. He courts controversy. And, let's face it Martyn – at the end of the day, the problems facing a load of women who have been attacked and brutalised has never really tugged at the heartstrings of the great British public. People tend to care more about abandoned donkeys, don't they?"

"But surely even the likes of Shaun Elliot would want to see you succeeding with getting your ladies back on track. Or am I sounding very naïve here …?"

The train's corridor door swooshed open and a giddy Liddy pranced through, cheeks aglow as a result of catching a case of north of the border excessively high spirits.

"Oh hello, Mother!" she shrieked. "There you are! I was worried that you might have thrown yourself out of the window and killed yourself. Because you don't like lots of noise, like what we're all making. Do you? See ya! Wouldn't wanna *be* ya!"

She span around and crashed through the doorway again. Back to her mates.

"Yes, you're sounding desperately naïve," I told him. "And whilst I can't really tell you what Shaun's motives are…"

I could attempt a bit of a guess on it. But I won't be sharing that one with you, Mr Pointer.

"… you're right to be worried, Martyn. This is going to be a real pisser, if he doesn't sign. I mean - what the frig *is* that total nobhead playing at?"

A tiny chink of silence. A wee reminder to me of Martyn's Jehovah's Witness credentials. Which I always seemed to somehow forget, in my conversations with him.

And then he sighed.

"I don't know, Rachael. As far as I'm concerned, Shaun Elliot never did have a strong moral compass. And these days it seems that it's all about the car, the status, the face in the media – all of this kind of thing being much more important to him than the original reason most of us went into this line of work."

I was tempted to comment on Martyn's one hundred and fifty thousand pounds' salary, plus pension, car, expenses da di da as head of New Banks. But I kept my gob shut.

"… Still, regardless of that, Rachael. Surely, he'll listen to reason if you contact him. Had a chat. You always got on better with him than I did."

Don't snort. Don't give it away, Rachael. Poor Martyn had never had a clue about all of that. Hardly anyone did, in fact.

"Look, I'm happy to give him a call on Monday, but I'm not ringing him today…"

Definitely not today. Because here, streaming towards Paddington Station, it already felt like it had happened a year ago. Although in fact, it had only been yesterday, when I had rushed to Shaun's office to confront him about his plans to close us down – and when he had ended up kissing me. And wanting something more; much more. So I was planning to stay as far away from him as I possibly could.

Because all of that had been a momentary lapse. A happen-stance hangover. Silly bint.

"Fine, Rachael. Monday will be fine."

"And I'm not begging him, Martyn."

"Of course not. But do use that legendary charm of yours. People like you, Rachael. And you're much better looking than I am – ha-ha."

There was a sudden burst of applause from the train compartment. A jarring cheer and a couple of inebriated 'Wa-heys!' I wondered what Lydia was up to now.

"Right. Look, I'd better go and rescue that lot from Lydia. But yeah. If you've not managed to get his signature by Monday, I'll call him and give it a shot."

Bloody great.

The train was bang on time and my sister was waiting for us at the top of the platform at the station. Lydia launched herself at her aunt and Vicky lost all the usual reserve that she kept for adult company, plastering Liddy's neck with lipsticked kisses. She gave me her usual, almost stand-offish, hug and then glanced at a rather expensive looking watch.

"Right. Let's get a late lunch. Plenty of time before you said you were going to meet your … uh … 'friend.'" She cast a quick glance at Lydia. "Uhm. Yes. That friend of your mum's who's going to drag her round all of the boring museums and do… cultural stuff… the kind of thing that kids really… hate."

We found a small cafe just outside the station. After we had ordered the food we continued to struggle with adult conversation, thanks to Lydia's constant tirade of questions in relation to policemen, red buses, homeless people, taxis and the inevitable;

"Why does everyone in London wear black? Do people keep dying here or what? So… do you still have the Bubonic Plague here? Are there rats in every toilet?"

Vicky was doing her best to extract information on who I was going to be staying with, but having Lydia around was a useful excuse not to go into too much detail. She knew that there was a man involved in the equation of big sister's jaunt to the Capital and she quickly gathered that I wasn't willing to part with any more information.

It wasn't that I didn't trust her to be aware of the Me and Michael thing. Vicky was the sensible, grounded sort. Not easily impressed by celebrity or status. I was pretty sure that she wouldn't get all blabbermouth about it. And it wasn't that I didn't want her to know that I was seeing someone. In fact, Vicky had been aware of what had happened between Shaun and myself so soon after losing Adam - and she hadn't judged me for it. No, instead, she had directed one hundred per cent of her disgust in the general direction of Shaun, ratcheting up her ancient hatred for him by another notch or two. If that was at all possible.

So, my need to keep quiet wasn't about Vicky. It was all about my own issues; my own reservations. That East-Mancunian born and bred default to negativity-tendency, again.

Don't get your hopes up, lass.

After a quick farewell, I finally set my face towards the Underground and then cast a glance over my shoulder. Lydia was instructing my usually far too sensible sibling to "Skip!" away from the station. I left them hopping and jumping towards the bus stop, and made my way down the escalator. As a prejudiced northerner, I noted that it was good to see at least two people in commuter-belt central who weren't looking like the usual dark-clad and dour-looking miserable sods who tend to hang out there.

I battled with the little suitcase on wheels, trying not to trip people up with it. Adam had always hated such contraptions – he would insist on picking them up and carrying them.

"They're a completely selfish and dangerous invention. Designed to cause accidents or to inconvenience pedestrians. They're like … the Hummer of the travel and luggage accessories world. But a lot smaller. Obviously."

A burst of sadness flowered in my chest. At the thought of Lydia and Matthew going through the rest of their lives without these silly little memories. They would never be able to recall any of Adam's random pet hates; taxi drivers who beeped their horns instead of *"getting off their fat arses and going to the door,"* Manga cartoons, cling film, swimming hats, Steve Wright in the Afternoon, cottage cheese, talcum powder. A whole set of encyclopaedias could have been commissioned; 'The Life and Dislikes of Adam Russell'. How could just one man feel so personally affronted by the bizarre trivialities of everyday life?

By the time the tube had reached Westminster station, I had managed to override the melancholy and smile at the memories. The glum looking passengers sitting opposite me clearly thought I was a loon.

Adam on our honeymoon in Madeira as he grabbed a hosepipe and drenched a huge bush filled with cicadas because;

"That non-stop bloody chirping is driving me mental!"

The clang and the creak of the high-security turnstiles at Westminster station jolted me back to the present moment. Cold air slapped my cheeks as I reached street level again, and the brassy tones of Big Ben informed me that there was at least another hour to kill before I was due to meet Michael in Parliament Gardens. Thankfully I had a few caseworker reports to check over before he was scheduled to put in an appearance. Yet at twenty-five past he still hadn't arrived, and I was beginning to tell myself that the whole promise of scorching hot sex on the menu for this weekend had been too good to be true. I resorted to checking which tube line would be the fastest in order to take me back to Vicky's place. But at that very point, I heard a soft tread from behind me and a pair of hands suddenly cupped themselves over my eyes. A whiff of tobacco, of dusky herbs. An apology for lateness in those charmingly well-bred tones of his. Some banter. A lingering kiss. A promise of more. And then an insistent;

"Right. Tube station. And for God's sake, let me carry that suitcase thing for you. Bloody silly contraptions. Things like that should be outlawed in crowded places. I'll get onto the Ministry of Stupid Luggage, pronto."

I sensed a smile over my shoulder.

And I began to relax.

CHAPTER 3

Michael's 'second home' - his London place - was an elegant Georgian flat, based just around the corner from Bedford Square. It was cosy and tidy, with every room containing bookcases crammed to the hilt with paperbacks and hardbacks. He had made a point on several occasions of telling me that he was;

"A bit of a technophobe. And I'll never do e-books. Over my dead body. Never."

The London apartment had quite a different feel to the earthy, more bohemian cottage back home in his constituency. Michael's other home was in Mottram - a sweet little village nudging rural Derbyshire away from East Manchester's urban sprawl, although my dad has never been a fan, "Wouldn't live in Mottram for a gold bloody clock. Full of your traffic and your green welly brigade with their Range Rovers."

Mottram had been the subject of 'we need a bypass' bickering for some fifty years now. But despite local conjecture - that the crossroads where L.S. Lowry had once ambled about had somehow morphed into Birmingham's Spaghetti Junction - Michael's flat in central London was still a world apart from his Mottram place. Here was the roar of the traffic, the ever-present drift of honking car horns, the sounds of emergency sirens. Here there prevailed no wildly overflowing cottage garden, no Morning Glory going crazy. No random bits of Michael's motorbike scattered about the hallway, or yellowing towers of The Guardian. But in many ways, I thought, as I noted a six-foot-long African tribal spear leaning next to the fireplace, it was just as child-unfriendly. And that was one of the other little dilemmas that I had been struggling to deal with.

Michael Didn't Do Kids.

And personally, I would also like to have done Less of the Kids. But I had very little choice in the matter, these days.

The view from the front of the flat was of a typical formal Bloomsbury street scene. At the back however, there was a private and expertly manicured quad shared with the other buildings, accompanied by a remarkable vista, taking in some of the more superior architecture of north London. You could even see the top of the London Eye. I murmured my appreciation;

"This is hardly what you led me to believe, Michael. The view, I mean. Dead pigeons and fire escapes is how you described it…"

"Well. I knew that you wouldn't grace me with your presence if you thought it wouldn't meet your own peculiar form of inverted snobbery. You seem like the kind of girl familiar with dead rodents and back door exits in grotty alleyways."

"Oi!"

"Shush. Now. How about we finish the property inspection with a little look at the bed itself…?"

He pulled me to him and his hands travelled to the back of my jeans. Squeezing my bum with his fingers. I sighed.

"God, that feels good."

"It's better with less clothing on, you know."

"We could always try that."

"I've missed you."

"Have you?"

He moved my hand to his crotch and murmured;

"Can't you tell?"

"Show me the bed then."

An hour later and we were snoozing in each other's arms, with my cheek on his chest, squashed up against a sprinkling of springy auburn and grey hair. But Michael suddenly sat up in bed, causing me to wonder if my semi-conscious state had resulted in me inadvertently slobbering on him.

"Bloody Hell!" He said. "It's just gone five o'clock! And I'm taking you out for the evening, in what…? In about twenty minutes. So, you'd best get yourself ready. Get changed - put some girl-clothes on etcetera."

His eyes met mine, hesitating for a moment.

"… Not that you don't already look ravishing. In your, erm… Black Sabbath t-shirt and, well. No pants on at all. But women usually want to faff about with make-up and hair and changing clothes and things…" I stared at him for a minute. No comment. He added. "Don't they?"

I answered with a shrug.

"The thing is… I don't actually have a change of clothes with me. Although I did bring a nice pair of shoes. Won't I do like this? Well, when I've got my knickers and jeans back on, of course." I glanced down at my t-shirt. It already possessed a dodgy looking stain from where Lydia had coughed her yoghurt drink all over me during the train journey. The jeans? Well, they weren't great either. They contained a wadge of stickiness in one of the back pockets. I suspected that this was a result of Matthew and his recently acquired fixation with Swizzel Drumstick lollipops.

Michael was biting his bottom lip. But then he tried to flash me an ebullient smile.

"Oh no. That's fine. Really. You look absolutely lovely in those. Don't worry about that for a minute. I mean, I don't mind if you don't. You look great. And Black Sabbath. Well. They're just fantastic, aren't they? Great rock band. Or metal. Whatever you call it."

I burst out laughing. He looked surprised. And then relieved.

"Oh – you! And that bloody sarcasm of yours! I've not missed that bit of your repertoire."

He grabbed me, pulling me back down and onto the bed. A kiss ("to shut you up!") as his fingers walked their way back down towards my thighs. I nudged him away.

"Look, if you really do want to go out for the evening, then yeah – I admit it. I need a good twenty minutes. So, you'd better stop this right now. And I do happen to have something with me that might make me look a little bit less like a dossy old trollop."

After a slapdash shower, slipping on a frock and adding a dab more slap to my face, I was ready.

"Right. Am I looking respectable enough?"

He cast a pair of appreciative eyes over me.

"Lovely. Perfect." Green-grey pupils travelled downwards and locked themselves onto my chest as he nodded. "And you'll be giving the busts at the British Museum a good run for their money there."

"Hmm. But it'll be nice to visit the British Museum again. I used to love wandering around the Elgin Marbles when I lived in London myself, many moons ago."

I hesitated. Very nearly confessing to him that the first time I visited the museum, I had been surprised to discover that the Elgin Marbles were not, in fact, great big round balls; bigger, shinier versions of the tiny glass things that you got in 'Ker Plunk'. But I didn't follow through. I didn't want him to think that I was a complete ignoramus; I'm not. It's just there are certain elements of information that don't get covered in your average northern comprehensive school education (i.e. artefacts in the British Museum) and certain stuff that does (whether it's possible to whip off the screws on your maths teacher's moped in the three minutes it takes him to have a fag break).

"Ah yes," said Michael. "Back when you were a mere slip of a lass and doing your assistant for MP's side of things. Larry Underwood, wasn't it?"

"Yeah."

"Lecherous leftie lunatic."

I punched his arm.

"Well, I liked him!"

His dimples twinkled;

"Well you would. Older men. In politics. Getting a bit of a track record, aren't you?"

I was about to wallop him again when he tapped his watch.

"Alright. Enough of the domestic violence, you hypocrite. Best be off then." He locked the front door and we made our way down the steps and into the chilled air of an early October evening. I asked him;

"So, what's this speech going to be about? Are you going to be revealing just how much of the contents of the museum - how most of our so-called 'British Heritage' - has been nicked from inferior and uncivilised cultures?"

"No. Not quite. Although I'm sure that your Marxist pals - like your friend Jake up in Manchester - wouldn't agree. It's exclusively about *real* British history; an archaeological thing. Roman excavations from East Anglia - military stuff, actually."

Should have known.

Something else that happened to provide occasional pluck at the strings of discord between us, was the fact that Michael also didn't Do The Pacifist Thing. Which Rachael Russell - former member of CND - definitely did embrace wholeheartedly.

He turned to close the gate behind him. I asked;

"Were you asked to do this speech because you served in the army - before you went into politics?"

"Sort of. But more so really because I've always had a huge interest in military history. My first degree at Oxford was in History. I specialised in ancient warfare and weaponry."

We were walking towards the British Museum, my arm linked through his.

"History?" I asked. "All career politicians plump for Politics, Philosophy and Economics, don't they? Jolly old PPE."

He shook his head. "Well you shouldn't make such presumptions. And I would have thought that you should already be aware that no one in politics likes to be referred to as a 'career politician.'"

"Ah well. I'm sure that you're all capable of getting over it…"

"…No, history was the first great love of my life. With the second being the military, the army, as you know. The third love must be politics, I guess."

I wondered what the fourth love of his life might prove to be. Embarking upon professional board membership. Most likely earning megabucks as Chairman of some huge multinational company after retiring from politics. Presiding over the inadvertent massacre of a rare breed of innocent penguin on the other side of the world in a desperate fracking bid, no doubt.

He interrupted my internal ruminations on the lives of the privileged with;

"And besides - you're wrong on the PPE front. Most people who end up in politics didn't study that sort of thing. Blair did History at Oxford, too."

"Great. Shame he didn't pay more attention. We might not have ended up with the Iraq side of things…"

We were strolling slowly through Bloomsbury Square itself, our fingers entwined together, but his phone rang. He let go of my hand and gestured 'one minute', whilst he took the call.

I perched on the edge of a wooden seat as he moved a couple of yards away, tucking the phone under his chin and managing to light a cigarette whilst tossing the empty packet into a litter bin at the same time. The bench and the bin suddenly reminded me.

Of Shaun and the Attack Of The Wasps. Of the huge barney that had taken place between us just a couple of weeks ago, in the park next to the Women's Centre. An argument that he had goaded me into, when I had refused his job offer. In fact, this had been rather a monumental row for me; the only time ever that I had let rip in such a direct way. I had told him, in no uncertain terms, just exactly what he had put me through in our relationship; both the first time around - back before I had met Adam - and then the damage that he had inflicted on me more recently, trucking up after the funeral and resurrecting our affair. Yes, Round Two proved to be even more devastating for me, because our sequential attempt at sneaky sexual shenanigans had somehow involved him forgetting to tell me of one small fact. That he was now married to Saint Jess.

Yet even the insects buzzing around the litter bins during that lunch time slanging match hadn't managed to sting him. Shaun Elliot; both Teflon coated and wasp resistant. Was this the fault of his adoptive parents? Had they unintentionally taught him that he was God's Gift? Or was the bugger just lacking the cognitive ability to process emotional empathy? In the past, my best friend Kate had veered between referring to him as either 'an overbearing emotional illiterate' or 'your typical moral coward.' When she wasn't calling him a 'total and utter dick', that is.

CHORLTON-CUM-HARDY, SOUTH MANCHESTER. SEPTEMBER 2001

"Jesus Christ, Rachael! Jesus! Look at that!"

Shaun lay on his back. My cheek squished against his chest. Fragments of glitter – my lipstick and his sweat - sparkled along his torso, down to his belly button and beyond. We had planned a secret early afternoon liaison at my place in Chorlton and it had been a busy lunch hour so far. Thanks to the joys of flexitime. In fact, it was rare for us to ever stop and pause, to snooze for a minute during our encounters. Rabbits had nothing on Shaun and me.

"What?" I groaned, all semi-slumber. "Post-coital telly-viewing is incredibly impolite, you know, Shaun. Especially if it's the bloody news."

"Shush!" he growled and sat up. Nudging me to one side and grabbing one of my pillows. For one minute I thought that he was going to smack me round the head with it – start a play-fight. But instead, he clutched it to his chest.

I followed his gaze. The picture on the TV was of an enormous building – a skyscraper –

azure skies behind it, above it. But there was a squall of white smoke billowing out its side. And then the camera jerked. And the tower collapsed. Just went.

My first thoughts were of Fred Dibnah. Britain's most legendary expert on all things detonation and tall chimneys. Fred lived just a street away from my Uncle Will and Auntie Sue and he was more northern than a slab of parkin. My Dad's claim to fame was that he had once bought ol' Fred a pint of dark mild in the Talbot Arms. He was a real character, was Fred.

"Oh, my God! Shit!" said Shaun. "Jesus. Shit!"

Shaun's outburst shook away all thoughts of what Fred must be up to these days.

"What's... what?"

"Twin Towers in New York. How did we miss...? One just collapsed – about an hour ago, they said. And looks like... we just saw the other one go."

I removed myself from his chest and sat up in bed, my eyes blinking away the blurriness, peering at the screen.

"You're kidding!" I said. "How the hell would... can that have happened?"

"Plane hit the first one a bit ago, they said. And then another plane flew into the second one. Few minutes ago. They've both... gone."

"No way! No! That's just – that would never happen. Are you sure that's what...?"

"Shush! Let me listen!"

So, we sat there, spellbound. Propped up against the crappy MDF and foam headboard, huddled underneath my purple paisley duvet. Shaun was rarely stuck for words or for opinions. But here we were, both captivated, both horrified as we watched the re-runs of the footage of planes colliding, of buildings collapsing. Over and over; again, and again. I got out of bed at one point to make us both a cup of tea. But Shaun let his go cold. And then we heard reports that another plane had smashed into the Pentagon.

At around three-thirty PM, I commented;

"Now this is all a bit different for us, isn't it? I mean, we never get the opportunity to watch films together in bed, do we? And this is real life. Bizarre or what? And far more morbid and horrible than the usual crap action films that you're always going on about..."

At that moment, we both jumped at the sound of loud rapping on my bedroom door.

"Shit," Shaun said.

"Jake's back already," I whispered. "That's a bit weird." Shaun glanced at my bedroom door. It didn't have a lock.

"Rachael, honey?" Jake called. "Are you in there? I just saw your car outside. Is everything alright?"

"Yes, fine, Jake. Everything's fine."

"Because I've just been doing some visits on Moss Side and came past and noticed that you're home. You're sure you're okay?"

"Yes. Course I am."

"Only... I just wondered. What with you and all of that listening to Celine Dion a bit too late at night when you're on your own... and... and oh - the news just now! Have you heard? Isn't it awful? New York! They're saying that it's those Al Qaeda lot who've done it."

19

"Yeah. It's terrible. Terrible."

"Can I come in? Are you decent?"

"No. Not really, Jake."

Jake was surprisingly slow on the uptake today, but after a few seconds of silence we heard;

"Ah. Oh. Oh, right. Right. I'll be… I guess I'll be off then."

"Yeah, ta. See you later."

"Right. Sure. I'll return home, when…" his voice became flatter, "in whatever amount of time might allow Shaun sufficient leeway to be able to cover his tracks. Yet again. Do let me know when it's convenient for you both - for me to return to my own flat - won't you?"

I heard the front door slam and then, a few seconds later, his car engine start.

"Dunno how you can stand living with Bamber-boy," Shaun muttered. "Thinks he's your mother."

"Yeah, no doubt she'd have a negative impact on my sex life, too, if she shared this place with me."

"Shush," said Shaun. Eyes back on the TV.

"No, I won't 'shush'!" I poked his ribs with my thumb and then gave his stomach a sloppy kiss. "What's wrong with you? We took the afternoon off to be together. I'm not at all happy about your bloody terrorists, interrupting my afternoon of rampant sex!"

Shaun shifted himself upwards and away from me. He folded his arms. He looked straight ahead and then I saw the spark of light in the brown-black pupils vanish.

"Poor you," he said.

And then I realised what I'd said – what I'd done.

The TV blathered on. A woman - early forties, maybe – an office worker from the City, in London, was being interviewed outside a dreary British workplace by a journalist.

"I mean, people from our company work in those buildings over there in… I mean, I'm on the phone to them every day. I know all about their kids, their lives, their... It's just. I can't get my head round it. I really can't. And to be honest… I just want to get home and to my family now. On a day like this, you just want to be with your family, don't you?"

Fifteen minutes later and Shaun was back on the other side of Chorlton. At home with Jess. And with Ozzy the cat.

And that was the last time. That we were together.

For some twelve years.

End of Round One.

Sixteen years later and I still hadn't quite figured out Shaun's overall psychological profile. But one thing was for sure: his natural tendency towards egocentricity central had mushroomed even further as his career reached loftier heights – matching his six foot five inches frame. But, if I'm going to be brutally honest about it, what naffed me off more than anything else was the fact that an ever-present sexual frisson remained between us. No, that's the wrong word. Not frisson. I had frisson with Michael. And with Adam it had been deep love and camaraderie. What did I have with Shaun? Something akin to a binge-purge cycle. Hardly sounds attractive, does it? Unless you've been there yourself. In which case, you'll be catching my drift.

Michael had finished his phone call.

"Chief Whip. About today's vote. And he's heard on the grapevine that the News of the Nation journos are still after my blood. God knows why. You'd think these muck-rakers would be more interested in your B-list celebs rather than an old duffer like me."

Only a handful of people happened to know the identity of the newspaper mystery gal. They included Dawn, the woman who we rescued from getting beaten up by her partner, Vinnie Murray, and Shaun - who had recognised the mole on my shoulder in the photograph and who chose to further ratchet up the pressure on me by accusing me of jeopardising the reputation of Sisters' Space and his local authority. Oh, and then there was also this other bloke who calls himself the 'Prime Minister.' Along with his top PR aide, Alex The Twat (a name that I bestowed upon him after he referred to me as 'The Merry Widow From Manchester'). Still, Michael – a man possessing an unusually blasé attitude to political life – seemed only to profit from the tabloid tattle; enjoying the fact that the narrower minded souls of the British population were now commenting along the lines of; 'and we all thought that he was gay! The little tinker!'

Ha-bloody-ha.

"Oh, God," I said, trying not to nibble at my already worn-down nails. "Don't tell me that Simone Shaw and that arse-wipe of a newspaper think that they've got something else on you?"

He slipped his phone back into his pocket and took my hand, pulling me up from the park bench.

"Oh, no. Nothing to worry about. The Brindleford Biker story is yesterday's news. Although I'm still receiving plenty of cryptic messages from colleagues in relation to Michael and my mystery squeeze."

"Well, thank God that you could only see my back in the photo…"

"And a very nice back it is too," Michael added. "That dress that you've got on does it superb justice. I'm looking forward to getting you out of it again after we've had dinner…"

I wobbled on my heels and nearly fell over. Can a shoe with a quarter of an inch wedge be counted as a 'heel'? For a woman who has dyspraxia and who lives in walking boots for most of her life, believe me, it can.

Iron railings girded the hulking mound of the British Museum. Michael had told me that we were attending a private reception. An exclusive little soiree for intellectual military history buffs.

As the last dregs of the tourists exited the grounds, the invited guests clip-clopped in, white cards clutched in their hands. I couldn't fail to note the expensive standard of attire adopted by The Romano British Military Appreciation Society - as they liked to refer to themselves. And there was I – clad in my charity shop frock. But these days I was surprising myself. It didn't really bother me. These days I felt every bit as attractive and as nicely turned out as the London lot. Perhaps Michael's endless reserves of happy self-assurance were rubbing off on me.

As people began to smile and nod at him, I also noted that my initial fears of being 'out there' as the Minister's current squeeze were fading too. A few weeks ago, when the photos had appeared in the press, I had been adamant that I didn't want my identity to be revealed. This was mainly because of my family. Michael did happen to be my parent's MP after all and my dad and his mates – not fellas to mince their words – were none too keen on what they referred to as 'that slimey upper-class, nancy-boy, right of centre pillock.' Yes, they have quite a little group of pseudo political-intellectuals down at the Stalybridge Allotment Society. And, the thought of what Adam's parents might think of me having another relationship had been a cause for my concerns. Plus of course, there was Lydia's classmates to consider; "Lydia's mum is shagging some posh old bloke in London! Bleurgh!" - Yes, seven year olds can be cruel.

But now? Now the attention and the buzz heralding Michael's arrival at the British Museum was proving to have a rather unexpected effect on me. An aphrodisiac charge. In fact, I was seized by an impulse to offer him a fast and furious quickie right there and then in some random public lavatory. But he dampened my ardour somewhat by turning to me and muttering;

"Right. I'll go and chat to the incontinence brigade. You wait with Brian."

"Brian? Who's Brian?"

"Who's Brian? You are joking, aren't you?"

I shook my head. Michael looked skyward again. "Brian has been following us ever since we left the flat."

He stabbed a finger and I glanced over my shoulder. A burly looking man, dressed in dark colours, was about eight feet away from us; sporting an ear piece. Michael crowed;

"A-ha! You really didn't notice him, did you? I've said this before, but I'll say it again. You do have dreadful observational skills, Rachael Russell. You'd never do well in the army."

"I'll take that as a compliment then. So… Brian. He's another Trevor, is he?"

Trevor had been the security man on the evening that I had stayed over at Michael's Mottram cottage. Poor Trevor got to sit outside the house and watch out for recalcitrant bombs whilst Michael and I enjoyed copious amounts of red wine and - later on - a bit of how's yer father. Well, I say 'poor' Trevor, but Michael had assured me that "the guys from Special Protection aren't your usual minder-sorts. They're highly skilled and are paid an absolute packet. More than MP's, you know. Risk involved and all of that."

"Yes," Michael nodded. "Brian changes shifts at midnight with another fella. Trevor's back on tomorrow morning for me."

"So, has… was he walking behind us the entire time?" I lowered my voice. Not wanting Brian to realise just how slow on the uptake I can be at times.

"They never leave our sides. Whether we're in the car, or on foot."

"What…? Hey. Hang on. Even when we met outside The Commons, earlier on?"

"Of course. Following your senior Ministers about has to be taken a lot more seriously back here in London than in the constituency. Because, despite the odd happening north of Watford, most terrorists are surprisingly lazy. They prefer to have a pop at you in the capital."

His eyes moved from mine to Brian's as he beckoned the man over.

"Brian – Rachael. Rachael – Brian. Although Brian's colleagues do like to refer to you as 'Giant Haystacks', don't they?"

"'Fraid so." A surprisingly high-pitched voice for such a mountain of a man. I held out my hand and he shook it;

"Well, I think that that's very rude of people to say that, Brian. I saw Giant Haystacks in a wrestling tournament at Hyde Town Hall back in the '80s. And you're much better looking than him. And a lot less sweaty. Less hairy, too."

Brian stared at me, unsure as to how to reply. But Michael answered breezily;

"Oh, never mind her. She's a northerner. No airs and graces. Now Brian, do keep an eye on Rachael, won't you? She's been fretting that no-one will talk to her because she doesn't own a pashmina."

He gave us both a wink and then wandered off to a group of fawning elderly ladies, one of whom appeared to have a dead peacock stapled to her hat.

I grinned at the bodyguard;

"So, Brian. Can you show me how to do an elbow-drop on Michael, then?"

Poor Brian. Gobby, common bird for companionship, nothing but farty little canapés to nibble at and a lecture on rotted military corpses from over two thousand years ago. Still, as Michael was forever claiming, Brian and his type were apparently paid more than your average MP was to put up with this sort of thing.

I already knew that the Minister was a gifted orator, and his speech went down well. But to be fair, it would have been hard not to please this room full of folk who were enthusiasts of all things short and stabby from several centuries ago. Afterwards, Michael ushered me to the museum courtyard and to where a government car had mysteriously manifested and was waiting for us. Brian was to be our all-singing and all-dancing driver, bodyguard and romantic chaperone for the evening. He drove us to one of North London's most fashionable restaurants – Bella's. I had never heard of the place.

"Not Bella Pasta, then?" I chirped. Michael looked blank. He had probably never experienced the joys of other 1980s fast food chains, either. Wimpy and Pizzaland would have passed him by during his Oxford days; it would have been Brown's or The Randolph or dining in halls kitted out in scholar's cap and gown, for the likes of him.

I tried to relax and enjoy the meal, but the atmosphere of Bella's – the blindingly white table linen (soon covered in my food and wine splashes), the swathes of air-kissing women in their designer what-nots and the minuscule portion sizes - soon had me fantasising about a proper bacon butty back at Holmfirth's key tourist attraction – 'Compo's Café'. Along with a good old fashioned milky coffee to wash it all down with.

Adam always made out to be Compo the Tramp – drinking his spilled tea from the saucer - whenever we visited our favourite haunt. I would tut at him and he would tease me further, leering; "Show us yer wrinkled stockings, Nora. An' I'll let you have a fiddle with me ferret."

Lydia could remember those laid back, laughter-filled Sunday mornings very clearly. She had recently asked me if it "would be a nice thing to do – to leave a big bacon butty and a cup of Yorkshire Tea on top of Daddy's grave." I had nodded, "Lovely. But we won't take Matthew with us. He's such a little greedy-guts. And there's probably a law against consuming things that people have left on top of graves."

Michael whispered to me;

"Is that beatific grin because Colin Firth just sat down at the table behind us?"

I shook my head and decided not to tell him about the fantasy fry-up at my husband's headstone.

"No. I'm smiling because the great thing about these small portion sizes is that you can scoff them all really quickly. And then you can bugger off back home, for more sex."

Michael looked surprised. But he was clearly happy to oblige as he began to clear his plate furiously.

And I can't deny that bumping into the likes of Ewan McGregor, Jude Law and Mr Darcy himself that evening had me feeling somewhat friskier than a ferret myself.

Shafts of sharp autumnal light spliced naked legs and crumpled sheets. We lay together, gazing out at a teal-blue Bloomsbury sky. We had made our recreation.

24

Time and again. Pink-fleshed, blue-veined; a few stretch marks (mine) and greying hairs (his) between us. But there was still plenty of charge there. Hardly Gone To Seed yet. And the only noise pollutant - aside from our own grunts and murmurs - came from the lustful cooing of the pigeons, their interim pecking at the windows as they stabbed for the Autumn dead-leg wasps. (Damn those wasps, reminding me of the row with Shaun. Again.)

My eyes roamed the sparseness of the whitewashed walls for a while.

"Michael – this place. Your flat here. It baffles me. It's so very different to your cottage in Mottram…"

He hoisted himself back onto one arm and double-bent a pillow, propping his head up against it, as he gazed at me.

"How do you mean? Because there are no marauding Stalyvegas types? No die-hard constituency evangelists like Graham the Griper - getting his knickers in a twist about the latest scandal over the timing of traffic lights and cars that queue-jump the outside lane on Mottram Moor?"

I smiled. "No." He kissed the hollow between my collarbone and neck. "No, silly. I mean that your place in Mottram is a bit more… well. Mad. Messy…"

He shrugged.

"I suppose that that does seem rather peculiar. Given that I spend a lot more of my work time in London than up in the constituency. You'd think that *this* place would be a bit more of a bomb-site, wouldn't you? But actually, I'd say that my home here is less about me. More detached, if you like. I always feel that…"

But his words were interrupted as my phone began to beep. I shuffled off the bed and rooted around in my bag to switch the sound down. The constant pings and burps of emails and texts had irritated me all night, after retiring to bed, but I hadn't had the wherewithal to leave the arms of Michael in order to tackle it.

"Oh, bollocks. Just look at this!" I brought my hand back out of the suitcase pocket and showed him the phone. It was covered in something brown and sticky. "Before we left the house yesterday, I asked them both to help me with a quick tidy up and one of them - Matthew probably - shoved a piece of 'Marmite toast' into the pocket."

The little git had also stashed away some broken chalk in there. And a popped balloon.

"God, even my suitcase is a shambles. You should see my house, Michael. I mean, how the hell do people manage to keep their homes clean and tidy? How do you keep your place here so pristine?"

"Easy," answered Michael. "You make a very conscious decision never to have children because they're horrid, demanding little things. And instead, you opt to hang about with the slutty sorts who can't even keep a clean and respectable suitcase – but who at least you can get a good, hard shag from once in a while…"

His fingers beckoned me back to the bed and I shook my head.

"No. Bugger off. You're a right one, you know, Michael. Most people who aren't keen on kids at least try and pretend to like them when faced with the parents of small children…"

He considered this.

"Well, I'm not a complete ogre. If there did happen to be a couple of kids hanging around the place today, I'd at least try and be nice to them. I'd let them go and sit outside in the ministerial car with Brian, or whoever, for twenty-four hours."

I crawled back onto the bed and he began to kiss the back of my neck, but the mention of Special Protection outside reminded me;

"Do you ever wonder if the flat could be bugged?" Michael moved his face away, looked around the bedroom and then whispered in my ear;

"Does it matter? Can we not be a bit exhibitionist about these things? Would it really bother you if someone was listening in?"

I chewed my thumb. "I don't know. I've never really had to think about it before. Well. I wouldn't want my parents hearing this. Or my children. Or the woman next door…"

"It's a man next door," said Michael "He's very high up at City Hall. Good pal of the mayor."

"No. I meant the old lady. The woman who lives next door to me. Mrs Finnigan," I replied.

"Well what on earth would Mrs Finnigan be doing here in London?" he asked, nibbling my earlobe.

"Oh, stop it!" I answered. "No – not the earlobe thing. You can carry on with that. I mean, joking about being bugged. I can't believe that you could be so blasé about that kind of thing."

He half sat up, but moved his hand to my inner thigh and murmured;

"Yes, well. It goes with the territory, I'm afraid. Unpleasant as it is – the thought of someone listening to us right now - it's hardly like we're talking government secrets, is it? It's not like I'm in bed with the Secretary of State for Home Affairs, is it?"

I scowled at him.

"So, you don't mind – because you're in bed with some bit of fluff from Up North. Someone whose brain wouldn't be able to retain a state secret, if you happened to mention one …"

He dropped his head to one shoulder and fixed me with the steely-Chiswick gaze. The one he liked to whip out of the bag for evil journalists and members of the Opposition.

"Actually, Rachael, I don't mind being 'listened in to' anytime. Because in my opinion, if you're going to get to the top of this profession, you'd be pretty stupid not to think that you aren't – sometimes – being listened to by others. You have to think ahead in this game. For example, if you assume that every conversation is being overheard, well, it can put you on a different playing field to the rest of the amateurs...."

I prodded a finger into his chest.

"Get you – Mr Politician Big Shot. Mr Risk Taker... Mr Bring 'Em On!"

He shut me up by pinning me down and attempting to tickle me. I only managed to get him off me by threatening to wet the bed. Well, it always works for Lydia when Grandad is getting a bit silly with her.

We spent the rest of Saturday morning horizontal, but headed out for a lazy lunch in a local coffee bar. By the end of the afternoon, as the light was fading, we were back in bed and remained there, ordering a pizza delivery - rather than leaving for the outside world again. I wondered how Michael was managing to ignore his mobile phone, but he simply said;

"This is one weekend that I decided to have a proper break from everything. So, if they want me, well – the people that really matter – they've got my landline number."

So much frenetic sexual activity was accompanied by the best sleep that I had had in nearly two years.

Adam and I had barely found the time for sleep - never mind the opportunity or the energy to have sex – during our last couple of years together, what with the jobs and the kids.

But Shaun and I? Well. We found the time for sex, alright. At the price of a considerable chunk of my sanity.

On Sunday morning I awoke to a peculiar cooing noise. But it was just the pigeons again. I squirmed up against Michael, snaking my hand around to the small of his back, my fingertips brushing up against the welts of scarring. "War wounds," he had joked - the first time that I had noticed them. But he hadn't elaborated on his comments. I kept meaning to ask him about them but the time never seemed to be right.

My phone began to trill and I scrambled out of bed - a naked scamper over to my bag.

"Rach?" It was Vicki. "There's been a bit of an accident."

At those words my spine seemed to crumple.

Somehow, I found myself sitting on the bedroom floor. Trying to speak, but only managing a half-croak – *What?* - into the phone as it very nearly slipped from my grasp.

There was a pause as Vicky collected herself.

"No, sweetie - nothing bad! God, no – don't worry – not that type of… Oh, sorry petal, no. It's just me. I got out of bed, half-asleep, to let the cat out and I tripped down the stairs. They think I've broken my ankle."

"Oh…Oh, thank God. I thought…"

"I know. I'm sorry… for making you think…"

"No, it's just that…"

"No – no. No. Really – it's just me. I should have… Sorry. Look. We're okay. We're at the A and E now. Me and Lydia. Liddy even phoned for an ambulance for me - bless her. She's been a little star." I could hear Lydia's voice in the background, protesting;

"And I've had no breakfast yet. Nowt!"

"So, they're just going to x-ray me and see what's what. But I can't really look after her for the rest of the day. And… I think I could do with a bit of help getting home from the hospital…"

"Oh. Of course. Thank God. Sure." Relief pouring through my veins. The blood began to pound in my ears;

Left, right, left, right. Like soldiers marching a drill in my head, as my heart tried to unscramble itself. Back to normality.

Michael shuffled to the side of the bed, concern etched into his face.

Return to Logic, Rachael. Rationality, please.

"Okay, Vicky," I folded my hand over my eyes, trying to screen out Michael's piercing gaze. Trying to dredge up a semblance of privacy. "So, Vick… tell me where you are? I'll come and get you. We'll get a… we'll taxi you back, or whatever."

From having lived in London many moons ago, I knew that St. Tommy's was just a hop and a skip away, on the Northern Line. I promised her that I would be there ASAP. Then I hung up. At this point, all attempts at mustering some sort of dignity collapsed. My hands began to flap at my face as I tried to gulp down oxygen. Michael moved off the bed. He was kneeling beside me;

"What's happened?"

I tried to explain, but the words didn't seem to be arriving in the correct order. His hands were on my shoulders.

"Jesus. You're freezing, Rachael. You're… you're shaking like a leaf."

A rapid spooling back from my subconscious. To the day when the police arrived on the doorstep. I suddenly remembered all of it.

I had been catching up on The Archers - although Lydia had been drowning out the crisis over effective silage as she watched her DVD of 'Cats' at top volume for the umpteenth time. Matthew had just tried to eat a fading poinsettia because Lydia had told him it was a magical plant from Father Christmas.

We were due to attend the birthday party of some random kid from Liddy's class – a child who I had never even met. But all of a sudden, it was a change of plans.

The female police officer had urged me to take a seat at my own kitchen table. She had a small hole in her black fifty-denier tights, just below the knee. I thought:

Bet she bought them from Primark in Leeds. Because I tried to get a pair that were ribbed like hers were, the other week. And Huddersfield don't offer the same range. And it's not like I want to go all Harvey Nicks but it'd be nice if provincial towns got a look in on a decent hosiery selection, once in a while;

This blokey copper-fella wants to tone down the aftershave a bit. And it's true what they say about the police looking younger these days. Bet he's never even heard of Adam Ant;

I've just spent a fiver on a crap birthday present for a five year old kid who'll never get to see it. Who can we give it to, instead? Or should I just send it in via school in the morning with an apologetic note – sorry for our absence yesterday - but Daddy had just been killed and I didn't fancy chatting with competitive mums about SATs scores and gluten-free biscuit products.

The policewoman had been nice, though. When I kept repeating different variations of the sentence; "this is all my fault for winning the toilet roll competition – I shouldn't have entered it. I never fancied the idea of a trip to South Africa," she finally took my phone from me and called my parents to come over.

The policeman, I was less partial to. He didn't take his shoes off at the front door. And he left the toilet seat up afterwards. Adam had been an all-rounder sit-downer. Men should always ask the lady of the household about their preferred bathroom etiquette, before they go and pee in your loo.

I fought for air; a descent into blackness.

But Michael was on the case. He hoisted me off the floor and back onto the bed. Then he ran to the other side of the room, bringing back a dainty paper bag, embellished in green and purple swirls of paint. The colours converged before my eyes as he thrust it under my nose, and for one dreadful moment I thought that I was either going to puke all over the expensive bedspread or be sick into the natty, little bag. (Big turn off, Rachael.)

"Breathe in. Breathe into it. And out again," he instructed. "You're just hyperventilating. That's all. Come on – you can do better than that. Big breaths," he urged, whilst rubbing my back.

After two minutes, the dizziness and nausea cleared. I crept back under the bedsheets, drawing them up to my chest. Excruciating embarrassment; shy suddenly - at the acres of bare skin that existed between us.

I thanked him and wiped my nose with the back of my hand, because the dratted thing seemed to be dripping. He fished out a tissue from the box at the side of the bed and handed it to me. I dabbed at my face.

"Well, it was… it's just our bloody Vicky falling down the stairs. Done her ankle in… Liddy's fine. She's fine. God, I feel like such a… pranny now. Total idiot. Total numpty."

He smiled, with such grace. Rust-tinted eyelashes flickering downwards. And yet he was still naked, still clearly at ease with the conversation, the circumstances.

"So, tell me. Does that happen to you a lot?" he asked. "Is this the normal course of reaction for you, every time your sister embarks upon something particularly... silly? I suspect that something else was going on for you there?"

I nodded. The first time that I had seen this skill, this ability to talk so naturally about such monstrously massive issues, had been that evening in his cottage when I had recounted the tale of Adam's death. My eyes blurred and I tried to focus on the beautifully embroidered eiderdown.

"Well, Vicky isn't the kind of person to spring this sort of thing on me – on anyone. She's Ms. Independent. She doesn't do the ditzy little sister act. And yes… this has never happened to me before. My reaction, I mean. Maybe all of that was some sort of a panic-attack thing."

He nodded.

"I mean, if either of the children had been with me, I don't think that I would have reacted like that. It's just that this is the first time since Adam…Well, since I've been away from them and with... with someone else."

He rubbed my shoulders hard and I sighed, my stomach finally relaxing. The flash of nausea had passed and my insides were grumbling – but this was now with hunger. Michael poked my belly and commented,

"We need to get something to eat before we go and rescue your sister. Sort your blood sugar out."

I was still clutching the crumpled-up bag, so I attempted to straighten it out and handed it back to him.

He furrowed his brows. I liked the lines that lived there.

"Hmm, well. Thankfully I removed what was in it before you started manhandling it…. Hang on."

He got off the bed again and ambled, naked, to the other side of the room. My eyes lingered on his body again. Broad in his shoulders and a more than pretty-fit physique. I knew that he went for runs and worked out regularly at the Westminster gym. But his body didn't smack of vanity, thank God. Padding back towards me, I grinned lustfully, suffocating it into the duvet. It was hardly the given mode of behaviour; getting all hot and bothered again about another man, so soon after having experienced some sort of panic attack – a flashback – about the death of your husband.

He placed a square, black case in my hands. And coiled inside it lay a thin, gold necklace; a tiny, delicate chain with an oval pendent. It glittered in the early morning light.

"It's beautiful." I paused. "Is it for me?"

"Of course. It probably wouldn't look so good on me, now, would it? Here, let me help." He reached over for it and I dipped my head forward as he fastened it around my neck.

"… I hoped that you might like the whole… idea of it. But after buying it, I realised that I've never seen you wearing any jewellery - so I've been fretting a bit - that you might have an allergy or something. Or that you could have conscientious objections to precious metals… I know that you Up The Worker sorts can get a bit sniffy about where you buy things from."

I shook my head.

"I did stop wearing jewellery when I had Matthew, because he had a good go at breaking every little bit that I've ever owned. But – oh. Michael. It's gorgeous." I held the pendant between my finger and thumb. "It's so dinky! What is it? A yin-yang symbol… or something?"

He cocked his head to one side. "Can't you tell, Rachael? I would have thought that you, of all people, would have realised."

It was a semi-circle. As though someone had spliced a tiny egg into two halves. With a slight dimple in the centre. I shrugged.

"I can't believe that you don't recognise it! It's a cocoa bean, of course."

"Oh. Oh, wow. That's so… that's just so lovely. You found a shop that made these? That's just…"

I played with the bean between my finger and thumb and pulled it upwards in order to look at it again more closely. We had plenty of sample cocoa beans knocking about at work, and the walls of Sisters' Space were plastered with photographs of the women in Ghana that we sourced our cocoa from, as they lugged enormous sacks of the fair trade beans about. But I had only ever seen the things in their varying shades of brown, mocha, tan. It was the gold that had thrown me.

Michael heaved himself off the bed and began to pull his clothes on.

"Ha, no. I didn't find a shop that made them. I just happen to know this fantastic goldsmith. So, I asked him to design me one… you know… look up some photos and do it. And he's made quite a natty little job out of it, don't you think? But the only snag being… that I forgot about you and your evangelism for ethical trade. So - it might not be your right-on sourced gold or whatever. But you can always flog it on EBay if it doesn't meet your human rights' standards. Ha ha."

"Don't even joke about that, Michael! It's just… Well. It's lovely."

"Goodo. Right." He clapped his hands together. "Now – I'm going to get a few pieces of toast on the go. We'll slap some marmalade on it and we'll grab a quick bite and a strong cuppa before we set off to liberate your family from the clutches of the NHS."

He moved off to the kitchen, as I remained sitting on the bed, tracing my finger over the necklace. I was aware that it must have cost Michael more than double – perhaps even triple - the Russell household's average weekly food shopping bill to buy this little giftie. But that wasn't the element that shocked me.

It was the inevitable comparisons.

What had Shaun ever furnished me with?

A second-hand book on research methodology, during the 1990's.

And that pair of socks he once left at my house. By mistake.

Mind you, he *had* sent me flowers for the first time ever, just the other week. But the bouquet had been sandwiched in between him trying to bribe me with a job and then informing me that he was going to pull the funding plug on Sisters' Space.

So, the flowers didn't really count.

Did they?

CHAPTER 4

Stepping into St Thomas' A and E, I immediately heard my daughter's not-so-dulcet tones. Standing with one hand on hip and the other pressed up against a pane of glass, she seemed to be advising someone about the exploitative tendencies of vending machines. An elderly gentleman was attempting to feed money into the coin slot with his tremulous hand. Lydia was brassily directing at him;

"Whatever you do, don't go for B1. Its eighty blummin' pence - for a packet of crisps! That's, like, nearly a whole week's pocket money! You'd be daft going for that one. And crisps won't fill you up as much as a nice healthy snack would. You should have thought ahead today, shouldn't you? You could have brought something from home and saved your money. You just need to plan a bit better." Echoes of my dad in her phraseology there; 'Tightwad Terry', as my mum referred to him, was never one to pay over the odds for anything.

Rheumy eyes bulged in disbelief at Lydia. But she was unaware, squishing her face against the glass of the machine.

"So, go for a C6 then. Flapjack, I think you'll be wanting. Press C6. Go on. No! Don't press *that* one, you daft...! That's a B – you don't want a B now, do you?"

The old man looked around anxiously. Yearning for another grown-up to assist him with standing up to the tiny tinpot dictator. My daughter's eyes followed his, flicking towards me.

"Mummy! You've come to rescue us! They've put a pink potty thing on Auntie Vicky's leg. It stank to high heaven when they wrapped it up with that wet stuff. And she's in a wheelchair too." Lydia pointed to a corridor. I couldn't get a word in edgeways. "It was a little bit scary when she fell down the stairs. With no other grown-ups about to help us - and she wasn't even drunk, you know!" Two nurses strolled past us and sniggered.

Lydia turned her attention back to the machine, but the man had seized the moment and deposited his coin. His purchase fluttered to the bottom of the vending machine and he began to push open the plastic flap on the machine. Lydia was there in a flash;

"No - not that one! I told you not to get the crisps! Honestly! You'll be all hungry and grumpy again in an hour!"

She snatched the packet off him. He tried to take it from her, but she held them behind her back - out of his reach. I flinched;

"Lydia Russell! How dare you be so rude! Give those back - right now!"

The pensioner looked at me wearily. Not angry. Just resigned to his fate.

I thought; imagine this for three hundred and sixty-five days of the year, my friend.

But Lydia had changed her mind. She suddenly tossed the crisps back at the man and grabbed between her legs with a howl;

"Ooooh! I need a wee!"

I stabbed my finger towards a door marked 'Ladies. 'As she made a fast exit, the old man shook his head, opened the packet, crunched a crisp and eyeballed me.

"Right funny little 'fing. Full of it, ain't she?"

I smiled, always grateful for small mercies where social embarrassment induced by my kids was concerned. At least he hadn't called my daughter an 'arsey, precocious little sod.' Even if he was thinking it.

"Sorry about that."

"Well, she'll be runnin' the country this time next year, the way she carries on. An' she'd no doubt do a better job than *this* government. Bunch of shysters that lot are. Bunch of…"

"Oh, I don't think that's very fair," came Michael's clipped tones. He had caught up with me after trying to help Trevor with finding a space in the hideously busy hospital car park. "I beg to differ," he continued. "We're not doing a bad job, given the mess that the previous lot left us with." Arms folded and standing next to me, he nodded towards the hospital exit; "Although I'm now thinking that perhaps we should be helping the NHS out a little bit more with its parking problems, eh?"

The old man gaped, mouth open. Half-chewed crisps on display. A Michael-recognition moment.

"Hey! Ain't you – that – Cheesewick bloke? That Minister of… of whatever?" he asked, spitting soggy potato fragments in our general direction.

Michael nodded indulgently. "Yes. That would be me. Minister of all-things potholes and council tax. How do you do?" He held his hand out to the old man, who wasn't quite sure what to do. Fingers greasy with crumbs, he proffered a wavering hand to Mr Politician.

"Pleased to meet you," Michael nodded again. "Now. I need sugar. Excuse me whilst I purchase a rather unhealthy snack." The older man continued to gawp but as Michael moved towards the coin slot, the lavatory door burst open and all a flurry, Lydia dashed back towards us. Michael was saying;

"So, I'm afraid that it's going to be chocolate. Do you want some too, Rachael?"

My daughter flung herself at the machine, barricading it with her arms.

"Oi - no! You can't have any of the chocolate in there! It's all bad chocolate. Children in Africa are put down chimneys for that stuff. Just so that people like you can get even fatter!"

"Ah. It's Lydia." Michael looked down at her, pausing with his pound coin a few inches from the machine.

Lydia narrowed her eyes, trying to fathom out where she'd seen him before. Michael pursed his lips and nodded.

"You're rather like your mother, aren't you? With that chocolate fixation. During one of the first conversations we ever had, she presented me with a gift of her ethically-traded chocolates and then condescended to warn me off eating them. Fearing that I was already treading the path towards obesity, no doubt."

I smirked, remembering that encounter on Michael's doorstep, only a few weeks ago. But Lydia glowered. She hated not to be in on the grown-up information. She was now slowly sliding down the front of the vending machine, her eyes half-slits of suspicion. But then it dawned on her.

"Oh." A gruff whisper. "You're the man off my fridge!"

"Am I?"

I groaned inwardly. Let this be a lesson to you, Rachael Russell. Newspaper clippings of random people that you might – one day, end up sleeping with – should never be attached to your kitchen-white goods.

"Yes," scowled Lydia. "And you Skyped us. I remember. You said that you were at a very boring party-thing at the seaside. With just a lot of very ugly, old men and no ice-creams or donkeys."

Michael's mouth twitched. "Well, I do remember that I Skyped you from our party conference in Brighton last week. Although I don't quite recall using that turn of phrase. But, still. She's got an impressive memory though, hasn't she?" Unfortunately, this only served to annoy Liddy further.

"Who's she? The Cat's Mother?"

"Lydia!" I barked at her. Michael attempted to dampen down the atmosphere.

"Quite right, Lydia. One should always address the person that one is speaking to. Now, I really am desperate for something to eat. But I would hate to purchase an ethically-unsound snack. So why don't you furnish me with some discerning advice, as to which product possesses the most principles?"

Lydia – although being Ms. Verbally Gifted herself – was knocked a little off-kilter by Michael's use of language. I wondered whether he was just doing it deliberately or whether he really was hopelessly unskilled in the art of communicating with small children. Either way, Lydia had now stopped sliding down the glass and was, instead, pointing out the flaws in the contents of the vending machine, demonstrating to Michael an example of leftie parental-brainwashing.

"… And really - we should buy the chocolate that the ladies at Mum's place make. 'Cause they get the cocoa things in it straight off the ladies in Africa. And Mum pays them a proper nice price and doesn't rip them off or turn them into slaves, or whatever. But this machine doesn't have any of my mum's stuff in it… Hey! Why's that, Mummy?"

Michael answered for me;

"I imagine, Lydia, that your mother's social enterprise hasn't yet reached sufficient economies of scale to be able to start marketing their products effectively to large-scale contractual —"

"Right," said Lydia. "But whatever you're on about, I don't think that no one should go for the chocolate in here. Or the crisps." Here she looked pointedly at her elderly friend; "You want to watch that crisp-eating stuff, you know. You'll end up having a heart coronation…"

Michael tried to bring her back to the task in question;

"How about a nice flapjack? More nutritiously balanced, I suspect."

"A flapjack would be okay," said Lydia. "If it *were* a nice flapjack – but those ones in there aren't nice. They're from the health food shop places where Auntie Vicky goes. And they taste like poo."

Michael shrugged. "Well, this really is a dilemma, eh, Lydia? We're faced with examining both quality of product and corporate social responsibility criteria. Bit of a palaver, I'd say."

Lydia nodded. Palpably clueless for once. But then Michael performed the coup de grâce.

"So. Given all of this. And that we all want to scoot off home and away from these premises ASAP. I say this; why don't I just get one of these bars of chocolate here after all. You can have some, eh? And we simply won't tell anyone about our purchasing habits of today."

"Okay," Lydia agreed. "But you'll be wanting two quid, won't you? Rather than one… if you're going to be buying me some chocolate too…"

Michael searched in his pocket for another coin and looked at me, commenting;

"Clever little thing." With a slight twist of forbearance. Or was it sarcasm?

After grabbing both bars and handing Michael his with a ceremonial flourish, Lydia flipped a casual "Adieu - and remember your fruit and fibre intake!" to the old man. She led us down the corridor and to where Vicky was parked up in a wheelchair. My sister had been busying herself with her phone but looked up on hearing her niece's voice. She gave me a relieved grin and reached from the wheelchair for a hug. I kissed the top of her head. Her hair smelled like pomegranates.

"You daft sod. What're you like?" And then I began to snigger. The much more stylish sibling was, today, clad in a pair of purple sweatpants, bright pink bed socks, a 'Little Miss Naughty' t-shirt and a lime green cardigan which our Auntie Jan had knitted for her. And which I knew, for a fact, she used as a blanket for the cat's basket. She cast her eyes down at the leisure-wear and smiled apologetically;

"Ah. Well. I normally just sleep in my undies, as you know. But before the ambulance came, Lydia fetched me some warmer clothes to wear. It's a bit worrying though, Rach. She's clearly inherited your dress sense. But hey, how did you get here so quickly?"

"Cadged a lift off a friend."

I glanced over my shoulder. Michael and Lydia were now behind me, scoffing their chocolate bars. Vicky had to look twice. And then again.

"Yes – a lift." I squinted and tried to telepathically convey the message of *'Indeed. The friend that I'm referring to here, happens to be the Government Minister for Communities. And yes, it is nine o'clock on a Sunday morning. But let's say no more about that, eh?'* Vicky frowned.

"Rachael - is there something wrong with your contact lenses? You're blinking rather a lot."

I scowled at her.

"Ooh – they look like they're really hurting you!" she added.

But then she snapped into dream Our-Kid mode, flashing a beatific smile at Michael;

"Hello there. Nice to meet you."

Michael stepped forward and shook her hand. Lydia decided to outline, using her best manners;

"This is some bloke; what Mother happens to know from work."

"Yes. I can see that," said Vicky as she nodded at Michael. "Oh, and I must apologise for my attire. My niece has been an absolute star - but she isn't very well trained in early morning dress assemblage. Although I must say, Rachael, that it was Lydia who dialled 999. She repeated the address to the ambulance operators. And she even stood at the front door to wave them over to us. She was a little darling." Lydia glowed.

Vicky had broken her ankle. Not a bad break. But enough to keep her from her usual tube-commute on the Northern line to work. In addition to the pot on her leg, she had been provided with crutches and was told to use a wheelchair to exit the hospital premises in case her early attempts at crutch-control failed. Michael took charge;

"Right. Let's get you back to Dulwich." And then he lowered his voice, "Before any of us catch MRSA or whatever they're now calling the latest superbug thing that Bob Porteus' Ministry is failing to control. But don't quote me on that one, please."

He moved behind the wheelchair and ushered us all outside. I knew that if security procedures were being followed correctly, Trevor should have followed Michael into the hospital. But perhaps this little venture was deemed to be of low risk. After all, even Al-Qaeda or ISIS couldn't have pre-empted a pussycat inflicted accident laying low the sister of the Minister's latest squeeze during the wee small hours of a random Sunday morning.

A traffic warden was hovering next to the ministerial car which had been parked on double yellow lines. By the looks of things, 'the VIP discussion' had already taken place with the man, who was no doubt hanging about to see if the scary-looking driver had been telling the truth. Trevor got out of the car and helped Michael to assist Vicky into the back seat. Lydia and I climbed in behind her; Liddy's eyes all agog at the sight of Trevor. And at the enormous space in the back of the car.

Trevor and I had finally met and enjoyed a brief chat on the way to the hospital. He was younger than Brian and less bulky, but considerably taller and he looked every inch the security man sort. He sported a buzz-cut, which Michael had been joshing about, on the drive to the hospital;

"When Trevor first came to work for me, he had an Afro but it ended up as a flat-top, didn't it? What with all of the sitting in the car. He's incredibly fashion-conscious, is Trevor, and couldn't cope with having a flat-top. So he decided to get it all shaved off – despite him feeling like he had betrayed his ethnic origins."

Trevor just gave him a look.

"Yehmon," he answered. "And I smoked ganja and played Bob Marley to him, all the way up and down the M6 until Michael pointed out that I was actually British by birth, that I was doing far too much of the Afro-Caribbean stereotype. And that he was going to get his Minister mates to revoke my citizenship if I didn't stop playing the black man."

Michael guffawed and told me;

"He's actually an enormous Stevie Wonder fan." Trevor shook his head again. These two clearly had a bit of a crack going on.

Vicky, however, was less interested in the lad-banter and more thrilled by the car.

"You know what? I'm really surprised that it's a Beamer. I would have thought that all of your ministerial cars would be Prius' by now."

Victoria Russell was a cool cookie indeed. She hadn't batted an eyelid at being introduced to Michael. There had been no indication of the fact that she had instantly recognised him. And yet within minutes, she was making chit-chat about the brands and models of government cars. She might be a bit of a smart-arse at times and could be incredibly rude about my parenting style, personal appearance and my taste in men, but that little sister of mine could always be relied upon to rise to the occasion.

CHAPTER 5

Michael called back to Vicky, from the front seat.

"The cars tend to vary. Last week it was a Merc. This week a BMW. All fleet stuff, generally. But the PM gets the Jag. And there's always talk of Prius' of course. I own one myself – it's back at home in Mottram. But I'm told that for the government they're a bit more… But, hey - Trevor, my friend, now then. Come on. You're responsible for the welfare of three ladies today. So, do keep the speed down, won't you?"

Trevor attempted not to smile, shaking his head wearily at Michael as he stared at the gridlocked traffic ahead of us. Occasionally his glance would flick up at the Russell girls in the back. He had hot-cocoa eyes. I was reminded of Shaun. But, even so - not even these peepers were quite as dark as Shaun's.

My meandering thoughts were interrupted by Vicky;

"You must be in demand quite a bit then, Michael. Popular with a certain type of folk, I mean - what with the armoured windows and the bullet-proof glass. No doubt a Kevlar-lined compartment. And I'm pretty sure there'll be explosive-resistant steel plate underneath. It's hardly your bog-standard government-issued car now, is it?"

Vicky never showed any interest in politics or in social issues, but her knowledge of modern cars had shed some interesting light on the level of Michael's seniority in government. She wasn't trying to show off though. She just came over all geeky when it came to mechanical contraptions.

Michael shrugged his shoulders, playing it all down.

"Oh, well. I haven't a clue who gets allocated what - or why. I'm only interested in who the drivers are. Trevor's main skill set is knowing where the best greasy spoons are. And how to avoid knocking down and killing too many anarchists - hey, Trev?"

"Ja, Baas." Trevor didn't miss a beat.

Michael grinned and then asked;

"Enjoying your weekend in London, Lydia?"

"Yeah! It's getting even better now - I've never been in a car what's got a TV in the back before! And isn't that a sort of little fridge thing? Is there any Pepsi in it? Can I have one? Oh, Matthew is going to be so soooo jealous! Can we watch some cartoons?"

"No," Michael replied. "I only allow the Parliamentary channels on in my cars. Cartoons would just distract Trevor. I don't even let him listen to Radio Two. Especially Steve Wright in the Afternoon."

"But that's not 'cause I'm lacking in concentration skills, Michael," Trevor lobbed back at him. "It's 'cause the guy gets my goat up. Bloke's a total wan…"

The blare of a taxi horn outside drowned out Trevor's adjective. Certainly, his choice of words to describe Steve Wright were not ones that tended to feature in the DJ's own radio jingles. Adam would have immediately warmed to Trevor. Bound by a mutual dislike of ol' Wrighty.

Lydia prattled on.

"But yes. London. We've done it all. Buckingham Palace, Traffy Square, Tower of London. And today was supposed to be me and Vicky going to the big wheel thing on the river. But it's all gone wrong, 'cause stupid old Cubus turned up when I was asleep and started shouting at Auntie Vicky through the letterbox. Going on that he really does loooooove her - more than the smallpox, even. And he would even marry her if she would go and live in Ifrica with him. Wherever that is. And after that, it went quiet. And then Claude the Cat wanted to go out. And then Auntie Vicky fell down the stairs after him."

I looked at my sister.

"Smallpox?"

"She probably means the Springboks".

"Blimey." I added, "A South African bloke said that he likes you more than the rugby? Wow. Never mind the offer of marriage – that says it all." She nodded woefully;

"He was totally steaming, Rachael. He'd been at Covent Garden all night. Some big works do with a load of the other guys up from Jo'berg. You can't believe a word that a bloke says, when they're like that…"

Both Michael and Trevor snorted. There was a privacy panel located between the front of the car and the passengers in the back seat. I leaned over and snapped it shut.

"Excuse me!" Michael rapped on the glass screen. "Just whose car *is* this?"

"Belongs to the Great British Public. Us ordinary tax payers," I called (or rather yelled) at him, then turning to Vicky, I added;

"Did he really say that stuff? The marriage bit?"

"'Fraid so," she admitted with a hitch of her shoulders, as though in her book it was the height of shame to have a marriage proposal drunkenly garbled to you via your letterbox. "And if I'm going to be honest, I've been getting a bit sick of the whole long-distance thing. That's why I was happy about using Lydia as an excuse for not spending time with him this weekend, whilst he's been up from Jo'berg again. I mean, he's top-notch in terms of knowing his stuff on field applications and the latest digital advances. But the only other stuff that he wants to talk about is sport. Or getting off his face. And I'm thirty-six now. I'm a bit past all of that."

"Right. So, his widgets and gadgets no longer hold you in thrall."

"Exactly. And even when I told him that I'd be looking after my niece this weekend – he turns up drunk in the middle of the night and starts bellowing through the front door. A door that I happen to share with other leaseholders in the damned building! And if he thinks depriving me of sleep and freaking out a little kid… meaning that I'm so bloody knackered later that I end up tripping down the bastard stair. Sorry." She directed the apology to me. I batted it away. Lydia knew plenty more profanities than that one, but was usually canny enough not to use them.

"So, he doesn't know about what happened to you? You didn't call him?"

"No way. The state that he was in? I'm hardly going to call a drunken dickhead to come and help me. Anyway. Lydia was a hell of a lot more use than he would have been. He's probably still sleeping it off on a park bench somewhere. And I'm not forgiving him for causing so much noise. The people above me are lesbian librarians and they're not used to that sort of behaviour."

"What's a lesbian librarian?" asked Lydia. "Are they like normal librarians – but only, even scarier?"

We both ignored her.

"Are you sure? I can call him, you know."

"No. No way. No thanks."

She folded her arms and stared at the back of Trevor's head. I wasn't going to probe any further. My sister and I had always kept abreast of each other's love lives, but we didn't intrude.

Or I had thought that we didn't intrude. Because then she asked me;

"So how long has this been going on then?" Not meeting my eyes, as she nodded towards the front seats of the car.

"Vick…" I gave her my warning voice. I didn't want my daughter to be privy to this kind of conversation. But Lydia seemed to be distracting herself with a packet of Tic Tacs. She was trying to throw them into the air and catch them in her mouth. Adam used to do that. Perhaps she had remembered this.

"Oh, I don't disapprove, Rachael. I think it's time. I mean, you didn't do yourself any favours after you lost Adam. Doing the whole rubber-ball thing - bouncing back for more with that tosspot Sh…"

I cut her off by clearing my throat loudly. She got the message.

Lydia said;

"We should buy Matthew a bouncy ball. One with a Union Jack on it? He'd like that. Might shut him up from being such a little whinge-bag."

And then she started singing and bopping along to 'Rubber Ball' by Bobby Vee. My parents must have been over-exposing their grandchildren to their Crap Songs from the Sixties CD again.

I glared over Lydia's dancing curls at my sister.

"Yeah, alright. I get the drift, our kid. I'll keep my gob shut."

Fifteen minutes later and we were rolling up to Vicky's place in Dulwich. Trevor steered the car between several wheelie bins that some London larkster had decided to push over for a Saturday night laugh. Michael opened the window panel and asked us if we had had a nice little chat about men and handbags. Lydia yawned;

"I wouldn't worry about not hearing what they said. It was reet dull. Even God in his heaven was probably exquisitely bored off his trolley face."

Michael raised his eyebrows;

"Lydia does have a remarkably eclectic grasp of language…"

"She's an avid reader," I said. "And we can also probably blame her numerous Famous Five audio books for the words that she sometimes comes out with."

Vicky smirked, adding;

"And her father's genes, of course. Not the Stanley family's. None of us lot are big readers. But Adam was. A real clever sod, he was. He was wasted in computers. He used to hate me for saying that, but it's true."

I reached over Lydia to squeeze my sister's hand. Hardly anyone talked about Adam so freely and so full of natural affection as Vicky did.

The men assisted the invalid out of the car whilst I unlocked her front door, intending to whizz around her home to make it as disabled-friendly as possible. Lydia had already had a good attempt at messing up her Aunt's usually immaculately presented abode. The living room floor now comprised of an elaborately woven tangle of Vicky's beads, bracelets and belts, scattered with what appeared to be pot pourri. Liddy had no doubt been creating another one of her Magic Circles, inspired by her recent interest in Wiccanism and too many day trips to Hebden Bridge. After I kicked the pile of crap to one side, Trevor entered the living room carrying Vicky in his arms.

"Blimey, Trevor," I said, "You're earning your wages today!"

"No probs," he replied; "She's a mere slip of a lass, your sister." He flashed her a brilliant white smile and gently manoeuvred her onto the sofa. Lydia was galloping behind them both, screeching "Me next, Trevor!" Michael trailed at the rear and then leaned against the door frame, watching me scurry around moving random pieces of furniture. I thought that he might at least offer to help me with things. But then he astonished me;

"Look," he said. "Why don't we get Lydia out of your hair for an hour? Whilst you make the place more suitable for Vicky."

Lydia curled her lip at him.

"I'm not in no-one's hair. Like I'm a nit or something! That's well mucky, that is."

"Sorry Lydia – I was just using an idiom. Something I would have thought you would have mastered by now, given your verbal gifts."

"And you shouldn't call me an idiot, neither," said Lydia, deliberately throwing Michael another language related curve-ball. Michael ignored her, and I moved through to the kitchen. He followed me.

"So, Rachael – what do you think? Lydia could come out with Trevor and me. Just for an hour. We could nip down to the Embankment. Can't really get tickets for the wheel at this stage, but we can at least have a look at it. Get her an ice-cream or something."

"Oh. You don't have to do that…" I began. And I could see that he was already wavering about the suggestion himself as he glanced at his watch. But then Liddy Loudmouth broke in;

"Oh, yes he flippin' well does! I'll have a Mr Whippy one with a flake. Definitely not a sicky-yellow hard one. And lots of sprinkles…"

I picked up the kettle and looked around for tea bags. Then I checked out the clock on the kitchen wall.

"It's ten o'clock on a Sunday morning. And it's pretty chilly outside. Ice-cream?"

Trevor appeared at Michael's shoulder now, smirking at Lydia.

"Where I grew up - not so far from the beach at Southport - we always said that it was never too early for an ice-cream. We even had it for breakfast in the summer. My dad used to say 'Well, it's all dairy – innit?'"

Lydia nodded furiously and began to embark upon her begging mode. This was a recent development of hers. It involved hands curled over in the fashion of furry paws, a protruding tongue and a lot of panting. If we had been at home on our own together, I would have told her to pack it in and stop acting like such a mentalist. But instead, I said;

"Well. Go on then. But Michael…"

"I know. I know what you're going to say. But we'll have to bring her back to you – even if you'd rather that we lose her…"

The two men turned to leave, with Lydia scampering behind and yelling "Oi – cheeky chops!"

I put the kettle on and dished out the green tea for my sister and then the bog-standard for me. Then I set up a small table at arm's length distance from her, so that her various electronic devices, remote controls and painkillers were close to hand. She commented;

"Hey – you're not as crap at this mothering malarkey as I thought you were. I've got all of my basic necessities right here, in the space of a few minutes!"

"Huh," I replied. "Well, you'd better tell me where you hide your vibrator. 'Cause you'll be needing that after buggering things up with Cubus…"

Vicky grimaced. "You're so vulgar. What's a top-class man like Michael wanting with someone like you?"

I smiled. All smug.

"That's classified info, Vicky."

"Well. Whatever. It's been a bit of a turn up for the books. Normally, something like this happening to me would have had me in a really foul mood. But you trucking up with your Minister-man was a welcome distraction. Nice - getting a lift home in a government limo, too!"

"Pleased to be a source of titillation for you, Vicky."

She mused on the edge of her cup as I plonked down next to her, disturbing Claude the Cat, who had been perching on the back of the chair. He jumped onto the carpet and stretched himself towards his owner. She reached over, scratching his ear.

"You two must have something... well. Something good going, Rachael. If you can trust him to cope with Lydia the Lunatic."

"Nice way to talk about your only niece. And of course I trust him! He's a politician, isn't he?" Vicky snorted and began to plait her chestnut-red hair. But then her expression suddenly altered. She said;

"Hey, hang on. Oh, my God!"

CHAPTER 6

She stopped, clapped her hand over her mouth and then pointed her finger at me, accusingly.

"*You* were that woman in the papers, weren't you? It only just occurred to me now. The 'blonde girl' they were all talking about - that someone took a photo of him with."

I swigged my tea, letting her continue;

"Christ – I don't believe it. We had a copy of that News of the Nation, in the coffee lounge at work that day. I was actually reading it out to a colleague and laughing. Saying how he's Mum and Dad's MP and… well - how everyone in his constituency always thought that he was gay!"

She began to chuckle to herself;

"That's so funny! I mean, you're not like - all tan and teeth, are you? You're more like a dirty, mousey sort of blonde. And I mean – you haven't been a girl for decades! Hardly some young bimbo like they've made it out to be. Ha-ha! If only the journalist scumbags at the News Of The Nation knew it was someone as boring and as serious as you are. Ha-ha! Classic!"

"Cheers for that, Vicky" I commented. "Yeah, thanks for describing me in probably the most unflattering terms that anyone ever has done. Faded, old, dull, etcetera..."

"Oh, come on," she teased me. "Don't tell me your confidence can't be sky-high now. Landing a catch like him! I mean, he isn't really my cup of tea – but he hasn't exactly been beaten with the ugliness stick either. I can see how he might appeal to you. And as dad would say 'And I bet he's probably worth a bob or two as well…'"

"I wouldn't know. And I haven't been out there fishing for people or landing catches as you ever so elegantly put it. It just so happened that I met him through work." I stared out of her window. But it was difficult to keep up the pretence of being all sniffy and offended when, in the upstairs flat of the house on the opposite side of the road, there appeared to be a semi-naked, middle-aged man doing tai chi exercises. Slow motion arm waving.

It had been a long time since Vicky and I had had a heart-to-heart. She had moved to London only a few weeks before Adam was killed and although the telephone had kept us talking, it was no substitute for a face-to-face relationship. For the hugs and the hands-on help that I had needed over the last year and a half. With the phone, it was always too easy for her not to see the swollen eyes, to note the sleep-deprivation and, of course, for me to turn the dratted thing off anyway, or to ignore any incoming calls; to cocoon myself in the routine of everyday task-list ticking. And although I missed the company of other adults at home, for over a year I had felt well and truly stuck - rendered unable to reach out for even a simple chat, to ask for help when I needed it. (Not that I'd ever been any good at it, before losing Adam.)

So, at long last, here was a chance to spill the emotional beans with my little sister. I moved quickly on from the affronted posturing and instead outlined the events of the last few weeks. She listened to me in silence, nodded every few seconds and then finally erupted into a full-blown belly-laugh as I outlined the latest part of the story;

"Priceless, Rachael! Good bloody God! So, Mum and Dad actually believed you – that you wanted to come to London on a retreat for recently bereaved spouses? Bloody amazing. Wonderful!"

She finished her tea and placed the mug primly on a granite coaster. "So, I'm best keeping my mouth shut about anything to do with what you actually *did* do here in London? No mention of you and your… some sort of burgeoning relationship or whatever you want to call it."

"Please."

"And is that what Michael wants?"

"No. Not really. He's not quite thinking along the same lines as I seem to be. In fact, I can't fathom it out. He says that he doesn't care what people think about him – with regards to his personal life, at any rate. That there's nothing that he needs to hide. But my feeling is that he's… maybe not being careful enough about it all. Especially after that mystery-blonde photo thing in the media."

Vicky reached behind her head to close the curtains. The morning sunlight was blinding me and I was having to shade my eyes with my hand to see her properly.

"Well - if as you say - he's lived the last few years with these daft 'Michael Chiswick is gay' rumours, perhaps now he's happy to disprove them. It sounds like you're the one worrying… about being seen with *him*."

"Well, I…" I looked at my watch. It had now been forty minutes since Lydia Had Left The Building. "… I – yeah. Maybe you're right. His career is so important to him. I guess that my concern is that him… hanging out with me - some working-class trollop from up north - will…"

"Damage his professional credentials. Typical you. Freaked out that you might end up feeling responsible for someone else's ill-advised choices in life. Especially if they happen to be far more well-bred and therefore worthy of having everything in life handed to them on a gilt-edged platter."

"Jake would admire you for saying that."

"Well, that'd be a first. I've only met Jake a few times and he didn't exactly endear himself to me by calling me Queen Victoria the Second and telling me that my sympathy with tax exiles was uncannily close to the imperialist fascism that my namesake had peddled out across the Empire."

"Aw. Jake. He's quite fluffy when you get to know him better."

"Well, anyway." Vicky picked up a pen and pad which I had placed on the table next to her. She began doodling tiny sketches of chickens and miniature daisies. An odd habit of hers. "Yeah – anyway. I think that you're neglecting to tell me the real reason here."

"And what would that be?"

"I think… Yes. I think that you suspect that Minister Michael mustn't be totally right in his head. That he's… actually got a screw loose for wanting to be with you."

I shrugged. She was good. No point in trying to deny it.

Vicky was now drawing a massive daisy. Its stamen was filled with mini-chickens. She shook her head thoughtfully.

"Classic again. Classic 'Rachael Mustn't Tempt Fate.' Because from what you always said to me - or rather didn't say - Shaun's approach to relationships was enough to cause anyone to grow even more doubtful about themselves than they already happened to be."

"Meaning me?"

"Yeah - meaning you. I was the one born with the excessive confidence levels, as you always love to tell me. You're the one who missed out on the inner poise. And the high self-esteem."

I gave her a sarcastic glare.

"But it's true," she pouted her bottom lip at me. "And Shaun messed with your mind even more. Playing games. Secrets. And no need for it. For any of it. Total freak, he was." She looked down at her nails and sighed. Falling down the stairs had led not only to a broken ankle but to a broken nail. Horror of horrors. She looked up at me and added quickly;

"And I reckon, if you hadn't put yourself through the Shaun experience again, after Adam died – well. You might be able to relax and enjoy yourself more now. With Michael, I mean. I tell you," she looked over her shoulder, scanning the lounge for her ever-present manicure set, "If I ever get hold of that Shaun, I'll rip his bloody head off."

Vicky wasn't prone to such violent outbursts, or passionate words. But she was loyal. Always loyal to me, at any rate. She shifted uncomfortably.

"Got to hand it to you, Rachael, though. Your Lydia really was a dream kid to have around during an accident. She flipped into adult mode. Ambulance man said it was like having another paramedic in the van."

"Yeah, well. We're not bad during crises in our family, are we? That's maybe one of our redeeming features."

FIRST AID TRAINING COURSE, MANCHESTER TOWN HALL, OCTOBER 1998

Our first real, up-and-close attempt at flirtatious banter had taken place during a mind-numbingly dull first aid training course in Manchester Town Hall. Sure, we had been working together for a few weeks beforehand – me as the trainee 'shadowing' Shaun, who back in those days was the assistant manager for housing in Whalley Range. And sure, until this point we had always had plenty of the repartee going on. What with him hijacking my (then) maiden name - 'Stanley' - and forever referring to me as 'Stan The Tomboy Lass.' And what with me taking the mick out of the posh grammar school that he had attended in Ilkley or Harrogate or wherever. Yeah, the joshing came free and easy. But the first real witticisms with a sexual undertone that had been uttered between us took place on a day that I still remember with sparkling clarity. We were stuck in the basement of the glorious Manchester Town Hall; a stunner of a building in itself – a true architectural smack in the gob for you Mancunian-doubters out there. But if you happened to be your average payroll pleb, and on a shit training course, it wasn't the best location in the north of England to be. I could almost feel the clammy atmosphere of the ten-by-eight underground training room; no windows or natural light. Parked right up against the council canteen. Wafts of catering-sized Heinz Minestrone soup and Spanish omelettes fanning themselves down the corridor towards us. Shaun had said;

"Everyone says that working in social housing is great, because no two days are the same. Well that's not true, Stan. This training course is even shitter than the Equal Opps one. At least on that one, we got to have some good arguments about whether Britain would be overrun by immigrants by the year 2000."

"No doubt you wound everyone up on that one."

"Too right. If I had had a quid for every dickhead who was going 'I'm not racist but...' Yeah. I told 'em all that Britain should be a damn site more worried about lard-arse benefit scroungers – your native Brits who've never done a day's work in their lives - than these so-called foreigners."

"Bet that went down well with the course tutor."

"Just a bit. But there's no debate to be had in this bloody First Aid course. That's the problem with it."

"Yes, well. Even you, Shaun, can't argue with an expert from St John's Ambulance as to the best way to deal with a heart attack."

"I wouldn't mind, but it's the same as it was three years ago - when I had to do this bastard course for the council back then! Nowt's changed. Why waste my time?"

"So now that you're assistant manager you're too important to be reminded of the rudimentary basics of First Aid?"

"Shut up, Stan. Look – meladdo trainer, there - wants you to go and French kiss his dummy or whatever you lot in East Manchester are calling that kind of thing these days. And if

I'm lucky, you might get to practice the same thing on me —"
  "Excuse me? In your dreams, mate."

I toyed with the idea of telling Vicky about my most recent Shaun-encounter of several days ago. But then I thought better of it. A moment of weakness. A wee wobble that my little sister didn't need to be aware of.

"You know," I said. "There's this thing with widowhood. For women, I mean. I've been reading a book about it. Society has to… put women into a widow's 'purdah'. Otherwise we're a threat. Might steal someone else's man and mess up the capitalist status quo."

"Bloody hell, Rachael, now who sounds like Jake the Trot? Have you been hanging out with him again? Has he finally forgiven you for having children and not being able to get off your face with him every weekend down on Canal Street?"

"Well, I did see him the other week, actually. Although it was all about work – this woman called Dawn that we're trying to help. But seriously - men who are widowed, tend to receive more sympathy from society. They get mothered. They're even perceived to be a bit more virile. Sexier. Women, on the other hand, become social pariahs. And that's certainly been my experience. Like, for example, we hardly ever get invited to kids' parties since Adam died. Poor Matthew hasn't even been to one in the last…"

She raised a perfectly waxed eyebrow and answered;

"Could just be because no-one likes Matthew."

"Very funny. It's more to do with the fact that I'm some sort of a social leper now. So, God forbid that I have a sex life! That people know about it. It's a huge taboo. If I do anything like that, I'm instantly being unfaithful to Adam's memory."

Vicky's nostrils flared. Not impressed.

"Soz, sis, but if you can't hear him, then I can. Yeah, I can definitely hear a certain brother-in-law of mine, right now… speaking to me from across the Great Divide. And he says that you're talking bollocks. Total and utter crap." She sighed and then carried on with, "So what? So what if the odd opinionated bugger thinks that you should keep your knickers on forever? Adam wouldn't have expected that of you. He'd want you to be happily shagging away. I'm sure of it."

"God, Vicky, you're such a romantic."

"No. Never have been, as you damned well know. But Shaun… he messed with that logical bit of your head which, quite frankly, you were never much cop at anyway. And you need to get over it. Now."

I smiled. Vicky had known Adam so well. Had always appreciated his rationality, his black-and-white approach to life. But before I could respond to her delicate pearls of wisdom, there was a thud. And then an accompanying crash as the door flew open.

Lydia bounded into the room. Her hair was wild – the curls had morphed into little devil horns. She had red stains all around her mouth.

"Sorry, Auntie Vicky! I forgot about the door again. You should really get it fixed though, so I don't have to keep kicking it, to open it. But anyway. It only looks like a little dent, that one."

Michael trailed into the room after her, carrying a pink heart-shaped helium balloon.

"Here, Lydia – you can have the balloon now. It won't float away again, now that we're back inside. Do try and remember what I told you about the properties of helium though, won't you?"

"Look what Michaelmas got me, Mum! I kept asking and asking and finally he coughed up for it!" Lydia thrust the balloon at my face, hitting me in the eye with it.

"Yes, but I told you that I would take it back to the stall-holder if you persisted in launching it into people's faces, Lydia." Michael looked weary. He sat down on the other armchair. I suddenly noticed that he wasn't wearing any shoes.

Lydia ignored his comment, telling us brightly;

"We've had quite a fun time really. Apart from what happened to Michaelmas of course. And to Trevor. That was all a bit misfortunate…" I looked at Michael. He shrugged and half-smiled. More grimace than a grin, though. Lydia elaborated;

"Well, I ran away from Trevor as a joke. Because Michaelmas said it was Trevor's job to follow us. So I thought - when we were near the river Thames… I thought 'I bet I can run faster than Trevor and get away from him!' So Michael and Trevor ran after me and Trevor grabbed me when I was climbing over the iron fencey thingy next to the river. I mean, I wouldn't have been so daft as to fall in. But Trevor grabbed me anyhow. And my elbow sort of hit him in the nose. It bled. A bit."

Oh crap. Lydia had now attacked a member of MI5. Or the Close Protection Unit. Or Special Protection. Or whatever the spook n' stake 'em out agency employing Trevor called themselves.

Michael said;

"Trevor's in the bathroom. Cleaning himself up."

"And then!" Lydia continued "Michaelmas had to chase after the balloon. Because I let go of it when I was trying to cuddle Trevor better. And Michaelmas ended up having to get a bit wet. Because I was crying 'cause it flew over and landed in a fountain. He thought that he could reach it without getting his feet wet. So I tried to help him but sort of nudged him."

I stood up. Hands on hips.

50

"Lydia. When someone takes you out and treats you to… that's an appalling…"

I was lost for words that didn't include child-inappropriate profanities. I turned towards Michael. "I am *so* sorry… I never would have dreamed that she would have pulled a stunt like that."

For once my daughter had the decency to look embarrassed. She moved behind the sofa and began to fiddle with the curtains. Michael did his best to remain positive;

"Oh, I don't know. Rachael. I've seen much more appalling displays of behaviour in my time. Prime Minister's Question Time generally has more…" But Lydia, possessing the attention span of a gnat, suddenly blurted;

"Look! There's a naked dancing man in that house over there! And speaking of dancing – guess what, Mum? Michaelmas might look clever and talk clever and be all posh and he went to that Oxfid school, but he hasn't a clue about musicals. He doesn't know any of the songs from The Lion King. Or from Starlight Express. Even High School Musical – which is, like, well old." She sounded quite concerned at this revelation. I turned to Michael, explaining apologetically;

"I think that I've already mentioned the musicals-obsession to you."

"You did do. But I hadn't realised just how marked it was. I mean, bringing her to London without going to see a show, Rachael? It's sheer cruelty. It's tantamount to shoving a bag of heroin under the nose of a hardcore addict. And Trevor pipped me on that one. I never realised just how many shambolic musical scores he knows off by heart."

"In-deedy!" added Lydia. "He won you pants-down. Trevor is well cool. But Michaelmas is okay too. I suppose. So I've changed his name for him. 'Cause he says that at his Oxfid school they're too posh to say the word 'Christmas' and so they call it 'Michaelmas' and it's spelled a bit like his name."

"That's not exactly how I described the historical nomenclature of Oxford term-dates to you, Lydia."

"Well, whatever. But you're still not as clever as Auntie Vicky. The Oxfid school wanted her to go there and she told *them* a big fat N – O. Get lost, she said."

Michael glanced at me.

"It's true," I admitted. "Our Vicky is one of the few girls from darkest East Manchester who chose Scotland and Strathclyde instead. She passed all the entrance exams and then turned them down."

"Really?" Genuinely taken aback.

Vicky was nonplussed.

"That's not exactly what I said to them, but yes. Strathclyde was far superior in terms of engineering. And had a lower suicide rate. And many, many more men… of course."

"And less of your upper-class inbred sorts!" I added breezily.

Michael muttered; "Someone really does have to sort out that working-class chip on your shoulder you know."

"Speaking of chips, Rachael - would you mind leaving me something out for lunch before you go? I love you both to bits of course, but all of this has left me feeling kind of exhausted…"

"She hardly minces her words, does she?" I asked Michael as I headed into the kitchen and slapped together a cheese sandwich for Vicky. When I was scraping the breadcrumbs away into the bin, I noted that an enormous bouquet of pink roses had been shoved head downwards into it. Poor Cubus.

Just as I was furnishing Madam with her sandwich, Trevor emerged from the bathroom. His nose looked fine but his shirt was splattered with blood. He grinned at Vicky.

"Aren't we two the accident-prone ones today? You going to be alright in this place on your own? At least it's ground floor, I suppose."

Vicky twirled a twist of hair around one finger.

"Oh, sure. I'm the resilient sort. Main problem for me is going to be boredom. But hopefully they'll let me work from home ASAP."

I fetched Lydia's overnight bag. We both kissed Vicky goodbye. Michael shook my sister's hand, telling her;

"It was lovely meeting you. And I'm sure that Oxford is all the worse off for not having had the pleasure of you studying with them." Vicky rolled her eyes as we clattered towards the front door and calling to us from over her shoulder;

"Look. I'm hardly doing badly in life, am I? I earn far more than your average MP does, I'll have you know."

"Ha-ha – that's just like you, Trevor," Michael goaded.

"Well. Anyway – just look after our kid, alright?" We heard Vicky's voice coming down the corridor after us.

"Will do!" Michael called back, as we closed the front door.

"That's a silly thing to say," Lydia grumbled. "Mum doesn't need men to look after her. She's got me!"

Followed by a rather audible sigh, courtesy of Michael.

CHAPTER 7

Lydia and I settled in the back of the car as Michael climbed into the front with Trevor.

"Right then, Trevor" he said, "Let's crank up the floor heater if you don't mind. Dry my shoes out. And now," he carried on, calling over his shoulder, "Given that we've received an unexpected addition to the party, I thought that we might do something a little bit more child friendly than the er… the things that we've been doing for the rest of the er… weekend…"

Trevor sniggered. Michael shot him a look.

"Like what?" I asked.

"Well, the Foundling Museum is just around the corner from my place."

Trevor interrupted;

"The Fondling Museum? I thought you wanted to do something a bit different to what you've —"

Michael cut him off.

"You see, I've never actually been to it. Or into Coram Fields – that's sort of a park really – but it has this odd rule that you're only allowed in if you're accompanied by a child. Which, thankfully, I've always managed to avoid. Until this moment in time."

Trevor was chuckling. Darkly.

I grinned.

"Yes. Let's exploit my daughter. It's usually the other way round, after all, in my household…"

"Oi!" said Lydia.

Twenty minutes later and we had parked. Lydia scurried ahead of us. Trevor tailed behind and I took the opportunity to apologise to Michael for our aborted weekend.

"Listen," I told him, as Liddy became distracted by a terrier out for a walk with its owner. "I'm so sorry. I thought that I had everything planned out with the kids for this trip. My family have a way of doing this…"

Michael's eyes darted over to Lydia. She was grilling the dog's owner about the pet's date of birth, preferences for doggy snacks and the pooch's bowel habits. Satisfied that my daughter was sufficiently preoccupied, Michael lent over and kissed me softly on the lips. Then he placed a finger over my mouth.

"No apologies. What is it the TV people say? Pets and children. Nothing but expense and trouble. And neither animal nor infant has anything sensible whatsoever to say in relation to the European Union and common economic policy. Give me adult presence any day. But, crikey. Your lips are cold. Let's head into the museum."

"Eew!" Lydia cried out. "It just wee-ed on my shoe!"

The Foundling Museum had been preserved in memory of Thomas Coram, an eighteenth-century philanthropist who set up a hospital and school in order to take in abandoned children. It was all quite revolutionary and ahead of its time, and Lydia was captivated by the place. I deliberately avoided explaining some of the more tragic tales that featured in the exhibition because my daughter might act like a gruff and uncouth gobshite, but she had a bottomless capacity for over-sensitivity. Still, despite my attempts to lead her away from the more depressing tales of woe, some of the Victorian illustrations of feckless gin-smitten mothers caught her attention;

"Mother! Why's that lady dropping her baby on its head? Why would someone draw a picture of something … so flippin' weird?"

Michael was standing beside us, his fingers discreetly toying with the top of my jeans, stroking the small of my back. He chipped in;

"They didn't have cameras in those days, Lydia. And received opinion was not particularly altruistic towards the destitute in society."

I interpreted;

"… yes. Some rich folk didn't care about poor people. They didn't understand why they came to be poor. And they didn't really want to know the real truth, either."

Michael smiled blankly at me. Still not catching onto the whole 'pitch it at a kid's level' approach. So, he continued;

"Yes, so in order to convey the message that the poor were feckless or undeserving of charitable aid – they employed artists to create illustrations… demonstrating for newspapers, and the like, the notion of a despicable underclass in society. Of course, this alleviated any hitherto sentiments of empathy - or even of Christian propriety."

I began to try and explain, but Lydia cut straight in with;

"Yeah, I get it. They believed what someone drew in a picture. And they were a bunch of tight-wads. Just like Mum is - and that's why we never have any nice new clothes."

Michael burst out with a public schoolboy guffaw. Lydia pouted. She wasn't trying to be all jocular. She was just stating the facts available at a certain postcode. But she carried on with;

"Those drawings... it's a bit like... at my school. Every Monday, when we do our 'What We Did At The Weekend Report', Travis Walker always draws pictures of monsters eating his mum and dad up. He says it really happens - every weekend. And Mrs McCauley always has to say; 'No more monster pictures today, Travis, please'. Because – like - no one's stupid enough to believe him. No one. Not even Malaga Maysfield who's a bit..."

I flashed her a look. She checked herself.

"...Who's got problems and all of that. So, if some rich person looking at those newspapers... if they believed it all just because they saw it in some drawing, then... they must have been as big a spanner as Travis Walker is."

We both burst out laughing. Lydia narrowed her eyes and flounced into the next room.

With the daughter gone, Michael's fingers attempted to find their way down the back of the waistband of my jeans. He murmured in my ear;

"Poor Travis Walker. And rotten old Mrs McCauley! What if Travis is desperately trying to convey a coded message to social services? And his teacher's just written him off as some snotty-nosed little attention seeker, when actually - his family home is filled with violence?"

"You could be right about that," I considered. "I've seen Travis' mum deal with the other parents over your usual playground scuffles. And she scares the shit out of me."

In the next room was a panel outlining 'Famous Orphans in History'. Lydia turned around to see us approaching and asked;

"So, Mum. What is a norphan exactly?"

"Not 'norphan'. 'Orphan'. With an 'O'. See?"

I pointed out the spelling. Then I said, "Oh, Lydia. Come on. You must know what an orphan is? How many stories have we read with orphans in them? It's a child who has no parents."

Lydia was one step ahead of me.

"Well, I like it with an 'N' better. That's how it sounds when you say it. But anyway. Lots of them weren't norphans, were they? 'Cause they had mums what dropped them on their heads. And then left them here. Didn't they?"

Michael was checking his phone. The ever-present lines on his forehead more ingrained than usual, but he chose to answer her;

"Actually, I used to be a junior minister in International Development, so I know a bit about this kind of thing. There is, indeed, a proper definition in terms of overseas development work," he informed Lydia, who had commenced with picking her nose. "One uses the term OVC – for 'Orphaned and Vulnerable Children' - when one speaks in terms of global issues of poverty and well-being."

Lydia had cocked her head to one side. Finger up nose still. Michael perambulated on;

"And in the developing world, an orphan is often a child who, yes, still possesses a sole, surviving parent."

The finger withdrew itself from her nose; a disappointing lack of bogies currently available. Liddy exhaled. A discernible hiss. Sibilant excitement.

"Oooshh. So, I'm a norphan then. Am I? 'Cause I've only got Mum alive, nowadays! And Matthew… yeah – our Matthew is a norphan too! I can't wait to tell him!"

I hadn't anticipated this. And I tried to search for the right words as I stared at the black-and-white photographs of doleful little girls wearing starched and pristine pinafores, sitting straight-backed in a 1920s classroom. Michael stepped in, surprising me.

"I think, Lydia - that in a developed nation such as Britain or the USA - that the definition of an orphan always has to be someone who has lost *both* of his – or her - parents."

"Why? Why do you have to have both parents die? If you live here in England. To get to be an orphan. That's not fair."

"Well." He looked slightly flummoxed. I had gathered my wits enough now to be able to chip in with;

"Liddy – it's probably because losing a parent if you live in a poor country is much more of a… a sort of… disaster. Whereas here, where there is a bit more money to go around, it's seen to be less…"

I had obviously said the wrong thing. A Lydia temper flare-up.

"What? So, you're saying it's not a preposterous disaster for me? For my daddy to be dead? Just because I have nice water to drink and no-one's trying to make me into their slave? Or making me eat just rice rice rice all of the time? That I'm not allowed to be all norphaned?"

Once again, Michael tried;

"I completely agree with you, Lydia. It seems very silly that we use the same term for different circumstances. I know that when I was little and my dad died…"

"What?" Liddy had put the brakes on. She looked taken aback. "Your daddy died too?"

"Yes, he did. And it was awful. But no one called me an 'orphan' because - like you – I had a nice mummy to take care of me and my sister."

This was the first time that Michael had successfully dampened down his excessive verbosity and had managed to showcase the 'child appropriate language' thing. Hal-le-bloody-lu-jah.

"Right," said Lydia. "So how did your dad die then?" Straight to the point.

"Oh. It was… cancer."

"Everyone says it's 'cancer' when you ask what's killed them."

"Ah, but sadly, cancer is rather common."

"What is cancer anyway? Like some sort of a Great Plague, or whatever?"

"Gosh. If we're going to be precise about this, Lydia – you might want to be aware that 'cancer' is the generic term for dozens of different types of manifestations of abnormal cell growth that tend to be degenerative and —"

Well. Perhaps he hadn't quite mastered the child appropriate language thing yet.

"So, it just kills people?" Lydia finished his sentence for him.

"That's right. But not always. These days, if preventative medicine such as chemotherapy or radiotherapy can be utilised, most people can survive it. But —"

"Your dad didn't."

"No." Michael shook his head. "Unfortunately."

"Bummer," Lydia agreed. She wandered over towards the life-sized black-and-white photographs of the foundlings on the walls and placed her pint-sized palms against them.

"I feel sorry for them. All of them. And I feel quite sorry for myself, too. Nearly being a norphan. And for Matthew, too. Even though he always smells of pickled onion Monster Munch."

Michael looked at me to gauge my reaction. I tried to do a *"Kids! The Things That They Say,"* sort-of smile. But it must have come out a little bit too melancholic, as he took a step towards me and combed his fingers against the back of my hair lightly. Lydia looked round and caught him.

"Oh!" she exclaimed. "And you too, Michaelmas. I feel sorry for you too. You would have been a nearly- norphan too! Come here. Group hug! Group hug!" She wrapped one arm about my leg and the other about Michael's. He looked inordinately surprised and didn't quite know how to respond. At the same time, two elderly ladies trundled into the room, flashing sentimental smiles over what must have looked like a familial display of affection. I heard one of them whisper to the other, "That minister – you know the one who…"

Michael cleared his throat, extracting himself from my daughter's pincer-like embrace.

"That's very kind of you, Lydia" Michael eventually said "What a charming little girl you can be."

Lydia headed for the stairs and turned, stabbing her forefinger at Michael;

"Well maybes… if you hugged people a bit more, you might actually have got to be the Prime Minister by now – rather than you just being some old minister-vicar who just waffles on about stuff."

Michael looked at me and added;

"Less of the 'charming,' perhaps."

After touring the exhibition, we had lunch in the museum cafe. Lydia sat at the table with us for only five minutes, having declined any of the choices of sandwiches.

"Why can't they do plain old cheese? I'll eat summat later." She sashayed away in the direction of the museum shop. I smirked to myself. Michael asked;

"What's so amusing?"

"Oh, just thinking about Bev. One of the women who comes to Sisters' Space. She makes it her mission in life to put me off my lunch every day."

"How so?"

"Well, every day – without fail – she asks me what kind of sandwich I've got. And then she always concocts some kind of disgusting comparison… and re-names my lunch for me."

"Like?"

"Like last week, she said that my corned beef butty looked like 'VD scrapings.' And then… she said that my coronation chicken looked like the contents of her toilet bowl after a dodgy curry from the Brindleford Bismillah."

Michael's eyes widened. "Interesting woman."

I nodded.

"But I'm getting good at anticipating her take on things now."

"So, go on then. What would she say about what you've chosen for lunch today?"

I shook my head. "You don't want to know." But he persisted.

"Okay." I took a slug of coffee. "Bev would say something to the effect of… that my hummus and tzatziki pita bread combo resembles a nasty vaginal discharge plastered onto a piece of cardboard."

Michael laughed. "And mine? What would Bev say that I was consuming for lunch?"

"Well… some might call it bratwurst with lemon mayo; but Bev would say that it looks like 'someone's bell-end got infected and that they're pissing custard.'"

Michael coughed as a remnant of his sandwich got lodged in his throat. His eyes began to water and he gulped some of his water.

"Sorry, Michael. But you did ask. Has the ghost of Bev's culinary comparisons put you off your lunch?"

He shook his head and grinned, licking the mayonnaise from his lips. "Not at all. I've got a stomach of steel. I've eaten some strange things in my time in – "

"Yeah – dead rats in Afghanistan or in the trenches of The Somme, or wherever."

His eyes glimmered. "You're clearly getting to know me rather too well. But tell me, Rachael. Or rather – please don't tell me - that you've put this Bev character in charge of the menu-setting for your cafe and chocolatiers?"

"Ha, no. She takes a back seat on the food side of things. We were getting too many references to 'the brown and sticky' way back when we were developing the chocolate side of things."

Michael reached over for my hand. He paused for a second and said; "You truly love that job of yours, don't you?"

"I do," I confessed, finishing the remnants of my pita bread. "And it's getting even better now that we're not under the threat of closure. Although we're still a bit under the cosh. We need to get the signature – from the council – for our social enterprise loan. For them to agree to sell the building to us."

Quick as a flash, Michael was back at me, curling his lip. "Oh, yes, I can just imagine this. A signature which will no doubt have to come from a certain Shaun Elliot. Who happens to be an ex of yours. Who happens to have recently been spouting off about me and my depraved government department, thanks to our ever-so obliging national media."

I looked away. I wasn't in the habit of talking about Shaun, to anyone. And especially not to Michael. I noticed that Lydia - who had previously been happily poking around the museum shop - was now hovering in the doorway of the café. She was talking to the two elderly ladies that we had encountered before. Probably trying to extort money from them for a crap pencil sharpener.

"Yes, that's it, I'm afraid," I admitted. "And I don't get why he's stalling. It makes perfect financial sense. It cuts the burden of the Women's Centre from the council's budget. And gives his lot much needed capital so that they can purchase more dog wardens, or whatever."

Michael cocked his head to one side. "Ah, well, I think that you're playing the Rachael factor down here... what about that job offer of his, the other week?"

"Yeah, right. Shaun's playing games to try and win me back. In your dreams, Michael. It's never so straightforward with him. He's never been after any kind of... normal relationship – not with me, at any rate."

"How do you mean?"

I exhaled and gripped my coffee cup.

"... He had this really bizarre thing about us not being seen in public together. I mean... this was a time before either of us were married... when there was no real reason at all, for all the secrecy. So, I hardly think that he's going to start prancing about, refusing to sign documents for Sisters' Space, to get my attention. Lovely, though I am."

"Well... you'd be surprised what men in love - or in lust - will..." He was interrupted by his phone. "Sorry. Got to take this."

I stood up, smiling briefly at Trevor – Mr Gooseberry Bodyguard, who had been sitting all on his lonesome at the table next to us. I strode past him, towards my daughter. As anticipated, Lydia had indeed managed to wangle something out of the two elderly ladies. Not a pencil sharpener however - but a badge with the museum's logo on it.

"Mother! See – what these Londoners bought for me! It's going to be a coat badge. I'm going to put it right next to my 'Jesus Loves You!' badge here. I'm all about God and orphans today. I'm going to start a badge collection and I might nick some of Matthew's superhero ones for it. But don't tell him…"

I apologised to her new-found friends, but they refused to take any money from me, saying;

"Not at all. We've both always quite liked your chappie and his opinions on society. Although we both could have sworn that he was gay. But now we see that he clearly bats for the other side. What with you and your little girl. Bit of a shame. Far too many heteros in this world eh, Annabel?"

She winked at me. She pinched her friend on the arse. And then they left the building.

Interesting place, Bloomsbury.

We joined Michael and Trevor at the museum entrance.

"Michael, I've just been chatting to two elderly ladies who Lydia befriended. It turned out that they were very disappointed with regards to your sexual orientation."

"I won't ask," he replied, eyeballing Lydia. "Now, look. I know that you were wanting to get the four o'clock train back, Rachael… But I'm in a bit of a pickle here. The PM and his lot were wanting to pitch up at my place in the next half hour. Stupidly last minute. But important stuff. And I can't really say no."

"Really? That's a bit… wouldn't you normally get summoned to Number Ten, rather than him coming to you?"

"Normally. But Jane – the PM's wife – she's gone into one of her mad as a hen rages. Is insisting that he shall no longer neglect his family on a Sunday. Wanted him to go for a little walk with her and the baby. So, this way, he gets to keep her sweet - and he can also pop in to see me."

"Clever chap."

"Has to be. With a woman like Jane for his wife."

"Look, it's fine. Neither Lydia or I will fly into one of our female hormonally-induced rages." I gave him a pointed look and for a second his eyes wavered with doubt. Had he overstepped the mark with Ms. Feminist pushing Forty? But then I smiled. "But no worries, Michael. I can chuck my stuff into my bag in a couple of seconds and we'll get off to Paddington. Pronto."

He shook his head.

"No. It's not fine. Not at all. I want to squeeze out every last minute that I can be with you. And the PM says that he only needs fifteen minutes or so - on pain of death from Jane. So, you and Lydia can just kick your heels back, watch the TV or whatever, until they've all buggered off again." He jerked his head towards Lydia, who was prattling on to Trevor, ahead of us, as we descended the steps of the museum. All about the horrors of morphemehood. And Jesus.

"And maybe… if we can distract Lydia with the TV or something… we can find time for a last little tête-àtête…" His hand deliberately moved to my breast, giving it a gentle squeeze as we walked towards the boundary of Coram Fields. Lydia's sixth sense must have kicked in, because she whirled around;

"Hey, Michaelmas. Do you want to see my new badge? What those old ladies bought me? I've got two badges on my coat now. See?"

"Very nice, Lydia. But I think that I definitely prefer the museum one."

Lydia glowered as she peered down at her lapel. "Why? What's wrong with my other one?"

"Well, nothing per se. It's just that it offends my ethnic sensibilities. I'm more of a cultural… a secularly-orientated Jew, you see. Not a religious inclination in my body. But even then – I'm none too keen on being informed that Jesus loves me."

Lydia dismissed his words. "Well. If you don't want to be loved by Jesus. And… as well as you being a sort-of norphan too… All I can say is that I feel very sorry for you. You must feel very unloved. And lonely." I heard Trevor laughing to himself. Lydia was playing to the crowd now;

"So, when you're frying in hell with the devil… Don't come crying to me and asking me for help!"

Michael's eyes caught mine and he whispered;

"Is she learning the Christian fundamentalist beliefs from her school?"

"Hardly. The most that they do in relation to religion at Liddy's school is to teach them that there were seven commandments rather than ten. They've dropped the ones about murder and sex and theft. We can't afford to put ideas into the kids' heads, apparently."

"Bloody hell. Well… perhaps you're brainwashing her at home then."

"Yeah, right. The last time we went to church was shortly after Adam's funeral. And whilst I do have my own beliefs – I don't bother discussing them with Lydia. She'd just tell me that I'm wrong wrong wrong. 'Yes. Jesus did rise from the dead. No two ways about it, Mum. You don't know what you're talking about.'"

"I see. Well. Does she still believe in Santa Claus?"

"No. She's never believed in him. Far too cynical. She's so very unlike Matthew, who believes anything you tell him. Like…. we told him that Bob our postman lives in next door's wheelie-bin. And that he likes leftovers."

"And yet she can't see the similarities between the myth of Santa Claus and of our so-called 'Christ'?"

"She's seven, Michael. She's seven,"

He sighed.

"And sadly, so very sure of her spiritual convictions. Too many like that in this world."

"Well, fair do's, Michael. It's her generation that'll be in charge of running the nation before you know it."

"Hum."

"So, if you can't take it, don't dish it out. Or would you prefer for me to start calling you, 'Satan's Plaything'?"

CHAPTER 8

We returned to Michael's flat. Lydia drank in the pristine burgundy carpets, the vast bookcases and the complete absence of Early Learning Centre toys and for once, seemed a little bit overawed. I told Michael that online games were the best way of keeping her occupied. He showed her through to his office and presented her with a choice of tablets, laptops or a good old fashioned PC. She slumped into an armchair with her chosen screen.

Michael went through to the kitchen to put some coffee on, whilst I nipped back into his bedroom. I began to fling things into my overnight bag, hoping that Lydia wouldn't ask any awkward questions about where I had slept for the last two nights. Michael then arrived, closing the door behind him. An ominous smile on his face. He handed me a small, shiny gift bag bedecked with ribbons and feathers. It turned out to be a nightdress. Black silk, with a delicate cream-lace edging. 1950s baby-doll style. He shrugged, looking slightly abashed, as I laid it out on the bed to look at it better. I said;

"It's beautiful. But it'll be covered in Marmite and Vimta stains before you know it…"

"Ha. No. I don't expect you to be wearing it in the presence of your children, you know. But, go on - do try it on for size."

I looked at him, askance.

"Now?"

"Yes. Now."

"That sounded a bit too much like a command for my liking. You're not going all Fifty Shades on me are you, Michael?"

"Fine. Whatever," he sighed, flapping his hand at me. "Would you feel more turned on if I opted for the pleading? If I went for a bit of pathetic degradation?" He glanced at his Breitling and continued; "Because we've still got a few minutes before our visitors arrive… Oh, alrighty then. Please, Rachael. Pretty, pretty please!"

"Oh, no. Crap, no. Stop it with the begging thing. Doesn't do it for me at all. Okay. Give me a sec."

I headed to the en-suite and threw my clothes off. The nightdress was a perfect fit. I eyed myself in the mirror, hands on hips like Liddy does when she's posing. I didn't look half-bad for once. Even with the red socks (which I duly took off). I was all set to make my exit and demonstrate to him that he had achieved full marks on memorising my vital statistics (via the Coppafeel form of measurement) when I heard the trill of his mobile.

"Sorry – I'd better just get that," he called through the door. 'Back in a minute."

I left the bathroom, trying not to feel a tad bit jaded at the fact that he had egged me on to parade myself in front of him like some old slapper - but had instantly abandoned me for a chat about Council Tax reform or whatever. So, I decided to make the most of the time and began lobbing my bits and pieces into the suitcase, hoping that Lydia wouldn't wander into the room and catch Mummy all got-up like a slightly gone-off-the-boil, more burlesque version of Doris Day.

The sudden squall of a baby echoed up from the street outside. I moved over to the window to have a nosey. But my heart skipped a beat, as I looked down to see Lydia, standing on the pavement below. She was bending over a baby's pushchair, helping the child's mother to tuck a blanket in. Somehow, she had managed to get out of the flat and was chatting to a random stranger. And this wasn't West Yorkshire - where you could trust Bob the Postman to look after your kids for ten minutes whilst you try and free a sheep caught on barbed wire at the back of your house. No. This was That London. Where anyone could nick your kid from under your nose and have it sold off to child traffickers via Luton airport before you could say boo to a goose.

I dashed out of the bedroom, sliced my way through the lounge and yanked open the front door. Sticking my head out, I called down the flight of steps to Lydia. She looked up.

"Oh, hello, Mother! Come and look at this baby. He's called Toby. And he's a little sweetie-pie - aren't you, Toby-Woby?" She turned back to the baby and started smoothing his hat down.

"Lydia!" I yelled - my jaw locked in anger. "Come back here, right now! That was very naughty of you – letting yourself out of the flat like that!"

But Lydia just replied;

"Sorry. Can you bring me my coat, Mum? It's freezing out here isn't it, Toby-Woby?"

She chucked him under the chin as a familiar ball of fury in my stomach began to form. I can just about manage cheekiness, crabbiness, the biting and the attacking of siblings, but I have never reacted well to being ignored. The woman glanced up at me. She smiled sympathetically at this strange lady peeping out of the door, who clearly wasn't much cop on the disciplinarian front.

"Best go back to your mummy," I heard her say. But Lydia just carried on fussing the baby.

I pushed the door outwards, hoping that Lydia would recognise it as a threatening gesture - evidence that I was going to sort the sassy little sod out. But a sudden gust of wind yanked the handle from me. As I struggled to grab it back, I lost my footing and stumbled down the first few steps. The wind slammed the door shut behind me.

Thank God, though - I managed to grab the banister before carrying out a repeat of my sister's performance of the night before. I exhaled and then steadied myself. The woman's eyes were fixed on me - all concerned.

"Are you okay?"

"Fine!" I answered breezily. "No worries!"

And then, I recognised her face from the television. This was Jane. That Jane. Famous-for-being-wife-of-the-Prime-Minister-Jane. Her initial look of anxiety had now melted into one of shock. Because here was the mother of this friendly little girl – teetering in bare feet on a stone staircase. And all kitted out in rather slinky night-attire.

I thought;

"Holy crap, it's cold."

And then;

"I can't believe that Michael didn't even notice that Lydia escaped! What planet does the man live on?"

Always helpful to blame someone else when you could quite happily expire… Cause of Death being Misadventure By Embarrassment. I hoped to God that the PM's wife didn't get out to meet the general public very often. If so, perhaps she might think that parading around in your skimpies was the kind of thing that most of us plebs got up to of a Sunday afternoon.

Lydia looked up again. And stared hard.

"Ooh, Mum - that's a pretty nightie! When did you put that on? You had your jeans on, only a minute ago, when you made me sit in Michaelmas' office so that you could get me out of the way."

She turned back to the baby and started pulling goofy faces at him, as he gurgled away at her. I flashed Jane my broadest 'everything is fine and dandy!' smile as I tiptoed back up a couple of icy steps and rapped on the door. No answer. I tried again. No answer. So, I slammed it with the palm of my hand. Still no answer. I remembered that Michael had an intercom system at the bottom of the stairs. I was about to call out to ask Liddy to buzz it for me, when a bumble of voices floated around the corner. Several men in suits arrived. And wouldn't you just know it – but one of them happened to be the Prime Minister. He was dressed less formally than the others; wearing a bright red fleece. Which just seemed – *wrong* – somehow. Lydia looked over at them and flung out a greeting;

"Hey! You're that man, aren't you? The famous one."

The Prime Minister's expression wavered into a bewildered smile.

"Well, I might be. Perhaps you've seen me on the TV?"

"Yes," said Lydia "The Prime Minister. You're normally being very bossy and in charge. Like a vicar. Or a monk. But not as special to God, probably."

The Prime Minister had the grace to look amused. The five men who were with him - two of them I presumed were bodyguards, given their earpieces and their similar stature to Trevor - burst out laughing. One of the others - a man so blonde that he was bordering on the verge of albino - commented;

"Out of the mouth of babes or what, PM?"

Lydia narrowed her eyes. She had taken an instant dislike to this one. But she chose to ignore him and, instead, held out her hand graciously to the Prime Minister.

"Well, I'm Lydia. And that's Mother, over there. We're from all the way Up North on the train, we are. And we're visiting Michaelmas. He's another of your minister-vicar sorts."

The Prime Minister took her hand and shook it. He nodded, realising who she was referring to.

"Ah yes, we've also come to visit Michael. If you don't mind us intruding on you, that is?"

Lydia smiled prettily, wrinkling her nose with a 'no'. And for a few seconds I experienced one of those oh-too-rare moments of overwhelming love and pride for my little girl as she greeted the leader of the land. It dissolved in seconds, however - morphing into *Michael Open The Sodding Door* desperation again. Because as always, Lydia's impeccably sweet manners were accompanied by a barbed edge;

"... But you'll have to help Mum to get back into the flat first, I think. We're locked out. And she's only got her new knicker-nightie things on."

Until this point, the men hadn't noticed my presence but as Lydia pointed her finger towards the steps, seven pairs of eyes looked up at me. I shivered a cheery smile and hugged my arms across my chest, hiding any gratuitous nipple-action.

Seconds suspended in time. No-one moved a muscle, apart from a gangly chap with sticky-out hair. His mouth dropped open. It took Jane to break the silence. She turned, snapping at the men.

"Can't you see that she's going to catch her death? Can't one of you be a gentleman? Give her your bloody coat, for Christ's sake!" The baby screamed – all excited - at the sound of animation in his mother's voice. He brought up a slick of luncheon.

"Eeeuuw!" said Lydia "Mum, look what Toby just did! He just puked all down his front!"

There was a scramble as the four men, each of them eager to please the PM's wife, tried to take their jackets off, but gangly man was the first off the mark. He sprinted up the stairs and hesitated for a second – uncertain as to whether he should fumble with a scantily-clad woman whom he had never met before. But he draped his mac around my shoulders and I thanked him through my clamped teeth. The coat was wonderfully warm and was scented with menthol cigarettes. I clutched at it, and my cold fingers attempted to clumsily button it up. Then, still seemingly wavering as to what to do next in order to help, the man gave me a little pat on my shoulder. Reassurance for the phantom female flasher. He called down to his colleagues;

"Guys, guys – buzz the intercom. Flat six."

"We are doing," said Albino-boy. "No answer."

"Right then," he replied. "I'll call him. Emergency line, I think. Definitely an emergency."

He winked at me and smiled. Meanwhile, the PM's wife was sounding even more stressed-out. She was shrieking;

"Wipes! Wipes! Can someone get some wipes, please? Can you not see what just happened? Honestly. Men! What's the matter with you all?"

Her husband now leapt into action, thrashing his arm about in the bottom of the pushchair's storage area. I wondered if Jane was as highly strung as she was appearing to be, or whether she was doing her best to distract attention away from me. Either way, I was grateful for it. My new male friend winked at me again as he held his phone to his ear;

"Don't worry. Michael's got a special landline. Emergency government stuff for if the mobile networks go down. He'll pick up. And if he doesn't pick up, the PM'll sack him." He gave me a cheeky grin, setting in motion the crow's feet around his eyes. Closer up, I could see that he was a lot older than I had originally taken him to be. And then the landline must have been answered, because he glanced away from me and spoke into the phone;

"Mike. It's Marv. Open the door, won't you?"

Five seconds later, the door was yanked open and Michael's eyes were blank buttons.

"Rachael! What on earth have you…?"

I made a dash for the bedroom, ripped the nightie off, threw my clothes on and then huddled myself into a small human ball on the edge of the bed as I tried to thaw out. My cold arse had lost all sense of feeling by now. But this was the least of my worries.

Oh shit, I thought. Oh shit, oh shit, oh shit.

Voices drifted from the sitting room. The odd chuckle. No way on God's earth could I ever face any of them again. As I began to contemplate climbing out of the window and down the fire escape, the bedroom door opened. Michael entered; a peculiar look on his face as he pushed a mug of coffee towards me. He was sucking his bottom lip and wouldn't look me in the eye at first. But when he finally did, it was with that ever-so-slightly boss-eyed expression. The one that I found so very endearing when I had first noticed him doing it at Miss Simpson's flat. It was the very same squint that Matthew did when he was conjugating a big silly fib for Mummy as to whether he had been trying to spit through the letterbox again.

Michael motioned towards the drink. As I took it, his lips twisted. He was unsuccessfully trying to hide his real reaction.

"If you're laughing at me, Michael – I will never speak to you again!"

"Not… laughing."

"Because this happens to be the most embarrassing moment of my life."

His shoulders were shaking, but he managed to regain his composure.

"Drink up. I thought that you could do with something nice and hot. After… after…" He erupted into full-blown laughter. I glared at him. He stopped and wiped his mouth.

"Look. I imagine that this has probably upset you, Rachael. But believe me - having the PM and his posse catching you in your undies… Well. It's hardly a tragedy. In fact, you've probably just made the chap's day. He's let it slip on a number of occasions just how little sex he's been getting since Toby came along."

I was about to bark back at him something along the lines of I couldn't care less about whether the Prime Minister was getting any or not. And that also - perhaps his wife wouldn't have been too pleased to know that her husband was sharing the details of his lack of love life with senior cabinet colleagues. But then I glimpsed my reflection in the bedroom mirror. Shoulders hunched and fat bottom lip. Ms Wounded Pride about to embark on a hissy fit; whilst Michael – once again – was showing his magnanimous side.

So instead, I said;

"Right, so… you're not… not a bit pissed off with what just happened?"

"Of course not." He sat next to me on the bed. A hand reached to stroke my neck.

"You really do need to get to know me better if you think that something like that would upset me. And anyway. You looked stunning in the nightdress thing. I'm quite glad that they saw you! You should be too."

I gave him the laser beams don't-mess-with-me-I'm-a-militant-feminist look.

"Stop it. Stop trying to make me feel better. You're digging yourself into a hole. And you're sounding like a total perv. Whilst I'm sitting here, feeling like a prize tit."

He kissed me on the nose and added;

"Well. I think that lucky old Marv was the only one close-up enough to be tempted to have a feel of Rachael's Prize Tits. But come on. Let's forget about it. Pop your head around the door and say a quick hello."

"No way! I couldn't, Michael. Not after…"

"Don't be silly," he nuzzled my hair. "Rise above it all. Just like a certain part of me seems to be doing right now. Yet again."

"Hey, stop that. Enough." I pushed him away. "Go and have your meeting." He laughed as I shooed him out of the bedroom. I was grateful for his concern, but all too aware that I didn't have too much choice in the matter. I mean, I could hardly sit in the bedroom simmering away with an adolescent pout on my face, whilst the UK's biggest VIP was sitting only yards away.

So, what the hell, I thought. I would never have to see this bunch again.

I turned the door handle and plastered a brave smile onto my face. I'd become a bit of a master at this kind of thing, since Adam died. Eyes flipped up from various bleeping phones and I stuck my hands into the pockets of my jeans. All casual, like. I shrugged.

"Sorry about that folks. Bit embarrassing to say the least."

Michael had been leaning over Marvin, peering at some message or other on the other man's phone. He grinned at me. And Marv winked again. The Prime Minister was sitting near to the window; a bodyguard standing behind his chair, scouting the street outside for random Scud missiles, or something. He leaned forward in his chair and swayed his big, bear-like head at me.

"No, not at all. We're the ones who should be apologising - for having to wait for my wife to tell us to cover you up. She's already given us a bit of an ear-bending about that. Hasn't she, lads?"

Nods all round. Apart from the near-albino bloke who shook his locks instead. Perhaps in disgust at me. Or at The Wife. The PM carried on;

"And Michael should also be apologising to you too, for not looking after you and your daughter. I certainly wouldn't be employing him as a babysitter, any time soon. And he should also be ashamed of himself for yacking away on his mobile - like a girl – for so damned long – so that we couldn't get through to him. And for being a cheapskate and not paying to have his bloody intercom repaired!"

I smiled, grateful for the empathy. And I managed to overlook the patriarchal, sexist comments.

"Oh, you're good at making excuses," I told him. "I can see why you got to be the Prime Minister."

Everyone laughed, except for the same bloke, who seemed to possess some sort of humour bypass and who was much more interested in fiddling with his phone. The PM noticed this and commented;

"Phones down, Alex. Meeting about to start."

Ah. So, *this* would be Alex the Twat then. A fella who I had taken an instant audio-dislike to, when Michael had told me about his 'Merry Widow,' dig. Yeah, this Alex - whom I had heard so much about, in terms of his influence in all-things PR and PM - was proving to be as annoying in person as he was in the third person narrative. I caught a momentary flicker of irritation in his eyes at his boss's order. But then I suddenly realised;

"Where's Lydia?" I turned to look at Michael. He shrugged;

"Gosh. I… er. In the study, maybe?"

He jogged over to the relevant door. Then to various others.

"How odd. I've really no idea where…"

Brilliant. Things were going from bad to worse. First of all - whilst I had been pandering to Michael's underwear whims - he hadn't even noticed Lydia sneaking out of the flat. And then - after yours truly had gotten herself locked out and had holed herself up in the bedroom in humiliation - the kid had gone AWOL again. Of course, I knew that Michael prided himself on not being interested in children, but he could at least have tried to pretend to be keeping an eye out for her.

Bloody good job that I hadn't brought Matthew with us after all, I thought. My youngest would have burned down the Houses of Parliament by now if Michael had had anything to do with it. I was about to say something along these lines to him but then remembered that we weren't on Rachael's stomping ground. The usual; 'I tell it like it is - 'cause I'm from Stalybridge' perhaps wouldn't cut the diplomatic mustard in Michael's Ministerial circles. And besides, I noticed that Alex the Twat was staring at me through lemon-lashed, narrowed eyes. Radar a-beeping for discord in Michael's love life, no doubt.

But at least the PM helped us out;

"See what I mean? Michael would make Fred West look like Babysitter of the Year. Seriously, man, I can't believe that you ever held such high rank in the forces. You're a thoroughly irresponsible adult. But anyway, I," the PM continued, now addressing me and smiling; "at least know where your daughter is. She wanted to tag along with Jane and the baby for a walk around Bloomsbury Square. Jane said that they'd be back here for half past. And that she'll… Well. She'll be none too pleased if this meeting isn't over by then… So. Let's crack on, eh chaps?"

For the first time since encountering him, I noticed a chip in the confidence of the PM. He glanced at the other men, checking out their reactions. They all seemed to be deliberately donning emotionless faces. Apart from Alex - the only one who seemed unable to mask his take on things. He sucked in his cheeks ever so slightly. Yeah. Behind every successful man was a nagging, fishwife-y old bag of a woman. That's what The Twat was thinking.

But I had more important things on my mind than whether Jane had an excessively grumpy side to the otherwise smiles-and -simpers public persona. I mean, I have never been precious about who I can palm my kids off onto; I have never felt the need to run a Disclosure and Barring Check on Bob the Postie for example, but the attitude of this particular group of men to child-care and kiddie-oversight, was just a tad bit too blasé for my liking. Still, I pondered, their political precedents were hardly any more impressive. David Cameron had forgotten his own child and left it in a pub, after all.

So, I bit my tongue and replied slowly.

"Right. That's fine. So long as your wife can cope with her. I'll leave you to your meeting. Nice to have met you all."

But as I closed the bedroom door, I heard a voice saying;

"Becoming a bit of a habit, the last few weeks, isn't it? Seeing her without her clothes on."

And then Michael's voice came right back at him.

"Yeah, well, Alex. If it wasn't for *her* and the 'trivial distractions' of my romantic life in the tabloids as you happened to refer to it the other day, this government would have had a hell of a lot more negative publicity over what we're trying to square off in the Middle East. So maybe you should be thanking her, rather than making snide remarks."

Then the PM's voice.

"Now, now ladies. Settle down."

CHAPTER 9

Back in Michael's bedroom, I flicked on the TV and distracted myself with watching a Sunday afternoon current affairs programme. Twenty minutes later, I heard the buzz of the front door, followed by the sounds of my daughter rampaging up the stairs. Pre-empting a Lydia-moment, I moved back to the lounge. Sure enough, the girl had already cornered the nation's Numero Uno. She was presenting him with an acorn;

"... Which I picked out from the dirt in the park all by myself. It's a Peter Pan thingy."

The Prime Minister looked rather disconcerted. Perhaps a long time since he had read any J. M. Barrie. Lydia prattled on;

"But don't be thinking that I want to kiss you or anything. I'm not a girly-girl like that Wendy. And don't be letting Toby eat it, will you? Or he'll get diarrhoea. Or even worse - maybe die. Which would be awful, wouldn't it? As he's ever so lovely."

Perhaps it wasn't the most delightful statement that Lydia had ever come out with but it also didn't warrant Alex wincing and murmuring "Nice kid, eh?" to one of the other aides. Either way, Lydia - who had already identified him as a twat (not in so many words – as she wasn't quite familiar with that particular noun just yet) - was subsequently given licence to ramp up the West Yorkie accent, turning towards him.

"D'yer know what? The colour of your hair makes you look like someone tipped a bowl of rubbery, old custard right on top of it. I bet yer were right bullied at school, weren't yer? About yer hair… And yer eyes are a well-weirdy too…"

Michael made a conversational rugby tackle before I managed to bellow my objections. He gave a curt;

"Right. Thank you very much, Lydia." But I noticed that he had a bit of a twinkle in his eye as the men trundled out of the flat and down the stairs to a toe-tapping Jane and a lactation-obsessed Toby. Alex cast a glance back at me however. He was whistling a tune under his breath. And it wasn't until ten minutes later that I realised what the melody was: The Merry Widow Waltz.

Twat.

Marv stayed for a few more minutes, so I thanked him for trying to save the last remaining scraps of my dignity, and Michael chipped in with;

"Oh, Rachael. You might also want to express gratitude for the other week. Marv's my very own PR guru. It was he who sorted out those nice little positive stories about me, to counteract the News of The Nation mush."

"Bloody hell, yes." I said. "Cheers, Marv. Seeing that photograph of us… Talk about wanting to crap myself!"

Marv's mouth curved upwards and, now that the stifling air that had surrounded the PM and his cronies had evaporated, I launched myself forward, giving him a bear hug and a smacker on the cheek. Perhaps he was too used to London air-kissing – was unfamiliar with northern manhandling - because his gangly, goofy persona suddenly reared its head again, along with the hint of a speech impediment that had probably laid dormant since his public-school days.

"Oh – n-no probs. That's m-my, part of the j-job." But he quickly managed to flip himself back into politico mode. "And in terms of the photo that they used - I must say that you're much more attractive from the front, than from the behind. Oh. Oh sorry. Sh-shit. That didn't come out the way that I meant it to…"

Michael sniggered.

Lydia said, "Hey, Marvy. Why's your face gone all purple?"

Half an hour later and we were in the car, being ferried to Paddington station by Trevor. Michael sat in the back with me this time, informing Lydia that he had decided to;

"Grant you the very unusual privilege of being able to ride upfront with Trevor," although he then whispered to me "Don't be thinking that I'm doing this to pander to her constant need for entertainment and attention. I just wanted one last chance to fondle you…"

Lydia, however, was oblivious to this and was on top form, wittering away to Trevor;

"It's funny how black people like you are much better looking than everyone else. Mind you, the brown ones are prettier too. White people look like pigs, I think. Especially my mum when she's not got her make-up on."

Trevor laughed.

"Yes," she carried on. "And oh – the not-white babies are just adorable, aren't they? Although Toby is very sweet. I'm glad that he looks more like his mum though. His dad's no oil painting. That's what my grandad would say. And also – that Toby – he's way nicer than my own little brother, Matthew. Matthew stinks of the infant school's boys toilets. And he steals everything. Especially my collections. Like my badge collection, that I'm now starting. I'm going to just *love* collecting badges. I gave Toby one of them actually, as it seems to me that Toby's quite a grateful little chap…"

Michael snapped the screen between ourselves and the front seats, shutting out Lydia's monologue.

"Good God, Rachael. I don't know how you cope with it," he muttered "the child talks utter…"

I frowned.

"You were going to say 'utter tosh,' or 'utter crap,' weren't you? Well, maybe you should be encouraging her to go into politics then."

But before he could disagree with me, we arrived at the station and there was only time for a quick hug and a semi-formal farewell. As Liddy was watching us.

The train journey back to Reading was quieter. No Scottish football fans this time. Lydia seemed tired and - unusually for her - contented herself with looking at her comics and drawing pictures. Back at my in-laws, they told me that Matthew had been "... beautifully behaved all weekend." But Julia then back-tracked slightly;

"Well. Most of the time. There was just one little incident… when he had a tiny tantrum in church. Bit silly really, looking back. I thought that he might like to help with the collection plate. But Matthew wasn't happy with handing the money over to the vicar. It took me and both of the sidesmen to calm him down. And I don't think that the Brownie leader was too impressed that he managed to bite through their flag."

Malcolm screwed his nose up;

"Actually, Julia from what you told me, it sounded like the worst bit was when he climbed up onto the font and was trying to lap the water, like a dog."

Matthew looked unabashed though. Matthew always did. He gave me his most handsome could-charm-the-pants-off-every-lesbian-in-the-world grin (that crooked smile, the one that Adam had won me over with.)

It took only ten minutes to swap the children, luggage and coats over, during which time the battle for armchair supremacy had begun; (Lydia had always objected to the fact that Malcolm had his 'own favourite chair' and wouldn't even allow small children to sit in it). But I left Julia to sort out the spat between elderly toddler and bossy granddaughter.

Matthew and I were soon back in the car and streaming up north on the M1. I listened to Gardeners Question Time on Radio Four as Matthew dozed. The panel were rambling on about the kindest and most organic way to kill slugs. I kept shouting 'Salt! For Godsake! What's the matter with you lot?' But my mind was wandering. I kept trying to feel positive about the fact that I wasn't one of those poor, jaded weekend commuters, returning to a Monday morning in London from a weekend away of northern-loveliness and now jammed nose-to-tail on the opposite side of the carriageway. But for most of the journey back to West Yorkshire, I felt on edge. I couldn't quite fathom out why. But there it lay.

A dubious dredge of something or other at the pit of my stomach.

CHAPTER 10

Monday morning proved to be better than the usual kick-off to the week though, with just the singular child to wrestle out of the front door and into a crisp and cloudless Autumn morning. We only had one small battle, when Matthew wanted to take a toy to his day nursery. We had been having this argument rather a lot recently. At first I thought that I had convinced him not to do this, by saying;

"Best not, Matthew. I mean, that Archie is a bit of a klepto, isn't he? He nicked your LEGO ninja. Remember?"

However, when I dropped him off at the brightly painted front door, he whipped a small Marvel superhero from his underpants and proudly presented it to Pink Trinny, his favourite nursery nurse.

"It's Batman. For you. To borrow. 'Cause your hair's pink. But your face is all black and your arms are too. Like Batman."

As per usual, Trinny didn't miss a beat;

"Wow. Thanks for that, Matthew. Just what I've always wanted. A Batman that smells like your bum."

I love that nursery.

I arrived at work, checked the staffing schedule and re-jigged the rota, because one of our volunteers had called in sick. Then I met with the steering group – a small band of the women who were responsible for co-ordinating the launch of Charlene's Chocolate Factory and Café. So far, I had managed to keep any of my previous worries in relation to the threatened closure of Sisters' Space away from the service users and from most of the staff. Things were looking a lot more chipper for us, since Shaun had dropped that particular little bombshell on me several weeks ago. Still, I had decided not to regale them with any jubilant tidings of our new social enterprise loan and freedom from local authority control. I would be playing all the cards close to my chest, until I had the signed documents in black and white.

The steering group consisted of the usual suspects. Me, my deputy Gill, along with Marsha - one of our caseworkers – and then four of our 'regulars' at the Centre. Firstly, there was Bev. She was full of the smutty jokes as per usual, which I always managed to forgive her for, because she had a knack of following them up with a few cracking ideas. Shirley was there too - our newly trained master-Chocolatier and our oldest and most sensible participant - as well as also being our most badly abused service user in terms of domestic violence; totting up a score sheet of forty-five years of hell. And then there was Jade and Gemma - two of our youngest women who had radically differing attitudes in relation to Sisters' Space - their respective outlooks being reflected in their answers to a recent service-user questionnaire; when responding to 'Why do you come to Sisters' Space?' Gemma had replied '*I like the solidarity and learning about male oppression. And it beats turning into a vegetable, sitting at home and watching crap daytime TV.*' But Jade had replied, '*Cuz I like yr biscits and cn save on the heating bills and yr loo flushes proper here.*'

I started the meeting and we began to iron out the details for the launch day. We finalised the logistics; which stall holders had confirmed their attendance, how much coffee and chocolate we could be expected to sell, which guests had responded to our invitations so far – and then we all jumped as the meeting room door was booted open.

It could only be Dee.

"Soz for bein' late. Alarm dint work. Police had us up till three AM. Our Tony's been taken in for questionin'. Over that break-in at the mattress factory. Anyway. I'm well fucked-off about it. They won't leave the kid alone. Always on at 'im, they are!"

Bev was all sympathy.

"Wouldn't worry about it, Dee. If he gets banged up at Strangeways again, you'll have one less for Christmas dinner. He told our Simon that he always has a better Christmas inside - than he does at your house, anyways."

Dee sneered;

"Oh, fuck off, Bev. At least some of us know how to cook a proper Christmas dinner, rather than just givin' your kids some fuckin' microwave meal from Lidl!"

"Oi! Pack it in you two! Rachael's trying to run a meeting here!" Gill bellowed.

They both instantly shut up and morphed into sulky mode. Because Gill was scary enough without the additional attribute of having recently shaved her entire scalp. Adam had always referred to her as 'your classic butch lesbian' – but I'd told him that there was nothing classic about Gill. She made her own way in the world and followed no fashions or lifestyle advice. And anyway, I had said to him: "You, Adam Russell, are simply jealous of the fact that Gill has a way-cool sports-bike and you're not allowed to have one anymore, since you became a father." Ha.

Which was all kind of ironic really, because despite me putting my foot down about the biking-thing, it was still his yearning for them that had brought our kids to their current fatherless status.

My thoughts must have been drifting towards Adam and bikes, because I caught Gill glancing at me, with a quizzical expression. We wouldn't exactly call ourselves 'friends' outside of the office, but I had the measure of her and she often seemed to be able to read my thoughts. A mutual respect, perhaps even an affection for one another.

"Rachael? You were saying about the invites…"

"Sorry. Yeah. If you still want me to – like you all said last week – I can try and get hold of Michael Chiswick's constituency office. See if he can make it. They might think it's all a bit too last minute, though."

Dee snickered;

"Hey – why don't we sack Rachael? We per-spiffically instructed her to do those invites last week, dint we? And we're a co-operative so she should be doin' as she's told… Bet she's not done the Mayor's invitation either! Or that giant-bloke's."

Dee was getting underneath my skin now.

"Excuse me, Dee. But I have had rather a lot on the last few days."

Although to be honest, the delay on my part was more because I had been doing my best to put off the rather uncomfortable proposition of inviting Michael to my workplace for a second visit. Especially given that we were now experiencing carnal relations.

It was Bev's turn next. But at least she was trying to defend me;

"Yeah – in't the lady entitled to a break every now and then? She's been to London, haven't you, Rach? Did you try and shoot any of the Royal Family or 'owt? I would have done. Shower of shit, that lot."

"Anyway," I interrupted. "I'm going to do the invites as soon as we can get this meeting finished. So please…"

"Hope so," said Dee. "'Cause Bev fancies the arse off that Shaun Elliot bloke. Even if he does look like Lurch off The Addams Family."

Bev was straight on the defensive;

"Look. For once and for all – I do not fancy that miserable get. I like his clothes and I like the fact that he speaks his mind. But I prefer a bloke who's got a sense of humour. I wouldn't touch someone like him with a barge pole."

"Ha! He's that friggin' tall that you'd never reach the top of his head with a barge pole!"

Now Shirley joined in.

"Well, I think that Michael Chiswick seems to be a much nicer person to invite. He seemed to really care about what we do here. And I also felt sorry for him. When all that tabloid muck-raking was going on, the other week – about him and his bimbo on Brindleford."

"Ha!" Dee spat. "Now, he's one – he's one bloke what's *that* posh – it's like… he's got a barge pole rammed up his arse!"

Previously, when my colleagues and service users had trotted out ill-informed gobshite opinions about the two men whom I had happened to have dalliances with (unbeknownst to them, of course), I had parked myself in 'rabbit caught in headlights' mode. This time, though, I was having none of it.

"Look. Like Gill just said. Will you all just shut up for a minute? Can we please just have this meeting over and done with? I'm sure that you've got as much to be getting on with as I have today."

Dee couldn't stop herself and squeaked a quiet; "Ooooh. Get Miss Important here…"

I moved the meeting back to the agenda. For the last two weeks, I had spent a great deal of time briefing others on the need for even tighter than usual security systems. Given the fact that this would be the first time that men would be allowed into the Centre - and that lots of publicity had already appeared across the borough about the occasion - I felt that we couldn't be too careful. Our volunteer receptionists had both offered to work on the morning of the launch. They were familiar with the usual protocol, but as we prepared to embark upon our new venture, they knew that we would have to be more vigilant than ever. We already kept photographs available to reception on the computer system in our 'Violent Partner Parade' and we agreed that the receptionists would continue to use the CCTV camera at the front door, in order to vet people through the entrance, before allowing them inside on the big day. Any sign of problems, or recognition of one of the men from the mug shots, and staff would contact the police immediately.

I reminded the others that security would be hiked up even further if Michael Chiswick was going to attend. And that he would also bring his own government protection guards with him. This gave Bev and Shirley licence to indulge themselves in a bit of drooling over Kevin Costner in 'The Bodyguard'; an old favourite with the ladies, so it seemed.

After trying to bring the conversation back from the fact that, yes, it really had been 'that many years ago,' since Whitney Houston had died, I decided to abandon Stupid Meeting Anonymous and return to my office. I checked my mobile. There was a voicemail from Martyn;

> "Rachael. Still not got the forms signed and returned from Shaun Elliot, after many attempts at my PA trying. I even told her that I'd sort it out myself. But the man won't return any of my calls. Not that he ever did when we were lowly housing officers in the past. So why change the habit of a lifetime, eh? Anyway. I think that, if by close of play… we haven't heard from him… we'll need you to work your charm on him a bit. Call me if you come up with any better ideas."

No better ideas. Unfortunately.

And then - because I had been instructed by my fellow colleagues – and because we were supposed to be a co-operative after all, I rattled off the VIP invites, added in the e-signature of our Cynthia, our chairperson, and emailed them off to Michael's lot, to Shaun's PA and to the Mayor's office. Next, I called the nursery to remind them that the underpants we had borrowed from them had been washed and placed in Matthew's Shaun the Sheep rucksack. Following this, I rang the bank to tell them to stop calling me in the evenings about my overdraft and my ever-spiralling personal debt problem, because every time the phone rings "you wake my children up and it's going to be *me* taking legal action against you lot - as opposed to vice versa - if they both continue with being even more bad-tempered than they usually are in the mornings…"

By the time I had hung up, there was an email in my inbox. From Shaun's PA, or rather his PR. His Pet Rottweiler, Renee. It confirmed that – yes - Shaun would be available to attend as VIP at the launch.

But the Rottweiler's email contained the obligatory snotty endnote;

> 'Of course, an invitation at such short notice would usually be impossible for someone as busy as Shaun Elliot. In the future, Mr Elliot would appreciate it if you could give us at least two months' notice of any requests for attendance at events.'

So. Shaun was around and about, after all. He was available enough to give Renee a specific go-ahead in relation to the invite to Sisters' Space. But he wasn't available enough to respond to Martyn Pointer in matters appertaining a signature required for our loan paperwork.

Interesting.

And frigging annoying, too.

CHAPTER 11

For the next hour or so, my mind continued to skip from one minor item to another, on the never-ending task list of work and of home, but just after midday I was interrupted by a soft tap against my door.

"Come in," I called. But there was no answer. I stood up and opened the door. It was Dawn Hibbert. Ferreting in her handbag for something or other.

"Are you after me, Dawn?"

She glanced up and I inhaled sharply. One eye was horribly swollen. Purple and bloodshot.

I had first met Dawn over two weeks ago; the day on Brindleford when Vinnie – a rather cerebrally-challenged chap, to say the least - had mistaken Michael for the more religious sort of Minister. Which, to be fair to him, our Lydia also did from time to time. But then again, Liddy is just seven years old. Still, Vinnie's misconceived awe at Michael's spiritual occupation succeeded in preventing him from kicking the crap out of anyone else on that afternoon.

And so, this is how I got to know Dawn. A sparky, confident woman in her mid-twenties who had managed to procreate early on in life (young Mason), had gotten hooked up with Vinnie (outcome being West and Poppy-Rose) and then who had ended up trapped in your typical but tragic cycle of 'relationship violence.' As us smug do-gooders at Sisters' Space refer to it.

During the last few weeks, I had been all fingers-crossed and touchy-wood that we had finally helped Dawn to break the pattern of abuse. Thanks to Martyn Pointer and his team, we had found her a New Banks housing association home - away from Brindleford estate and at an address closer to Sisters' Space. And we'd also been trying our damnedest to get her to take out an injunction against Vinnie.

But now this. Fan-bloody-tastic.

She looked at me wearily.

"Yeah. I know. I know what you're gonna say. Like what all the other women sat in the kitchen are saying. I should've sorted the friggin' injunction out."

The Dawn that I had been getting to know – the zippy, mouthy, belts-and-braces Dawn – had clearly evaporated. Stuffing knocked out of her. Her shoulders were slumped, clothes creased, even her hair looked lank and in need of a good wash. But she had been trying to disguise the dishevelled look; had applied far too much foundation which only served to render her a strange shade of orange. She took a bottle of perfume out from her handbag and was spraying some onto her wrists, across her collarbone. Trying to pep it all up a bit. Keeping up the appearances. I told her;

"I'm not your bloody school teacher. And don't predict how anyone might react to you. You're not a mind-reader, either."

She half-smiled. I asked her where the kids were. Her mouth drooped and she closed both her eyes and inhaled. And then coughed at her own OTT application of perfume.

"They saw it all. Last night. Mason's gone to school but West were really freaked out. Wanted to stay at his Nan's today. Poppy-Rose is down the corridor. In your crèche."

I took her by the arm, guiding her into the office but as I did so, she winced. Some other, non-visible injury. Se we sat there, facing each other, on two scruffy but comfortable armchairs, at the far end of my office. Seats that had soaked up the stories from dozens of women during the past couple of years in my time as manager at the centre. As she relaxed into the sagging cushion, Dawn's head flopped into her hands. She said nothing. I resisted the temptation to try and fill the silence. Instead, I waited to see what she might want to say. After a short while she finally looked up.

"I've 'ad it. I can't do this no more." Shaking her head to herself. "'Fing is. I was right – right sorted about it all, I mean - when you got us the new house the other week. Made sure there was no ways Vinnie could find out the address. Bribed the boys with some new Xbox stuff, to make 'em keep their gobs shut. But then all last Thursday and Friday… and Saturday… Vinnie kept sendin' me these dead nice texts. And I didn't have no credit on me phone. So, I couldn't even have texted him back to tell him to shove it up his arse."

She looked beyond the office window, to the park's playground. Toddlers were flapping mitten-clad hands and shrieking with joy.

"What did his texts say?" I nudged.

"Just… just nicer stuff than usual. He never apologises for 'owt, does Vinnie. But he sent one sayin' he were dead sorry. First time I've ever had that from him. Asked if I could maybe forgive him?"

"Right."

She puffed a breath of air. Exhausted carbon monoxide. The scent of watermelon chewing gum.

"Anyway, yesterday tea time, I'd arranged to see me cousin – you know – our Katrina – the one what married SFB - Shit For Brains – you know, Vinnie's cousin."

"Yeah. I remember you mentioning him, before. Great name."

"So, yeah. Anyways, our Katrina – poor cow – well, she's always got Shelly Murray's fat arse stuck to her sofa…"

Shelly Murray was Vinnie's aunt. And you couldn't meet a nastier piece of work. A lady who was quite happy to use a machete on innocent neighbours who might have parked their car in the wrong place. Or who she felt were daring to challenge her family's entitlement to Brindleford rule. She'd once even tried to punch me in the face, back in the day when I had been a housing officer on the estate.

"So yeah. 'Cause it were West's birthday – he's just turned eight – our Katrina wanted to give him his pressie. So, we agreed to meet just off Brindleford – at The Lantern. We used to go there a lot, me and her. Play darts an' that. An' anyway… we're sat there havin' a drink. Kids were fine – messin' about in the games room – and then some bloke comes over to us, to say there's someone outside askin' for me. Turns out it were Vinnie."

"So… how did he know you were there?"

"Well, I'm guessing that fat slag, Shelley, must have gotten hold of Katrina's phone somehow. Seen about me and her meetin' up. She's sly. Fuckin' sly, Shelley is. Probably saw the birthday pressie for West an' all. Put two and two together."

I could picture that. Shelley had taken a photo of Michael riding Vinnie's motorbike through Brindleford and sold it to the News of the Nation.

"So, first of all, like - I weren't gonna go outside to see him. But then I thought… it were like, showin' me a bit of respect. weren't it? Him not comin' and gobbin' off at me like he normally would do. So… maybe he really were sorry. I thought."

I could see where this was going. I also suspected that Shelley Murray might have given her nephew a pep talk on the correct strategy when approaching a woman who you'd recently assaulted and who also happened to be the mother of your children (i.e. don't punch 'em in the face straight away, our Vin - leave it for an hour or so).

"An' then our West – who were earwiggin' as per usual – twigged that it were his dad outside, so he ran out to 'im and it were all tears and 'I miss you' and all of that. So, I went out to the front door of the pub to tell West to get his arse back inside. But Vinnie were givin' him his pressie. New tablet thing. An' he'd got Poppy-Rose this tiny pair of sparkly pink trainers. An' a load of cinema vouchers to give to Mason, what he'd got from somewhere or other…"

"And then?"

"An' I bet you're thinkin' 'You stupid cow!' Like, 'ow could you go outside and see him, after all the stuff that you lot at Sisters' Space 'ave been doin' to help us out?"

I interrupted her.

"Hey. Pack it in with the mind-reading act, will you?"

She nodded. A pause. She reached into her handbag for a bottle of day-glow orange pop. And then wrinkled her nose.

"Whatever. So… there were West cryin' and all of that. It's his birthday. And he just wants to see his dad. And there's Vinnie going 'Please – please can I spend some time with the kids?' And the kids were all going 'Please, please' and so I said - yeh – alright. You can see 'em for a couple of hours inside the pub. But I'm sittin' behind the bar - with one of Katrina's mates what works there. Stayin' away from you." She cleared her throat. "Thought I'd be alright with that. Plenty of people about in the pub."

We both glanced outside. A child had fallen off the swing and was screeching for its mother.

"So, he came in and he were playin' darts with Mace and West. An' they were lovin' it. Playin' dead nice with them he were. An' in the end I'd had a few bevvies myself. Still sat behind the bar. And they were all askin' me to go over – 'cause everyone knows that I used to be the best on the ladies' darts team. An' so, we all ended up 'avin a few beers together. So, by now it got to half-nine and I thought, we should be goin' back - 'cause it were school the next day, an' that."

Half past nine on a Sunday night in the Russell household must clearly operate on a different time continuum to that of Dawn's family. By then, both of my children have already been nailed into their respective bedrooms for over two hours. But there you go. Horses for courses.

"An' so we tried to set off. I was gonna get a cab from the taxi rank round the corner. Our Katrina had slipped us a tenner to get one. But he kept followin' us. Askin' us where we were livin' now. An' I could see that West were just about to blow it all - an' tell him where we'd moved to. So, in the end I just shouted back at him to fuck off and stop followin' us. But he wouldn't. So, then I shouted that I were gonna get an injunction out on 'im and ban him from seein' the kids. An' that's when he lost it, proper like. Went mental. You know?"

I knew.

And I could have asked her a dozen different questions. Why did you have to meet in a pub just around the corner from Brindleford? Why didn't you call up a radio cab to come to the door of the pub? Why didn't your dimwit cousin keep her phone on her at-all-bloody-times with a nutter like Shelly Murray hanging about at her house for most of the day? But I kept a lid on it.

She was quiet. Lost in thought. I said;

"So, stop me if I'm asking a silly question here, Dawn. But – did you report it to the police?"

An incredulous laugh. "Ha. Whadder you think?"

That'd be a Nah, then.

She coughed. Took a swig out of the pop and suppressed a belch;

"'Scuse me… But yeh. It could have been worse, I s'ppose. The kids started screamin'. Five of the blokes in the taxi office legged it outside to us. Even Vinnie's not fuckin' stupid enough to take on five. So, he pissed off – fast. Mace said he jumped on a bus what was headin' for Levenshulme."

She wiped her nose with her sleeve. Was she crying? No. Dawn wasn't the type to "do tears." I'd heard her self-proclaimed pride herself on that one, before now.

"And. Well. I just keep thinkin'. Why does it always happen? An' I... God. I can't believe I'm tellin' you this. We did it. Actually, did it. Shagged - had sex, I mean. In the pub. In the bastard men's toilets! After we'd been muckin' about and playin' darts. Jesus Christ. I'm such a stupid, stupid bitch! I bet you can't believe what I'm sayin' to you here!"

I could. And I could well imagine doing something like that myself. Not with Vinnie. Obviously. Good God, No. But I knew what she was talking about. That sort of story. I just gave her a sympathetic shrug and a shake of the head. She continued;

"He just... he's got some sort of hold over me, sex-wise. Magnetic or whatever."

I nodded.

"Me mum just can't get it. She reckons I've got a bit of me brain missin' where Vinnie's concerned. But I can't explain it to her. She can't get her head round the sex thing. I keep sayin'... with me and Vin it... it's really just like when you see it in the films. Proper passion. Proper intense. So, then me mum goes 'Oh don't fuckin' talk to me about sex again! You should have got over all of that by the time you were eighteen, Dawn!' Which is actually dead funny really. 'Cause her latest bloke is about the same age as me."

She screwed her eyes up in pain, as she moved her arm too suddenly. Drinking from her bottle again;

"An' I just always," her eyes flashed bitterness at me. "I always fuck it up. I always just give in to him. Give him that one little minute. To explain. Even if I'm well pissed off with him. I sometimes just feel sorry for him... And before you know it, we're laughin'. He always makes me laugh. An' then. An' then we're shaggin' each other's arses off."

I knew that tale, too. Her head snapped upwards as a baby at the other end of the corridor began to wail. The crying stopped and she suddenly stood up, with a slight groan and bit her lip. Pointed a finger at me.

"'Fing is. You've got to see Vinnie. When he's at his best. He's well fit. He's dead funny. He's hard and he's quiet and he's cool. And... like... He's a bleedin' drug and he draws me in, and I get off on it. I can get off me head on it." She was a lady in sore need of some validation. So, I said;

"I do know what you're saying."

"Yeah?" She gingerly picked up her bag and moved to the window, pressing one of her palms against it. Jules the cleaner wouldn't be happy about that. She'd have a go at me for that, later on. She was proper scary, was Jules. I said;

"Yeah. You know what, Dawn? There's a lot of elements that make up what and who you find to be sexually attractive. Physical, emotional, genetic things...

like… like endorphins. That we're not at all aware of."

"Endorphins? Thought that was to do with athletics and that?"

"Well, yeah. It's similar. Hormones. Brain chemicals. The feel-good stuff. Pheromones. You're not aware of your own and how they might – instantly – mesh with someone else's. They can be pretty addictive. Dynamite, even…"

But I was drifting again.

Dawn laughed, breaking my mood.

"What? Like some big sex bomb? Ha ha!" We both smirked.

"Well, the love songs are always talking about chemistry, eh? The invisible stuff. And if you're lucky – or unlucky enough as some people might see it – to experience that kind of 'Wham Bam' with someone, well your endorphins might end up going ga-ga. Getting addicted to the hit. Developing a habit."

Dawn chewed her gum, contemplating.

"Bad choice of words that, Rachael. Hit."

I smiled. "Sorry. But what I'm saying - in essence - is that a lot of couples start off with massive chemistry to begin with. And then when they settle down and have kids, it tails off. It's just the job of evolution - making sure that we reproduce effectively, look after our children and all of that, rather than going at it like rabbits half of the time – whilst the kids starve to death." She smiled.

"Well, it never tailed off with me and Vin. But like what you just said - maybe that's 'cause we never settled down."

Another little kid outside tumbled off a swing. Splat. Dawn continued;

"See, I met Vin when I already had Mason. He were just a toddler then. So, course - there was me havin' to look after Mace. Meanin' that we never had the chance for a proper romance – hearts an' flowers an' goin' out to Nando's, all of that. He were back an' forward on army leave. We had to grab our moments together. Speakin' of which…Yeah. You sound like a lady who knows a bit too much about all of this…"

I frowned, but she carried on with, "Is that what… you and that Shithead I saw you with in the park the other week… were like?"

Were?

Dawn had witnessed Shaun trying to ladle on the pressure with me, when he had realised that I was Michael's mysterious co-star in The News of the Nation. Neither Shaun nor I had realised that the argument had been overheard. Later, Dawn had confronted me about it, telling me that yes - she might be able to make a few hundred quid of your tabloid-pounds out of this knowledge, but she reckoned that I deserved better than national disgrace and losing my job (see why I like Dawn?)

I shook my head slowly. Adopted the oh-so-professional mode.

"This isn't about me, Dawn…"

She grunted. "Yeah, right. Fair enough. Mind your own business, Dawnie.

So." She turned round again, to look out onto the faded playground equipment. "Me and Vin... after I got pregnant and we had West, Vinnie did one. Pissed off back to the army. And then we didn't see him for God knows how long. Said he were stayin' over at his mates - Liverpool way for a bit. And then... yeah he lived with us for about four months. That were two years ago, when I got pregnant with Poppy-Rose..." She shrugged her shoulders. "That's why there's a bit of a gap between her and West."

"So, you never lived in the barracks with him? With his regiment - the other families?"

She barked a laugh and brought out a packet of cigarettes from her bag, wincing as she moved her arm

"Yeah, right. Do I look like your army-wife sort? Brindleford might be a shit place to live, but at least me family and me mates are all there. Once - early on - Vin asked me to move into the barracks with him, but it were over near Sheffield and nah. I can't be doing with Sheffield. Hills on every street corner over there. Try pushin' a pram round that place."

"So, he was never really around? For... that tailing-off of the passion - to happen?"

"Nah. An' actually... maybe that's exactly why, come to think of it. If he'd thought that we'd lose all of that sex stuff. I reckon he would have fucked off for good. Cause it were him what always talked about gettin' off his head on me." She mimicked his voice, exaggerating the Mancunian nasal twang; "'Dawn – you're better than friggin' H. Heroin ain't got noooo appeal when I've got yooouuuu'." She fiddled with the packet of cigarettes, adding quickly;

"But I hated him sayin' stuff like that. Talking up skag like it's summat cool. I know I drink and smoke too much or whatever, but I've always hated drugs. They did it for my dad, see? But I used to tell myself that if he could just kick the drugs and stop knockin' us about a bit. That we'd be okay."

She pulled a cigarette out and tapped it against the packet. I stood up too, as she prepared to leave the room. I needed to push her a bit. I wanted this to be one conversation that had a proper conclusion.

"But now?"

"Now, the kids... have seen too much. An' like Bev were sayin' to me before, in the kitchen. If I don't get my act together, social services are gonna end up taking me kids off of me, anyway."

"So," I moved closer to her and touched her shoulder gently, the one that didn't seem to be causing her too much pain. "Can I finally convince you to commit yourself to keeping an appointment with one of our caseworkers? To get the ball rolling on an injunction? I don't like to nag anyone but..."

Dawn popped the cigarette between her lips.

"Go on then. But only 'cause Bev said she'd be the next one to give me a good slappin', if I didn't."

And then, with a mischievous grin on her face, she gave me a "Ta, chick" and headed outside to Smoker's Corner.

Bless that Bev. She might have put me off my lunch yet again that morning, by informing me that my potted beef panini resembled 'Our Simon's undies when he's got a case of the skiddies'.

But she was undoubtedly a good 'un.

CHAPTER 12

After Dawn left, I ruminated as to whether the crew at Sisters' Space would be able to convince her to report the attack to the police. Of course, it would have been better if she had immediately made the phone call by herself. But that aside, it would still be the only way for us to sort out getting an injunction drafted. Plus, according to Dawn, Vinnie already possessed a criminal record, which would be another big help in persuading the guy to keep his distance. Still, I knew damned well that someone with Vinnie's history of violence might not always be deterred by an injunction. Sure, if we did help Dawn to take legal action - in the longer term - Vinnie could even end up in prison for this incident, but that would all be dependent on whether the taxi drivers who had helped Dawn were willing to give evidence. And I didn't feel too positive about that side of things. Because over the years, Vinnie and the infamous Murrays had spawned a culture of fear and intimidation on Brindleford. They did their own thing - they did it their own way. Everyone knew it. And their reputation extended beyond the boundaries of the estate.

I had been involved in countless cases like this before; when you had finally managed to piece it all together, hacked your way through the organisational silos, made a pact with your colleagues in housing, in social services and with the law enforcement bods. When it seemed as though you had all of your ducks in a row; when it was looking good, with the victim being supported to either appear in court or to continue with the case; when the evidence that you had sweated to collect had been parcelled up nicely, all neatly. And then - just one hour before the trial - someone would end up 'getting to' a key witness and the entire thing would come toppling down.

Tits n' bollocks n' all. Was always an understatement in these circumstances.

It was perhaps the most infuriating part of my job at Sisters' Space. Equally frustrating for the Crown Prosecution Service. And certainly, for the police. But then, as so many potential witnesses had said to me, on so many occasions;

'Well, would *you* do it? They know where I live! An' the coppers are never round here when you need 'em. I've got [delete as applicable] kids/elderly parents/pets/a car/a dicky heart/a nice garden/a desire not to get burned alive…'

Of course, I had sympathy for them. But in my own mind, I had always hoped that if ever faced with testifying against such violence, that I would somehow find the courage from somewhere, to dredge up the necessary mettle and to be able to go through with it.

Probably not though. I mean, I don't even like telling our milkman when he makes a mistake and brings us the skimmed instead of the semi.

Despite Bev's attempts at ruining my appetite, I managed to complete my lunch and was crunching into an apple when the phone on my desk jerked into action. It was Kevin Harris, New Banks' housing manager for Stepping Vale, the area of Medlock where Dawn had only just relocated to. Marsha had persuaded Kevin's team to part with one of their newly available void properties and Dawn was more than happy with her new location, an anonymous cul de sac, a good few miles away from Vinnie and his lot.

But Kevin Harris wasn't.

"Bloody hell, Rachael," he grumbled. "What the hell've you given me here?"

Straight to the point as always, Kevin was yet another housing professional that I had worked with over many years.

"What's the problem, Kev?"

"Your lot told us that this Dawn Hibbert would cause no problems for us. But today I'm being told that she's had her face smashed in again. Just two weeks after bloody moving into one of ours! Hardly the 'Happy Houses, Happy Homelives' corporate shite that your mate, Martyn Pointer, expects us front-liners to somehow magically procure for him."

A chunk of apple scratched my throat, causing me to wince. I cleared my voice;

"Sorry, Kev… maybe I'm being a bit pedantic here, but I would have thought that a woman having her face smashed in was a bit of a problem for *her*, as opposed to you…"

"Well, yes. You know what I mean."

I gave Kevin the benefit of the doubt. He had never even tried to pretend to be part of the politically correct brigade, but at least he meant well. I tossed my apple core towards the bin. Missed it. He carried on;

"Another tenant of ours - a neighbour - just told us about it. Saw the family coming home in a taxi last night. Saw the blood all over the pavement this morning Saw the state of Dawn Hibbert's face this morning when she left the house. The neighbour's concerned that Dawn's type might have an adverse effect on the standing of the street. It's one of our better areas in Manchester, is Tranmere Avenue…"

A bolt of anger coursed through my veins.

"Well, it's nice to know that New Banks Housing is more concerned about curtain-twitchers obsessed with their neighbourhood standing – as opposed to a young woman getting the shit kicked out of her by a total nobhead."

Kevin interrupted me; a dreadful, hacking smoker's cough. The symphony of phlegm lasted for a good ten seconds.

"Eew. Sorry about that - trying to cut down on the ciggies, but after forty years... you can well imagine. Anyway. Look. Let's not get funny with each other about this. I'll level with you. I'm a bit pissed off that your Marsha promised us there'd be no bother with this nutcase..."

"But you've had no bother from him. Not on your patch, anyway."

"True. But *she* has – Dawn has. And Marsha reassured us that the two of 'em had split up. So how long, Rachael - before Mr Charm Himself turns up on Tranmere Avenue, kicking her door down?"

I sighed. It was fair do's really. I'd worked on the other side of the fence for long enough to know that at the end of the day, a social landlord had to look out for both the property and for the rest of the neighbourhood. Nosey Nimby next door wasn't the only one who didn't want to see the area going to the dogs. None of us want a bloke like Vinnie and his family around. But Kevin decided to answer himself;

"I mean, Rachael – you know as well as I do that managing property - per se - is a piece of piss. It's all the bloody people living in the bloody places that send it all to cock... if I could be... if you could just..."

"Just what?" I rubbed my eyes and glanced at the clock. I hadn't had enough sleep last night because Matthew had been up at four AM ("I just had a cool dream about Chewbacca eating a Jabba The Hutt pie. Can I watch Star Wars now, Mummy?")

"... you know. Be assured that she isn't going to bring it all home with her. This neighbour who..."

"Grassed her up."

"Whatever. This neighbour also said that Dawn Hibbert's kids are pretty feral too... you know, bad language... not at school every day... out on their bikes till all times of the night."

"Well – Mason and West are a bit sharp around the edges maybe, but that's to be expected. Hardly junior werewolf material. And sure, perhaps Dawn isn't the most vigilant of mothers..."

I bit my lip. Pot. Kettle. Black. I could hardly claim Mother Of The Week Award now, could I? After all, it was only yesterday that Lydia had tried to jump into the Thames whilst accompanied by two strange men. And shortly after, had managed to escape from Michael's flat, whilst Mummy had other slinky negligee priorities to be distracted by.

I changed tack.

"Look. We'll do our absolute best to press Dawn to report this latest incident to the police. That way we can sort the injunction out. And then everyone's on safer ground. And sure – I'll tell her to be more mindful of the kids. And the neighbours..."

This seemed to satisfy him and the conversation meandered off into

91

chocolate Hob-Nob land (apparently, a sure-fire way to beat the nicotine cravings, but unfortunately you end up gaining thirty-six pounds instead).

After five PM had hit home, I signed out and headed off for the day. I cut across the A6 and just fifteen minutes later I had passed the invisible boundaries that carried me over Manchester's Lancashire, through a few miles of Derbyshire and then into West Yorkshire. Back home. Home to Holme. The name of our little village never ceased to make me smile. Before we were married, when we were looking for a house together, Adam had been hankering after moving to another wryly named little village in nearby Derbyshire (*"Cause it's hilarious, isn't it? I mean, I'll never get bored of saying 'I live in Hope'"*). I counted my blessings as I drove. Of course, it's always easier to do that, when you live right next to the most stunning moorland in the world. Yes, I thought - I might have lost my husband and been left to bring up two kids on my own; but I had a great job, the support of my parents, good pals and I was currently enjoying some steamy sex sessions with a government minister; as opposed to wandering round with a smashed-in face and a violent bastard like Vinnie Murray on my tail. So, I was all light spirits when I stopped at the childcare providers to collect Matthew. According to Pink Trinny, Matthew had experienced an okay day.

"Yeah, we only had half an hour of him refusing to wear clothes today. Not as bad as last week. Problem was though - when the younger kids started copying him. 'Cause it meant that at one point, we had five of them naked whilst they were eating their elevenses. And wouldn't you just know it? We had our surprise Ofsted inspection today."

"Oh, God. Really? What did the inspector think?"

"She seemed alright about it. Joked that they should have sent a nudist hotel inspector instead of her."

"Oh. Oh well. No harm done then…"

Trinny shrugged;

"Matthew did get a bit fresh with her though…"

Matthew, now fully clothed and ready to head home, realised that his performance was being appraised;

"I didn't, Pink Trinny! I just showed her my willy and asked if I could see hers."

"Matthew!" I was horrified. "I hope that you didn't! And you know very well that women don't have willies!"

He scowled at me.

"Well, I thought that she might. 'Cause she was all ugly and looked like a man with a moustache,"

Trinny rolled her eyes and commented;

"Well, Matthew, if we've dropped from 'Improving' to 'Poor' in the Ofsted star-rating and when no one wants to send their kids here anymore, we'll know whose mummy to blame, won't we?"

Matthew pranced towards the door and then turned to Trinny, blowing her a kiss. He sang;

"You're just jealous 'cause you've got no willy…"

I strapped Matthew into his car seat, pretending to be cross with him, whilst stifling a grin. But as soon as I was back in the front of the car and driving to our house, my mood became tinged with a sudden sadness. It shouldn't have been like this. I was supposed to have returned home with Matthew, fed him a breadstick or two and then commenced the conspiratorial whispering with Adam. About the boys in the Russell household; their obsessions with willies. And their blatant disrespect towards women who happened to possess facial hair.

But Adam wasn't great on the old two-way conversations these days.

I missed him. Bloody, bloody missed him.

CHAPTER 13

Tuesday morning and still lacking a Lydia to dawdle over her Coco Pops, Matthew and I were out of the house bright and early. By eight-fifteen AM, I was already at my desk, wondering if I would, indeed, need to call Shaun that day. Hopefully not.

The night before, I'd enjoyed a rather fruity phone conversation with Michael. It had largely involved him trying to persuade me to 'do a selfie' and to send him photographs of 'Rachael posing naked in new coffee bean necklace.' He had done his best to try and convince me that this would somehow be of use to him;

"… on the dark and lonely nights, down here in Westminster." I told him to get a grip on himself. Or to hire a prostitute to perform that little deed for him.

"I'm too well-known to visit ladies of the night, these days," he joked. "And I don't want any more slip-ups in the press for the next few years, thank you very much."

Famous last words.

At eight-thirty AM, my phone buzzed. A clipped message from Michael. He had used a 'caller unknown' SIM card:

It's Me. Seen News of The Nation?

Nothing else.

Oh, God. Here we go again.

I was just about to bring up the online version of the newspaper on my computer, but then remembered that we had recently had various news and views websites blocked, because one or two of the more work-shy elements of the team at Sisters' Space had been idling away the hours, reading the less worthy sections of the press and generally frittering their time away on social media. So, I decided that the fastest course of action would be to resort to the old-fashioned black and white version of the day's events. Thankfully everybody else in the building was too busy to notice my sudden need to nip to Mrs Singh's to buy a 'rag-for-the-lobotomised,' as Adam used to refer to the tabloid. I hurried out of the office, my heart a-skittering. Given the events of the previous few weeks, an image had already semi-lodged itself in my mind. Me, adorning the front page. Clad in slinky nightdress and stumbling down Michael's stairwell.

But then, as I'm often found to be lecturing my daughter;

"It's not all about Me Me Me now, Lydia, is it?"

Although, in a strange way, it was this time. It was all about Lydia. Or at least generated by her. On page four, the headline shrieked; "PM Pins His Cross to Mast!"

The Prime Minister has been hiding his religious preferences under a cloak of hypocrisy – causing an unholy war of words to erupt between Britain's religious leaders. Despite his frequent claims of 'not following any religion,' this week, baby son Toby was spotted wearing a lapel badge which declared 'Jesus Loves YOU!'

Expert in Contemporary Religious Studies at Sussex University, Dr Winifred Williams, told the News Of The Nation; 'The wearing of this badge is very significant. It proclaims not only the Christian faith, but that its wearer follows evangelical Christianity – a set of beliefs which has strong right-wing affiliations. And as in the case of George Bush and Tony Blair, it is difficult for any world leader to follow such strong doctrines without it impacting on their political actions. This badge tells us that the leader of this country feels strongly about issues such as abortion or the death penalty and that they believe that their actions should be led by an entity other than themselves. A child wearing this badge would seem to belong to a family who practise evangelical Christianity. I imagine that the Prime Minister would rather keep his true beliefs hidden in order not to alienate non-Christian voters."

Leader of the 'Jesus Tribes' church movement in the UK, Pastor Samuel Bannerman, told the News Of The Nation; "It's great to see the man in charge of the country proclaiming love for the Lord! But it concerns me that the Prime Minister has felt the need to hide his faith until now. If our leader is a Jesus-Lover, he shouldn't fear the darkness of Satan and those who are morally rudderless. He shouldn't be trying to pedal the usual liberal wishy-washy interfaith rhetoric. Christianity is our British heritage! Let's be proud of it! Let's see the Prime Minister standing on the roof – never mind the doorstep - of Number Ten! Let's see him out there - punching the air for the Lord!"

Imam Amin Yousef from Brixton Islamic Revival

Mosque, commented; "Given the legislation that this government has recently been trying to force through in order to further persecute Muslims in this country, I am not surprised to hear this. Born-again Christians are nearly always anti-Islamic in their attitude. This means that now, more than ever, Muslims in the UK need to unite against the next inevitable wave of prejudice and persecution against us.

Next to the article was a close-up photograph of Toby. His little face was all pixelated out – the prerogative of having famous parents – but the reader could clearly see a badge pinned to his coat. I knew that badge very well. A cute little cartoon elephant, trumpeting out the now infamous words; 'Jesus Loves YOU!'

For the second time that month, I performed a News of the Nation-induced zombie march back to my office with a copy of the so-called newspaper. I sat in the armchair next to the window overlooking the park, shaking my head at the craziness of it all. I remembered that Lydia had been wittering on about giving Toby a badge, at the very point when Michael had shut the screen in the car so that we didn't have to listen to her anymore.

However, in the great scheme of things, I thought, it was hardly a big deal, was it? Lydia collects things. Badges, keyrings, shells, adult conversational skills – and she sometimes enjoys bestowing them upon others (unless Matthew is suggested as the beneficiary, whereupon the worst of Lydia's Yorkshire tight-arse attributes are inevitably displayed).

I sent Michael a quick and apologetic message;

Just saw it. Lydia's generosity, eh? All ok?

I sat at my desk for a moment, wondering whether I should call him directly or whether he would be busy trying to untangle yet another Russell family-induced media mess, but then my mobile trilled. It was the in-laws. Julia's voice; all feathery, all concerned;

"I'm so sorry to bother you at work, Rachael – but it's Lydia. She's been wonderful so far. But we've just had a bit of an argument. Malcolm was watching the news on the telly and there was this thing about the Prime Minister getting converted, becoming a born-again, or something. Well, there was a photograph of his baby and they were all going on about this little badge that he was wearing."

"Right…"

"And Lydia was in the lounge… and she told us that the baby was wearing her badge. Well, of course, we said that it might be *like* hers. But that it couldn't possibly *be* her actual badge. But then she started insisting that she'd met the baby the other day. That she'd given him the badge! So, Malcolm told her not to be so silly and not to tell fibs. And she got very cross. And she's now upstairs crying. She's refusing to talk to us at all. Is she going through a phase of making up stories at the moment?"

I groaned inwardly.

How the hell could I explain that I had overlooked mentioning the fact that Liddy and I had been hanging about with the PM and his family at the weekend? For a split-second I contemplated telling Julia that – yeah - Lydia had recently turned into a right lying little sod. But then the phrase 'what a tangled web we weave' sprang to mind. So instead, I took a deep breath and said;

"Well actually… Lydia isn't making it up. Really, I should have mentioned it on Sunday. But it was all a bit of a rush whilst we were swapping the kids over. Yes, we sort of… bumped into the Prime Minister at the weekend. And Lydia did tell me that she'd given her badge to the baby. So…"

There was a pause as Julia took in the news. Then;

"Really? Really and truly? Well. I never did. I really… never did. How did you end up meeting the Prime Minister then?"

Think fast, Rachael. But don't lie to your nice mother-in-law.

"Oh… just through someone that I know. Someone from work. No point in asking Lydia about it though, Julia. You won't get much sense out of her. Ha ha – I mean, I think that the entire weekend morphed into some kind of Lydia-focussed Hollywood blockbuster for her. You know; 'Lydia Stars in London!' 'Lydia Saves Auntie from Tragic Accident!' 'Lydia Meets the Prime Minister!' That sort of thing. Ha ha!"

Julia was quiet. We had never really shared the same sense of humour.

"Right. Gosh. Hmmm. I suppose we owe her an apology then, don't we, Malcolm?" I heard a murmured exchange between Adam's parents. Then Malcolm took over the phone;

"So, it's true then…? Christ on a bike!"

"Yes – that's him. But he was on a badge, this time round."

Malcolm chortled.

"Oh, bloody hell, Rachael! Only Lydia could meet the Prime Minister - and end up creating news headlines!"

I had to wait a few seconds until he had calmed down. Then he cleared his throat and carried on with;

"… I mean, how bloody stupid the world is today! These news programmes – they've been wheeling out every religious expert under the sun! All of your Muslim crackpots coming out of the woodwork… they're saying that because of all of this, there's going to be more prejudice against them. I mean, it's hardly like us Christians are the ones blowing people up and training terrorists up there in the Lake District, now, is it? I mean…"

He carried on in his usual ill-informed, sound-bite manner. His favourite form of media had always been the dreadful Star News Channel; part of the same massive corporation as News Of The Nation. I loved Malcolm to bits, but I had always felt it to be pretty tragic - that such an intelligent man didn't engage himself with more challenging material when it came to current affairs. For a moment, I considered reminding Malcolm about the IRA. Or the UVF. Or the UFF. Or various other terrorist factions all over the world who considered themselves to be 'Christian' and who would quite happily slaughter people in the name of their religion, their cause. And of course, that the vast majority of ordinary Muslims felt that committing murder in the name of Islam was a blasphemy. But hey. This was Malcolm. And this would need to be a discussion for another day. Or rather – one for Lydia and Matthew to deal with when they were arsey students - and where the discourse would be aided by the buffer of a generation-removed. So, instead, I cut him off mid-rant;

"Sorry, Malcolm. Yes, I really should have mentioned it. Maybe you should just tell her that you were wrong. And that her mum also says she was sorry. That I should have told you about it. But yeah… if I were you, I wouldn't try and ask her for the details of how we met the Prime Minister. She'll just think that you're trying to prove that she's lying, or something."

He seemed to accept my solution to dealing with the problem of a tear-sodden granddaughter and passed the phone back to his wife, and after making the arrangements for Lydia to be returned home at the weekend, I hung up.

Despite my clever remarks designed to dissuade the grandparents from grilling the girl, I still had to wonder if Lydia would voluntarily mention Michael to them. My stomach twisted, as I recalled the nightdress incident. And imagined a Liddy-embellishment; ('Mummy has a new friend. She was wearing a little lacy nightie in his house. And she was showing it to the Prime Minister, too!')

I didn't think that Julia and Malcolm would expect me to remain in mourning forever. But there was a time and a place to break new romantic developments to them. If Michael and I did end up becoming something more than just a flash in the pan, I had hoped that I would be the one to break the news to them, as opposed to a Lydia version of events.

I snuck out of my office and went to find a consolatory biscuit. Or twenty. For the rest of the day I managed to distract myself with work, meetings and plans for the launch. But I kept popping back to my desk to check the news on the internet. Sisters' Space has access to the BBC websites at any rate; I like to make concessions for quality reporting as opposed to half-baked titillation for the masses. The story was still sticking. In fact, it was growing. The Archbishop of Canterbury had responded to a statement provided by one of the more rabid far-right Christian leaders. And then the President of the Humanist Society stirred up further controversy with; "What's all the fuss about? We're just talking about a baby wearing a badge. A badge that contains a nice, fuzzy, warm statement. A fitting analogy for all simplistic and medieval modes of thinking - such as religion – I think."

Yes indeed, the whole situation was becoming increasingly surreal.

By three PM, following another email nudge from Martyn, I could no longer avoid the other burning issue of the day. Forget badges, babies and bizarre news stories. Chase Shaun.

First, I tried his mobile. It went straight to voicemail. He was probably in one of his oh-so-important Medlock Council meetings. No doubt, the Lord of Local Leisure and Communities Department would be presiding over high-level strategic direction i.e. whether the authority should be culling innocent lollipop ladies or, instead, torching blameless librarians.

So, I decided to call his office. Steeling myself for the officious, icy sneer of The Rottweiler.

"Renee McCauley."

"Oh. Hello. It's Rachael Russell here from Sisters' Space – the women's centre. Could I speak with Shaun Elliot, please?"

"I'm afraid he's not available right now. Can I help you?"

"Yes. You can tell me when he would be *available.*"

Renee and I had already had a little run-in recently. I had managed to sneak past her kennel the other week, whilst she had disappeared to chomp a bone. She had inadvertently allowed me access to the Sanctuary of Shaun, Overlord of All Dark Things Municipal, also known as 'Shaun's office at Medlock Town Hall'. And she wouldn't be forgetting that little trespass for a good few decades.

"Well, Mr Elliot is a very busy man. It would be quite difficult for him to find time to speak with you. Can you tell me what the nature of your enquiry is? I'm sure that I'd be able to help." After hell freezes over.

I gritted my teeth.

"No, I'm sorry. But I don't think that you can help. It's quite an urgent matter - one that only he can deal with. I do need to speak with him directly."

"Well, Mr Elliot is a very busy…" I cut her off.

"I know. You said. He's very busy and he's very important. You say that quite a lot, actually."

She snapped. Spitting acid;

"Well, there's no need to be rude. My job is to intercept communications for Mr Elliot which are of a less… essential nature and which can be dealt with by myself."

My voice was already dripping with sarcasm.

"And yes - you really do cross all of the I's and dot all the T's - with regards to your job description. But never mind all of this. I happen to be one of the privileged peasants who *does* have possession of his mobile number. Which kind of indicates that he's more than happy to speak directly with me. Don't you think?"

"Well, if you have his mobile number, then why are you trying to reach him on the landline?"

"Because… because I do. I need to find out where he is. His mobile went to voicemail. And this is a very pressing matter. So, I need to speak to him. Urgently."

Now the Rottweiler was flashing the sarky tone back at me;

"So, if it's as – *pressing* – as you say, then I'm sure he'll call you back very soon."

"Look. Can't you at least tell me when he'll be free to speak? Or where he is?"

"I'm sorry. I couldn't possibly let someone know his whereabouts over the phone. It wouldn't be…"

I snorted appalled laughter at her;

"Oh, come on! What is this? I mean, we're not exactly talking about the President of the United States now, are we? He's the man in charge of community centres and council leisure facilities! Are you terrified that I'm going to try and drown him in a swimming pool during the local Brownies' sports gala or something like…?"

Right back at me, "Look. If you're going to continue to be abusive towards me, then…"

I cut her off.

"Listen, lady – don't *ever* use that word – abusive – in relation to someone getting snotty with you over the phone. If you want to know what real abuse looks like, then come and visit the women's centre and listen to what a hell of a lot of females in our country are putting up with. That'll jerk you out of your municipal cosiness, you…"

But she had hung up on me before I had managed to call her a 'daft, jobsworth bint.'

Which I concede, would not have been very professional or particularly 'pro-women' of me.

CHAPTER 14

I took a late lunch and tried to distract myself from the altercation with Shaun's pet pooch by googling 'best pets for kids when their parents can't be arsed.' The search engine came back with 'sea monkeys' which sounded to me like an awful lot of bother, what with us living nowhere near an ocean and what with you needing a Dangerous Wild Animals licence to own a simian if you happen to live in the UK.

But before I could investigate this any further, Bev wandered past my office, on her way down the corridor to the other end of the centre. She stuck her head around the door;

"Alreet, Rach."

"Hiya. What you up to?"

"Just on me way to the barista training."

She noticed my sandwich.

"And before you ask, Bev. It's an egg and cress wrap."

"Bleugh. Looks like someone blew their nose on your gusset."

"Leave me alone. Go and play with your frothy milk jug – or your bean to brew ratio or whatever tosh those coffee-freak trainers are trying to convince you is actually some acceptable form of artistic expression."

She pulled a face at me and wandered off.

The phone rang. It was Michael.

"I'm sorry I couldn't call earlier. It's been somewhat manic here. Are you okay, Rachael?"

"Yeah, I think so. The only fallout, so far, seems to have been around Adam's parents." I outlined what had happened and then asked him how it had been playing out for him.

"Well, not too bad, strangely. It's a little bit like the other week with the Minister-biker story. This whole Jesus-badge thing is proving to be a very convenient distraction... We've got lots of other stuff happening at the moment in the Middle East; juggling the Yanks and the Saudis - which we'd rather keep away from the press."

"Right. So, the Prime Minister isn't too pissed off about it all?"

He burst out laughing. The knots in my stomach relaxed.

"No – not at all. The PM finds it all quite amusing actually. That anyone would think that he - Mr dyed-in-the-wool atheist - might believe in such a load of old tosh about God."

"Charming. Not at all patronising."

Michael carried on breezily. "Yes, and doesn't it just go to show you? All of these crazy religious sorts - jumping onto the bandwagon in the press. Your dodgy demagogues and your rabble rousers."

"Well, not all of them, Michael. Several hundred thousand Anglicans don't really view the Archbishop of Canterbury as some kind of dodgy demagogue."

He tutted.

"Well, not him of course. And … he's another one who knows how to play the game with finesse. In fact, this is very convenient for Lambeth Palace too. They've just had another big run-in with the African Anglicans and their usual homophobic objections at some conference or another. So 'The Baby And The Badge' is a nice little side-show for everyone. Nothing to worry about."

"Good. That's a relief."

"But," he continued, "With regards to all of that, I do need to ask you something. The PM's office want to release a press statement explaining that the badge hadn't been pinned onto Toby's coat by his own parents."

This surprised me;

"Really? That seems to be a bit… over the top. Does it really matter that Lydia gave him the badge – and not his parents?"

Michael's voice was weary – but still cheery – down the phone line.

"Oh, it's just that the PM's people are thinking that there does need to be a response of some sort. An explanation. And that the best bet would be utilise a sort of 'naïve source' for outlining where the badge came from…"

I stayed quiet.

"So, Rachael. We were thinking… that it would be better if we were straight up about it. Told the truth."

"The 'we' bit meaning that Alex the Twat… is angling for this?"

A sigh. Followed by;

"Look. I know that the guy is a complete prick. But he does have a crucial job to do… to provide damage limitation. And I've also got ministerial obligations myself - to the PM…"

"But hang on. You just said that the whole thing was a helpful distraction. A side-show. So, I don't understand why putting out a press release that… 'tells the truth' as you put it… is so important?"

Michael tried to interrupt me, but it was too late. The bit about ministerial obligations had particularly naffed me off. What about my own obligations? To my children? To my in-laws? To my own wavering spiritual or religious beliefs - or whatever the hell crumbling remnants were left of them these days? My indignation flared and the fireworks began to start;

"No! I don't see why Lydia's name has to be dragged into all of this. I know

I'm not some kind of celeb or a bloody Royal or whatever… But no. I don't want my child being flashed all over the papers. I don't want her name on the TV! She's just some daft little girl with a badge-fixation, for God's sake!"

"Well, what I was —" Michael tried to say. But I was on a roll.

"Sorry to say this, but I'm not that bothered about the Prime Minister's family in all of this. Toby's face will always be pixelated until he's eighteen. Little Toby will get all of the privileges associated with his family name. *He'll* get the private education. *He'll* go to Oxbridge, without ever having to fret about paying back a crippling student loan. *He'll* get fast-tracked to some City job… earning hundreds of thousands a year just because of who his parents happen to be."

"Let me just —" Michael began. But I raced on;

"Lydia won't. *She'll* just get her fifteen minutes of fame in some shit tabloid newspaper. And then she'll get bullied for the next ten years at the local comprehensive school because she'll have starred as some weird little kid in a religious controversy. As opposed to gracing the stage for Britain's Got Talent. Or shagging a League Two footballer."

"Rachael, I can't believe — "

I barely took a breath.

"Still, whilst you're at it. If your lot want this badge to be seen to have originated from a 'naïve' source… Well. Why don't you put *this* in your press release; that it came from a kid who lives up north… and who probably subsists on a diet of mushy peas and pudding. Who is probably obese, a bit backward and so who'll no doubt believe whatever bollocks you tell it about - when it comes to matters of religion."

"Okay. Enough." Michael's voice was more than clipped. Trimmed with an edge that I hadn't heard directed at me before. "Have you quite finished?"

Like he's my headteacher or something. Yeah, actually. I have finished. And so what? I'm not on the other side of the sodding Commons. Bugger off with your ministerial obligations and your hoity toity manner.

But I had run out of steam, so I gulped a breath in order to reply. He got in there first.

"For your information, Rachael. We weren't going to suggest that Lydia is mentioned. I wouldn't dream of giving the nod to that. I was just going to ask if you were okay with us simply saying that another child – who the family had met that day – gave it to the baby. And that therefore, it would have been impolite for Jane and the PM to refuse it."

"Oh. Right."

Silence descended.

A bit of back-peddling needed.

"I thought you meant that they… would. You know - put her name in the papers or something."

A very palpable quietness at the other end of the line.

"Look, Michael. That might have sounded like a bit of an overreaction there…"

"Just a bit."

"I should have realised. That you wouldn't have allowed her name to be mentioned. Of course. It's just that —"

"Nobody trusts a politician, right?"

Was he genuinely offended?

"No… Michael. I'm not saying that. The Archbishop of Canterbury might be a dab hand at it… playing games. Politics. The press. But I'm just… some ordinary woman. I'm Joe Public. I don't know how all of this pans out…"

"That's not entirely true. You've had experience yourself in Westminster; when you were advising civil servants. You know how this sort of thing works."

I half-laughed. It turned into a recalcitrant snot moment.

"Oh, please - I was a policy advisor! I gave the government tips about social policy. The welfare system. How to stop grinding the poor down even more. I wasn't a spin doctor!"

"But you're a canny woman, Rachael – you always —"

"And when your own child is under threat, you know what, Michael? You do tend to get a tad bit defensive about things. But you wouldn't…" I trailed off.

He completed the sentence.

"… understand. Because I've never been blessed with the joys of having children.'

I swallowed. Trying to explain myself better.

"It's not that. I just hate this attitude… that I seem to be hearing. This 'we' stuff. The government. The men. The voice of the secular establishment. It feels like you belong to some… Big Boy's Club. Playing out your strategy with the press and the innocent public. Yeah – sneering at people who are religious. And that's people like me. People who do have some kind of a faith. Or whatever you want to call it."

"That's ridiculous. We have plenty of women in government these days. And you know my own background. I'm Jewish. Jewish-Catholic for Christ's sake! Educated at a Roman Catholic seminary school —"

"Yes," I snapped. "But your family were secular Jews. And you told me that all of the religious stuff at Ampleforth put you off it for life."

"Well, I'm sorry if you feel that we're – I'm – sneering." 'Sneering' was cast back at me with rather a lot of venom. "… But, Rachael, if people of faith – or religion or whatever – can't handle a bit of criticism… Can't handle the fact that the vast majority of us reckon that they're all deluded - believing in such preposterous fairy tales then —"

"Fine, Michael. You just said it all. So, let's go with it. And hey - if it makes it easier for everyone all round, I'm quite happy for me and mine to be alluded to as a bunch of simple-minded born-again Christians, who are clearly emotional cripples and who need to imagine a God to enable them to get through life. The sort of people who randomly accost others and provide them with Jesus Loves You badges."

"Well there's no need to —"

"So, sure. Fire your press release off or whatever gung-ho military jargon you'll all be using. But I've got to go. People with real problems in life. Maybe speak later —"

I heard him replying with a pointed, "Maybe…" as I hung up.

For the rest of the afternoon I functioned on autopilot, the anger still seething throughout the journey back home. None of this was assisted by Steve Wright's inane banter, so I changed the channel to Radio Four instead. But then jabbed the button to 'off' when the Prime Minister's voice came on. Alright, he was railing on about the decline of the steel industry, as opposed to his religious affiliations. But whatever. I was sick of the whole lot of them.

Matthew was duly collected from nursery and if he had been banking on double the motherly love and attention given Lydia's absence, the kid would have been one very disappointed child. A few chunks of cheese and a jam sandwich was tossed in his general direction for supper, but he didn't seem to be too upset about it. As always, kiddy-TV let me off the hook for an hour or so. I tried not to look at my phone, tried not to stew about the fact that Michael hadn't called me or sent any messages. By seven PM, we had watched the Christmas episode of Sooty and Sweep for the eighth time and I had been forced to come to a conclusion.

That this was It. End of story. That the Right Honourable Michael Chiswick MP, cabinet minister, ex-army officer, born of uber-posh Berkshire stock, would never be the kind of man prepared to put up with gobby, easily offended and religiously inclined, common northern birds. (Even if I am a dead good shag.)

So, I lay on the living room sofa, drifting off into a strange and uncomfortable sleep. Matthew had given up on the stuffed animals with hands up their arses performances and was wielding the remote control by himself, channel-hopping from one unsuitable programme, to another.

The room seemed to be rocking gently as I half opened my eyes. There was a hazy atmosphere, a scent of something that I couldn't quite place. The smell of tar – of roadworks? No, more like a garage. Motor oil.

For a split second I saw Adam.

He was sitting on the chair opposite the sofa. Bum plonked on a tea towel issued by The

Wife, because he was wearing his bike overalls; "And our sofa might be second-hand, Adam, but try not to make it look any shittier than it already does."

He was holding his head in his hands. He was muttering one of his favourite expressions of frustration with Rachael Russell nee-Stanley.

"Aarrghh... someone PLEASE kill me before I do it myself!"

This was an utterance that I usually heard several times a week. It was Adam's standard response to what some might call my spirited and challenging nature. Or as Adam chose to view it, "your stubborn-as-a-sodding-pig, sheer bloody-mindedness."

I jerked out of my snooze and tried to sit up, but the imprint of Adam had vanished and instead had been replaced by the oh-so real flesh and bone incarnation of his son. Who, for reasons unbeknownst to us mere mortals, had been rocking my head from side-to-side whilst singing 'Yellow Submarine.' He had also precariously placed his cup of milk between my legs. It sloshed all over my jeans.

Matthew pressed a grimy finger onto the tip of my nose. Squashed it down.

"Ha. Ugly Mummy. But I'll still kiss you."

I puckered up and obliged. Then he moved onto providing me with a strange version of a head massage. It involved wiping rather more jam from his gloopy sandwich into my hair than I would have hoped for. I ignored the sticky hair issue as I tried to enjoy a rare-son snuggle.

And then I cried. Naked self-pity.

I cried because of my inability to reign in that wilful and volatile streak; a character flaw which had caused me – yet again - to mouth off at a man who genuinely seemed to care for me. A man who I had been getting far too keen on. Even if he was one of your posh, parasitic politicians.

And I cried for my children too. By rights, they should be sitting here with Adam – not me - rubbing jam into his hair, sloshing milk all over him. And then more; tears fell for Adam's parents too. Doing their best to hold it together, but both empty husks of the people that they had once been. Losing a child – whether a nipper or an adult - brings a pain that no one can ever come to terms with.

And finally, back to me again. I cried because I missed Adam. I missed the way that he would simply walk off in the middle of an argument because he – quite correctly – felt that "This isn't a row – this is a rant. And you're monopolising the oxygen around here." I cried because I missed his inconsistent generosity; the way that he would quite happily devour half a dead cow purchased from his favourite farm shop in Holmfirth with no sense of guilt whatsoever, but would stop the car and pull over if a butterfly got trapped under the windscreen wipers. I cried because I missed every night in bed with him – never any awkwardness between us. I cried because I missed the way that he would bite into pens and pencils and end up breaking them. Because of his ridiculous habit of opening a dozen different cereal packets at a time; "Because I like to make life more interesting by having a different cereal every day. You're the boring one - you - with your Marmite toast."

When I cry, it's never just over one thing.

And although Matthew knew what an adult's leaky eyes signify, it didn't seem to bother him. He simply wiped away my tears with his fingers, dabbing them with the corner of his jammy crusts, whilst he still continued to stare at the TV, pondering; "Poor Mummy. You're silly, you are."

Children have an uncanny ability of being right about things, sometimes.

One hour later, Matthew was in bed and I had decided to take a bath, aiming to console myself with a large glass of wine and a chubby candle purchased from the pound shop in Holmfirth. Lydia had proudly presented me with it on Mother's Day. It claimed to be 'lavender and patchouli scented', but unfortunately smelled more like I had accidentally melted a bottle of Toilet Duck in the bathroom, so I quickly snuffed it out and lobbed it into the bin. The fifteen minutes in the bath, though, had proven to be useful. I had shaken off the crippling wave of grief and had been engaging in some serious self-talk. I had decided to come to terms with the fact that my relationship with Michael had been just a brief thing; one of those in-betweeners.

Yeah, it was still too early to get involved with somebody else. I would buck up and concentrate on the kids, the café, the chocolate and the women at work. That little lot needed me, a lot more than Mr Up Himself Politician and his London-Luvvies did, anyway.

Yeah. Sod the men. Focus on the people who really deserve the help.

CHAPTER 15

I yanked the plug from the bath, put on my dressing gown and wandered downstairs, glass of wine in hand. Pausing at the TV in the living room, I contemplated whether it would be sensible to torture myself further with more media details on the unholy row that my daughter had unwittingly released.

The doorbell chimed. Probably Mrs Finnigan from next door. She tended to do this of a Tuesday night. It was bin collection day and she enjoyed engaging me with a regular bitch-fest about the wanton mess, destruction and general negligence operated by the yobbos who masqueraded as our municipal refuse collection team.

But it wasn't Mrs F.

And it appeared that the issue at hand wasn't going to be about the effective collection and disposal of household waste.

A flickering orange streetlight emphasised the slight bend in his nose. An injury inflicted on him many moons ago when some kid at Ilkley Grammar School had kicked him in the face during a particularly rambunctious rugby match.

All six foot five inches of Medlock's head honcho happened to be standing, oh-so-casually, on my doorstep. Immaculately suited and booted. At least he had the courtesy to look just a tad bit sheepish. (Which was unusual for him.)

"Not interrupting you putting the kids to bed or anything, am I?"

There was only a light rainfall but the wind was beginning to whip itself into an autumn squall. His coat glittered with tiny jewels of moisture.

"No."

His eyes left mine as he glanced down at the doorstep. An empty yogurt carton was rolling around there, rattled by a gust from the north.

"Would you look at that?" I said, half-wondering as to why I was sounding so apologetic. "Bloody binmen. But no… It's just Matthew here at the moment. He should be asleep by now."

Sick to the back teeth of the usual Power Ranger or Marvel Superhero storybook shenanigans, I had demanded that Matthew listen to some nice, old-fashioned fairy tales before bedtime. But whilst the kid himself had experienced them to be "as boring as poo," they must have struck a chord with me. Because I could now imagine certain sibilant words as they floated down the stairs from Matthew's bedroom, towards the front door.

"Little pig, little pig, let me come in…"

Shaun wiped sparkles of rain from his brow.

"Alright if I come in, Stan? It's right nippy tonight. Looks like it's going to freeze over."

My hackles rose. No bugger else ever called me that - 'Stan.' Shaun felt that it was his exclusive prerogative. But I did my best to ignore it and stepped back from the door, allowing him over the threshold. He took off his coat and hung it over the back of a kitchen chair. Then he loosened his tie.

"Just been to a conference in Leeds. Dull as hell. One shitty, long day of it. Thought I'd forgo the M62. Drive back over the tops instead."

"Yeah?" I picked up a random sock and a set of plastic vampire teeth which Matthew had left on the kitchen table. "Surely it would have been more direct to drive back to your side of Manchester through Sheffield? Holme isn't exactly on the way."

"Well, you can't beat the hills over this way, can you? Holme Moss... it's always been my favourite drive. Better on the bike of course, but leathers aren't the best sort of apparel for my line of work these days. Not the image, really."

"Right. So, is that you thinking that your average Council Tax payer in Medlock is daft enough to be taken in by a senior manager who wears Armani and drives the latest Lexus? As opposed to someone who might come across like a normal person? A bit less of the aesthetics and more of the humility might not go amiss with your local residents."

"I'll ignore that comment, Stan." Then he gestured to my glass of wine. "Any of that going?"

"Aren't you driving?"

"Just one will be fine. I'm a big fella. Remember?"

I took a glass out of the kitchen cabinet and poured him a drink. My hand was shaking. He took the drink from me and nodded at my dressing gown;

"Like the leopard-skin print. Classy."

"Cheers."

"Goes well with the slippers." I glanced down. I had forgotten about the slippers. Enormous furry dog-shaped things that Lydia and Grandma had conspired to purchase as a birthday present for me. My mother knew that I would hate them. She liked to do things like that.

He followed me through to the living room and sat down on the sofa. Sipped his wine.

"Not bad stuff, this. Must be paying you too much at the women's centre if you've started partaking of the finer things in life. And far too nice to be drinking on your own, it must be said..."

"Must it? Because funnily enough, Shaun, I don't have much of a choice these days. In case you hadn't noticed."

I looked – deliberately - over at the family portrait that hung on the wall.

It had been taken only six weeks before Adam was killed. We didn't normally go in for that kind of thing as he had always objected ("too cheesy – too chavvy. And you're too hideously unattractive Rachael…") but one of my little hobbies had been entering competitions - and it turned out that I had won the portrait sitting thanks to a local newspaper prize draw. I must have been on a bit of a roll at that point in time. A stroke of good luck. Because it had been the same time of year when I had won the toilet-roll trip to Cape Town. A holiday that Adam had ended up going on with his mate, Big Jim, instead of me; "I'm not bloody dragging the kids to South Africa, Adam. Imagine Matthew airborne for over twelve hours! No – you can go with Jim instead. You'll have more fun anyway, doing your boys-stuff, without me dragging you around museums and the like."

So, I had won The Holiday Of A Lifetime. Which really, should have been billed as The Holiday To End A Lifetime. An impromptu vacation where Adam had vanished from us, for all eternity - thanks to that damned freak accident.

But at least the photo-op had been a good little win. I had persuaded Adam to "get over your wanabee upper-class prejudices, you great big snob. What are you waiting for? Someone to commission a royal artist to paint a portrait of us lot?" And the picture was indeed a beaut. It captured all four of us laughing out loud – even toddling Matthew - whose predominating facial expressions were either a grump, a grimace or a cacked-in-his pants gurn. Adam's shirt sleeves had been rolled up during the photo session because he had arrived to meet us at the studio after tinkering with Big Jim's bike. Oil stains on his cuffs, along with a tell-tale combo-whiff of diesel and Theakston's Old Peculiar; "It's bloody Saturday, Rach. Helping a mate out. Give us a break and smile for the camera – you miserable old tart!"

Shaun followed my eyes. He had the decency to look slightly abashed. But only for a split second. Self-assurance in spades.

"Well… that was more of a reference to your recently acquired taste for other… finer things in life."

"Meaning?"

"Meaning Mr Chiswick. You told me last week that you were going to London for the weekend, didn't you? So, then. How was The Big Smoke?"

"Nice. But then you should no doubt be aware of that yourself. Always hurtling to and from your important London stuff, in your first-class West Coast train compartments."

"Yeah, well, not so much these days. Cutbacks mean that we've been seeing a lot more meetings taking place in the regions."

"Ah, yeah. Leeds – like you said. Slumming it. God, poor you."

"Anyway. I'm not here to talk about that. You left a message. And I seem to have received lots of missed calls from you. Renee said that you were trying to get in touch. That you were claiming that something was urgent."

"Oh, so she does pass messages on then, does she? If she feels that they might be worthy enough to warrant the attention of her Lord and Master."

"She also said that you were very rude to her. Not like you, that…"

He crossed his arms and showed me a sardonic grin. So, I told him;

"Yeah, well. Your Renee got as good as she gives. You should send her along to Sisters' Space sometime. She could definitely do with attending one of our courses about passive-aggressive behaviour. We also do training on how to implement the principles of co-operation when working with other females."

"Jesus. Training on 'women and co-operation'? No wonder you're short of cash there. Wasting your budgets on that sort of crap. Once Roger retires and I end up stepping into his shoes, pointless training will be the first thing out of the window in Medlock."

For all of his opinions and bluntness with regards to anything and everything, the one thing that Shaun *didn't* do, was engage with me in the gender war of words. Whether my observations were intended as light-hearted conversation, or whether they possessed profound meanderings in relation to misogyny or the patriarchy, Shaun just didn't bite the bullet.

"It's boring," he had told me, shortly after we first began working together some sixteen years ago. I had been recounting my disgust at a particularly vile girlie calendar that adorned the walls of a local housing repairs contractor. I had said how offensive it was, how it made me feel very uncomfortable, but Shaun had just responded; "I take your point, Stan, but — it's just boring. Dull. I mean — there isn't even a debate to be had. Men that get off on having photos of lasses like that up on their walls. Well, they're just thick-as-pig-shit Neanderthals. So why bother stressing about it? You're not going to change the opinions of pillocks like that. Get over it."

I'd said, "But it's totally wrong! Stuff like this should be banned from anywhere — especially a workplace! Just allowing it… it's reinforcing the fact that it's okay to view women as sexual objects."

"Well, as much as you don't like it, Stan, a hell of a lot of men do see women like that. And by taking their girlie calendars off them, you're just encouraging them to go and buy a wank-rag from the corner shop so that they can drool over lasses in secret. And the way that the internet is going — one day pretty soon - any bloody building contractor will be able to copy something onto a phone or whatever and shove it up his sleeve. Have a sneaky little tommy-tank in the corner of the office whilst your back is turned. Surely, that would be worse?"

"Whether women are viewed like that in secret or out in the open isn't the issue. What I'm talking about is changing the mindset of future generations —"

"I'm bored," said Shaun. "I've stopped listening. I'd rather go and sort my rent arrears out."

He rubbed his eyes and winced, revealing a sudden glimmer of tiredness. This surprised me; Shaun looking weary. Of course, he had a growth of stubble on his chin, but that had always been present. And these days it marked an act of defiance, two-fingers to the clean-shaven versus beardy brigade trend that predominates. But back in the day, Shaun had mastered the unshaven look as a badge of honour; Mr Tough Yorkshireman Doesn't Need to Shave For You Mancunian Lot. And the tired vibes were not a result of his get-up either. The pristinely ironed shirt, the pressed tie, and the gleaming shoes were as they had always been, even when we'd worked in social housing, patrolling some of the grottiest properties in Manchester.

Maybe it was a work problem. Maybe Roger - Medlock Council's CEO - was an evil git to work for, after all. As opposed to being the buffoon in a one hundred and eighty thousand pounds post that everyone else took him to be. But viewing Shaun - even with the slightest sign of his defences being on the wane – had always thrown me off guard. I was about to soften the conversational sparring and ask him what the problem was, when his phone suddenly rang. His eyes flicked towards it; starting that tell-tale involuntary muscle spasm in the corner of his left eye. His finger nudged the 'decline' button. In the past, I would have avoided the issue, but these days the wheel of fortune had left me in a rather different position. These days I had nothing to lose. So, I said;

"Was that your wife?"

With the emphasis being on the noun.

The noun component of the sentence was a comparatively new state of affairs. And one which Shaun had neglected to inform me of - whilst we had been tearing at each other's clothes, parked up in his Lexus and squirrelled away in some grubby Mancunian car park, some fifteen months ago. How the hell you can forget to tell the person you're regularly screwing, that you've just gotten hitched to someone else, I don't know. But Shaun had had a pretty good try at that one. And looking back on it, his explanation about the recent tan – that he had received it courtesy of a long weekend at Bolton Abbey, as opposed to their week's honeymoon in Fiji - had also been one hell of a classic.

So, yeah. I had been engaging in official adultery, without realising it. And it had only been two weeks longer, before I discovered the truth. A former colleague from Whalley Range housing office had bumped into me in the frozen food aisle of Medlock's Sainsbury's and had happened to mention that Shaun had finally gotten wed to his long-term girlfriend. "Nearly twenty years, the poor woman's waited!"

Brown-black, almost pupiless eyes - moved back onto mine. He wasn't responding to the dig.

"Maybe you're needed at home," I said.

With the emphasis being on the noun again. A reference to the cosy suburban nest that he and Jess shared in Chorlton-cum-Hardy; the most bo-ho town around Manchester. I had lived there once. But my experience of Chorlton had been rather different to his way of life. Some fourteen years ago, I had moved in with Jake Bamber, in an attempt to try and deal with the roller-coaster ride that involved – even then – a secret relationship with Shaun. Jake had been another colleague of ours and was the only person in our office who had been aware of what was going on between us. He had done his best to cheer me up; urging me to flog copies of Socialist Worker newspaper around the Arndale Centre with him and he had also roped me into helping with the organisation of Manchester's Gay Pride parade. But his efforts proved to be futile. Most evenings seemed to culminate in me drinking far too much Malibu and finding myself sobbing along to various Celine Dion tracks. Which is always a bad sign, for anyone.

So, my own memories of Chorlton were rather depressing. A woodlice problem in one corner of my bedroom. Constantly having my Vauxhall Astra broken into by various scumbags. The excruciating commute along the demonically named A666 to Bolton where I happened to work as a housing officer at the time. Jake and the never-ending stream of gorgeous gay blokes interrupting me at seven AM in the bathroom. Me also possessing a fair bit of pulling-power back in those days; blokes on tap in the bars and boozers at the corner of Beech Road, or in the nightclubs of Manchester. But me only wanting…

And Shaun? Shaun's version of life in Chorlton-cum-Hardy had furnished him with a four-bedroomed house, a double garage and a ten-minute commute to work. And Jess.

And Jess?

Jess had a garden office. And Shaun, of course.

He stretched out his long legs. His movements had always been lazy and languid. But lots of the bravado managerial body language was just for show. At heart, he was still a fidgeter;

"I need to move this bloody light. It's right in my eyes. Feels like I'm being interrogated. Did one of the kids bend it over like this?"

I nodded. Matthew had attacked the angle poise lamp earlier on in the week, so that it no longer retained any 'poise' and instead, looked more like a contorted stick insect. Shaun jerked the lamp away and muttered;

"Nice lamp, that. You shouldn't let them play with it."

I gave him a thin smile. There is nothing more guaranteed to get the back up of a struggling parent than a non-parent providing their expert opinion on how a child should behave. Most non-parents however, possess the sensitivity and the sensibility to realise this before they open their gob and stick their size twelves in. But not Shaun. Or perhaps he was trying to nark me. Getting me back for my nudge about The Wife.

"You rather neatly sidestepped my question there, Shaun. About your home life." I was perching on my favourite armchair and had tucked my legs under myself as I slowly swished the wine around in my glass. I was enjoying being on my own territory for once; every recent encounter with Shaun had been tainted with the age-old feeling of power imbalance. (Always in Shaun's favour.)

He gave me a don't-give-a-toss shrug, put his mobile down on the arm of the sofa and commenced with cracking his knuckles.

"Yeah, well. Doesn't feel like my home much, anymore. Feels more like it belongs to Jess' parents. 'Cause they're moving house. Living at ours for a few weeks till the chain's sorted. And giving her loads of grief over various things. Mostly to do with me being a crap and absentee husband. So, it's not a barrel of laughs there, right now."

"Sorry to hear that," I said, trying to keep the smirk out of my voice. "But the absentee accusations are striking a chord with me. Because if you're as difficult to get in touch with for those that you live with - as you are for those that you're supposed to be working with – I can understand why that might piss people off. I mean, all that I've been trying to sort out with you is getting your signature for our loan. Time's running out."

Shaun burst out laughing. He seemed to have located some profound hilarity in what I had just said.

"Stan, I can't believe you. Seriously. I offered you a top job the other week. First the money. Way more. And then I said that you can do whatever the hell you want – in effect. And you said no. Got all these principles these days - you said. And now you seem to think that a route out of your own personal money problems is to get your social enterprise backed by Martyn? Some loony Jehovah's Witness freak who suffers with short-man syndrome? You're crazy, Stan."

Bam.

The mention of my own financial mess was way below the belt. In a moment of weakness shortly after Adam's death, when Shaun and I had resurrected our affair - I had admitted to him that there had been no life or accident insurance payment. I now bitterly regretted letting that one slip. It meant that Shaun would all too often whip it out and try and use it to get the upper hand. But this was not the time to show regrets or irritation. I tried to gloss over the embarrassment; kept my composure.

"No. You're the crazy one. I've told you that I'm not interested in that type of career anymore. And not just because I have the kids, or because of losing Adam. But because, I would rather spend my time doing things that I enjoy. With people that I like. As opposed to chasing some corporate – or council - job title. As opposed to giving myself a heart attack brought on by the stress of working with self-important, parochial, small minded borderline psychopaths who only give a toss about their final salary pension scheme…"

A pause. No response. So, I continued;

"Or whether they got invited to make the keynote speech at the Local Government Association Conference last year..."

Shaun took another gulp of wine.

"Directed at me by any chance?"

"Gosh. Who knows?"

"I know. And I think that you're being a bit out of order, Stan."

"Yeah?"

"Yeah. Cause I've only ever done the keynote speech for the Local Government Association, just the one time. And even then, what I said – apparently - upset a lot of the sort of people that you seem to despise these days. So, I doubt if they'll be asking me back in a hurry. I would have thought that you would approve of what I do. Of how I do it. Would like us to work together. Again."

And that was where he couldn't see it. Shaun Elliot lived, breathed - would probably die courting controversy. I remembered the press coverage on that particular one. It had been just after I learned about his wedding. Shaun had been all-out, guns a-blazing; he had gotten a massive kick out of telling the great and the good attending that particular conference – and a certain Minister named Michael Chiswick who had delivered the opening speech just moments before - exactly what he thought of them all. That senior employees in the public sector had had 'a cushy number for far too long' and that 'let's face it – over half of you lot are a pretty talentless bunch'. Shaun had lapped it all up and if it had resulted in him being barred from all such conferences in the future, it would have been an endless source of delight to him. I tried to clarify;

"Oh, forget you - and your daft rabble-rousing speeches. Even if I did want that kind of job; why the hell do you think that I'd want to work for someone who treated me in the way that you did?"

CHAPTER 16

Silence.

There should have been the sound of a clock ticking. No, really. There should have been.

I narrowed my eyes and peered at my great-grandfather's Victorian mantelpiece clock. It had been beautifully restored and presented to me by my father on my wedding day, with much ceremony; "Make sure that you look after it better than you do your car. Never seen a filthier interior. Your upholstery's a disgrace," but now it appeared to have a jam butty wedged into the opening at the back of it. Not conducive to tick-tock mechanics.

I stood up and strolled to the clock. Removed the butty, lobbed it into the waste paper basket and then walked over to the window. Red lights that marked out the pinnacle of the Holme Moss mast were winking a warning to low flying aircraft in the near vicinity.

I placed my knuckles on the window sill. Shaun hadn't replied. Perhaps he was taking my question as a rhetorical statement and was choosing to ignore it. Perhaps he was shocked by the fact that I allowed my children to insert food items into nineteenth-century antiques.

Or perhaps he was just bored again. That oh-so easily bored, Shaun…

And then the house phone burst into life. I wasn't going to bother getting it, so it tripped into answering machine mode. Julia's sing-song tones echoed across the living room;

"Rachael, love, it's me. Just letting you know that Madam is all settled down for the night now, after a rather unusual day. We did as you said – we didn't ask her about the badge and the Prime Minister – and she managed to get over her sulk about it all. But I'm still tickled pink about it! And I can't wait to hear about how you met them all and how she came to give it to his baby. Did you get to go inside Number Ten then? You lucky thing! Anyway. I'll say nighty-night now. Give Matthew a kiss from us all. Oh – and with regards to us dropping Lydia back with you, I…"

I wandered over to the answering machine and in the most nonchalant manner that I could summon, I switched the volume off.

But Shaun didn't miss a trick.

Shaun never missed a trick.

He went straight for the James Bond eyebrow.

I also engaged in a bit of the Hollywood Facial Expressions Show Time; instinctively flashing back at him a 'what you looking at' face. Probably resembling Mr Bean, myself. But what the hell.

And he said;

"Jesus wept, Stan. I mean, Jesus! Don't tell me that you've dragged Lydia into all of this now? Your —"

"Into what?" I replied. All innocence.

"Into… Frigging headline creation! The stuff that's been all over the show today! About that pathetic excuse that we've currently got for a Prime Minister… about him being 'outed' as a born-again Christian. I mean, I know you went down to London to hang out with your Cabinet fella, but I wouldn't have thought that you… that you'd have levered Lydia into the midst of your seedy Whitehall liaisons."

I drew breath. Ran my tongue around my teeth.

"First of all," I spat. "Don't you *ever* accuse me of dragging my daughter into anything to do with *my personal life*. If I ever happened to get the time to be having one. And second of all…"

I couldn't think of a second of all. So, I just glared at him. Trying to plaster over the humiliation and the fury that I was now feeling, thanks to being rumbled over Badgegate.

But Shaun had already moved on. He had adopted his best Bruce Willis expression (I'm-trying-to-be-compassionate-here… but-I'm-still-gonna-shoot-your-Nanna-in-sixty-seconds-flat). It was accompanied by;

"… And this is yet another reason, why you can't get me to sign your loan paperwork. It's like I said to you the other day. If you and your family are going to be running around in the national press; how can I put my name - put the local authority's reputation at risk – by agreeing to a business venture that might well end up being run by a woman… who's become a public laughing stock?"

"What? You're totally blowing stuff out of proportion here. This is just about some little daft badge that Lydia gave to a baby!"

"No, Stan. Can't you see how much you're lacking judgement here? You might have a lovely, fluffy social enterprise idea that – yeah – might even make sense on paper. But if I give the lenders the assurance that I think your women's centre, your management - meaning your leadership - is viable… and it turns out that —"

"How dare you criticise my managerial abilities!"

"… and if it doesn't work out, thanks to your Barbara Windsor and your Carry On Up The Tabloids act. Well, it'll be me that looks like the prize dickhead at the end of the day."

I was quiet for a second but then murmured.

"Oh, don't worry about that. You do the prize dickhead thing perfectly well, all by yourself. Without any assistance from me and mine."

I stared hard out of the window and managed to focus on the radio mast and its blinking scarlet spot. I tried not to blink, tilting my face upwards slightly so that any moisture wouldn't be seen; that the damned things wouldn't spill over, that they would melt invisibly back into the tear ducts. Over the years, I had found that this was always a cunning way of disguising upset. But the only trouble with this, is that the tears end up coming out of your nose instead.

So, I wiped my nose with my sleeve. Shaun had now morphed into his Hollywood Hero Number Three expression; the Robert de Niro gurn. This was the one he always whipped out of the box when trying to express either disgust, or his 'I-don't-give-a-shit' attitude. Perhaps he had been revolted by my snotty dressing gown sleeves. With any luck.

But instead, I heard a sigh.

"Stan, look. Let's forget the Jesus badge thing. And I can even ignore the other one – the running around half naked in the press with your Minister pal thing. And yeah – I know that I might come across as being a tough arse at work at times. But I've had to be – in order to get to where I am now…'

I sniffed. And reached for the wine. He carried on.

"And yeah, I know that you've had a hell of a time of it… That you think that I made things worse for you. But…"

His words petered out. I wasn't replying. I was watching the lights of a night flight as it arced its way around Holme Moss and towards Manchester airport.

"… Well. You know that I don't do apologies, Stan. Too much apologising going on in the world these days. But, okay then. I can understand why you feel like you got a raw deal out of everything. I *do* get that."

I moved my arms away from the window, folded them tightly and then turned to face him. Trying to keep my voice steady.

"It's not about me getting a raw deal, Shaun. It's not even about what happened the first time round - when there was no excuse to be sneaking around. Hiding from Jess. I mean – you weren't married. And I was bloody single!"

He looked at the wall and then away again, eyes quickly moving from the family portrait and over to a mess of elastic bands and paper clips that Matthew had woven around the base of the angle-poise lamp.

"It's about, Shaun - it's about how it never made any sense to me. Jess not knowing why you'd actually moved out! You not telling her about me. You leaving her – with no real explanation, with her thinking that you were having some kind of early mid-life crisis at the age of twenty-eight, or whatever. Until - for some reason - you decided that you were missing your cushy life in Chorlton-cum-Hardy with her. And you moved back in with her again. And then, you… applying for a job working over in Preston and nowhere near me."

"You make it sound like it was all really calculated. It wasn't."

"Well, that's how it all felt to me. So, then another eight or nine years passes. We maybe saw each other at the odd motorbike rally or whatever. And then suddenly you pitched up at our wedding reception - along with your other bike chums. Just 'cause you happened to have done the odd ride with Adam and his bike club. You only knew him to have the occasional beer with at the Snake Pass. You turned up at my wedding reception, Shaun! Where you deliberately waited to catch me coming out of the loos and then you tried to —"

"Had a bit to drink. We all had."

"And then a few more years on and my husband has just been killed. So you trundle over here to give me your condolences. And we end up…"

I turned back to the windowsill and picked up the glass of wine. I slurped some. He did the same. Then I faced him again as I smacked my forehead with the palm of my hand.

"I'm so… stupid! We end up… in secret again. Whilst you conveniently forget to tell me that you're about to get married. At last – at long bloody last - Jess gets her disgustingly expensive wedding over there in Harrogate. So yeah, I mean – let's not tell Rachael the bimbo about that one, eh?"

I moved to the sideboard and poured myself another glass of wine. I resisted the urge to take a swig from the bottle itself.

"I'm talking about morality here, Shaun. About treating people who you're supposed to care about with a bit of respect. It's not about you having to think of me as some pathetic widow-woman who's had a shitty deal in life. About you giving me some half-arsed tosh about how you're trying to understand me. It's about you having the decency to de-code stuff for me. Am I really so lacking in worth that…"

There was a wobble to my voice and my vision was blurring even more than before. No amount of face-tipping would help this one out. But he stood up, suddenly - ducking to avoid the lampshade - and moved towards me.

I looked away. Matthew appeared to have shoved Lydia's stuffed Scooby-Doo down the back of the bureau. I tried to focus on Scooby and the Gang. Velma wouldn't have cried. Daphne probably would have done, but not Velma. Think Velma.

Shaun had paused to examine the sole of his shoe, having inadvertently stepped on a small pile of sultanas that Matthew had picked out of his cereal that morning and had deposited on the edge of the living room rug. I used the opportunity to brush away the recalcitrant tears. But then he moved towards me again, looking almost-chastised - if that was at all humanly possible for him.

A muffled complaint came from above. Matthew wasn't used to hearing adult voices raised at home. Shaun looked towards the door leading to the stairway and spoke quietly, urgently. His hand reached out to my elbow, trying to explain himself;

"Right. I do hear what you're saying. I wish that…"

And now he stepped closer to me, so that the tip of my nose was only inches from his chest. I said nothing. I let him continue.

"Okay. So. You're serious about this? About me signing this stuff for you? You really think that you can make a go of it; turn your women's centre into something successful? Bring the money in big time. You're certain of it?"

"I know I can."

His hand moved to my hair. He tucked the strands behind my ear, smoothing them down.

"I think – know - you can, too. If anyone can make it happen. You can."

His hand continued to stroke my hair. A slight rustle of starchy shirt as he moved even closer to me. I inhaled a puff of fabric conditioner - but beneath the domestic overtures, I breathed in his scent. The traces that had first spiked my own lunatic pheromones some sixteen years ago, were still there - powerful and sweet, behind the citrus tones of proudly pressed cotton and of designer aftershave.

"Look, Stan, I didn't mean to mess you about like that. In the past. And in many ways things… are okay between me and Jess. But I just… miss you. I miss the fire. Your fire." His fingers began to massage my shoulder gently. It felt good to be touched by him again.

Damn. Shit and Bollocks.

He continued;

"I don't understand it myself… how I've behaved before. And I know that it's not been the usual way of ... being involved. Me and you. Having a relationship, or whatever you want to call it, I mean. But I can't imagine the thought of the rest of my life. Going without you."

His fingers moved up to my neck. To my earlobe. I stood, rooted to the spot - as the ritual began. This wasn't supposed to be happening; not ever again. I'd sworn off this – I had gone cold turkey for long enough now. But paralysis to any resistance was setting in. A dark, velvet-coated voice whispered to me, to go on. To forget about the bitterness, the disappointments of today, of the last few years. That it would be easier to give in and to enjoy something that I hadn't felt in a long time.

Remnants of my conversation with Dawn began to drift forwards from the recesses of my mind. Endorphins and chemicals. I tried to think about de-coding again, about common sense and psychological insight. Logic can be a very powerful tool for changing one's behaviour of course but…

His bottom lip brushed against mine, urging me to kiss him back. He was drinking me in before he devoured me. He always did that.

I didn't push him away.

But I didn't respond either. Even though he was the instigator. Was I testing him - or myself?

His fingers toyed with the opening of my dressing gown as his mouth moved

120

to my ear, hushed tones;

"You want your loan. You want me. And I want you. Let's not have any more talk about you having had a crappy deal of it in the past. Let's make a better arrangement. One that works for us both. I'll sign over the loan for you and you can… "

His mouth was back onto mine as he nudged my backside against the window sill.

Bad move, Shaun.

Because I suddenly remembered that Mrs Finnigan might be able to see us from her kitchen window and that this little performance would certainly scandalise her more than the recalcitrant bin men ever could.

And then Matthew joined in the moment; a lusty bellow echoing from upstairs;

"No! Not jam! I want Marmite! Not Hovis! White bread!"

I broke away, knocking the edge of a wine glass with my elbow and hoping that I hadn't knocked red wine all over the living room carpet. Well, sod it if I had. Perhaps even a mollycoddled-Shaun was capable of finding some kitchen roll and a cloth. I took the stairs two at a time. Normally I would ignore the odd night time call-out from my son - especially if it was only about Marmite as opposed to mutating monsters, that he might have accidentally been exposed to on a fifteen-rated film last week. But fortune had granted me a reason to get away from Shaun for a few seconds.

Matthew was fine. He was the kind of kid who often shrieked out strange connotations of conversation in his sleep, but Shaun wouldn't know this. Shaun's only experiences of nocturnal interruptions involved Ozzy, his cat, scratching the front door to be let out. Or an over-enthusiastic accordion player going for it big time on Chorlton's Beech Road.

Matthew was fast asleep, nestled against a rather uncomfortable-looking bed fellow – a large cardboard cereal box which contained four dummies that he hadn't seen in over a year. Little swine must have found where I had hidden them in the back of the pantry. Rosebud lips puckered as he slumbered; a smooth brow and that chunky little chest rising and falling beneath his Incredible Hulk onesie. So much like Adam when he was asleep. He even used the same deep sleep posture; on his back, arms raised above his head as though he was halfway through doing the Mexican Wave.

I tiptoed into the bathroom, locked the door and took out my mobile which I had stuffed into my dressing gown pocket earlier on. (Good move, Rachael). I jabbed my finger onto the word 'Kate'. This was definitely the kind of situation that required a check-in with my oldest pal.

Kate and I had met at Saint Christopher's at the age of eleven when, lured by surplices and song, I had started attending the choir. At first, we had been churchy-rivals, her having been chosen to be the Rose Queen and me not even getting a look in. This was because her mother was very much involved in the church and happened to be dead good at sewing. Yes, Kate's mum had pledged to the Rose Queen committee that if her daughter was elected as Queen, she would be able to run up dresses for the Queen and her retinue - no-problemo - because she was already a seamstress and ran the big-knicker stall on Stalybridge market. My mum, however, couldn't even be bothered to make a pitch to the committee as to what our little family could offer the church, advising me;

"You know full well that we don't have a sewing machine. And that your dad won't allow you to stick paper roses onto his Datsun. And he'd never let you sit on the car – for fear of you denting it. In fact, this time next year you'll be even bigger if you carry on with the Mars Bars like you're doing at the moment. No. I can't help you, I'm afraid."

At the time, I had felt rather embittered about her lack of interest in my ambition to become a local celeb - plus her blatant ignorance on such matters; because everybody knew that Rose Queens represent Christ on Earth and are dignified in all manner of church and civic affairs. Yes, everybody across the whole of the North West knew that it was the Carnival Queens who did the car bonnet thing; who got to sit on the front of their dad's car when it had been plastered in a bed of fake roses as they toured every Mancunian summer Sunday festival. These lasses had velvet capes, fake crowns and they waved demurely at the crowd. They were surrounded by a procession of local performers - kazoo majorettes - or those long lines of girls who wore lots of medals and slapped their mini-skirted thighs in time to the music. (Now there's a talent that we no longer fully value in today's society.) Yes. The Carnival Queen scene was all very secular.

Later, however, I was relieved at my parents' lack of interest in Anglican society. Because after Kate had been crowned - during one of the beetle drives to raise funds for the Rose Queen minibus - her dad was caught with his pants-down; having it away with the mother of one of the retinue girls named Becky Kavanagh. The fornication took place in the vicar's vestry. And the congregation only discovered their philandering ways when it turned out that Nosey Norman – the church warden – had installed a fully functioning video camera in the poky little room; a mission to catch the person who had been pilfering communion wine and the Cadbury's crème eggs for our Easter service distribution. On hearing the scandal, my dad had commented to me;

"See love – it's a funny old world. Your mother always knows best. If I'd let you plonk your arse on the bonnet of my car and be the Rose Queen – it might have been me having a bit of rumpy-pumpy with Becky Kavanagh's mother in the vestry. Come to think of it, she's not a bad looking woman actually…"

I had said;

"Dad! Don't you know anything? It's the Carnival Queens with the car bonnet thingy! A Rose Queen is…"

But my mother had shot him a filthy look, so he quickly changed tack;

122

"Mind you, Becky Kavanagh's mum is a bit on the hefty side for me. And speaking of arses, how the hell she managed to fit that one of hers - into that tiny little vestry at all - is beyond me…"

So, it had been a fast 1980s divorce for Kate's parents. And an early political awakening, involving much anti-royal sentiment, for Kate. Plus, a lifelong hatred of the Anglican church and fondant-filled chocolate eggs.

The phone rang out for what seemed like forever and then she answered with;

"Oh. It's you. All shagged-out from your rampant sex sessions in London? Finally decided to pick up the phone and call your best mate?"

Kate, Vicky and Jake Bamber were the only people aware that I had been seeing Michael. Although Shaun had clearly cottoned onto the whole thing.

"Later, Kate. I'm in the middle of a bad situation right now. I need some advice."

"Well, it better be good – 'cause I've got a stack of parents' reports to write for my year twos again. I'm boring myself shitless with having to put things like; 'He's been trying really hard this term' when what I *really* want to put is 'Can't stand the little git, what *were* you thinking? Had you never heard of the Abortion Act?' Plus, Rachael, guess what? I've got headlice again. I seriously need to change careers —"

I cut her off with a hissed;

"Kate! Shut it. This is an emergency!" and then gave her a twenty second update. An outline on the argument with Michael and that Shaun had just called round to see me. She gave me calm and unbiased words of wisdom;

"What the frig? Get him out of the house! What the hell are you thinking of? Tell him to sod off back to West Didsbury or wherever he lives - and shove some stuffed olives up his arse or something!"

"I can't, Kate. I'm in a real palaver here. I've got to get him to sign these documents - saying that the council are going to back our social enterprise loan. And if we don't get the loan… we go bust - 'cause the council can't fund us anymore."

"Oh, right. So – I'm guessing that Shaun is playing around with you here. Maybe asking for a piece of the action in return for his signature —"

"Hey - God, you're good at this —"

"And are you tempted?"

"He sort of… kissed me."

"You don't sort of kiss someone, Rachael. And… oh, whatever. Look. I know you. And I know all about him and you and just how bloody stupid you can be when you're around each other. So, okay. And you don't need to answer me on whether you're tempted or not. I'm not a total div. But just stop and think for a moment. I mean - what happened to you and Michael? It sounded good. Positive."

"It was. But Lydia ruined it all with her Jesus badge."

"Come again?"

"Don't you watch the news?"

"No! I'm a teacher for Christsake! I'll check it out at three AM or something. But look… whatever. This is Shaun that we're talking about! Fair enough, we've all got our womanly drives. But come on! Not Shaun. If you end up doing that, I mean sure - you'll get the signature that you need. But you'll be back there again. Broken your vow. Dancing to his tune. Back in his pocket. At his beck and call. Every cliché in the book. Every sad case scenario that you warn your women at the centre about."

"I know, I know. But…" My phone bleeped and I saw 'Michael Calling' flash up on the screen. I told Kate this.

"Take the call! Take the call, you daft sod! I'll hang on – keep me on the other line!"

I obeyed, answered the call and immediately Michael's voice came on;

"Rachael. I just wanted to say that I'm profoundly sorry for all the misunderstanding today. I didn't mean to upset you and —"

I interrupted him, gabbling,

"Michael – I'm really sorry too. And I'm so glad that you called. But I'm just having a bit of a crisis right now with Matthew. I'll call you back in ten minutes, I promise."

His voice sounded surprised, but not hostile, "Yes, of course. Fine. Speak in a bit."

Back to Kate.

"He apologized, Kate. Things seem okay. I've got —"

"Great. So, ring Michael back in a bit, when you've got rid of Shaun," Kate told me. "Now. I've just been thinking. We're… what? A good fifteen minutes' drive from you. But. Ah. Hang on. Yes. Listen. Just stay in the loo for another ten minutes. I think that we need a double whammy here. Yes. Stay in the bathroom for ten. And then go downstairs and tell Shaun that Matthew has the squits, something terrible; and you need to go and sort out the mess that's everywhere. A good dose of diarrhoea usually dampens the ardour of most randy buggers in my experience. And then… you need to threaten him. So's that he'll sign your document thingy."

"Threaten?"

"Yes. Bribe him. He's done it enough times to you over the years, in his own very particularly charming and manipulative way. And from what you just said, he's still clearly happy to engage in a bit of that this evening."

"I'm not sure how… I could."

124

"Oh, come on Rachael. Stop being so bloody naïve. You *tell* him that if he doesn't sign, you'll turn up at Jess' workplace or whatever. Present her with the evidence. From back in the old days. And that you'll let her know about the stuff that happened between you two again after the funeral, last year…"

I breathed hard. "But I couldn't, Kate. That'd be… just nasty. Horrible. I'm not that sort of a —"

"Tough shit. You probably wouldn't have to do it. 'Cause the tosspot is a coward at the end of the day. A total and utter, twatty… twatty-arsed moral coward. And what's more important? Playing your hand with a bit of bribery? Or keeping Sisters' Space open?"

"Well. Hmmm. Right. Yeah, right. You might have a point there…"

"You know that I bloody well do. Now, man up. Grab a cold shower or whatever - just in case meladdo tries it on with you the minute you open the bathroom door. And I'll be calling you in a bit. So, you had better answer the phone. Don't ignore it. You've done that to me before, Rachael - when you explicitly asked me to ring you if you were at risk of having a shag yet again, with His Nibs. So, you bloody well owe me for that. Okay?"

"Okay."

CHAPTER 17

I side-stepped the idea of a cold shower. But never one to waste time, I spent the next ten minutes cleaning the bath. Shaun would be getting annoyed a bit by now. Good.

And then I returned to the lounge. Shaun had propped himself against the windowsill, awaiting my return, but he had turned the TV on and was watching Channel Four news, arms folded. He pointed the remote at the TV and switched it off. Held his hand out to me; let's resume matters.

No. I'm staying put.

"Sorry about that," I shrugged and offered up the fib; "Matthew's got diarrhoea. It's an awful mess up there. I've had to put him into my bed, but I do need to go back up to him. It's going to take me ages to sort it out. I've tried scraping the worst of it off the sheets, but…"

The outstretched hand now flipped into Stop mode. "Spare me the details." Shaun didn't do chatting about bodily functions unless it was dirty sex talk, slap bang in the middle of the carnal action.

I scrunched my nose up.

"Yeah. I probably stink of shit myself! Ha! Anyway. I'd best get back to up there. But before you go home, let's sort out the signature thing…"

He shook his head. Taking a stance.

"No go, Stan." His eyes twinkled. "Unless we come to some other kind of agreement. Like we were talking about just now."

But I breezed right on, wind beneath my sails for once.

"Okay. Well. I've got another kind of arrangement in mind. Just after getting the worst of the crack off the sheets upstairs, I had an idea. I used Matthew's Spiderman notepaper to draft a little missive. As you know, I've got a cracking memory for random things like phone numbers and Andrew Lloyd Webber song lyrics. And it also works for times, dates and places."

He sighed. What's she on about now?

"So yeah, Shaun. I thought that Jess might appreciate a letter – or two – about all those times. You know. When she was away on her religious retreats or when she was skydiving to raise money for lepers in the Congo. I've even got a wee list of B and Bs that we stayed at. I can dig out receipts as the proof, too. You know that I've always been a bit of a hoarder."

He jerked forward from the window ledge; I carried on

"And for our more recent liaisons, I've even got a long list of car parks. With the exact dates of when we frequented them and where you told me you were *supposed* to be. And of course, the fact that I know where every mole and every birth mark on your body happens to be located."

I saw his fists flex, but he tried to resume with his usual unruffled mode. Pretending that the words hadn't hit their intended target. He said;

"You wouldn't do something as underhand as that. You're not that kind of — " But that muscle at the corner of the left eye was a dead giveaway.

I shook my head and finished the sentence for him.

"... a person. No. But needs-must. Think about it. As much as I've enjoyed shagging you over the years, keeping Sisters' Space open is a little bit more important to me. For the women. Other people's jobs and – my job too. Ensuring that my house isn't repossessed."

I gave him a big smile. See? He clearly didn't, so I carried on;

"So, if I can find a way to do this, that makes me feel empowered - as opposed to what you're offering me – which sounds worryingly like little old me having to perform blow jobs for you - entirely on your terms - then I'd be an idiot *not* to do it, wouldn't I?"

No reply.

"Even if it means screwing up your marriage, which – incidentally, Shaun - I actually don't give a shit about. Sorry and all of that. But you're leaving me with no other option."

He rubbed his head, nails grating against the number two haircut.

"There's no way that you'd — " he began again, but his words got no further. Instead, his head suddenly whipped around. He slammed his palm against the window and shouted;

"Oi!"

And then he ran out of the lounge.

He clattered down the hallway and tore open the front door. I followed him. A ferocious wind rushed into the house, knocking over Lydia's bike with a crash. I heard Matthew yell again from upstairs but I went outside, ignoring him. Shaun was stalking around his car, hissing into the wind.

"Fucksake! Look at this! Just look!"

I peered through the darkness. The whole front of the Lexus's bonnet and the windscreen was swathed with pale yellow globules. They were swimming in a runny liquid.

"Eggs!" he said. "Fucking eggs!"

"And..." I put my finger gingerly on the bonnet. "And flour too. Bizarre."

"Not fucking bizarre, it's fucking vandalism!"

For Shaun, this was tantamount to disaster. The Lexus was his pride and joy and he upgraded it every couple of years. I used to find it highly amusing that wherever we went in his car (when I wasn't ducking down and hiding from being seen, that is) he entertained extreme paranoia about getting it bumped, scratched, vandalised or stolen. Motorbikes and cars were Shaun's babies. Probably came above even Jess and Ozzy the cat.

He had found a torch in his glove compartment and was walking about the car now, shining the beam on his beloved and trying to discover any hidden damage.

"Do you want me to ring the police, Shaun?"

"No. What's the point?" he huffed, having made at least five routes around the car.

The beam of his torch moved onto me now.

"I need to get this crap off right now, before it freezes and eats into the paintwork. And eggs are a fucking nightmare on windscreens."

I flip-flopped back into the house in my ridiculous slippers and filled the bowl from the sink with some warm water and washing-up liquid. I lobbed a sponge into it, brought it outside and handed it over, telling him;

"See? I'm still a nice person, Shaun. It's just that you've backed me into a corner. And I don't really want your marriage to take a battering... like your poor car has just done..."

But at that point I lost the plot completely. I had to return to the porch and try to stop myself from giggling too much. Shaun was shooting me evil looks every thirty seconds or so. The wind was icy and it made his mission an utterly miserable one. I stood in the porch and in between trying to stifle my laughter, called out;

"I'd honestly help you – but I really need to keep my ear out for Matthew!"

I shivered as he sloshed water over the car and mostly over himself. He swore repeatedly and finally handed the empty basin back to me, saying;

"I'll have to wash it properly when I get home. Get it to the car wash first thing in the morning."

"No doubt."

"If I'd only been five seconds faster I could have caught the bastards, right in the middle of it all. I saw the back of two mopeds racing off. Bunch of freaks you've got - living round here."

Through the gale, I could hear Matthew shrieking in his sleep again. I grabbed Shaun's coat from the back of the kitchen chair and handed it to him.

"Look, I have to go and see to Matthew. Can't you hear him screaming? Some of us have more precious cargos than cars, to think about."

"Right. Fine."

He opened the vehicle's door and a gust of wind threatened to rip it off its hinges.

"And Shaun?" I called out. "I don't want to come over all Poison Penelope with my letter. I mean, really I don't. So you *will* sign and send the documents to us tomorrow. Won't you?"

He was shaking his head as he folded his frame into the driver's seat but despite the wind, I could make the words out clearly enough;

"Whatever, Stan. Whatever."

I turned away, closing the front door. Warmth from the house and from liberation, leaching into my bones.

Matthew had managed to turn himself around and get stuck at the bottom of his bed. His head was now inside the cardboard box. He was still fast asleep, despite the yelling at whatever X-Men mutations he had been dreaming about. I was glad that he didn't really have the trots. I hated having to share my bed with either of my two kids. Lydia wriggled and talked non-stop in her sleep and Matthew was a fighter and a farter. I straightened him out and then went back downstairs as my mobile phone bleeped. It was Kate.

"Ha. You answered. Kept your promise to me for once. So, did you do it? I don't mean you not-screwing Shaun – I'm taking that as read! I mean - the blackmail."

"I did."

"Attagirl! So, he took 'the hint'?"

"Oh yes. I did what I had to. But Kate… How did you *do* that?"

I could almost hear the silent mirth down the phoneline.

"No idea what you're talking about. I've been sitting here, conjugating lies about Olivia Ogden being a 'pleasant child' when neither the kids nor the teachers like her. In fact, the Lollipop Lady tried to get the kid run over last week by the…"

"Shut up! I don't mean what did *you* do. I mean what did *you and yours* do?"

"Haven't a clue what you're…"

Nothing to do with your moped-loving husband then?"

Kate was still trying it on with the innocence.

"Whatever do you mean? Bob's not here. He's round at Bigsy's this evening. Watching the footie."

"Hmm. Would that be Bigsy who happens to live just a mile down the road from me?"

"Could be."

"Bigsy who also has a moped? And who has about a dozen hens in his back garden? Bigsy who is always very generous with his egg surpluses to friends and family?"

"Yeah. Did I tell you that he named his latest hen 'Motherclucker?'"

"Don't change the subject, Kate."

"Well, some people just don't like asking for help, do they?"

"Hmm. Fair do's. You might be right on that one. But old Mrs Finnegan next

129

door isn't going to be impressed. Tomorrow morning she'll take one look at the state of the road outside and be onto the refuse collection team again. The bin men are usually messy sods, but even they can't be blamed for the frozen omelettes all over the tarmac."

"Yeah, but Rachael, if she had realised what her nicest neighbour was faced with – she wouldn't mind… Oh. Ha. Get this. Just got a text through from Bob. It says; 'Tell Rach that Moped-heads beat Biker-boys. Every time."

"Hmm. Well. I suppose I should say thank you to him. Not that I needed rescuing, mind."

"You? Need or ask for help? That'll be the day, pal. Anyway. Go and ring your Michael, fella."

"Oh crap! I totally forgot… "

The tickle of a glow that had been kindled by Kate and Bob's loyalty began to fade as I dialled Michael's number. What if Michael was going to get all cool, all condescending again? He might even think that I had delayed returning the phone call just to toy with him. Thankfully, I didn't have too long to wait as he answered after a few rings. We both commenced with trying to apologise to each other. Michael began;

"I'm so sorry about it all. It must have sounded like I was trying to railroad you into party political concerns or… And, I mean, I do realise that you're a bit of a free spirit. Very down to earth. And now I… see that you're proud of whatever, er, kind of faith – religious thinking or whatever it is – that you have. And that you've been around the block a bit, what with one thing and another. And you can get quite prickly about —"

"Prickly?"

"No… Sorry. Wrong choice of words. That you're quite sensitive… and very self-aware, so that you don't want to feel that you're at all kow-towing to the 'powers that be.' And you know, that's one of the reasons that I find you to be so damned attractive…"

"Gee, thanks Michael."

"Not at all. Oh. Are you being sarcastic again?"

I laughed.

"No. Not really - but you're not helping yourself here. You're coming across as though… you've got a bit of a penchant for religiously obsessed, pikey old slappers."

"Oh. Ha. Sorry. Again."

So, the ice had been broken and the fire had been stoked again. For the next half an hour we talked politics and poll ratings. With the odd smattering of smut in between.

But I still went to bed wondering whether I should have provided him with the truth about my evening at home. Although perhaps, when it comes to burgeoning relationships with a senior cabinet minister, the phrase 'less is more' might be the best approach to adopt.

CHAPTER 18

On Wednesday morning, I fired off a quick email to Martyn Pointer:

> Martyn
> Tried my best to convince Shaun E. But until the forms arrive here at our place, or with you lot – we'd best not hold our breath, eh?
> Bye for now
> Rachael

Only a few seconds later, I received:

> Rachael
> How are you? All good, I hope.
> Thanks for trying. I think that I'll have to contact Cllr. Casey if we don't get the papers by close of play.
> I don't like to pander to the politicians, but sometimes desperate measures are called for.
> Kind Regards
> Martyn

I bit my lip and scowled. Kath Casey was Chief Politico-Supremo in the fair land of Medlock. Leader of the Council. And she was not a big fan of Sisters' Space. In the past, she had referred to the women's centre as a 'Leftie Feminists Coven,' so she was the last person that I would want to be begging favours from. Shaun had also previously advised me that it would have been a complete waste of time asking her if the council could grant us a measly one hundred quid to pay for a face painter or other forms of kiddy-entertainment for our launch. Plus, Gill had also told me that Casey's husband was a bigwig in Medlock's property development circles; that he had had his eye on our building – a former primary school – for some time. Mr. Casey's specialism happened to be converting existing non-residential properties into flats for 'young professionals.' So, no, Kath Casey probably wouldn't give a toss as to whether her council backed a loan for Sisters' Space or not. Martyn would be better off praying to his God about all of this, rather than cosying up to the politicians.

During the lunch hour, I headed down to the reception to see our new display. The women's art group - led by our chairperson - had recently won an award from one of the North's most prestigious galleries. Cynthia had been over the moon about it all and she and the lasses had just finished hanging their pictures in our foyer area.

Bev was sitting behind the reception desk, indulging herself in cursory half-spins on the swivel chair.

"Crikey," I said. "They've managed to hang all of that lot up there pretty quickly. Where have they all gone? The art group, I mean."

"Pub. To celebrate. Again."

"Right. Don't blame them. And where's Stacey?" I asked, referring to the receptionist.

"I said I'd cover for her. She's buggered off to TK Max on her lunch. They've got a load of new candlesticks in – and she's well-weird about havin' candles in all her rooms, is Stacey. Even in her toddler's. Which is just askin' for tears before bedtime, if you ask me."

Dee, who had (allegedly) been on a volunteering shift at Sisters' Space in the new café, also happened to be hanging about in reception, waiting for the rain to stop, before she dared to venture outside for a smoke. Bev hissed at me that Dee was now;

"On her eighth fag break of this mornin'. She's a right pillock. She bought all her new e-ciggy equipment the other day. Were raving about this Jamaican White Rum flavoured one, but… what a load of bollocks! 'Cause she's back on the Benson and Hedges, already. No bloody stayin' power."

In between twirling around on the chair, Bev was taking the incoming phone calls whilst reading the Manchester Evening News, which was spread out in front of her. I peered over her shoulder for a gander. But there was nothing more interesting than a decapitation in Prestwich, followed by a geography teacher who had been stalking his students via the internet and finally - the inevitable feel-good story; a burned-out, former Coronation Street star who had set up a 'Shabby Chic' shop over in Ashton in partnership with a chap who used to play one of the Teletubbies.

I called over to our mutual friend:

"So, Dee. What do you think of the paintings? They're good, aren't they? Especially when you consider that they've only been studying art with Cynthia for just a few months."

Dee didn't even bother to turn around and look at the paintings.

"Load of shite. Don't know why they bother. I mean – that Cynthia's supposed to be, like, a proper artist or whatever. From Bristol or Brighton, or wherever they reckon they're a cut above the rest. But I don't reckon she's got a bleedin' clue. Like – that one over there that she actually did herself… it looks like. Like urghh…"

The ever-eloquent and adjectively-gifted Bev finished Dee's sentence for her;

"Like someone shat on a bit of canvas, got a three-year-old to glue some clippins' from 'Hello' magazine onto it, ripped up a pair of tights, stuck 'em in the lumpy bits what look like shit… and then gave it the ill-ustri-ous title of; 'Female Eunuchs; A Northern Eulogy.'"

Dee snickered and Bev actually grinned at her. I was impressed; I had never seen either of them enjoying each other's company, or sharing a co-commentary on life before. Normally they were all bicker-city and at each other's throats. I flirted with the idea of conveying this to Cynthia. That her work of art had led to a reconciliation between the Dee n' Bev War of Words. But then I thought better of it. Cynthia's heart was in the right place but, well. Art Is Art and not really to be ridiculed, is it? No, it wouldn't be wise to piss off our well-connected chairperson by informing her that Bev had compared Cynthia's very own personal portrayal of the patriarchy - to a big pile of poo.

I returned to reading the Manchester Evening News over Bev's shoulder, only to be interrupted by the sound of the buzzer. Bev stabbed the intercom;

"Yeah?"

A husky velveteen voice answered;

"Hi – can I get access please? I'd like to see the hot babes that hang out at Sisters' Space. That is - if I'm not interrupting your pole-dancing-whilst-making-a-latte class - or whatever bizarre combination of training you've got on there today."

"Yer what?" Bev asked, peering quizzically at the screen in front of her. The computer showed the image of the person standing outside the door, as captured by our rather swish CCTV camera - one of the few modern attributes belonging to our fraying-at-the-edges building.

Dee said;

"Who the frig's that weirdo, then?"

Bev brightened;

"Oh yeah – I know now. It's that mad mate of yours innit, Rachael? Your buddy from the housin'"

"Yep," I answered. "Jake Bamber. Let him in."

"Eh? We can't let a bloke in," said Dee. "We hate blokes, don't we, Rach? That's what you said to that Michael fingy that time. That Minister fella. You said that Sisters' Space is 'sclusively for women what have been knocked about. And no blokes allowed. An' you told him – din't yer? That we were havin' none of his Smack Me Bitch Up attitude round 'ere."

Even Bev was shocked by Dee's brazen distortion of the facts.

"She never said nowt of the sort! Don't you remember? Your posh MP,

Minister fella were givin' her the usual 'Oh! So why don't you hahlp male victims of domestic viohlence then…is all of thaahs really an effective use of public monah' thing…"

I was speechless. Bev had Michael down to a tee. More clipped, more horsey – but she'd even picked up the way he used intonation in his sentences. I was about to smile and then realised that going all-dreamy and la-la à-la Michael might give the game away. Bev continued;

"And then after that - Rachael were a right sarcastic bint with him, weren't you?"

She did have a point. Quipping to the Minister for Communities on our first meeting – after he'd asked me whether Sisters' Space would ever help a man who was a victim of domestic violence - that, no, we'd never help a bloke out *"Even if he was bleeding to death and shouting, 'Help me! Help me!' through the intercom. We'd just ignore him, of course,"* perhaps hadn't been my finest attempt at winning a VIP over.

But thankfully Michael seemed to have warmed to my particularly East Mancunian dry sense of humour. Dee clearly hadn't been following the plot though.

"Don't you remember that, Dee?" said Bev – all Mother Superior tone. "Don't you remember that Rachael were a bit cheeky with him? But that - then - she explained properly to him, our policy towards protectin' women. An' that we don't discriminate against men."

Dee shrugged. And yawned. So, Bev decided to answer her own question.

"Yeah well, Dee. You were all tammied out of yer head that day, weren't yer?"

"Oh, Piss Off, Bev," Dee growled. "At least *my* eldest weren't banged up for dealin' to kids at Medlock High."

"No. Your eldest were banged up for nickin' computers from the same bloody school – and not even havin' the friggin' brain to notice that the police van were sat there, watchin' him the entire time…"

Temporary truce forged by mutual dislike of shit-art display was already over, then.

"Look," I said. "Will you just let Jake in? It's piddling it down out there. And he's got lovely hair."

A few seconds later and Jake Bamber was shaking his now less-immaculately-coiffured-than-usual locks at us.

"What took you so long?' he asked me. 'I mean, I know that I owe you a few bottles of vino but… trying to drown me… is simply not cricket, my girl.'

"Ooh get you!' sneered Dee. 'Simply not cricket!' Not heard that one since I last read me Enid Blyton!"

"Can you read, then, Dee? Well, wonders never cease." Bev was back on for an all-out war. But Jake stepped in, placing his car keys on the reception desk and giving it a touch of the teeny shoulder-twitch. He liked to dredge up the camp affectations when it suited him.

"Hmm. Well. Rachael enjoys a man with a bit of finesse – don't you, chickie? A man who's rather well-bred."

I gave him a filthy look. Don't Jake. And certainly, not in front of the service users.

Dee winked at Jake as she started fiddling with her lighter and leered;

"You two shaggin' each other then?"

Bev burst out laughing, spraying the telephone handset.

"Jesus! Talk about 'as thick as pigshit!'"

Jake - whilst not having had the pleasure of meeting Dee before - was a housing officer and therefore was a quick judge of personality, temperament and of atmospheres that were about to lead to either the decimation of someone's shrubbery or to cold-blooded murder. He reached over to Gobshite Central and took her hand, stroking it gently.

"Sweetie," he said to Dee. "If I'd be shagging anyone in this room right now, it'd be you my darling. Not these two skinny old trollops." Dee coloured slightly. Jake was an extremely good looking man. Fine featured. All latino eyes, fringed with flutteringly long lashes.

"Ha!" said Bev. "Skinny's summat I've never been insulted with before." Jake continued.

"But unfortunately, I do have to tell you that much as I admire the female of the species, they don't really happen to be the gender that dingles my dongle, as it were. And that – oooh – your bracelet! Isn't that a Pandora? I love Pandora! I *adora*-Pandora!"

Jake had expertly diffused the situation. Dee was now showing him her shiny stuff and waxing lyrical with her new friend about bunny-shaped trinkets and the like. I gave them a minute and then cleared my throat.

"'Scuse me, Jake - for interrupting your attempt to convince us that you moonlight as a presenter on the Jewels for Fools TV channel - but one of the old trollops here is wondering; to what do we owe the pleasure? Of your visit, I mean."

Jake stopped tinkering with Dee's bracelet and answered.

"Oh yes. Just been trying to track down one of your service users at Sisters' Space."

He didn't say any more than that. Not politic – or professional to discuss - one woman's case in front of the others. I was going to ask him to come through to my office for a private chat, but then Bev waded in with;

"Bet it'll be Dawn, eh? What's up? You lot in housin' all ready to evict her just 'cause that piece of shit, Vinnie Murray tried to kick her head in on Sunday night?"

"Nothing of the sort, my love," Jake shook his head and I added,

"Down, Bev. Jake's one of the good guys…"

But Bev's butterfly brain had moved on.

"And hey up! Here's one of the bad bitches!"

I was about to remind Bev about our policy in relation to derogatory language towards other women, but I changed my mind when I saw the figure that appeared on the screen before us. The buzzer sounded. And Bev yelled at the intercom;

"Yeah – whoareyer and whaddyawant?"

I elbowed her. "You could at least try and remember some of your training…"

Bev sniffed. "I'm only *covering* reception. Not properly trained. And anyway. I hate her guts."

"Renee McCauley," came the all-too familiar nasally tones over the intercom. Her addition of;

"… From Communities and Leisure, Medlock Council," was nearly drowned out by an enormous thunderclap. The rain began to turn into hailstones.

"Jesus wept!" Jake murmured. "That was just like a scene from Twilight! Do you think that she made that happen all by herself?"

"Well, with any luck – she'll turn into a bat and fly off or summat," said Bev. "Can't stand the cow."

I peered at the monitor. Renee didn't appear to have an umbrella. So, I asked Bev;

"How do you know her then?"

She snorted. "I used to clean the Town Hall before they sacked off the contractors what I was workin' for and brought the Polish lot in. She's a complete bee-yatch – yeah soz, I know Rach – you'll be tellin' me off for horrible language about another woman – but… she is!"

"Oh, don't mind me, for once," I commented. I was going to add that my own preferred label for the woman was 'Renee The Rottweiler.' But then I remembered that Bev had a big, scary dog herself and might find the comparison to Renee, to be insulting towards her own prized pooch.

The buzzer sounded again.

"Is anyone going to let her in? It's awful out there," Jake asked.

"Oooh… I can hardly hear that buzzer above the weather outside!" Bev smirked. "But yeah. In a min. Those hailstones must sting like a bugger. Anyway. Yeah - at the Town Hall - my shift were at five o'clock and she'd always be out the offices, on the dot."

"Jobsworth," Dee nodded. I tried not to grin. If anyone could shirk the work, it was Queen Dee.

"And, so I'd always pass her in the corridor – every day – but she wouldn't even so much as look me in the eye."

"Maybe she's autistic?" Jake added helpfully. We ignored him.

"So, I'd just do my stuff. Clean around – always had to be ultra-careful with the Head Man's office – you know – the Shaun Elliot big fella. Hey, get this – he's that ginormous – he has to have a special chair and everything,'

"We know," said Jake. Quietly. Eyeballing me. "Rachael and I once had the pleasure of working with him. Many moons ago. He even came out on strike with us a couple of times. Before he sold out completely and fell for the trappings of capitalism. Power and wealth. Etcetera."

"Yeah," agreed Bev. "He's even got a massive rubber tree plant thingy in there – so I bet that they're payin' him a fair bob or two. And that's what I got in trouble for. Not dustin' his rubber plant properly."

"Jesus!" Dee sang. "Look at the size of the hailstones out there! She's gonna be piss wet through!"

"Does anyone – really – still own rubber plants these days?" Jake asked. "I mean, they're so 1980's, aren't they?"

"Shaun does. I saw it in his office the other week," I said. In error.

Jake's eyes widened. Mine mirrored back; Don't Ask Me - Right Here, Right Now. Or Else.

"So yeah. Uptight bitch out there - sorry Rach – grassed me up for not dustin' his plant properly. And then for fiddlin' with his pens."

I was intrigued. "His pens?"

"She always laid them out for him at ten to five every day. Ready for him for the next day. In a certain order. It was… let me see… it was from left to right – hum – red, green, orange, blue, purple. I remember it see, 'cause she wrote it all down in a report to my supervisor."

"What a rotten cow!" I couldn't contain myself anymore, adding; "Sorry. To all of you, I mean. For
using deroga…"

"Yeah, yeah." Bev flapped a hand at me.

"Well… that really *is* very autistic… very spectrummy behaviour," said Jake. "The pen-thing. Perhaps we should feel sorry for her. The pens. The lack of eye contact."

"The pens might not be her problem. They could be a Shaun-thing," I added. "You know… Shaun proving to himself that he's reached the dizzy heights of municipaldom. 'I can afford different coloured pens, me, I can."

Jake and I had been trying not to be too blasé about the mention of Shaun in front of the others, but by now we had given up, and me and my old buddy were chortling away. It was all going over the heads of both Dee and Bev thankfully, though. Dee chipped in with;

"Anyways – I don't see why we should have to feel sorry for someone, just 'cause they're autistic. Joel Patterson round the corner from us is well-autistic and he's just… like a sicko. He kills cats n' everything."

"Well, I've only ever known dead nice autistic people," Bev disagreed. "So, you might wanna watch what you're labellin' people with there, Dee. You're probably getting 'autistic' confused with 'psychotic' or summat. Like – my nephew Neil, what's autistic. He's lovely and he's well smart and he knows the entire bus network of Greater Manchester off by heart. Timetables and everything."

"Really?" asked Jake. "I love people who have gifts like that. So much more useful to society than a Theology degree from Cambridge!"

"Yeah, tell me about it," Bev continued, "so you just send him a text message and tell him where you wanna go and in seconds you get one back that says fifteen hundred hours, the number four-oh-nine bus, Buxton Road chippy stop, journey time approximately twenty-two minutes, watch the dogshit near the post office.' And then he'll text you again to advise you on the best route back home."

The buzzer rang again. And this time it wasn't stopping. We all realised that we were pushing it just a bit too far now.

"Oh, come in, then, won't 'cha." snapped Bev, jabbing the 'open' button.

A waterlogged woman carrying a plastic bag stalked into the reception. Her bottle green coat was pebble dashed with half-melting hailstones and her wiry black hair dripped onto its sodden collar. Her glasses hit instant 'steam me up, Scottie' mode as soon as she entered the building. She took them off to glare at us.

"Is there something wrong with your intercom?"

"Hello, Renee," I gave her my friendliest smile. God knows where I dredged it up from. But I remembered not to bare too much teeth. (Rottweilers don't take kindly to that.) "But no. The intercom's fine. It's just that – unlike working for the local authority – our service isn't cushioned by salaried staff and the like. We rely on the use of volunteers. So sometimes things take a bit longer." I patted Bev on the shoulder. "No offence, Bev!"

Bev smirked. "None taken."

"Anyway," I continued to gurn at Renee – smiling with the mouth and not the eyes. "Sorry about the little wait there. So. How can we help you?"

She shifted her handbag from her shoulder, attempting to juggle the plastic bag which was emblazoned with the logo of Medlock's finest delicatessen, providing Jake with a license to coo;

"Oooh! Lunch from Webster's! My favourite sandwich shop! Although it's more of a sandwich *experience*, as they like to call it. I haven't been there for ages. It's ever so expensive. But I can't really afford it these days on my salary. Are you treating yourself then?"

Renee gave him a blank look. And then peered into the handbag, looking for something. She had clearly not met Jake before and didn't know anything about him. If she had, she wouldn't have supplied him with yet more evidence of Shaun's nascent progression to recently becoming Satan's Capitalist Bum-Boy.

"For Mr Elliot. The Director of Communities and Leisure —"

I cut her off.

"And a Very Important Person, Jake," tipping him a subtle wink. Jake got the deal.

"Oooh, I can imagine. So, has the boss treated you to lunch as well, then?"

The Rottweiler gave us her best no-nonsense judder of the head, sprinkling more moisture onto the reception floor.

"I make my own packed lunches. I've got a wheat allergy. And I need gluten-free. I struggle with nuts too. Even with the most high-end food shops, you can never be too careful, when you suffer with a severe allergy."

"I struggle with nuts too. Especially the big 'uns." Dee was still flicking her lighter. Waiting for the storm to pass. I wasn't sure whether this was Dee being crude or whether she had a real issue with KP or Planters. "But anyway," Dee carried on "What's he got on his butties then?'

I had been wondering this myself. In the old days – the Whalley Range Housing Officer days - Shaun had always gone for cheese and tomato, white muffin, no onion and loads of salad cream.

Renee was irritated. She ignored Dee and continued to ferret around in her handbag, finally bringing an envelope out of it. I was enjoying the fact that The Rottweiler wasn't on her home turf. She passed the envelope to me. It was slightly damp but had escaped the worst excesses of the downpour.

"Mr Elliot asked me to deliver it directly to you, rather than you have to wait for the post."

Jake might not be aware of the current scenario in terms of Shaun's refusal to sign his support for the loan, but he knew about the past. The past the first time round – not the second time after Adam had died – I mean. But still, his eyes were burning into me. He was clearly thinking the worst. Meaning that it might be best if I opened the envelope in front of everyone, in order to get Jake off my back.

"Cool," I said, as I ripped it open. Realising that I must sound like Matthew when he's found a crappy toy in a packet of cereal. "But just dull financial stuff here, folks. No orders for our chocolate from the Town Hall. Which is a shame – as you'd hope that our local authority personnel would be the first to support us, wouldn't you?"

I smiled sadly at Renee. Jibes about voluntary versus public sector workers were above and beyond her. She was about to turn around and leave, when Dee asked again;

"So, come on. Tell us what the big bloke has on his butties, then. Not like it's a state secret or owt, is it?"

Renee pursed her lips. She wasn't used to dealing with members of the public. And certainly, not members of the public with a gob like the Mersey Tunnel. But she told us;

"Curried lamb and lemongrass. With cranberries. On Focaccia"

I was surprised. But then Shaun had grown up in Harrogate after all. Or Ilkley. Or wherever. And as people get older, they often like to resort to childhood comforts. I felt sorry for the old cheese sarnie on a white muffin. Not swanky enough now, for Mr Hot Shot Town Haller. I half-expected Bev to trot out her usual disgusting analogies on the contents of sandwiches, but she was busy scribbling away on a notepad next to the phone. So perhaps it was only me that ever happened to be the ungrateful beneficiary of her revolting luncheon comparisons.

"Right then," I said. "Give our best to Mr Elliot."

She nodded.

"And tell him," added Jake, "that we'll bump into him at the Local Government Association charity night in London. Oh no. Scotch that idea. We can't afford the train fare, can we Rachael? Never mind the two thousand pounds that Shaun Elliot managed to pull together for a table there last year… even without the wine bill."

Renee tossed her head and dappled us with droplets as she walked back to the front door, pressing the release button in order to exit. But Bev had decided to winch herself out of the receptionists' chair and was heading after her. As The Rottweiler pushed the door open, Bev caught up with her, handing her an envelope;

"Nearly forgot. Can you give this to Mr Elliot? Says 'Private and Confidential' there, see? So, that means that it's only to be opened by 'im. Yeah?"

"I *do* know what that means," came the frosty reply. And then the door clicked behind her.

Bev scooted back to her seat at reception whilst Dee slouched towards the door, finally moving out for a ciggie, now that the torrent had subsided.

"Well," said Jake. "Wasn't that fun? I almost felt sorry for her at one point. Yet another poor, deluded woman who has fallen for Shaun Elliot's charms."

I narrowed my eyes at him. Change the subject, please.

"So," he said brightly. "Let's go and see if you can help me find this service user of yours, who seems to have fallen off my radar…."

"You mean Dawn," Bev chipped in.

"Oh, pack it in, Bev," I told her. "And anyway – what was the envelope business all about? This letter thing for Shaun Elliot?"

"Ha. Just a few words from the wise. For 'im an' 'is eyes only."

"What do you mean…?" Jake and I looked at each other.

"Oh, don't be worryin'. I was going to tell old sour-faced cow herself, but I knew she wouldn't pass on the message. So, I thought that writin' it down would be best."

"What message?" As I do with Liddy when she's too engrossed with Dennis the Menace and The Beano to answer me, I swiped Bev's newspaper away so that she had to give me her full attention.

"Just a little bit of advice from the expert."

"What? What did you write, Bev?"

"Nowt. Nowt major anyway. I just wrote 'Lamb and lemongrass might sound very nice – but watch out for the cranberry bits 'cause they'll be the winnits from the lamb."

"You never did!" I yelped. Hand to mouth. Not sure whether to laugh or to throw up.

Jake said;

"Winnits? What's winnits?"

"Ha. Can tell you're not from round 'ere," said Bev. "Everyone knows what winnits are."

"Do enlighten me."

"The little balls of shit that hang round a sheep's arse. Did your mother never say to you 'always wipe your winnits off?'"

"No, she didn't," Jake beamed a glorious smile. "But this new-found knowledge has certainly made my day. Especially if it puts Shaun Elliot off his lunch."

Bev looked pleased with herself.

"And," she added. "Just in case he didn't know what winnits were himself – I added, like, a reference note. Like what you'd do in a dissertation. An' I drew a little picture for him. Of a sheep's arse."

"Oh, Bev," I said. "Please tell me that you're joking."

"Soz!" she said "All true. Now gimme me paper back. An' sod off and find Dawn."

CHAPTER 19

There had been no little, sticky Post-it notes added to the document that Renee had handed to me. No SWALKS or death threats. Simply Shaun's scribble. Actually, Shaun's rather violent moniker of a signature. I noted that the ballpoint of the pen had nearly gone through the paper.

That there Shaun, was Goddamned pissed - as the Yanks would have put it. Goodo.

Once we had Shaun's agreement to get the loan, things felt like they were on more of an even keel. Lydia came home the next day. It was a Thursday morning and she had been dropped off by Julia and Malcolm, who were on their way for a long weekend in the Dales. I had arranged for them to park Liddy at her school during the lunch hour, which served two useful purposes; firstly, it meant that they could be on their way to their hotel more promptly and secondly it allowed me to avoid any awkward conversations as to why I had been hanging around with the Prime Minister's posse.

I had been looking forward to seeing Lydia, but the girl was grouch-personified when I collected her from the after-school club. And on picking up Matthew from the day nursery next door the two newly reunited kids simply hurtled themselves headlong into the latest back-of-the-car sibling conflict. This one centred around whether Matthew should be allowed to listen to Thin Lizzy, or whether Lydia's preference for Starlight Express should prevail. I screamed at them both;

"For God's sake! You've only been together for three seconds and already you're making this car sound like downtown Beirut!"

Which I realise is a rather 1980s expression, but I don't get to read the papers a lot these days.

Matthew said;

"Do beetroots live in our town? I never saw no beetroot in Holmfirth."

His sister hissed;

"We don't live in Holmfirth, you little beast. How many times do I have to tell you? Don't you understand anything about towns and villages and even what your own address is or... Ow!"

Matthew had thrown an empty carton of apple juice at her.

"Oi! Just zip it, will you?" I barked. "We'll be home in a few minutes and if I see any more of this kind of behaviour once we get through the front door, there'll be no more special permission from your headteacher for extra holidays away from school for you, Lydia."

"Huh," from the back seat.

"And it'll be muesli for breakfast for you, Matthew!"

I glanced in the rear-view mirror. Matthew was already looking traumatised at the thought. s

Lydia gave me her usual scowl and folded her arms. She glared out of the window and I noticed that she stuck her tongue out at a passing cyclist, who wobbled his bicycle in surprise. I chose to ignore her behaviour and, instead, slammed some Robbie Williams onto the car stereo. Now, whether Robbie's artistic integrity would be offended if he thought that I'd used him as a compromise between '70s heavy metal and camp musicals, I don't know. But it did the trick on a quick mood alteration. And by the time Lydia had kicked her school shoes off and dumped her bag on the hallway floor, she cheerily declared;

"Oh well. More school tomorrow. And it's my spelling test. Hey – I wonder, Mum… if you ended up dying – like daddy did - if I'd get a whole year off?"

I like to think that she inherited her lack of diplomatic skills from Adam, rather than from her mother.

On Friday morning, the newspapers had more or less dropped 'Badgegate' and had resurrected the previous week's stories about the dispute over funding cuts between northern local authorities and the government. Shaun and Michael's names were scattered throughout, with the alleged 'spat' between the Greater Manchester authorities and Whitehall. For some reason, Shaun seemed to have been appointed as 'Anti-Westminster Spokesperson' for the Mancunian Mafia. My sister found the whole state of affairs to be hilarious and I was the recipient of numerous texts and emails along the lines of:

> VICKY: Ha! Russell Girls keeping press alive this
> week… Lydia's religious obsessions & now the boys r
> fighting over her ma
> ME: V funny
> VICKY: Yehyeh – they say it's @ 'cuts' but we all know
> it's @ who gets 2 feel u up
> ME: Don't b crude
> VICKY: Ha. Gone r yr leftie credentials. Yr contributing
> 2 Murdoch empire now.
> ME: Go & do something useful. Listen 2 The Archers
> VICKY: Archers? Ur so RURAL these days
> ME: Oh fuck off. Some of us r at work.
> VICKY: I'll forward that 1 to Mum, eh?

The following week passed quickly, but it felt like an age since I had seen Michael in London. Lydia asked about him several times. Would he like to chat with her on the telephone so she could advise him more on the best musicals to listen to? Could he get her her own House of Commons business card? That kind of thing. I felt a little bit antsy that she would mention 'Michaelmas' to her teachers, to the parents of her friends. Or even worse, perhaps, to my parents. But small children are rarely concerned with the same priorities as us adults. For Lydia, when her next wobbly tooth might appear and whether Matthew had stolen her joke dog turd and hidden it somewhere mysterious would always end up being the most pressing issue of the day.

Michael claimed to have had a 'bugger of a time' all week. The more senior members of the Cabinet had been summoned by the Prime Minister to Chequers for the week;

"Where no – before you ask – we didn't engage in dressage or clay pigeon shooting or whatever I know you're going to accuse me of."

"I wasn't going to accuse you of that, Michael. I was simply going to ask you how your little jollies at the taxpayers' expense went."

"Ah, well. It was worth every penny, I can assure you. I'm a big fan of Chequers."

"Who wouldn't be? Still. Doesn't exactly sound like a 'bugger of a week' – hanging out in the middle of the Buckinghamshire countryside in an enormous mansion. Wish I could take the women from Sisters' Space somewhere like that for the week. Do us all some good."

"Well, I'm sure that the government would love to offer it to them, Rachael - but your lot scared the hell out of me when I met them, so heavens knows how the PM would react to them. The poor chap is terrified of his own wife – never mind a troop of marauding Mancunian man-haters."

"Careful, Michael."

"Ha. Sorry. But no – really. We had lots of fruitful discussions about various bits and pieces that the Party has had to be fielding over the last few weeks. And no, Rachael, none of them were to do with God or Satan or anything that your daughter might unwittingly have caused a row over. Not to worry."

He returned Up North on the Thursday tea-time and had already been nailed by Graham the Griper for various constituency duties the following day. We had planned to go out for dinner together that evening, but it transpired that my mother had enrolled on a sugar-crafting class and that my dad was incapable of coping with both Lydia and Matthew on his own. Indeed, the thought of even having to spend ten minutes alone with the two of them, usually led their grandad to make a hasty retreat to his allotment to lie down on his emergency picnic blanket with a packet of dry roasted peanuts and a crate of Special Brew for comfort.

So, Michael tentatively suggested that;

"Why don't we all meet up? You, me and the children."

I mentioned a local soft play facility, not far from his constituency home, but his immediate reaction was;

"Christ, no! I've seen those dreadful places. They're full of screaming kids. And no doubt dozens of parents who'll want to kneecap me because my government hasn't reinstated universal Child Benefit, or provided them with free nipple shields on the NHS or something equally crucial to parenting."

Instead, we arranged to meet at tea-time at a local 'Family Friendly' restaurant, halfway between our two homes. Although I was looking forward to seeing him (my heart giving Skippy the Bush Kangaroo a run for its money) having the kids in tow was certainly not my ideal kind of arrangement. I threatened both children with;

"If I have any misbehaviour from either of you today, there'll be no more sleepovers at Grandma's. Ever." Which was a bit of a hollow threat – as banning them from the odd night at Mum's would simply be cutting off my nose to spite my face.

"Who are we going to see again?" asked Matthew as we pulled into the pub car park. Lydia replied;

"Michaelmas. Mummy's old friend. Me and Mum saw him in London."

"Yes – but he's not old!" I objected. "He's only er… I think forty-seven." I couldn't quite remember. The last time Michael and I had discussed ages we had been well into our second bottle of wine. I wondered whether I should grab my phone and do a Wiki on him. But I have never been a fan of Net-induced nosiness.

"Well, he's old to me," said Lydia. "And you're getting a bit too old too, Mum. 'Cause you can't remember the ages of your friends anymore."

"That's exactly the kind of smarty-pants remark that I don't want to hear from you for the next couple of hours."

"Ja, Mein Fuhrer."

"Liddy! You shouldn't say things like that! Has Grandad been making you watch 'Dad's Army' again?"

"No. That's just what he always says to Grandma when she's going on at him."

We were already fifteen minutes late. I fretted as I looked for a parking space. I couldn't see his Prius or any swanky-looking government cars. Just your usual Volvos and Mini-Coopers. Perhaps he had parked round the back. Or perhaps he had given up waiting for the Russell clan and was already heading back to Mottram. But as we entered the restaurant, I heard Lydia shriek "Michaelmas!"

He was behind us, following us in. Clad in bike leathers and boots and very nearly about to be bowled over by Lydia as she hurled herself at him.

"Gosh, well. This is all a very nice welcome, Lydia. But, erm. You can let go now."

He was standing all-rigid. He didn't seem to know what to do with his arms. Should he try and unravel Lydia? Or would that come across as being rude and unfriendly?

"Hello there," I said. And then whispered; "I won't kiss you in front of these two. You know."

He smiled stiffly and nodded.

"Sorry I'm a bit late. I ran up against a bit of a problem with the starter engine on the Triumph…"

He tailed off, remembering the bike issue. But it was difficult to look all serious and sensitive when a small child was trying to jiggle you up and down.

"Oh dear… So, who's your Special Protection today? Trevor?"

"No – Trev's on leave for a week. I've got Ross today. He's over there. He followed me over from Mottram. He's terribly shy though. So, don't expect a peep out of him."

Ross had already found himself a seat at the bar where he was keeping an eye on things. I gave him a little wave. He gave me a little smile. Leave it at that, I thought. Big blokes carrying firearms who claim to be shy. Why push them to be sociable?

"But I *like* Trevor!" said Lydia, still doing her boa constrictor act. "Why couldn't it be him today? We could sing 'Annie,' together. I know all the words now. For every song in the whole flipping' musical!"

"Lydia, let go of Michael, please."

"No. He loves it, don't you, Michael?"

"Well, er. It's very nice. But I think I've had my fill for today."

"Lydia! Let go!"

"No! It's nice to show that you care about people."

Michael was looking decidedly uncomfortable. I snatched Lydia's hands and began to prise them away from him. Liddy recoiled.

"Well, you don't have to pinch me, Mum! I was letting go anyway – 'cause Michael smells of old shoes!" She wrinkled her nose up in disgust. Michael was doing his best not to look too offended as he said;

"Well, perhaps it's the smell of the leathers, Lydia."

"Whatever. It's odious and well pongy. And anyway, isn't leather just like you wearing a load of dead animals all over you? That's well freaky."

Michael replied "I'm afraid that I don't have much of a choice, Lydia. Until they invent a more substantial material that keeps one safe in the event of a road accident, then…" He trailed off.

"Let's go and find a table, eh?" I gave him my broadest smile, trying to reassure him that I wasn't at all bothered by his comments. But then Matthew intervened. My youngest was usually rather standoffish with strangers and wasn't one for speaking until he was spoken to. Often, he would just growl if an adult that he had never met before asked him a question. But he suddenly poked Michael in the leg with a lightsabre that had accompanied him to and from preschool and nursery that day.

"My daddy's got a motorbike," he said.

"Has he? Er… I mean has…" Michael was struggling as to whether he should use the past or present tense in relation to Adam. I had managed to find a passing waitress who directed us towards an empty table whilst Lydia decided to help the conversational flow.

"Honestly! Matthew is so stupid, Michaelmas! He's talking like… he can actually remember his daddy. Matthew's rubbish! He's forgotten everything about him already. He's dead, Matthew! You shouldn't talk about him, like he's alive or summat. You little idiot!"

We had reached the table now and I had also reached the end of my tether.

"That's enough, Lydia!"

Matthew whacked his sister over the head with his lightsabre and snarled;

"Well, you'll be dead too!"

Michael looked appalled. Lydia grabbed a handful of Matthew's hair at which point I had to physically separate them; "Enough of that! The pair of you!"

Five minutes later and both children were in their respective Time Outs. Lydia had been made to 'stand in the corner', where she was busily dead-heading potted geraniums on a shelf next to her. Matthew was at the other side of the room, facing the floor-length windows and being forced to look at the car park. I noticed that he was flashing his belly button at passing customers.

"Yes," I said breezily to Michael, feeling a little bit more in control of the situation now that the kids were not so much in my face as previously. "I've tried every kind of disciplinary method going, but at the moment, I'm using Time Out."

"Does it work then?"

I noted the doubt in his eyes as we both looked over at the kids. Lydia had managed to catch Matthew's eye and was drawing her finger across her neck in a cut-throat gesture. Matthew responded by pursing his lips and spitting at Lydia.

"I'm ignoring them," I told Michael. "The hardest thing to do – but apparently the most effective - is ignoring bad behaviour."

"Are you supposed to ignore… well. Actual… spitting though? That's a bit…"

I was getting irritated with him now. Although, if I am going to be honest, the frustration was mostly directed towards myself. I was horribly embarrassed at the performance that the kids were pulling on me, despite my earlier pleas, bribes and threats. And I was annoyed, too, because I honestly couldn't remember if spitting *was* on my list of absolutely un-ignorable behaviours for this week. Hitting and biting definitely were. But as far as spitting and saying hurtful things? I had forgotten.

But Michael answered his own question. "Still… things are very different in terms of discipline these days, in comparison to when I was a child." I decided to head him off at the pass.

"Yeah, bring back the old thumbscrews and the rack, eh?"

Michael reached over the table and stroked my knuckles with the tip of his forefinger.

"Actually, I was thinking more of the Scold's Bridle when it came down to Lydia."

"Ha-ha. And how typically anti-female of you, Michael."

"Come here. A quick kiss whilst they're not looking…"

But before our attempts at lip-aerobics across the table could be fulfilled, a sullen-faced teenage waitress slammed four dinner plates down in front of us.

"Needketchuporsaucesorowtliketha?"

"I'm sorry?" said Michael. I translated for him;

"Do we want any ketchup? Or any sauces?" Michael looked blankly at the waitress. She was tinkering with a false fingernail.

"Why would we want ketchup or sauces?" he asked. "We've both got the masala."

The waitress looked at him as if he were an imbecile and then nodded at the Kiddy Specials for Lydia and Michael.

"Chipsnsausages."

I smiled and requested the ketchup.

Lydia and Matthew had noticed that their meals had arrived. They both voluntarily abandoned their Time Outs, with Matthew complaining that Lydia should have had two minutes longer than him; "It's one for every minute of her life!" he whined. He was right, but I couldn't be arsed discussing it with him.

"Just eat your chips, spanner-boy," Lydia hissed. The waitress slammed the ketchup onto the table and Lydia grabbed it, squeezing long, laborious laces across her food. Matthew seized the salt cellar.

Michael swallowed a forkful of his curry and addressed my daughter;

"You know, Lydia, you're supposed to taste your food before you add any sort of… seasoning to it."

Lydia had already shoved red-splattered food into her mouth and with gob open and chewed grub on display, managed to fire back at him;

"Well, you're supposed to wash your hands before you eat. But I didn't see you do it."

Michael looked at me. I wondered if he expected me to tick her off again. I didn't do it, however. Perhaps because of Bev, I've developed an aversion – a low tolerance threshold – when it comes to commentary and criticism about other people's food choices.

Matthew had already troughed his way through quite a bit of his food, although rather too much of it had landed on his lap because he was insisting on multi-tasking; lightsabre in one hand and head in the clouds.

"No singing whilst you're eating, Matthew."

"But it's AC/DC. My daddy likes AC/DC!"

"Here he goes again…" said Lydia. She prodded the side of her temple and made a circular movement with her forefinger; "Tap tap, whirly whirly – cuckoo-cuckoo. Hey, Michaelmas – what do *you* do… you know – what sign or what noise do *you* make – to show that someone's a total spanner?"

"Gosh, I don't know, Lydia. I suppose… Well. In the House of Commons – when the other side are talking rubbish. We sort of shout 'Bah! Bah!' at them."

"Ha yes, they do, Lydia," I said. "I've seen it myself when I used to work with the government in London. You can see it on the TV too. They go Baaaah Baaaah. At the people in the other parties."

Lydia eyeballed us both warily. "Like sheep, you mean?"

"Exactly."

"Sheep at parties? I dunno. And you're supposed to be the grown-ups." She shook her head. Matthew was knocking out 'You Shook Me All Night Long' at a decibel that threatened to rival the power of the best Marshall amp.

"Pack it in, Matthew," I said. "We don't sing at mealtimes."

There was silence for a few minutes whilst we all ate. Michael took the opportunity to murmur in my ear;

"So… do they always act like this in restaurants?"

"I've no idea," I muttered back. "This is the first time I've let them out in one. Why? Do you think that they're being really awful?"

Matthew was now fishing ice cubes out of his drink and lobbing them at Lydia, who was shrieking with laughter. I wondered whether ice cube attack could be counted as hitting, if the other child seemed to be enjoying it. No, I would ignore this one. Choose your battles wisely, as they say.

"It's just that… I've noticed two other groups of people now move tables. Away from us."

I sniffed. "Well, you should be glad of that then. Less chance of people recognising you and associating you with an unruly family".

He finally twigged that I was getting pissed off.

"I'm sorry, Rachael. Apologies. I imagine that there's nothing more irritating than someone who doesn't happen to have children – commenting on your chosen… parenting style."

"Ha!" I exploded – halfway through a mouthful of food. "Style? In my dreams."

"Eew, Mum!" Lydia commented. "You just spat rice on the table. So, don't you have any children, Michaelmas?"

"I'm afraid not."

"Why?"

"Lydia!" I warned. "It's rude to question adults about things like that." (Although at least Lydia had the guts to ask the question that I had been wondering myself.) But she carried on with another, 'Why?'

"Well," Michael offered. "Some adults – like me for example – only like children if they're served on hot, buttered toast. Yum yum!"

Lydia gave him a look.

"You really are weird sometimes, Michaelmas."

Matthew shoved his knife and fork to one side, lifted his plate up and began to lick it. I took it off him and gave him some of my food to finish.

"Were they boys?" Matthew suddenly asked Michael in between mouthfuls. "Did they like Star Wars?"

"Did who like Star Wars?" Michael frowned.

"Your children. Before you ate them."

"He's serious!" Lydia squealed. "Matthew thinks that you really did eat your children up! You two are both total freaky-deaky-pants together! Oooh, Mum! I need to wee!"

I scolded Lydia for - yet again - not pacing her bladder effectively enough and then led her away from the table. A few minutes later we returned to find Michael informing my son;

"The thing is, Matthew… there are several tribes in the remotest parts of the world where it's considered to be an act of the highest honour to eat the elders of the community. Now, we – you and I - might consider this to be a detestable atrocity – a hideous, barbaric act – but cannibalism is one of the…"

Matthew had his hands down his pants and was busily scratching his bum. He interrupted Michael with;

"So, when you ate *your* children – did you put brown or red sauce on them?"

Teen-waitress had followed us to the table with the desserts and was standing behind us, two plates in hand and two balanced on her forearms. And despite this, she was still managing to flirt unashamedly with a group of army cadets at the table next to us.

The waitress promised, "Laters, maybes see yers up Matley Lane?" to the lads and then plonked our plates down with an; "Oosdeathbychoclut?"

I translated. "Michael – you ordered the Death By Chocolate, didn't you?"

"Ah yes. And I see that the three of you have plumped for boring old vanilla ice cream. Does anyone want to try some of mine? It looks scrummy!"

"It looks like runny dog poo!" said Matthew.

"We don't eat bad chocolate, in our family. I told you that before, Michaelmas!"

Michael looked at Lydia and then at me. "Really? Is she having me on? Do you really refuse to eat chocolate that's…"

"That kills kids down mines and makes African children shoot people with guns," finished Lydia.

"Cool!" said Matthew. "Kids have guns in Africa? Can I go there, Mummy?"

I shrugged. "Well. As you know – it's what we do at Sisters' Space. We're all about fairly-traded chocolate. I mean, ever since we made the link with the women in Ghana… it's just been making me think a lot more. And I do believe that I should be practising what I preach at home – as well as at work."

"Gosh."

"Yeah. I know that I'm a laid-back parent when it comes to a lot of things… food wise – diet wise and all of that. But I do like to think that I have some principles that are of importance. That challenge the consumerist society. That help us – to support others out there in the world who have nothing like the standard of living that we enjoy. That's what I think. Anyway."

Michael gulped a wedge of his desert. "Well, thinking's dangerous when it comes to chocolate."

"Eeew!" said Matthew. "You just ate dog diarrhoea!"

Even though my children couldn't have been more obnoxious if I had asked them to try their damnedest, Michael gave me a fleeting kiss in the car park (whilst the kids weren't looking) and said;

"Please stop apologising. It's been fine. Come round tomorrow night – as planned. I might manage to have a conversation without a small person finishing the end of my sentences for me. Oh no – perhaps not. You'll be there though, won't you?"

"Ha. You calling me a short arse?"

"Precisely."

('Short arse' happened to be another one of Shaun's nicknames for me.)

The next day I drove over to my parents and dropped both kids off for the night. When planning over the phone for babysitting logistics with my mother the day before, I had finally admitted to her that I had a Saturday night 'date.' She had sounded surprised and even quite upbeat about it. But both of my parents were uncharacteristically quiet when I arrived at theirs. Although Dad didn't beat about the bush.

"So, who is this bloke then?"

"Oh, just someone I know from work."

True. All true. I hoped that they wouldn't ask any further questions. And whilst I knew that tomorrow they wouldn't be asking me, 'So did you make it home last night then?' or 'Did you get any?', I did suspect that they would probably try and press Lydia for some details as to whether Mummy Has Any Nice New Man-Friends. I hoped that Lydia would rise to the occasion and prove to be enigmatic. She could be annoyingly mysterious and evasive when she sniffed the whiff of desperation from any adult who was clearly trying to extract information from her.

CHAPTER 20

Michael was still trying to persuade me that it had been a bit of a heady week in politics, what with the new oil crisis, a renewed West African conflict and the Prime Minister 'accidentally' saying 'Fuck' when he gave a speech at an Evangelical Alliance conference. Michael told me that he had deliberately done this, to prove to them once and for all that he wasn't a fundy.

I just rolled my eyes and said;

"Don't believe you. Your claiming to be too knackered to take me out is a thinly-veiled excuse. You're actually too tight to want to spend a few bob on buying me a couple of pints down in Stalyvegas."

Michael had stretched out on the sofa and invited me to snuggle under the crook of his arm.

"Hah. More like I'm scared of being seen in public with you in these parts… after the experience with your two in the so-called 'restaurant'. The way that the other people were looking at us! Must have dropped me a couple of dozen votes, at the very least."

Thankfully we were distracted from our lack of common policy on parenting matters when Michael's phone rang. Again. He had told me that he wanted a peaceful night in – no phone calls other than 'urgent matters' - just chilling out and watching a few films, but despite the promise of 'No interruptions this evening, eh?' his mobile trilled out some eleven times (I counted). And his latest conversation seemed yet again to be 'urgent business,' requiring him to spend over half an hour discussing the history of block voting at party conferences. I mean – sure - I've always retained a very real interest in politics, but towards the end of the conversation when he was regaling facts from the 1970s about percentage shares of independent votes versus constituency, I ended up waking with a start, from a semi-snooze. Which unfortunately had involved me drooling a red wine stained patch onto one of the more expensive looking cushions.

As he hung up, I chucked the soggy cushion behind the back of the sofa, repositioning myself so that he could lie across my lap, as I played with his hair. It was more salt and peppered these days, than in past photographs that I had seen of him, but it was still shot through with strong, sandy shades. I wondered at the fact that he hadn't lost more of his hair by now. The stress of political life and all of that. And then I began to chuckle to myself. It had been so long – far too long - since I had found myself fondling another grown-up person's barnet, versus a kiddy's.

"What's up?"

"Oh. My chimp tendencies. I've just realised that I'm sitting here, doing the 'nit-sectioning' stroke that I have to do on Lydia and Matthew when we get an outbreak of too-busy mothers who can't be arsed to check their kids regularly."

"Found anything?"

"No. You've been a good boy and managed to avoid too much head-to-head contact with the grubbier members of the Cabinet this week."

"I thought that you only got head lice if your hair was clean?"

"Not true. They'll go for anyone really. Mucky or not. But – fascinating fact here - they especially like red-heads. So, watch it."

"Another reason to be keeping your children at arm's length from me."

"Thanks for the reminder. Anyway. I bet you, you've never had a lady-friend who automatically does this kind of thing for you, have you? Voluntary delousing, I mean."

"No. Can't say that I have ever had anyone in my life, quite so… offbeat as you are."

"Well, 'offbeat' isn't the worst so-called compliment that I've ever been paid."

"Yes, it's true," said Michael, reaching over me to grab a handful of popcorn from the side table "All my ex's were… shall we say… rather conventional. In comparison to you."

He proceeded to tell me about them. The girl that he met at Oxford and very nearly married; "Her father was very high ranking in the forces and it was a time in my life where I'd fallen in love with the military. But less so her, I'm afraid. Thankfully she did me a favour and ran off with a good friend of mine." He skated over a few dalliances that he had had during his army career; "No hamsters, no Arab prisoners – nothing too fruity" and then told me about Miranda – a New York fashion designer. They had shared a place in London for a couple of years just after Michael had left the forces. I asked him why it had ended.

"To be honest," he replied, wiping a trickle of beer from his chin, "Sorry - Christ, it's hard to drink whilst lying down, isn't it? Well, I'd seen – done – a lot of stuff. In various parts of the world. Of course, the army puts you through de-compression and all of that, but civilian life can hit you hard. And so… my head was rather messed up. Miranda wasn't… Well. She wasn't interested in what I had experienced. And she wasn't really the kind of person kitted out for living with a bit of a basket case. Which I probably was, back in those days."

"So… did you have Post-Traumatic Stress Disorder then?"

"Perhaps that's what we'd call it today. But back then it wasn't… But, no."

He trailed off and fiddled with the remote control, trying to pause the film that we had been trying to watch. Leonardo DiCaprio's face was now frozen in mid-rant at a suspected Indonesian terrorist. Poor Mr DiCaprio. I could never take him seriously in grown-up films after 'Titanic.' And he had always reminded me of a lad who worked at the petrol station in Stalybridge. Too youthful looking to threaten to cut someone's bollocks off. But might give you a good ticking off if you didn't put your hose back in the pump properly.

"I'm sure," he continued, "That I wasn't too much fun to live with at that point in time. Suffered terribly with insomnia. But..." he tried to balance a half-empty bottle on his chest and frowned at it, daring it to topple over as he tried to conjure up the right words. "Miranda's attitude didn't really help, I suppose. I overheard her on the phone to one of her friends one day." He mimicked a mid-Atlantic accent;

"*Well, Cherry - when I hooked up with Michael I really hadn't anticipated that I was signing myself up for never-ending sleepless nights with a nut-job wreck of an ex-soldier.*"

I pulled a face. Shocked that someone could be so callous. He carried on;

"Hearing her say that, did me a favour actually. Jolted me out of my temporary lack of direction in life.

After leaving the forces I had been feeling completely rudderless. Army life – the non-stop travelling. Being stuck in London - it truly had knocked me out of kilter."

"Whereabouts did you serve?"

"Oh – all over the bloody show. Name me a country with a dodgy dictator where I didn't end up doing my thing. But anyway. Back to Miranda. I asked her to leave. She packed her Prada suitcases and trotted off back to New York City."

He picked up the bottle again and laughed quietly;

"So – once she was out of the door, I grabbed the phone and made an appointment to see a top-notch psychiatrist in Harley Street. And I discovered that my problem was less about any underlying mental health issues – but that it was more about a lack of career direction. The psych helped me to unearth a childhood passion of mine. Politics. My family had always been political. I'd always been a member of the party. But in the forces, ideological affiliations are quite obviously discouraged whilst you're serving."

"Apart from the fact that the army exists solely to defend rampant capitalism, by reliance on weapons of mass destruction..."

"Oh, you're so old fashioned, Rachael."

But he grinned. I was relieved that he clearly thought so very little of cold fish Miranda. But my curiosity still hadn't been fully satisfied. Especially in relation to the scarring on his back; of how he had ended up with those white welts – those ripples. I wanted to ask him about it.

But then he grabbed a handful of popcorn again and sighed.

"But enough of me. Let's talk about you. Potted relationship history, please."

So, I told him about Adam. How we had met in one of the biker pubs that I often hung out at with Kate and Bob. How Adam had caught my eye and approached me with; "I like your handbag. Did you stencil that Judge Dredd motif on it yourself? Or did you get it off some crap market somewhere? 'Cause it looks a bit dodgy." Kate and Bob had brought along a friend of theirs; a bloke that they were angling to fix me up with. I was into guys with long hair at the time, but this one didn't do it for me at all (he reminded me of an old English sheepdog) and to Kate's horror, Adam had just proceeded to muscle right in on her nicely planned little foursome and continued with trying to chat me up. We had had our first date a few days later. A bike rally in Matlock; fish and chips and Nescafe. And after a bit we moved in together and had five years of marriage. All happy. All good.

"And then the children came along?"

"Yes. Quite soon after we got married really. I guess that I'm supposed to say that Lydia and Matthew were our finest achievements. Although after yesterday's performance, I'm not quite so sure…"

His dimples danced at me and he replied;

"Well, producing those two indicates that Adam must have had a great sense of humour. As well as excellent taste in women. But what about before Adam? After Adam… perhaps?"

I coloured. Flooded with a sense of foolishness.

"Well. A few casual boyfriends and one-nighters before I met Adam. But I guess really the main relationship that I had – in terms of length of time – was with Shaun. Who you've already heard of. Before. And after Adam. I'm sorry to say…"

Michael glowered.

"Ah yes. Mr Hotshot Knight of his own Tinpot Municipal Realm. Fascinating." He tried to half-sit up, propping himself on one elbow so that he could look at me more directly. Which I didn't particularly want him to. "So," he carried on; "don't you think that there could be a bit more to all of this 'posturing' then? Moaning in the media about my heartless government department? Trying to blackmail you the other week, over the photographs? Don't you think that this is all getting a bit too personally directed at me?"

"Er, no. This has nothing to do with the past. You're making it sound like some kind of 'Who's Got The Biggest Willy Contest'."

"Oh, don't underestimate yourself. Perhaps you're a bit of a Helen of Troy figure. History shows us that men have waggled their willies at each other, over women a lot more unpleasant looking – and much less charming – than you are."

I shook my head and rolled my eyes. Yeah, right.

"Well, whatever, Rachael. But you do have an interesting relationship pattern going on there. Shaun before Adam. And then Shaun after Adam. How did all of that come about?"

My defences were up. A very raw nerve had just been touched.

"Don't be thinking," I spluttered, aware that my voice had suddenly risen an octave; "that there was some kind of 'during' with Shaun. Shaun and I were over, *long* before I met Adam. I never would have…done that to…"

"Rach." He called me 'Rach' – just like Adam used to. "I wasn't thinking anything of the sort. And even if you did – even if there was… I'm not in a position to judge. I just wondered."

I decided to tell him the whole story. Factual rather than emotional of course. And that the strangest thing was this; when Adam and I got together, it turned out that he already knew Shaun – because they were both into their motorbikes. So, they knew each other from various biker clubs; Adam doing the Yorkshire side of the Pennines and Shaun on the Manchester side.

"There's an unusual trend here going on with you. Blokes and their bikes."
I shook my head. Couldn't deny that one.

"Sad but true. So yes, if you want to flog your Triumph in order to buck the trend, I for one won't be stopping you."

"Ha. It'll take more than your seedy past, before I part with the love of my life."

I stopped smiling. Nausea crept up my throat. Michael had used the exact same phrase that Adam had uttered - when he had finally caved in to my safety-conscious nagging. Me haranguing him about That Bloody Motorbike;

"Right, Rach, it's all done and dusted. The buyer's money has just hit the bank account."
"Hey – nice one, Adam. Well done. How does it feel to be a grown-up at last?"
"Very funny. I hope you're happy now. I've finally dumped the love of my life for a life of domestic drudgery with the naggy old trout and two evil pixies from hell."

Adam had been joking of course, but that craving – the desire to mount the bike and head for the open road had ultimately been the love that *did* take his life. That 'last day treat' in South Africa for him and Big Jim when they had hired a bike, that for one reason or another, decided to career off the edge of Cape Point.

Michael was staring at me. He tried to move the conversation on;
"And then Shaun reappeared on the scene again. After Adam died?"
"Yes."
"How soon?"
"Oh, pretty soon. Too soon."
"First to offer his sympathy?" Michael muttered, not attempting to disguise the disgust in his voice.

"Something like that. But he was still with Jess," I said quietly. It didn't sound good, however you put it. So then I admitted to him that I had been more than a little bit messed up. Befugged by the Valium. That one thing had led to another and that Shaun and I were back to the old days. Keeping it to car parks and the odd time when my kids weren't about. But that after six months, I had finally managed to put on the brakes on it all when I found out that he had gotten married.

Michael looked incredulous;

"Good grief. I mean, I *was* going to say that all of this was quite obviously – deceitful and calculated – behaviour. But, on second thoughts, I think that what he did to you is more… demonstrative of psychopathic tendencies."

I laughed and nearly spilled some of my wine onto Michael's shirt.

"Sorry. He *is* a bit of a spanner, that's for sure. Or a 'moronic nobhead tosser' as some might say, around these parts. But I don't think that you can put him down as someone who meets your psychopath criteria."

"You'd be surprised," said Michael, knowingly.

"Oh, God – don't start spouting off about the stuff they taught you in the army again. How to spot someone with borderline personality disorder at five thousand paces or something…"

"Does he have kids?"

"No. They still don't. Never asked why. She was always the Topic Not To Be Discussed. And the crazy thing is, even after losing Adam – Shaun was still more antsy about people seeing us together - than I was. I mean, you can just imagine the stigma that women face, can't you? Society has this attitude of… 'No sex for widows… forever!' But it had always been Shaun who wanted to keep the whole thing quiet. It sounds ridiculous – was ridiculous - how two grown adults were behaving; dodging and hiding."

"But then if he was already planning to get married… The stakes would have been quite high for him."

"I guess so. And I didn't put my foot down with him. Looking back, I probably didn't know any other way of operating in a so-called relationship with him. It's incredible how easily a human being can fall back into an old habit."

I suddenly laughed out loud as a memory resurfaced.

"Here's an example; back – first time round - when we were in our twenties, he had already moved out of their flat and one day we had parked up in his car in Altrincham, so that he could nip into a corner shop for something. And he suddenly spotted this other couple – a friend of his and Jess' – in their car. And he made me duck down. He threw a blanket from the back seat over me."

"And you still think that he's not unhinged?" Michael looked incredulous. "That sort of thing must have made you feel dreadful."

"Yes. Bit like a leper. Something wrong with me – about me; I'm embarrassing or not attractive enough, etcetera."

"Preposterous! The man's a fruitcake!"

"And honestly, Michael. Shaun is no nutcase. If you met him you'd find him to be a very sane, very balanced - somewhat flippant - bloke. He ticks all the boxes of a man about to hit the big time in terms of his career. But, when it came to me – both times round - he just acted like… well. He just acted oddly."

Michael sighed.

"Well, all I care about," he carried on, stroking my back; "is that there won't be a repeat performance. Is all of that – the attempt at bribing you, cutting your funding - then the bloody job offer, for God's sake - is all of that over now?"

I moved closer to him and thought for a second about telling him about what had happened when Shaun had turned up on my doorstep the other night. But I didn't want to admit to the fact that he had visited me at home. And neither did I want to confess to trying my own hand at a form of blackmail. So, I said;

"Oh yeah. All sorted. We're on our way to getting the loan. No need for any further contact with him, other than…"

"Than what?"

"Well, did your constituency office ask you about the official invite? For you to open Charlene's Chocolate Factory for us."

"Ah yes – they did. Graham the Griper said that there wouldn't be enough time in my schedule for it. He had me booked down for a visit to the WI in Marple on the same Saturday afternoon."

"Oh. That's a shame."

Or perhaps not. Perhaps a ruddy great big relief. No Shaun and Michael present in the same building, after all.

"Yes. But not to worry, Rachael. I told him to park the Marple trip and to invite the WI to your launch instead. The WI can be a scary bunch… you need ladies like them on board. Two birds with one stone. Ha – excuse the pun."

"Oh. Good. That's… great."

Hells Bells.

"Am I sensing that you're not actually too enamoured with my acceptance of your invitation, after all?"

I shook my head. "Well. It's just that… I had to end up inviting both of you. You and Shaun Elliot, I mean. Plus the Mayor of Medlock. Because we're a co-operative. The women wanted the local bigwig and you and… oh. It's just bloody silly really."

"Ah. Ah, well. That could be interesting. Both of us on the same territory. That could be very interesting indeed…" Michel trailed off. I tried to sound upbeat;

"So – if you'd rather say no. Now that you realise this - after all of the aggro that Shaun has been trying to whip up in the press, I'll completely understand."

He waved his hand in the air, dismissing me. "Not at all. Doesn't bother me in the slightest. So long as it doesn't upset you…"

"God, no. I couldn't give a toss about him and his lot. They've done nothing for us at Sisters' Space - other than to make life a hell of a lot harder than it needed to be."

"Good. Then there's nothing to worry about."

He put his empty beer bottle down.

"Still, Rachael. Don't be too dismissive of his character and of his motives. Men with an obsessive streak in their nature can decide to take on institutions - governments even – for all kinds of unfathomable and illogical reasons. Often for reasons that they can't even admit to themselves."

I began to laugh.

"Oh, you're a card, Michael. As no doubt your pals at Westminster would say."

He pressed my nose. Like Adam used to do.

"Say what you like, Ms Russell. I don't care. Just so long as I win."

"Win what?"

"The Biggest Willy Competition of course."

"Ha yeah. Dick-swinging. What are you lot like? Bloody men."

"You're so coarse. I love it when you talk dirty."

He picked up my wrist, kissed it and we kicked Leonard DiCaprio into touch, heading for the bedroom and for an earlier night than we had originally planned.

CHAPTER 21

Michael travelled back to London on the Sunday afternoon;

"Got to try and talk the PM out of this new Winter Tax for councils who aren't clearing the roads free of snow in time. It's all very well for him – he never gets a sniff of the white stuff in his Isle of bloody Wight constituency – but those of us representing you rough and ready northern sorts are always the ones to get the flak."

"Nice to know that disdain for The North has extended to the level where The Establishment is now trying to tax us for our snowflake consumption."

"Well, it wasn't my idea. I tried to persuade the Treasury to cough up for mass installation of underground heating for every acre of England north of Birmingham. But they were having none of it."

Despite the banter, I was disappointed that I wouldn't see him until the launch day itself. I thought that I had managed to disguise my feelings, but as we said goodbye, he pinched my cheek between his thumb and finger and then tried to force a smile out of my lips by stretching my mouth. Just like Matthew does;

"Chin up, Rachael. We can Skype or Facetime, or whatever. And I'll make it up to you. The next time that I'm back up here, we'll have lots of sweaty sex and trips to Bradford Industrial Museum so that you can look at trolleybuses. But for now, dull run-of-the-mill politics in Westminster must be the order of the day, I'm afraid."

And it was hardly going to be a scintillating few weeks for me, either. Despite the shot in the arm that the social enterprise loan was going to provide for us, I was determined that we shouldn't be reliant on borrowing. I had had enough of being forever in the red, with regards to my own personal financial circumstances. I didn't want it for Sister's Space too. I felt sure that some trust or charity or another, would be able to stump up the cash to help us to get back on our feet without having to do the pay-back thing. So, I carried on, with doffing my cap and tugging my forelock at people who were a million miles away from my own social standing (otherwise known as 'completing a funding application'). And when I wasn't grovelling to the people who possessed ownership of the much-needed moolah – when I wasn't dreaming up outputs and outcomes and performance indicator-ing myself into an early grave - I was engaged in empowering our service users to carry out effective decision-making in relation to the launch, telling the likes of Bev;

"God! I dunno, Bev! I couldn't give a toss what tricks the magician does on the day itself! You sort his repertoire out. I'm totally bogged down with funding applications at the moment."

And her replying;

"Well, Grumpy-gussets, all's I'm sayin' is that he might well have his DBS certificate, but a bloke what calls one of his 'illusions' the 'Weasel Out Of Trouser Leg' sounds like a bit of a kiddy-fiddler to me!"

"Yeah – and Bev should know," chimed Dee. "'Cause 'er Jordan's back on A-Wing at Strangeways and we all know the sorts that get banged up in that section."

Cue World War Three erupting.

During the next couple of weeks, Dawn turned up to the Centre a few times with Poppy-Rose in tow, but I was so busy that I didn't have time to do anything other than to smile, wave and to mouth the word 'injunction' at her. 'Yeah, yeah – I know,' came the response. Two weeks had passed since her latest Vinnie-pummelling and Gill told me that she was beginning to despair of Dawn ever filing for an injunction. She had now missed three separate appointments to complete the paperwork.

The centre-users who were most closely involved in the new enterprise were thriving on the buzz of the launch day preparations. Most of them hadn't been in employment for a long time and were enjoying the frenetic pace of plotting and planning. Dee was the only one who kept trying to sneak out for far too many fag breaks. Most of these, I noticed, involved a little saunter across to the park railings.

"Where's Dee gone? Yet again." Bev asked me. She was having to bellow over the clanging and the hissing of the espresso machine. It was the Monday before launch day and I had trundled down to the café to supervise how the latte art was getting on. We had paid a fortune for the barista training for both her and Jade and I wanted to make sure that we had been getting value for money.

"Oh, I think she's having a ciggie – near the park," I replied. "They've got some landscape gardeners there. Doing their thing with the shrubbery."

"Huh," Bev huffed. "No doubt Dee'll be hoping that they'll be doing *her*... with their *things*... in the bloody shrubbery."

Jade suddenly started giggling. Bev looked over. And yowled.

"Jesus Christ Almighty! What a waste of bloody money that was, Rachael - trying to get Jade properly trained! She in't the most talented latte-art lass, that I've ever seen."

By now Jade was in convulsions, dabbing her eyes in order to stem the flow

163

of goth-black tears. Bev carried on with;

"I mean, see… with the amount of blokes what Jade's had – at the ripe old age of – what?"

"Nineteen," Jade just about managed to say in between the hiccups of laughter.

"Yeah… with the amount what you've 'ad, you'd think you'd be a little bit better with the old hand-shakin' movement - when you're doing the artwork on the froth. See, Jade, I said to you before that it's all in the movement of yer wrist. It's only like when you're with a bloke and you're wan…"

"Enough, thanks, Bev," I said as I shook my head at her. "I'd like to be able to drink my cappuccinos without wondering what Jade was imagining, when she's producing the cute little pictures on top of the foam."

Bev took the cup off me and thrust it under my nose.

"Yeah well, Rach. Even her artwork tells you what she's thinkin' of. Look at that! It was meant to be a leaf! What does it look like to you?"

"Erm… like…"

"Like a nob! Like a big bloody donger! Honestly, Jade. You're gonna be here all week, practising this if you want to be half-decent by Saturday."

Jade said;

"I've wet me pants with laughin'! Need the bog!"

Gill wandered into the café.

"Rachael, I've just heard the radio in the kitchen. BBC Manchester news; all about our Big Unfriendly Giant at the Town Hall, having a pop at Michael Chiswick and his lot again. All the Greater Manchester authorities had some big press conference about it this morning. And apparently meladdo Lurch was gobbing off again. I mean, bloody hell. That'll look good, won't it? Bun fight between the boys on our launch day, next week."

She picked up one of the full cups that Bev had produced;

"Hey, that's really nice, Bev. Beautiful little love heart there. You've obviously got a knack at this malarkey. This one still seems warm enough for a…"

But before Bev could reply, Gill took a slurp. And then promptly spat it back into the cup.

"Oh, my God! That's rank! What the frig did you do to it, Bev?"

"Milk's off. We're only *practisin'* the latte art. Shouldn't matter if the milk's on the turn – or your coffee's shit, when you're practisin'."

"Well, thanks for telling me! God, that was hideous."

"Actually, Bev," I said, "I'm sure that the guy who trained you said that you should only use full cream, homogenised milk and you should make sure that it's totally fresh and from Sainsbury's and —"

"Yeah, yeah, yeah. But he was from Hebden Bridge. Started bangin' on about organic or soya milk or whatever shit they drink over that way. Was saying that his wife's a fruitarian or somethin' and they make their own sheep's yogurt and grow Goji berries or summat like that. Bloody weirdo. And I can't stand wastin' stuff, me, I can't."

She moved the cups to one side, picked up her phone and began tapping away.

"Checkin' the news for Manchester. Ah… yeah. You're right. Shaun Elliot just did this press conference… apparently accused Michael Chiswick of 'Nothin short of blackmail.' Oooh – get him! Handbags at fifty paces eh, Rachael? Pair of silly sods. But what if it all kicks off between them on Saturday? Should we tell 'em we don't want neither of 'em comin' now?"

I reached over to a lonely looking chocolate bar next to the espresso machine and broke it in half, handing it to Gill.

"Doesn't bother me. If it doesn't bother you lot. Here, Gill. That'll take the taste of your vile cappuccino away

Michael's comments in relation to the men both attending the launch, had cast away any doubts that I previously had in relation to the double-bill appearance. His own, very dismissive, attitude had filled me with confidence.

"All we have to do," I said, "is to remember that this is just boys in the playground, posturing. A load of froth and hot air. A bit of willy waggling so that they'll get their name into the newspapers a bit more."

"Yeah," Bev agreed. "Pathetic. Though I wouldn't mind having a sneaky peek at that Shaun Elliot's swingin' bits. But don't tell Dee I said that. She's got this thing about me fancyin' him. Always going on about it."

Oh well, I wasn't the only person with a taste-bypass problem in these parts, then.

Gill pointed her piece of chocolate at Bev;

"Which patently, you don't."

"Zactly. But anyroadup, bring it on, I say! Let them look like the nobsacks that we all know them to be. And then Sisters' Space'll get all the publicity around their bitchin' at each other, too."

"Absolutely," I replied, before realising that I had agreed with her that Michael was a nobsack. My phone began to bleep at me. It was Jake Bamber.

"Rachael, hun – sorry - but we've got a bit of a situation here. I've had to ask Martyn to come away from the office to see if he can try and get things moving. But it seems that even the kudos of our own CEO at New Banks isn't holding any sway…"

"Hang on – what are you on about?" I half-yelled because Bev was back at the espresso machine and the hissing and slamming down of jugs was drowning his words out. I moved away from the noise so that I could hear him.

"We've done our best, Rachael, but it's all gone a bit pear…"

"Sorry. I missed most of that. What's happened?"

"Look – just get your arse over here asap to the town hall. If anyone can sort this out, you can. And it's all… Well. A bit to do with you, really."

"Great. Sounds ominous…"

"Not too bad. But you're needed. We're at the old entrance. Not the new bit where all the offices are. We're at the back. Right next to the statue of Saint George. I'm stubbing my ciggie out on his shin, as we speak."

"Ha. Living Marxism. I'll be there in ten…"

I called back to the others that I was needed at the Town Hall and would be heading off home after that. But Gill's reaction was unexpected.

"Bleeuggh!" She had bitten into the piece of chocolate. Her face was a picture. "Jesus H Christ! What the hell's wrong with this? It's disgusting! Tastes like candle wax!" She reached for a serviette and spat it out. Bev picked up the chocolate wrapper, peering at it.

"Rachael, you pranny! You gave her one of the sample ones that we're supposed to put on display. No sugar or owt in it. I'm always scrimpin' an' savin', me, I am."

I grinned at Gill. "Sorry, Gill. Not your day, eh? See you tomorrow."

"Call this a café?" I heard Gill's voice as I headed down the corridor. "We'll be lucky if we don't get done for poisoning half of bloody Medlock!"

The town hall was only a short drive away. Martyn and Jake were loitering next to the statue that marked the entrance to the Victorian gothic monstrosity. The building had been erected in honour of Medlock's finest (and no doubt Masonically-oriented) municipal men. Martyn looked glum, but Jake had that dangerous chink of mischief in his eye. And he was clearly back on his old chain-smoking habit, flicking a cigarette butt nonchalantly towards the market ground as we turned to climb the steps up to the foyer.

"Judging by the smirk, Jake, this doesn't seem to be as serious as you previously indicated."

Jake flashed several thousand pounds' worth of Manchester's premium orthodontistry output at me, but said nothing.

"It *is* serious," pouted Martyn, arms folded and eyes narrowed as we stood at the top of the steps. It's…" he interrupted himself with an enormous "*Waah-choo*!"

"Mind if I move away?" I commented. "We've had enough back-to-school colds in our household, this term."

"Not a cold,' he sniffled. "… I tend to get a bit of an allergic reaction to perfumes and chemicals."

"Jake – have you been overdoing it on the Jean Paul Gaultier again?"

"Ha. Very funny," he responded. "No. It Vim. It's the Vim powder that the old lady chucked at us."

"*Waah-choo!*" Martyn added again.

"Right," I directed at Jake as Martyn smothered his face in a handkerchief. "Stop twatting about now. Tell me what the frig you dragged me out here for. It's been a bastard of a week for me…"

And then I checked myself. That subconscious desire of mine, to swear in front of Martyn, was becoming an increasingly worrying trait.

Martyn was busy blowing his nose, so Jake explained.

"Well Miss Simpson - you know, the old dear that you helped - along with your newfound fr…" he stopped himself just in time. Jake knew that the minister had been on the scene when I had helped to rescue the elderly lady from her flooded home in Mottram. He had also carried out some accurate guesswork in relation to what Michael and I had gotten up to later that evening. But he had been sworn to secrecy - and the look on my face halted him in his tracks. Jake had always been a tad bit afraid of the 'Rachael Scary Glare-y' as he referred to it.

"Yes…" he continued, mentally reprimanding himself. "Well. Shaun Elliot's lot at the town hall are still being stroppy about the whole thing; exactly as I said they would do. They told us that they won't pay for more than just the original two weeks stay for her at the hostel on their side of the Manchester boundary."

"So," Martyn put his handkerchief back in his pocket and took up the tale. "We pulled out all of the stops to get Miss Simpson's maisonette shipshape again. Anything to get Shaun off our backs. The man never needs an excuse to try and get one over on us. And the warden – you know Brenda, at Lancaster House?" I nodded. "Well, Brenda spent a good hour with Miss Simpson, explaining that we'd adapted the flat especially for her. You know, put some grab rails in for her, installed a panic alarm – even whacked a new heating system in. She told her that New Banks had even put new carpets in, to replace the water-damaged ones. That we'd help her to move her things back into the flat too. And that now that we're all aware of what an awful state her home – yes, her entire life, the poor thing - had actually been in…"

"… not to mention the dementia …" Jake chipped in.

"… yes, and all of that of course. Well, we're going to try to put a nice little parcel of support for her, in partnership with social services. Maybe a bit of help with her bathing and personal care. So, she…"

"Doesn't stink of piss so much," added Jake. Martyn frowned.

"So, Brenda – and Jake –explained to her that all of this means that there's no reason for her to be staying at Lancaster House anymore."

"And it also means that we can now tell Shaun Elliot to get off our backs and to Fuck Off."

"Tone the language down please, Jake,"

"This is Rachael, Martyn – she's hardly…"

Martyn ignored him. "But come D-day yesterday morning. Brenda found that

Miss Simpson was nowhere to be seen at the hostel. That she'd gone AWOL."

"Oh, shit!" I started. "She's so frigging vulnerable, Martyn! She's…'

Jake flapped a tanned hand at me. "Oh, you don't need to tell us that! We know! We had the police out looking for her. Bloody helicopters through the night and everything. One big search party – everyone worried because the temperature has dropped so much the last couple of days. But this morning we found her."

My stomach knotted. I'd spent an entire day trying to help Mary Simpson out. I'd even ferreted through her great and greying knicker drawers. I'd grown rather fond of her.

"Alive?" I asked.

"Oh, Christ yes. Very much alive!" Jake shook his head. "Do you think I'd be looking this amused if she'd kicked the bucket?"

Martyn glared at him. "None of this is funny at all, Jake – *Waah-choo!*" He reached for his hankie again.

"Sorry, Martyn. It was just… one of those moments."

I was getting really exasperated now but Jake was chewing the inside of one of his cheeks. Trying not to laugh. He flicked his head towards the inside of the building.

"She's round the corner. In the caretaker's broom cupboard."

"In the what?"

Martyn cleared his throat. "Well – Derek – the town hall's Technical Supervisor – he doesn't like to be called a 'caretaker', Jake."

"Whatever."

"Plus, he chooses to refer to his 'broom cupboard' as his 'office.' Well, Derek was most upset this morning, on turning up to work to find that a ninety-one-year-old lady had… *Waah-choo!*"

"… had somehow managed to get over from Manchester to Medlock," said Jake. "Early morning bus, probably. That she had seized his workspace. And that she's now claiming squatter's rights. She's locked him out. Viva La Revolution!" Jake gave me a delicious wink as he stroked his goatee with those immaculately manicured fingers.

"Yes," Martyn added. "Jake was summoned down here as soon as the police put two and two together and realised that she was our missing tenant from the hostel on Brindleford. And then I got roped into it all. And so, it was down to us - and to a duty social worker - to try and coax her out."

"No luck?"

"Well," Martyn huffed. "We thought we were onto something when she finally unlocked the door and opened it. But instead of permitting us to escort her off the premises she threw a load of Vim cleaning powder over the social worker."

.

He pointed to the freckles of white, spattered across his jacket; "And then she locked the door again, quick smart."

"Bloody hell, Martyn," I commented, "and here's me just thinking that you had a particularly bad case of dandruff today."

Martyn shook his head. "It really isn't as amusing as it all sounds. The social worker was standing in front of me and she caught the most of it. She was wearing glasses, so that stopped it from getting into her eyes, at any rate. She's had to go home to get changed."

"So, where's Derek the caretaker now?" I asked.

"He lost his temper. And stomped off round to the council offices to get..."

"... someone who isn't as fucking incompetent as we are," Jake added.

Martyn frowned.

"Well, those *were* his exact words, Martyn."

"Maybe, Jake. But the last thing we need is yet another run-in with Medlock Council over Miss Simpson."

"Speak of the devil..." grimaced my old buddy, as he nodded towards the bottom of the town hall steps.

CHAPTER 22

Shaun Elliot was striding up the stone town hall steps. Three at a time. His winter rain mac, the colour of soot, flapping behind him.

Very à la Darth Vader. Very Big Foreboding Fella With a Mood on Him...

The chill of the Empire was heightened even further, thanks to the presence of the Leader of the Council - Councillor Kathleen Casey - as she wobbled behind Shaun in her high heels.

Casey was in her early 60s; surely, she should have grown some footwear-sense by now, I thought to myself. She also appeared to be wearing a cowl – or some kind of a snood. I suppressed a snigger. With the sour-faced expression and the creepy hood-thing, she looked even more like Darth Vader's power-crazed little friend. The Emperor in stilettos.

Another figure jiggled up the steps behind them, panting and mopping his brow. This must be Derek the Caretaker. The third party involved in a rather marvellous Star Wars cameo. A short and stocky man, with hair sprouting from every visible orifice, the moustache, the beard, the Denis Healey eyebrows... the works. And even more so. He was growling every incomprehensible curse imaginable in relation to his perceived territory. Which had apparently been "Seized by a mad old cow!"

Yep. Derek portrayed the very image of an Ewok.

But Martyn had always been one to rise to the occasion – to stand on ceremony. He visibly shook the powder off his shoulders and declared;

"Good afternoon, Shaun. And nice to see you again, Kathleen." Martyn forced a smile as the party arrived at the entrance to the town hall. I noticed that he had hiked himself slightly up; that he was ever-so-casually teetering on the edge of his toes. Subconsciously, no doubt - because a good foot of height existed between Shaun and Martyn. Shaun had always mercilessly ribbed his adversary about his 'Little Issue' back in the days when we had all worked together at Whalley Range.

"Councillor Casey, this is Jake Bamber," Martyn informed the woman. "Jake is one of our senior housing officers at New Banks Housing. And this is Rachael Russell - the manager of the women's centre in Medlock. They do incredible work with women who have suffered abuse and who are turning their lives around. I'm sure that you already know about them."

Councillor Casey winced. Either it was a smile as forced as Martyn's, or she was experiencing a bout of wind.

"Yes. I know all about The Sisters' Place,"

"Actually – it's Sisters' *Space*," I corrected her. "And you really should stop by sometime, Councillor. We run some fantastic courses on…"

But Shaun interrupted my flow. Perhaps second-guessing that I was going to suggest some of our passive-aggressive training sessions to her. And even though Shaun could pip all of us at the rudeness game, he wasn't going to let me deliberately needle the woman who was, no doubt, the key to his coveted Numero Uno Chief Exec's post, once Roger Dawson had shuffled off into retirement sunset. He barged in with;

"So, Rachael. You've got it all sorted here then?"

I had always possessed the knack for reading his body language, but today I was struggling with it. His face was expressionless. His hands were stuffed into the pockets of his mac – but his eyes… his eyes danced over to Jake. He was checking out his reaction.

Ha, yes. That would be it; Shaun would be wondering whether I had confided in Jake about either of the most recent encounters between us.

Well, sweat it out, Shaun-baby…

"What do you mean?" I asked.

"I mean, surely you've sorted the old lady out by now?" He tipped his head to one side. Doing the cheeky Yorkshire bloke thing. "'Cause, wherever Rachael Russell's hallowed feet tread… she ends up liberating oppressed women of the borough. Whether it be OAPs or pregnant teenage druggies. So, I would have thought that you could have coaxed some pensioner out of the broom cupboard by now."

Councillor Casey stifled a giggle. I ignored the annoying old troll.

"It's not a broom cupboard!" Derek blurted. "It's my office! I've got paperwork in there! I've got a proper filing system and everything!"

Shaun narrowed his eyes at him. Shut up furry, minor Star Wars character. Then back at me;

"But, Rachael. When you do manage to extract your pal from the mop bucket, can you at least have the courtesy to check with us about where she goes to for her bed and board this time? Because *last time*, the Russell-rescue cost us a bloody fortune; when you drove her over to Brindleford. Never mind the accommodation charge that Manchester Council slapped onto us; that taxi fare you claimed for was truly extortionate. Was Prince William in the taxi with you? Or some other special VIP?"

Accusing me of wasting public resources was a purposeful red rag to the She-Bull. Even without the not-so-thinly-veiled allusion to the fact that Michael had been with me.

"Well, to begin with," I told him, "I wasn't even working on that day. As you already know – it was a Saturday and I just happened to be passing her house when a couple of kids told me that it was flooded. And – as you well know – all of the B and B's in Medlock were full that weekend. So, I had no choice other than get her over to Manchester to get her safe and dry and…"

But Shaun was now checking his phone for messages - had conjured up his best bored-on-purpose expression. He knew that I had played everything by the book with Miss Simpson. He was simply having a pop at me in public because I'd naffed him off over the way that I had managed to get him to sign the loan documents.

So, it would only be fair to have a swing back at him, wouldn't it?

"But you know what, Shaun? If the whole thing with Mary Simpson bothers you that much, I've got a better idea. The next time I encounter an incontinent, smelly and confused old lady who's about to die of hypothermia – I'll give you a tinkle on your mobile. You can come and pick her up in one of your cars. Maybe that top of the range Lexus of yours. Although I imagine that you'd be very concerned about getting stains on your seats…"

I caught Jake's eye. He flashed me a saucy grin. He knew a little bit about me, Shaun and sex in parked-up cars. But my jibe had soared over the heads of the others; Martyn being far too much the religious innocent to guess the back story about stains and car seats, Kath Casey being far too up her own arse to think that anyone else had a life. And poor Derek the caretaker being too worried about whether Miss Simpson was going to steal his paper clips or snaffle his Mr Muscle.

But Shaun just shoved his phone back into his pocket and deliberately made no eye contact with me. He turned towards his old-time career rival and decided to go for the double-pronged insult; a Two For One aimed at both New Banks fellas.

"So, Martyn… interesting choice of design for your suit there. Has Tinkerbell here - been sprinkling you with his magic dust? Have you got your boss flying alongside you and the other fairies yet, Jake?"

Martyn – to his credit – didn't rise to the bait.

"Actually, as I was just saying, we shouldn't really make light of it, Shaun. Of course, we all know that Mary Simpson suffers with dementia – but we can't really let her go round attacking members of staff, can we? I was quite worried about your own employee actually – that poor social worker… she caught the worst of it. And I seem to have developed quite an allergic reaction to the Vim myself…"

He snuffled into his handkerchief again. Shaun commented;

"Well, and there's me thinking that you always got your biggest kicks because of your Mr Squeaky Clean image." He paused, looked at us all and then suddenly slapped those large hands of his together.

"Right then! Enough. Someone's got to do something. No point in standing about gassing like a load of old biddies. Let's get back to the eviction days of yore – eh? Remember all of that - Bamber boy?"

Jake glared at him. Until this point, he had been uncharacteristically restrained about the Tinkerbell and the fairies comment. And the irony of the insult was that Shaun didn't possess a homophobic bone in his body. But he also didn't *do* politically-correct speech just to pacify others; especially when the mood of being rude about anyone and anything had seized him. Jake knew this and so he clearly didn't see the point in whipping out the anti-gay card and flinging it at Shaun. It wouldn't be accurate - and it would just be water off a duck's back. But Jake wasn't going to take any form of insult on the chin;

"So, you still enjoy evicting people, Shaun? Some of us always thought that you enjoyed kicking people out of their homes just a bit too much for your own good. Early signs of tinpot dictatorship, even back then —."

Martyn cleared his throat from behind his handkerchief, adding a loud cough for effect. Jake took the warning from his boss and stopped himself mid-sentence.

"Well," Shaun nodded towards me. "Seeing as though our New Banks colleagues have failed miserably in their attempt to remove one of their tenants from our local authority council property - I vote that me and Rachael here have a go. Bit of a blast from the past eh? She can show me how she works her magic on the vulnerable and marginalised in society. You lot wait here."

Martyn shrugged and snuffled. Jake rolled his eyes at the ceiling. Casey simpered at Big Brave Handsome Shaun.

"Derek," Shaun commanded. "Lead the way."

We turned a corner past the 'Medlock Council Members-Only' lavatories to find our way to Derek the Caretaker's kingdom. Or broom cupboard – stroke - office judging by its size.

"Here we go," said Derek, gesturing at a closed door. "Now, I've still got no bloody idea how she managed to get hold of a key. "He gestured at the floor. "See – there's all the disinfectant and cream cleaner what she threw at us… She just yanked the door open - made a right mess and… oh-ho – what's this?" He stooped down to pick up a piece of paper which had been pushed under the locked door and began reading it, lips moving silently.

"Bloody hell! Cheeky old sod's scoffed all of me stuff. I buy that meself!"

I took the paper from him. An A4 sheet embellished with a scrawly message;

"It says," I told Shaun; "'Simpson has enjoyed the fig rolls and the fondant fancies provided by Medlock Council, but must protest at the poor quality of the custard creams. Shop's own brands are always unwise in terms of biscuit choices. She demands that currant teacakes are delivered forthwith.'"

"She actually wrote that?" Shaun looked impressed.

"Why shouldn't she have done?" I gave him a dirty glance. "Just because she's elderly and because everyone is saying that she has dementia - doesn't mean that she lacks intelligence. In fact, both her handwriting and her spelling… and her sentence structure are far better than yours, that's for sure."

He scowled at me.

"Anyway," I said. "Let's stop fannying about here."

I knocked on the door.

"Miss Simpson? It's Rachael Russell here. Do you remember me? I helped you out of your flat the other week and took you over to Brindleford. In the taxi. Remember?"

The sound of shuffling feet. I hoped that she was moving towards the door.

"She's extremely deaf," I told Shaun. "I'll have to shout through the keyhole – although I doubt if she'll still be able to hear; she's not one for wearing her hearing aids." I cleared my throat and bent down, moving my mouth towards the door handle. "MISS SIMPSON? CAN YOU PLEASE PUT YOUR EAR RIGHT NEXT TO THE KEYHOLE HERE?"

I nearly toppled over when her voice came right back at me, straight through the keyhole and into *my* ear;

"I'M NOT GOING BACK TO THAT PLACE!" she shrieked; "THAT PLACE WHICH WAS ONCE A HOME! ONCE A CASTLE! BUT WHICH THEY'VE NOW FILLED WITH THEIR NEFARIOUS ACCOUTREMENTS!"

I shouted back. "SORRY… WHAT DO YOU MEAN BY 'NEFARIOUS ACCOUTREMENTS?'"

Derek the caretaker helped me out.

"Bloody bloke – your boss-man over there from the housing. That's what did it. He tried to coax her out, like – all nicey-nicey - by passing his phone through the door when she first opened it a bit. Showed her some photos of the work what they've done to her flat. Your adaptations and your grab rails and all of that. That's when she chucked the phone back at him. Along with the cleaning fluids…"

"Right." I nodded. Martyn had neglected to mention that part of the little tale to us. Meaning that both he and the social worker had misread the lady's personality. Miss Simpson was certainly not the type to let you fiddle about with her home and then to meekly shuffle back into her house and act the grateful beneficiary.

I addressed the keyhole again. "MISS SIMPSON!" I paused and tried to summon an inflection of positivity and excitement. "I KNOW THAT IT MIGHT SOUND… I KNOW THAT SEEING THOSE PHOTOGRAPHS MIGHT HAVE SEEMED A BIT STRANGE TO YOU. BUT HONESTLY. YOU'LL FIND THAT VERY LITTLE HAS CHANGED IN YOUR HOME. JUST SOME NEW BITS AND PIECES TO HELP YOU OUT."

Silence for a few seconds. Then;

"I DON'T NEED YOUR MARKETING SHENNANIGANS, YOU YOUNG STRUMPET, YOU! TAKE YOUR AVON CATALOGUE AND YOUR ENTRAPMENT LINGERIE ELSEWHERE!"

Bloody door. Bloody lack of hearing aids. Bloody refusal to acknowledge what was going on in the twenty-first century. Or whatever.

"Entrapment lingerie?" Shaun had definitely picked up on this one. "I know that you've been struggling for money, Rachael… but I didn't realise that you'd had to resort to selling pairs of knickers."

I ignored him and tried again.

"I've seen quite a bit of Dawn recently, Miss Simpson! You know – we got her and the kids away from that man who had been hurting them… and into Lockwood House on the same day as you. You got on very well with little Poppy-Rose, didn't you?"

A high warble came from the other side of the door. It was the chorus from 'Rose of Tralee'. I took this to be a good thing. Miss Simpson liked to sing. She seemed to enjoy interpreting the events that unfolded around her using words and phrases that struck a chord with her memories of the songs from a bygone era. She would probably get on with Lydia. Perhaps the two of them could become the next Andrew Lloyd Webber and Tim Rice combo; working together to produce 'Miss Simpson – The Musical.' Christ, that was a scary thought.

But in response to the singing, Shaun simply tapped his watch.

"Are you going to take much longer, Rachael – in showing me how well you work with vulnerable people? Because I've got an interview with a journalist in twenty minutes…"

I whirled around and took a few steps away from the door.

"Well, funnily enough, some things in life can't be earmarked into little pockets of time, Shaun. Some people need a bit more help than others. They can't be shoved from pillar to post… just so that you can do your whole darling-luvvie-boy of the northern-municipal-media thing!"

Derek was goggling at the two of us, enjoying the show. But obviously, Shaun wasn't too keen on one of his lowest paid underlings seeing a small, crabby woman speaking to the head honcho like this.

"Derek. Can you do one, please?" He jerked his head at the man and looked towards the entrance of the town hall. Derek shrugged and slouched away with a;

"No probs, Boss. Got quite enough on me plate with the one mad-as-a-hen female round here."

"Well, hey, Shaun." I said. "You're obviously skilled at issuing instructions to people. Maybe you should just have a word with her."

"Jesus! Alright then. If I must."

He almost had to double his frame over, in order to crouch down towards the door handle. I had a sudden urge to kick him in the arse and run away laughing, just like the kids do with me when I'm reaching into the freezer for something. But I resisted it.

"Hellooo, Miss Simpson," he projected bass tones through the door. "I don't normally shout through keyholes at people. So, if you don't mind – I'd much prefer it if you came out and we could talk face to face."

I tutted. "Well, that wasn't the best approach, Shaun. What you just said to her – that was all about *your* needs. That's not the way to communicate with someone. Although on the other hand, why change the habit of a lifetime?"

He ignored me and carried on with;

"So, come on out, won't you? Let's have a chat. Maybe make a deal. Or something."

"Ha! It's not like she's taken anyone hostage, Shaun. God, I bet you're still obsessed with watching your crap Hollywood films, aren't you? Still think that you're Bruce Willis or something." He turned his face back towards me, furnishing me with his best Robert de Niro gurn. *Shut it, Rachael.*

Miss Simpson shrieked;

"Well, it's just lovely to hear your voice, dear! It's been far too long. But I know that you move in higher circles than the rest of us these days. Simpson thinks that it's nice that you spare the likes of us any time at all!"

Shaun looked at me and tapped his forehead. Murmuring; '*Nuts. Never met her in my life.*' But he gave a little shrug and then responded.

"Actually, I *am* very busy today. I've got a press interview in a minute. So, it'd be helpful if you can come out now. And – didn't you say in your note - that you wanted currant tea cakes? Well – you know what? Our market sells them - just outside of here. Medlock Market's won awards for them you know. Best in The North. Golden Fork award, they call it. How about we… get you a dozen. Take them home with you."

I tutted. Patronising tosser. Telling someone as other-worldly as Mary Simpson about his oh-so important media engagements and trying to bait her with the promise of oven-bottom muffins and impressive talk about awards. Who the hell did he think he…

We heard the key turn in the lock.

Shaun looked surprised, but stood up and backed away quickly as the door opened. Perhaps thinking that he might end up getting sprayed with Mr Sheen.

Miss Simpson narrowed her eyes at us. She was wearing that same old, hideous polyester frock. Her hair – as always – stood on end; a wild, white mess of candy floss strands.

She moved towards Shaun. Seeing as though she wasn't armed with a can of fly-spray or a wadge of wire wool, he decided to thrust his hand out.

"Nice to meet you. Shaun Elliot."

She took his hand and then stopped;

A jaunty shake of her head.

"Oh, dearie me, no. You're not *he*, are you? I thought you were the other one. Gentleman from the news. With her," she looked towards me.

"I'm sorry, you've lost me…" said Shaun. His eyes were fixed on me now, but I shrugged. Shaun had seen the photos in the tabloids of Michael riding Vinnie's motorbike on Brindleford, of the two of us getting a bit up-close in his garden later that day – but I wasn't going to spell it out for him; that Miss Simpson had spent plenty of time with the minister and had taken quite a shine to him (mistaking him for a newsreader for some reason).

Yet how the hell she had mistaken Shaun's hoarse Yorkshire tones echoing through the keyhole - for Michael's clipped, cut-glass accent - was beyond me. But hey, the woman's mental faculties were failing, after all.

Tapered, crêpey eyes continued to take in Shaun, as he towered above her. To date, Mary Simpson had displayed an obvious disdain for most of the men that I had seen her encounter. And for me, the fact that when she had seen fit to try her own hand at verbally tackling Vinnie outside Lockwood House she had referred to him as 'a misogynistic miscreant' seemed to speak volumes. I had always imagined the never-married Miss Simpson to have been an early feminist; well-educated, middle class and - these days - fallen on hard times. A woman who would put up with no-nonsense from the male of the species – and, what with her being a female who had never married - perhaps she even held a romantic preference for her own gender. A slight tendency to snobbishness too. So, she would no doubt be disappointed that Michael hadn't been the chap to liberate her from the broom cupboard. Yes, Shaun was certainly going to cop for it now; was going to be in for an earful from her.

But Miss Simpson simply kept hold of Shaun's hand. I detected a smile dancing over the corners of the many creases around her mouth. And a glint in her eye. And then she bobbed him a little curtsey (for God's sake) and chimed;

"You're even taller than they let on, you know! And your eyes are like… like coal mines. As black as the coal mines of the Welsh Valleys. Burning coal. Sends me all of a shiver. So *very* handsome too!"

Shaun glanced over the top of her wispy locks at me. He looked a bit disconcerted. I shrugged at him again and mouthed;

"*Must* be dementia then."

And then he smiled at her. Not something that Shaun had ever had much practice in doing. And then he put his arm in hers and patted her scrawny old hand, moving her away from Derek's cupboard and towards the front of the town hall steps. I followed behind them whilst Derek – who had obviously clocked that the lady was about to leave the building – made a dash for his 'office' with an;

177

"Oh, bloody hell! Look at the shit tip that she's left it in! And she's drunk all of me fizzy Vimto!"

We found Martyn, Kath Casey and Jake Bamber still waiting outside. Martyn gave me a thumbs-up and burst forth with;

"Excellent - you did it, Rachael! I knew that you would!" I looked over at Shaun. A crooked smile was playing around his lips.

"Actually, it wasn't so much me, Martyn. It was Shaun… It was Shaun, here, who managed to persuade Miss Simpson out. And as you can see - it looks like - he has a new fan now..."

Jake gazed at The Giant and Geriatric Show in astonishment. But he managed to mutter;

"Hmmm. Well, that'd be his one and only supporter in Medlock." Martyn glared at him. Watch it, Bamber. But Jake swung back into cheery-professional mode.

"Well, all's well that ends well. And it's lovely to see you safe and sound, Miss Simpson. I think I'll just hail a taxi and we'll get you back to the hostel and then sort out getting you back home ASAP. All nice and cosy, eh?"

Mary Simpson shook her head fiercely and scowled at the housing officer.

"Only if accompanied by the regality of tea cakes. I'm a lady on a promise,"

Shaun began to laugh. It was a rare sound for all our ears. And then he tapped her hand and wagged his finger at her, all playful-like;

"Hmm, well. You had better promise me you won't be doing silly things like this again. You're a very naughty girl."

Miss Simpson chortled back at him.

"Girl Guide's honour!"

Jake gawped at me in mutual disgust at the display, so I stuck two fingers into my mouth and pretended to vomit into a potted plant next to me. It was unnecessary, it was childish – so it was probably entirely deserved - that at that precise moment Councillor Casey turned round and caught me doing it.

"Had fish and chips at lunch" I said. "Bit of a bone stuck… still feels like it's there…"

She didn't look particularly convinced.

Shaun was getting his wallet out. He pushed a fiver at Jake and jerked his thumb towards the market ground.

"Bamber - go and get us a dozen currant tea cakes from the inside market. Oven-bottom sorts. The pricier ones – the ones with more raisins in them."

Jake was about to protest - What Did Your Last Slave Die Of - but noticed the look on Martyn's face and instead, headed off towards the market hall. I felt sorry for Jake, being sent on a bread-buying mission, so I gestured to the grand entrance hall behind us and said to Shaun;

"Saw all your municipal trophies back there in the foyer, Shaun. But didn't see any for award-winning currant tea-cakes."

He avoided my gaze.

"Somebody vandalised it, when we had it on display in the tea-cake stall," he replied.

"Wooh. Serious stuff."

"We think it was a rival tea-cake producer in Huddersfield."

"That's my neck of the woods," I said. "We'd never stoop so low."

"Yeah, well. Your lot are pretty good at getting their mates over to trash people's cars when they aren't getting what they want. So, I wouldn't put it past the West Yorkshire Mafia to throw a wobbler over the fact that their oven-bottoms aren't as tasty as ours."

I let it go.

Kath Casey had walked to the corner of the building to flag a taxi down. The remaining four of us stood at the bottom of the town hall steps, avoiding puddles produced by the quick cloudburst which had showered Medlock whilst we had been inside. Nearly all the outside traders had dismantled their stalls, packed their vans and were getting ready to head off back home. A watery autumn sun had fashioned a vivid rainbow. It streamed its way above the market ground lending a hint of exotica to what had been the usual murky-in-Medlock day.

"Oh look!" said Miss Simpson. "'The Lord gives us a sign!'"

This was the kind of talk that Martyn always warmed to.

"He certainly does," the chief executive bubbled back at her; "A promise never to flood the Earth again! And that's a particularly pertinent sign, isn't it? Given the fact that your home was flooded the other week! I wonder what we can all learn from…"

But Miss Simpson just scowled at him, cutting him off with;

"No. That's not the sign that He means. Not at all!"

I tried to disguise my smile. As well as the singing, Miss Simpson also had a propensity to talk a lot of religious nonsense - but in my book, it was more purposeful and helpful religious nonsense than the stuff that Martyn Pointer's version of The Truth tended to consist of.

"And I'll be getting a sign myself,' I chipped in. 'From the local constabulary - if I don't get back in time to pick the kids up - and the child care providers have had to dump them by the side of the road in Holmfirth again." I fished in my handbag for car keys.

"Right. See you Saturday then," Shaun commented, as he stared out over the now nearly-deserted market ground.

"Yep, at the big launch," I answered. I turned to the old lady; "So, Miss Simpson, I really hope that things go well for you on the move back home. And

I'll make sure that I get Dawn to give you a call. I'm sure that she'd like to speak to you…"

Miss Simpson was still clinging tightly onto Shaun's arm and she nodded her head at me, beckoning me nearer. She reached out a veiny hand to the back of my head, poking yellowed fingernails into my hair as she drew me closer. So, near that I could smell the custard creams on her breath. She whispered;

"*You* know what the sign means, don't you?"

"Do I?" I mouthed back.

"Yes, you do!" she hissed, waving her forefinger at me, in an Elderly-ET-Go-Home gesture. "But the Lord of the Earth and Sky doesn't even know himself. So, who can tell? Who can say? Shall the chosen one be the Great Giant? Or the Man Off The Telly? It's causing a proper consternation amongst us all - it is."

"Is it?"

"Yes. And even a sacrificial tea-cake or two, might not appease the God of our ancestors."

I went to get the kids. They made a bit more sense. But only slightly.

CHAPTER 23

I was in the middle of a rather interesting discussion between Shanaz, Maryam and Dee, when reception called me away from the hall. It was eleven AM and fifteen women were assembled in the main body of the centre, all ready and waiting for the weekly belly-dancing lesson. Milly, the class teacher, was caught up in what sounded like a shrieking match with someone at the other end of her phone (probably British Gas; Milly never had much luck with utility companies) and Dee had taken the opportunity to saunter to the side of the hall, where I had been chatting away with Shanaz and Maryam.

Dee, hand on her more-than-fair-share of hips, was twirling one of the tassels on her 'designer' belly-dancing costume. It was already shedding little tinselled strands onto the hall floor. She cocked her head at the two women.

"You two gonna just sit, gassin' with Rachael, then? You not joinin' us?"

They shook their heads. Maryam replied;

"No, thanks."

Dee wasn't giving up;

"Don't see why not. You can still have a proper boogie in yer tent-dress things."

Both women were wearing niqabs. Shanaz shrugged.

Dee went on;

"You fastin' then or summat? Some religious rule that you'll faint if you have a freak-out?"

Maryam replied;

"No. Not today."

"An' anyways," Dee prattled on, "I dunno why you never take yer headgear off in 'ere. I know for a fact that you're allowed to show yer face and yer hair and all of that when there's no blokes about. An' there's never no blokes at Sisters' Space 'cause we don't let 'em in, 'cause we hate 'em all. Don't we, Rach?"

I was appalled. Dee was turning into a stuck record when it came to our policy about male visitors.

"Dee! You know that's not what we..."

But Dee was doing the hand-in-air 'whatevoh' at me as she turned and walked away to the front of the class. Milly had now returned to the job in hand, complete with an ominous smile on her face; a complaint to the energy ombudsman on the cards, no doubt.

"Sorry," I said to the two women as we were left alone again. "I don't suppose Dee's particularly familiar with what the Qur'an says about dancing and sexual movements in public… modesty and all of that."

Maryam's eyes narrowed.

"Nah," she replied. "It's not about that. That's not why we aren't dancin'." She jerked her head at her friend. "It's 'cause *she's* on the blob and she doesn't fancy leakin' all over yer hall floor."

Shanaz nodded. Her eyes deadpan. Her pal went on;

"And me? I'd rather slit me own throat than do a Dee – prancing around looking a blubbery, hairy old walrus. I mean. At her age! No bloody shame!"

Stacy poked her head around the hall doors;

"Rach. Got a bit of a problem on reception."

I moved away and called over my shoulder to the two women;

"Well, maybe not today – but if you ever fancy it, do feel free to lose the niqabs and join in with the dancing. No blokes about for a million miles."

Shazana shot back;

"We would do - if you'd sort your friggin' heating system out. We're freezin' our tits off here. Neither of us has as much lard on us as Dee does."

Those two. I never know when they're winding me up or not.

Reporting to reception though, it seemed that I had been wrong about the proximity of the next nearest male.

"Bad news," Sandra nodded towards the front door. "Got Mr Charm Personified outside. Demanding to see Dawn Hibbert."

"Oh great. Is it —."

"Yeah. That Vinnie Murray bloke. Recognised him. He's not bad lookin'. Shame he's such a nutter. God knows what that Dawn was thinking, getting mixed up with him."

She jerked her head towards one of the photographs on the computer that she had highlighted with her cursor. The system that we had named 'Our Violent Partner Parade' was beautiful in its simplicity and it came to be very useful at times.

I looked away and towards the CCTV camera screen, at the image of the figure standing outside of our heavy-duty security doors. He was just finishing off a cigarette. Stubbed it out against our brickwork and then lobbed it over the wall. This was followed by a hacking cough.

"Eeww," said Sandra. "Did you see him just greb on the path there? Dirty sod."

Then Vinnie Murray followed this up with his party piece. He simultaneously booted the door whilst pressing the intercom button.

"Anyone fuckin' in there – for fucksake?"

Such a gent. I took over from Sandra, speaking into the intercom;

"Hello, Mr Murray. You seem to have developed a nasty habit of attempting to kick doors in over the last few weeks. Would you like me to call the police in order to assist you with your little problem?"

Yes, I knew that it probably wasn't the best way to deal with a volatile thug like Vinnie, but in my role as manager of the centre, I didn't usually get to witness the actual acts of physical violence; it was nearly always the imprints and the aftermath that I had to deal with. But on that sweltering day, a few weeks ago, in September, I had personally experienced the real-time horror etched upon the faces of his kids, along with the physical marks that he had just inflicted upon his girlfriend. So, it was hard for me not to rein in the feelings of profound disdain and disgust.

Still, Vinnie didn't seem to possess the intelligence to realise that I was being sarcastic. And, ever so slightly, unprofessional.

"Oi – is that, that... blonde woman?"

"Which one?" I asked, followed by; "I believe that there are several million females in this country alone, possessing such hair colour."

A pause.

"Yeah, it's you alright. You were the one helpin' fuckin' Dawn out on that day. With that bloke who turned out not to be a vicar, but to be a governmental whatsisname."

I sighed. Vinnie wasn't the most erudite of chaps.

"Well," I began. "My colleague tells me that you were asking to see Dawn Hibbert. Now, firstly, we don't allow men access to our premises. And secondly, Dawn isn't here. And thirdly, we certainly don't engage in discussions with misogynists who have a history of beating their partners."

Sandra nodded in agreement. We gave him the opportunity to respond. But he didn't. He was probably trying to figure out which B-list celebrity rap star Ms Ojinist was. So, I continued;

"So, don't try and kick our door again. You're on CCTV camera anyway. Please leave our grounds immediately or we'll be forced to call the police."

Vinnie already had a lengthy police record, but despite that, you can never tell whether the threat of the bizzies will work with someone or not.

His voice came over the intercom again;

"Yeah well, you do that an' I'll just be back 'ere in a couple of fuckin' hours. I know she's fuckin' in there."

I looked at Sandra. She muttered;

"In the old days, we would have been quite within our rights to pour boiling oil on dickheads like him. Civil rights gone crazy, it is. This country's not what it used to be."

"Yeah, good job the Brexit vote went the way it did. I can't wait for the reintroduction of capital punishment as well, eh? And a spot of water-boarding for juvenile offenders." I spoke back to Vinnie now. "Look. Never mind the fact that Dawn's all set to apply for an injunction against you and all of that. Because the way that you're behaving here, right now – I'm thinking that we should be applying for a second one against you. On behalf of the centre."

"Fuck that —" he began, but then interrupted himself. His tone of voice completely changed. Raising itself from gruff aggression to almost polite enquiry. The attention span of a gnat.

"Hey, you know that politician bloke what you know? Mr Not A Vicar man. Have you got his number? 'Cause I'm needin' to sort me carbs out on the bike and he said that he knew this fuckin' good bike mechanic over in Mottram. Called Andy, he were, but I can't remember the name of the fuckin' garage now."

I snorted. In the space of thirty seconds, Vinnie had gone from threatening thug, to wanting to speak to the Minister of Communities about motorcycle maintenance. Yeah right, Vin – like I'm going to give you the Minister's personal mobile number, so that you can call him in the middle of Prime Minister's Questions about carburettors and ignition coils or whatever.

Sandra was giving me the eyeball. It seemed that I had been chuckling to myself. So, I reined my mirth back in again and answered him;

"No. No, I can't really help you with that. But – tell you what – tomorrow he's off abroad on an overseas diplomatic mission for a few years. So, if you're quick about it, you can call his constituency office in Stalybridge and ask them. I'm sure that he'd call you back about it all before he leaves the country. You'd best be quick about it though —"

Sandra whispered to me;

"A local government minister… going abroad for a few *years*? You're lying, aren't you?"

"No flies on you," I mouthed back.

Either way, we weren't sure whether Vinnie's rapid departure from our entrance porch was due to his imbecilic belief that a senior UK politician would want to chat happily with a wife-beater about bike parts. Or due to the coincidental sound of a police siren in the distance.

CHAPTER 24

Only a couple of days were now left before the grand opening. Sisters' Space was all aglow with positivity. Preparations for the launch seemed to have forged a new sense of camaraderie and I was beginning to feel very upbeat about things. Reet chipper in fact. And it seemed as though even my parents had caught the bug. My mother telephoned me to say that although they had originally agreed to keep the kids at theirs that day, they;

"Fancied having a little drive over to see what's happening with your battered ladies' festival."

Normally, the prospect of my own offspring (or indeed, my own parents) appearing at a work-related event was enough to make my blood run cold. But my mood was still buoyant, bobbing along on waves of optimism, so I simply agreed. Mum replied;

"Good. And I'll make some cakes for your cake stall. Parkin – it's that time of year after all. Plus, some salted caramel brownies for the more sophisticated sorts who live closer to the south Manchester side and who like their sun-dried tomatoes and their kumquats. But don't you go snaffling any of it yourself. You never really lost all of the baby-weight, did you? Different metabolism to Vicky-the-whippet, I suppose. Such a shame she can't get up from London for your little soiree, after all."

I did feel a bit down in the mouth about the absence of Vicky on the big day. The two of us had been having many more phone conversations than we usually did. She had informed me that my love life had proven to be a very interesting distraction for her; taking her mind away from her being 'Billy No Mates', stuck at home; 'It's driving me crazy, not even being able to go to work and shout at my team. Like, you can't call someone 'a Fuckwit' in an email, can you? They'll take you to a tribunal. I mean, at least if I do it in person, I can pretend that I said something in my Mancunian accent that they must have misheard.'

"… so yes," Mum continued, "I'll have the cakes all ready here for you on Saturday morning. They can be my little contribution for your Cause. And your dad – Stingy Sod here…"

I could hear the fuzzy grumble of my dad's voice as he objected to her words;

"Yes, Terry, there's a *reason* why people call you that. Along with plenty of other things, of course - well, your dad's contribution can be to stop moaning about the cost of petrol for driving just the eight miles to Medlock in order to support his eldest daughter. And her abused people's celebrations."

"Right, well. But go easy on doing so many different cakes, Mum. Baking can be expensive."

"Don't be daft. You sound like old misery guts here – I can already see him stressing about the cost of butter and flour. I don't give two hoots about the money. These days, people in our society don't do enough to help other folk. And no one likes to see women getting knocked about - do they, Terry?"

An indecipherable comment from my dad in the background indicated that he occasionally begged to differ on that one.

Thursday morning and at eleven o'clock, I was crouching on my office floor with Kirsty, one of our newest service users. I was attempting to demonstrate how to make up the different information packs for the event. I had presumed that this would be a fool-proof task for anyone to do – but she wasn't the most confident of women. Just being in the same room as her, made me feel like Two Ton Tessie. So, I was doing my best to speak quietly and to convince her that it really was as easy as cottage pie;

"See, Kirsty, you've got the four categories of guests. You've got 'VIPs', 'Professionals', 'Media' and 'Public' and I've written down which leaflets go with which category. Most are 'Public' of course. So, you just follow that and make up the numbers for each category that are listed on the spreadsheet printout. Okay?"

Kirsty nodded. But then she changed her mind and shook her head, wondering aloud in a small voice;

"What if I screw it up?"

I sighed inwardly. Years of abuse and bullying had knocked the edges off her ability to try out something new; even shoving some leaflets in an envelope. It was pathetic - but hardly her fault. Her eyes wandered uncertainly over mine, but I didn't want her to register my impatience, so I gave her a friendly nudge with my elbow;

"What's the worst that can happen? Is someone going to have a paddy because the odd leaflet on home security systems is missing? Come on, Kirsty. People won't even sodding notice!"

She shot me a bleak smile and I was about to ladle on more spoonfuls of reassurances when the office phone rang. It was reception.

"Shaun Elliot to see you, Rachael. He's coming through right now..."

This was of the blue.

"No… no! Stacey - he doesn't have an appointment with me. He can't just walk in here and —"

"Sorry – I couldn't stop him!"

A second later Shaun strolled into my office. Hands in pockets and head tipped on one side. He knew damned well that I'd be furious about the fact that

186

he hadn't waited in reception; our 'no men in the building' policy; the invite-only to male colleagues stuff.

"Alright?" he said. "Busy getting ready for Saturday, then?"

"Yes. And we didn't have an appointment to meet. So, I can't really speak with you right now."

"Won't take long. Do you mind?' he glowered at Kirsty. A look of puzzled anxiety etched itself across her face as she glanced at me. Shaun decided to spell it out for her benefit.

"Would you mind *doing one* - I mean." He jerked his thumb towards the door. Kirsty fumbled and then dropped the stack of leaflets that she was holding. They scrawled across the floor as she scurried off in the opposite direction, calling to me from over her shoulder;

"Sorry! Sorry, Rachael! I'll come and tidy them all up again in a minute! Sorry!"

I raced after her. She scurried down the corridor and into the kitchen, grabbing the kettle.

"What are you doing?" I asked. "Come back in! He's got no right to do what he just did!"

"He's that bloke in charge at the council —"

Her nervous tic - manic blinking in order clear her vision and to soothe her mind - had kicked in.

"I know, Kirsty – but I'll tell him to sling his hook. Like I said, he's got no—"

"No!" She almost shouted back. "I'm… I'm feeling a bit crap, Rachael. Think I've got a migraine coming on. Staring at all those leaflets."

I could tell that she was about to cry, so I put my arm round her and gave her a squeeze;

"Okay, love. You just get yourself some paracetamol. I'll be back in a minute."

I strode back to my office and slammed the door behind me. Throwing a look of utter contempt up at the lofty sod, I bent down and commenced with picking up the spilled leaflets.

"Who the hell do you think you are, Shaun? I've spent all morning trying to get her to chill out! To try and stop acting like the next man that she encounters is going to smash her face in. And in three seconds flat, you waltz in here with your size twelves and undo all of that!"

Shaun shrugged and parked himself against my office window. Blocking out most of the sunlight.

"That's not my problem. Whatever 'issues' your women have here at this place, they've still got to live in the real world. And in the real world, people can't be tiptoeing around them all of the time."

I crouched, carrying on with trying to put the leaflets back into piles, not even bothering to look at him.

"You always were an arrogant git. But these days, you surpass even yourself."

He coughed a half-laugh.

"Meaning?"

"Meaning – when I first met you – even *that* Shaun wouldn't have been so callous. Kirsty - the woman that you just acted like a complete tosspot with - was locked under the stairs for three days by her husband. Just because she dared to make an extra trip to the supermarket without asking him first."

"Yeah?"

"Yeah. Maybe all of your hanging around with the municipal great and good has made you forget that there are far too many people out there leading really shitty, dreadful lives. Don't you think that some people perhaps *do* merit a little bit of tiptoeing around? As opposed to being bullied?"

Shaun was nonplussed. Shaun always was.

"Don't be using the 'B' word with me, Stan. Bullying isn't anything to do with having a bit of conviction about the way you deal with people. I'm not the bullying sort."

I stayed quiet. Focussed on the leaflets. He carried on;

"But yeah – come to think of it, since you and I worked together way back when – I have changed. Maybe grown up a bit. Making decisions in senior management does that to you. Even people like your little friend there, who've – yeah, gone through shit – don't need mollycoddling. They need to toughen up, fast."

"You've not changed for the better then, Shaun. If that's what you think. If you'd been such a callous prick and come out with a load of claptrap like that when we first met… well. I wouldn't have given you a second glance…"

He tutted. Then sighed.

"Yeah well, then you must have changed too. In fact – yeah, you have actually. The Rachael that I used to know back in those days, wanted to make a real impact on society. She wouldn't have been into fannying about with community events and your fair trade hot chocolate or whatever it is you're peddling at this place this week. I mean, Jesus! Where's the business sense in it all?"

I just gawped at him. He carried on;

"Getting your women, a bunch of lasses like her, who jump out of their skin at the first person who speaks to them - to run a café and chocolate shop thing for you? It's mental. You'll be employing ex-drug pushers to sell your chocolate lollipops at the school gates next."

I stayed quiet. He wasn't getting the message;

"'Cause I've just been reading the leaflet that you printed – all about your do on Saturday. What you've got to offer the public. I mean - cake stalls, balloons, tombola, bouncy castle... Sounds like your average crappy church fete, for God's sake! I thought that you were supposed to be serious about enterprising activities here with your big ambitious business plan…"

I continued with stacking the leaflets. I let his little tirade peter out. And then I said;

"There's nothing more amusing than receiving a lecture on business and enterprise from someone who's only ever worked in the public sector. Whose entire career – his future pension scheme - has been cushioned by grants provided by the central government. Grants which he – incidentally – has never even had to put pen to paper to apply for. Never mind having to think about creating a real business plan or financial forecasts…"

"Don't get arsey about my career path, Stan. It's not much different to your own. Business is hardly rocket science —"

"Except that my post – and the jobs of people here – aren't assured by big fat government grants."

"Well, no jobs are 'assured' at the council these days, Stan. If you hadn't noticed… your man at the Ministry and his ridiculous cutbacks are causing a hell of a lot of job losses in local authorities."

"Yeah. But the jobs that are going are your lower paid minions. Your bin men and your clerical staff and your care home assistants. Maybe some of your middle managers. Can't imagine *you* fretting that *your* job is going to get axed. I mean, I spend half of my life writing funding applications and praying that someone will see what we've got here in terms of our service - in terms of our potential – that someone will 'get' the whole picture and will bail us out."

"Well, your little fan, Martyn's, done that for you this time round, hasn't he? Bailed you out with his social enterprise loan."

I ignored him and slapped one of the stacks of papers onto the office armchair. But he wasn't letting it go.

"He's always fancied a piece of you."

"Oh, fuck off, Shaun. Have you any idea… what a total twat you sound like?"

"You didn't used to like using the word 'twat'."

"I still don't, really. But actually - I can't think of a word right now that suits you better. Other than one that I find to be even more unhelpful, because it simply reinforces the fact that society has this mistaken belief that female genitalia are somehow more unclean and debase than male…"

"Christ almighty. Can't you just call me a 'cunt' and have done with it? Without having to turn it into a PhD thesis on neo-feminism or whatever you've recently been …"

"And anyway, Shaun. Going back to the subject of enterprise. I do happen to know just a bit about it all. Don't forget that for quite a few years, I helped Adam. He was self-employed – remember? I spent most of my evenings doing Inland Revenue stuff and putting together business plans with him."

Shaun's voice had a habit of becoming quieter whenever I mentioned Adam. But my deliberate reminder still wasn't stopping him;

"Well, whatever. I stand by what I said. You're hardly doing your women here any favours. Keeping them away from people who say it like it is."

I didn't bother looking up, as I replied;

"Oh, God. Here we go again. 'I'm Shaun, me, I am. I'm from Yorkshire. I speak my mind, I do. Call a spade a spade, I do. Bit of home truths for you lot la la la. But it's all because I've never grown up. And I think that the rules of discretion, subtlety and genuine consideration for others don't apply to me. Because basically I'm too fucking arrogant to rein my gob in.' And stop calling me 'Stan', will you? I changed my surname, when I got married. Remember?"

He chuckled; "Yeah, and that was a bit hypocritical of you. Hardly feminism in practice."

"Most feminists recognise that whatever name you end up with – it's still some bloke's. But I don't imagine that this would have even been a fleeting consideration for your Jess. *She* would have just done… whatever her parish priest had recommended her to do for the big occasion of hitching herself to you and your name - for life. No doubt. Poor cow."

Golly gosh, we were doing our best to needle each other now.

So he changed tack and next it was;

"Anyway. That's a bit of a blast from the past."

"What is?"

"You on the office floor. Waving your bum at me. You used to do that with the property files, remember? You said that there wasn't enough room on the desks to sort them all out. So, you did it on the floor. Subconscious arse waggling at me. Presenting oneself. The animal world thing."

I remembered all of that of course. Only too well. But I wasn't going to go there, because this was an office and this was a place for levity and for skilful maturity. Plus, the 'Fuck Off' and the 'Twat' insults and his own voluntary description of himself as 'Cunt' clearly hadn't worked.

So instead, I stood up and, with my arms folded, I decided to front it out.

"How's your car now?"

A pause.

"Fine, thanks. But if I were you, I'd think about moving away from that side of West Yorkshire. Ever since they killed off Last of the Summer Wine, the place's been going to the dogs. I've heard about all the aggro they have these days in Holmfirth pubs of a Friday night. You should move to Bradford. Even over there, they're a bit classier than your lot."

"Yeah,' I sneered. "It's like The Bronx for us, in the Holme Valley at the moment. The attack on your car was probably carried out by a couple of Japanese tourists who had come all the way from Tokyo to do the Summer Wine Tour and who were in a bad mood, 'cause Compo's Chippy closes at seven PM."

Shaun pointed his finger at me and said;

"Peeow. Still sharp as a razor, Stan."

"Yeah, well. Enough." I flipped my hand at him, dismissively. "Why are you here - wasting my time? Don't you have a photo op with some face-painted child from a local council estate to attend to, or something?"

"Well, for starters. Going back to your loan; a nice 'thank you' for my signature - wouldn't go amiss."

I gave him a withered smile.

"You've got to be kidding. I mean, you hardly signed the damned thing out of goodwill, did you now? You were more worried about a bit of argy-bargy with the missus!"

He winced. "See what I mean? You're the one who's changed, Stan. Talk about… bribery. It'll be corruption next. No doubt you've been taking lessons off your Chiswick pal. And that's why I'm here. A little bird has just let slip that you've asked more than just our Worshipful the Mayor and me – as the VIPs - to your launch."

I stuck my bottom lip out. So?

His voice boomed off the ceiling. He was finally letting rip. I was glad that the door was closed.

"I mean, fucking hell, Stan! What the fuck were you thinking?"

I gave him a long and hard stare. The face that Matthew does to perfection; the - I'm Superman and I'm gonna use my red-laser eyes to burn a hole through my snotty older sister - face.

"I was thinking that… that maybe some of us are not so messed up that we get all sweaty and terrified at the prospect of being seen in public with the person that we're screwing. I was thinking that maybe some of us have the balls to…"

He tipped his head up.

"Ha. So, you're admitting it now. That you're *at it* with him."

"No. I'm not saying that at all. He's our local MP. He's helped us in the past. He'll bring more PR and sales than you and the Mayor and your Medlock cronies combined could ever bring. *It's a no-brainer.* As you and your management mates would no doubt say. Duckie."

Flooded with sudden confidence and a growing sense of calm - I must have been, because I had called him 'duckie' - I noticed that Shaun was showing the opposite effect. Looking all ruffled. Fluffy duckie?

"A no-brainer?" he growled. "You've seen the exchanges that've gone on between his department and practically every single Greater Manchester authority the last couple of weeks."

"Spearheaded by a certain Shaun Elliot."

"Whatever. Have you totally lost the plot? Inviting us both? To a public event?"

"Well, as you like to say quite a lot these days, Shaun. *It's not my problem.*" I smiled sweetly, tapping my watch. Indicating that our conversation was now drawing to a close.

"How is this not your problem? You're the manager of this place. You make these decisions."

"Not quite. I'm the person whom our women's co-operative committee appointed to carry out their collective decisions. They were the ones who came up with the idea of inviting you both along. *They* seemed to feel that you lot at Medlock Council and Michael Chiswick's office could somehow rise above your high-powered handbags at fifty paces and do the honest and decent thing. That you just might be able to put the launch of a local social enterprise first… But hey-ho. What a silly bunch of bimbos they clearly are, eh?"

And then I winked at him. I actually winked at him. This surprised both of us. Because I don't normally lack self-assurance in the workplace and in life, but where Shaun had been concerned, he always seemed to possess this uncanny knack of being able to knock me off guard. Whether it was a professional dig from the early days; when he used to criticise the style in which I wrote my 'Request for Eviction' reports, or whether it was more to do with my own personal naiveté - such as the time when he laughed at me in a swanky coffee shop in Huddersfield for not knowing the difference between the type of coffee grain that you needed to purchase for a cafetière and the sort that you needed for a filter machine.

But this was the second occasion in the last few weeks where I seemed to have knocked the wind out of his sails. Time to launch the big ship on its final voyage, then. I moved towards my office door.

"You're really going to have to excuse me now. But, Shaun - if you'd rather not square up to Michael Chiswick, then you're best just telling me now. Perhaps you could… inform me… that 'something has come up'. And I'll scratch your name off the list. I don't even mind if you completely fabricate a reason. Like… you could say that Jess needs you to accompany her to an extra Mass on Saturday morning, or whatever."

I held the door open for him. He'd gotten the message. But as he made to stride past me, he stopped sharply, stooping and leaning in towards me. His mouth was dangerously close – to the naked part of my neck where he had left an invisible imprint on Tuesday night. A harsh whisper in my ear.

"Oh no. I wouldn't miss it for the world."

And then he left.

I went to look for Kirsty. She was perched on the edge of the sofa in the kitchen, nursing a cup of tea, her eyes closed. On hearing me approach, she opened them and commenced with blinking again, beginning to apologise, 'for messing things up in front of that important bloke.'

"Don't apologise, Kirsty. He's of no importance to us. And anyway, he's the one that should be apologising to you. For being so rude. How are you feeling?"

I wanted to add that Shaun was, in fact, an absolute tosspot whose capacity for compassion and emotional intelligence had gone AWOL many moons ago. But it wouldn't have been particularly professional of me. Or helpful to her. So, when she told me that her headache had gone, we both returned to my office and to the task in hand, doing our best to focus on the leaflet-juggling. But what with me being around the ever-jittery Kirsty, fielding several phone calls from the local fire station in relation to the launch and safety numbers and then Gemma confiding in me that she thought she might be pregnant - courtesy of her worthless scumbag of a fiancé - my own nerves were not what they had been when Shaun had left the building.

How quickly my confidence dissipates.

After work, I felt the rare need to talk the whole situation over with someone. Normally I'm a rather self-contained person. Perhaps spending the bulk of your working week with people whose problems seem to be so much more terrible than your own, does this to you. Or perhaps I'm just too proud to tell others when I'm really struggling with life. Adam always had a different spin on the matter, however; *'You just hate anyone ever fronting up to you and telling you that you're wrong, Rachael. And you are. A lot. Actually.'*

But I needed to confide in someone about my fears over the Shaun and Michael Show; about their celebrity appearance together in my very own workplace – about my anxieties over the huge risk of potential embarrassment on launch day. I tried to contact Kate, but she was ensconced in important educational activities - 'It's parents' evening, Rach. I've been practising my 'Aw, bless him,' smile. But I still worry that my Tourette's will kick in. Group of little bastards this year, Year Two were.'

My next port of call was even more unhelpful; Vicky wasn't answering her phone. Perhaps she had followed through with her stated threat of the other day - 'I tell you – I'm going to die of boredom. It's getting that bad that I'm even missing being felt-up by weirdos during the rush hour on the Northern line.' And obviously, talking to my parents about any form of romantic shenanigans was out with a capital O. In fact, I must have been feeling pretty desperate for any form of adult conversation, because when the inevitable hassling-me calls from the bank and credit card people started appearing after six PM – rather than bollocking them for ignoring my requests for no evening calls, I found myself saying;

"Yes, sorry about not making the payment. Got a bit of a cash flow problem at the moment. And it's not being helped by the problems I'm having to face at work this week. Have you ever had one of those days where you ...?"

But this evening, somehow, the phone calls seemed to end rather sooner than they usually did. It seemed that even the bank's call centre operators in Slough, had better things to do than listen to my tales of local authority politico-induced murkiness and projections of doom.

So, I really needed to talk to someone. I thought about contacting Adam. It might sound crazy, but if you have ever lost a person that you are indelibly close to, you might be aware that this can be a helpful therapeutic remedy at times. And that some people leave such an imprint on your heart and on your soul, that you can just carry on the conversation, regardless of time and space continuum. Or of mortality. So, there had been times – many times – after Adam's death where I had engaged in excellent two-way discussions with him.

Tonight, this didn't seem to be working however. Perhaps Adam was sulking because he wasn't keen on the idea of me being involved with upper-crust politicians. Or of me having run-ins with men who were taller and more Yorkshire than he was. Or maybe it just happened to be his turn to rub the Pearly Gates down with a tin of Brasso, or something.

I didn't want to chat to Lydia about the whole situation. Her mental agility was too sharp and her subsequent ability to quote any conversations (out loud, in public) that she had previously had with Mama were far too unpredictable at present. Plus, you're not really supposed to talk to a seven-year-old about your sex life. So, whilst she was watching her West Side Story DVD and screeching along with Natalie Wood next door, I decided to confide in Matthew instead. My youngest was splashing around in the bathtub as I perched on the lid of the toilet next to him.

"Mummy's feeling a little bit stressed about how things might go on Saturday."

Matthew squeezed a blue plastic turtle at me. It squirted water all over my trousers.

"What's Saturday?"

"Oh, you know, Matthew. You know what Saturday is."

"No, I don't. What's a Saturday?"

"Don't be silly. It's one of the days of the week. And please don't stick the turtle up the hot tap. It was bad enough when you managed to get your entire flannel up there last week."

He ignored me. I continued.

"But, yes. This Saturday is a special one for me. You've heard me talking about it. You know. Where we tell everyone about the new chocolate shop. At my work."

He was now drinking bathwater from a plastic yellow teapot.

"Matthew – if you've done a wee in the bathwater again, that's probably not the best thing to be doing."

He shrugged and asked me;

"So… is Saturday a boy or a girl? I don't like it if it's a girl."

"For God's sake, Matthew. We're not French you know! We don't have to assign a gender-label to everything!"

I sighed, watching him as he concentrated fiercely on pouring water from the plastic teapot into one of my exfoliation gloves. A little frown; an identikit of Adam. The same glower that etched itself on his father's face as he tinkered with a chunk of metal from his motorbike on the kitchen table. Just before I pow-slapped him for making such a mess.

I decided to spill the emotional beans.

"I guess, Matthew, I'm just worried about feeling embarrassed. On Saturday. And maybe… even… perhaps that I'll be acting with an element of hypocrisy. Because I guess, there's still quite a few aspects – about everything really - that I genuinely feel confused about."

Matthew jerked his shoulders again. I noted a hint of sympathy there, however.

"So, what do you think that I should do? If it all goes wrong on Saturday?"

He looked at me, narrowing his eyes.

"Haahm. Let's fink." I waited. And waited. I took the exfoliation glove off him and removed a Lego man from the pinky finger.

His brow was furrowed when he finally replied.

"Ahm finkin' you could maybe poo in your pants."

Some helpful advice there. Especially given that I was learning rather a lot about diversionary tactics from Michael these days.

CHAPTER 25

Before I knew it, it was far too early on a Saturday morning and there I was - swapping my kids for several trays of cakes and biscuits - at a certain Stalybridge terraced home.

I was about to pull away from the kerb, but then I stopped and wound down the window, calling out;

"Look. If it's too much fuss, don't worry about driving over to Medlock for the whole thing. It won't be anything very impressive. Just me. And a few stalls. And a bouncy castle."

Mum called back, "Oh no, love. We'll see you in a few hours. Wouldn't miss it for the world."

I flicked the radio on, trying to soothe the butterflies that were now looping-the-loop their way around my stomach with a bit of Radio Four. But someone had re-programmed all of the channels and the only radio presenter that I could summon up seemed to be that of Steve Wright on Radio Two. This had all the hallmarks of a Matthew-prank. The previous day, whilst I nipped into the corner shop for a loaf of bread and a tin of sardines, I had left him on his own in the car for only two minutes and on my return, I had noticed that ominous grin playing around the corners of his mouth.

Cheers for that, Matthew.

Listening to the inane banter of the UK's most one-dimensional resident was not something that I felt up for, at the best of times. And today my nerves were a-jangling enough as it was. I stabbed the 'off' switch just before Ol' Wrighty could furnish the British population with his views about whether the world was indeed a happier place when we had just four TV channels to choose from, as opposed to four thousand.

But this was ridiculous. Not Steve Wright, I mean – although he is patently a bit of a dingbat - no, I refer to me. To my attitude; to all of this. This kind of stuff was my bread and butter; my meat and pudding. I was used to giving speeches at conferences; at running workshops for terribly 'important' people - whether it be up north or for the Whitehall civil servant sorts in London. And this? Come on, Rachael. Get a bloody great big grip. In comparison to ladling out the spiel in Portcullis House, or on the terraces at the House of Commons, this was just some piddling little community event. A poxy little affair designed to help a few women who were probably incapable of 'getting' the bigger picture. And who wouldn't be grateful anyway, for all the efforts that I had gone to, to set up the whole enterprise for them.

Well, that had been the gospel according to Shaun Elliot, a few weeks back. When we had had a bit of an argument about my reasoning behind why I wouldn't change jobs and go and work for him instead.

But Shaun was talking bollocks. And I knew myself well enough these days, to realise that the jitters had rather a lot more to do with the fact that I had invested so much time and emotional energy in the initiative. And further; that the entire idea had been born from Adam's words. From the beloved bane of my life - who had prodded me to set up something; "based on your own chocolate and coffee addictions. But, you know - something that - maybe also helps your margarine-alised women out. Or whatever unflattering term you're using for your poor down n' out floozies these days."

So, in a way, today was all about remembering Adam. For me, at any rate.

But, still. If I was going to be entirely honest with myself, that unsettled feeling – the writhing nerves – was being stoked to an uncomfortable degree by the fact that Shaun and Michael would also be present in the same room together. Call me a prude if you will, but I think that it's a strange enough feeling for anyone; having to share a few square yards of space with two men that you have recently experienced carnal relations with, without all eyes of the press, public, your work colleagues and your family - also being on you.

So, no. I wasn't looking forward to the vibe. I was hoping, however, that both men would be able to find it in themselves to rise above the media-manipulating squabbles of the last few days. But Michael wasn't a straightforward bet either; having previously revealed an unpredictable streak when he had tagged along with me and Miss Simpson to the Brindleford estate and helped Vinnie out by riding his motorbike home for him. A touch of the old, reckless ex-army fella thing, perhaps.

And Shaun? Well, Shaun was Shaun. You could never tell.

And then there were my parents. Would Lydia point out – in public - to Ma and Pa, that it was *this* minister whose doorstep I had been prancing about on in my 'new knicker-things'?

No wonder I was feeling like Basket Case of the Year.

Just before leaving the house that morning, I had fired off a text to Michael. A tiny part of me hoped that he might have had to cancel his appearance. Goat running amok in the lobby of the Commons sort of disaster. Or Russian nuclear warheads discovered underneath the Trafford Centre. Or something.

> ME: *U still up for 2day?*
> MICHAEL: *Just onto M6. Wdn't miss it 4 the world.*

What *was* it with everyone not wanting to miss our launch for the bloody, sodding world?

As soon as I arrived, Bev was in my face. She was insisting that she borrow my keys to the Centre.

"'Cause thievin' scrotes always try it on at events like this. Don't be forgettin' that we've got laptops and shite in here," she told me. Over the last few years I had discovered that it was wise to pay heed to Bev, whenever she adopted that oh-so unusual serious tone in her voice. "It's called 'distraction burglary', Rachael. Only last week, our Tony and Leonie – who live just round the corner from here - had their entire kitchen taken out whilst they were watchin' 'Homes Under The Hammer.' I mean it. All of the units – gone - in half an hour! So, I'm going to do a once-round and check that every single door what we don't use today is locked up properly."

I handed over the keys and did my best not to smile at the irony of what had happened to Tony and Leonie. In five minutes, she was back again, rollocking me for several unlocked internal doors.

"You're slackin', Rach. You should be givin' Jules - that so-called cleaner of ours - a bloody rocket up the arse for not doin' this every night of the week."

I nodded, but disregarded her advice. Because Jules scared the crap out of me.

"Fine – but make sure you keep the fire exit routes unlocked, won't you? The fire officers bored me shitless about all of that sort of thing, the other day."

Dee trundled over to us, reeking of a potent concoction. It seemed that she had not-so-expertly disguised the cigarette smoke with a recent blast of Beyonce's Midnight Heat. She heard me asking Bev to liaise with the police, who had just arrived, to give the place a once-over because of Michael's presence.

"Hang on. Police? You're kiddin'! A load of pigs crawlin' about all over the place? I've only just had 'em round again – last bleedin' night! They reckon our Harrison were involved in the Aldi turnover…"

"Harrison now!" screeched Bev. "He's only thirteen! Are you goin' for a family record or summat? That'll be four of 'em banged up in the last two years if you…"

"Bev," I interrupted. "Just make sure you tell *either* the local police *or* the Special Protection officers who are part of Michael Chiswick's team – that apart from the two main fire exits in the hall, all of the internal doors have been locked."

Bev raised a hand to me;

"Awright, Miss Keks," and wandered off to find a bizzy. She called back over her shoulder; "Dee – best make sure that face painter's got non-allergic face paints. Last time she was here - your Drew got a bad reaction, didn't he? His face totally blew up. His nose ended up lookin' like a septic bell-end."

Dee narrowed her eyes but followed the advice and went off to steam-roller Flossie and her Face Paints. A nudge against my shoulder announced the presence of Gill, dressed in her weekend best. Combats, DMs from the 1980's and various shades of khaki.

"Rachael, I've just reminded Sandra and Cerys on reception that they're not to let any press or media into the building until after the event formally ends. About one o'clock-ish, yeah?"

"Nice one. Last thing we need is a bunch of tosspot journalists trucking up and playing to the crowds because of the spat between the council and the government."

"Yup. And I've gone over the changes with the two of them. Men welcome. New era, eh?"

Keeping our building safe and secure was paramount. We were going to continue to keep half of Sisters' Space 'safe' for women, with no allowed access to men. But the co-operative had voted that male customers would be welcome in the cafe and shop. Yet this decision had come with various logistical problems. The buzz-in intercom and video camera system at the entrance to the building were all well and good, but this wasn't going to be the best approach to running the new business and allowing the public in on a daily basis. What we really needed was a separate entrance and shop frontage, but this would require quite a bit more money than the social enterprise loan would give us. So, for the time being – and certainly for today - passing through the reception area to access the shop and café was the only way into the building for our new customers.

Our volunteer reception staff were not keen on the changes. They didn't want to take responsibility for 'buzzing in' customers. Sandra had tactfully put it like this;

"We can hardly say to every bloke who comes to the front door for the next few months; 'So do you want to buy some chocolate truffles? Or have a large latte? Or are you just here to smash your wife's face in?"

And then the other receptionist, Cerys - who had turned out to be far less PC than she had come across at her interview - told me;

"And I'm not being funny, but if we're having to scrutinise the blokes who want to come in here to use the café - to check that they're not dodgy - then it's going to be tricky differentiating. Some of the women here look more male and scarier than your average bloke! I mean, I know that Gill is your deputy and everything… but her current girlfriend or whatever you should call him-her looks like she's just walked out of HMP Forest Bank!"

To get round this dilemma, Martyn Pointer had generously arranged for New Banks to install some panic alarm buttons at the reception and in discreet locations throughout the building. We had also adopted a new policy to ensure that no woman should be left alone, when working in the café or in the adjacent shop during opening hours. And of course, we had the Violent Partner Parade photographs on hand at reception.

"But that still won't help us if they're wearing hoodies," Sandra had moaned.

"Well, we'll tell them to take off their hoodies," Cerys added firmly. "That'll send them off with their tails between their legs. People who wear hoodies are usually scumbags with no fashion sense. And they're always up to no good, those sorts."

"Cheers for that," I had said. (I had been wearing my own favourite turquoise hoodie, at the time.)

I moved down the main hall where most of the stalls and activities were set out and headed towards 'Marmaduke Magician'. We chatted about the best approach for his conjuring tricks that morning. Marmaduke turned out to think himself a bit of a wit - 'Don't worry, Missy. I've done my research about this place. No sudden noises. No pretending to strangle people with silk scarves. And I bet you wouldn't want me to bring out the other side of my business today. I do a Punch and Judy show as well!'

Ha Bloody Ha.

I completed my quick tour of the ten stalls. The notorious face-painter, the fake tattoos, the tombola, a second-hand stall, the Citizens Advice Bureau and an adult education stall. The usual suspects. I suppose we could have been a bit more creative, but I didn't want to detract attention from the Chocolate Factory and the café itself - the flagship baby of Sisters' Space where the 'posh chocolate' in its gleaming gift packs was ready and waiting along with the prerequisite bacon and sausage butties. And then of course, there was the ugly wanabee-Disney pink and yellow bouncy castle – now fully inflated – which was lurking in the corner of the hall. Some of the women who had turned up early to help, had already deposited their children on it. Cue a handful of somersaulting children, near-fatal crashes and a 'Shit – Mum, quick! Our Melinda's having a nosebleed all over her socks!'

Shaun arrived just as Gill and I were running through a final check in the cafe. He was looking sharp. New suit, no doubt. New haircut; a number one. There were few men that could carry off such a short style and look neither like a Neo-Nazi or a Mr Potato Head. But Shaun could manage it. The git.

The Mayor of Medlock sent his apologies. Apparently, he had experienced an angina attack. Although if the rumour mill was anything to go by, we all knew that it was his usual Saturday morning hangover. Instead, Shaun was accompanied by Kath Casey. She shook my hand à la wet lettuce and tried a bit of humour; 'Hopefully we won't have to try and extract any old ladies from cupboards today!' but the forced crinkling of her eyes and the constant glances at her watch said it all. Probably due a round of golf by midday. I was relieved to have Gill by my side when pitched up against these two, so I forgave her for whispering rather too loudly in my ear - "Shaun Elliot's stalking me – nicking my bloody haircut now!" But she was a good egg. She immediately resorted to her best professional behaviour, attempting to occupy Kath Casey in a bland conversation about the colourful bunting which the women had made. "It's very gay, isn't it?" I overheard her telling the council leader, with an impassive expression fixed to her face.

Shaun shook my hand and held it for longer than was necessary.

"Where's Pointless?" he said, referring to Martyn Pointer.

"I just got a message from his wife," I replied extracting my hand from his. "He's got the shingles. Nasty stuff."

Shaun grinned. "And it's Saturday. He must be gutted. Missing his shift - door-stepping people with his Watchtower magazines. But hey, fair do's, Stan. Credit where it's due. The place looks great. Good job."

The hall was filling up now, kids running around after the magician and fighting to get to the front of the ever-lengthening face-painting and tattoo queues. I caught a quick glimpse of Dawn's eldest – Mason – who had arrived on a striped scooter – all sparks and flashing lights - probably even turbocharged. He whizzed towards us at an incredible speed, clipping the end of Councillor Casey's shoe and causing her to grab her stilettoed foot. She winced with over-exaggerated pain.

"Sorry," I apologised on Mason's behalf. "They get a bit excited with this kind of thing, some of the kids." Although I doubted whether Dawn would have apologised for Mason. In fact, she probably would have told Councillor Casey that if she wore such stupid shoes at such a busy event then what the hell did she expect?

Shaun looked towards the shrieking kids on the bouncy castle and commented;

"Hmmm. Got a bit of a feel of an ADHD Childhood Convention, hasn't it?" Then he stuck his hands into his pockets and gestured at the stalls with his head, saying;

"Fake tattoos? I mean… *fake?* Was that your idea, Rachael? That's a bloody joke. Half of these kids probably have the real McCoy already. And maybe you should have been giving out free samples of Ritalin…?"

I gave him a look, but he ignored me, carrying on with;

"And I admire your vision for an Adult Education stall. But that's pushing it a bit when you look at the demographics of this lot." He turned to Councillor Casey. "You see? Rachael Russell's always been into her wishful thinking." Casey crinkled the corners of her lips and simpered;

"Oh, Shaun! You're always stirring the pot, aren't you?"

I turned away and spotted my dad. He had just entered the building and very nearly tripped up over Matthew, who had done his usual trick of 'I'll stop suddenly in front of a large adult - just because I can.' Councillor Casey's attention had been grabbed by someone who claimed to know her from 'years back in the Soroptimist Society' and so Shaun seized the opportunity, taking me by the elbow and gesturing towards the corridor. He wanted a word.

"Only if its quick,' I said. 'I've got better things to do than listen to you slagging off our event or brown-nosing the Leader of the Council."

CHAPTER 26

We headed down the corridor, me with my arms folded. All huffy, like.

"Just wanted to tell you about your Miss Simpson," he said.

"Right. So why couldn't you tell me in the hall?"

"Because. Well, Kath Casey..." Shaun shrugged, looking slightly disconcerted. But then continued;

"I visited her the other day. Your Miss Simpson."

"Look, will you stop referring to her as '*my* Miss Simpson'. She's not some personal geriatric project of mine that I've suddenly decided to take on."

"Well, whatever. I visited her at the hostel. On Brindleford. I've managed to get her a really good social services package; far better than the kind of thing that New Banks were aiming for. Gotten her Meals on Wheels or Neighbourhood Nutrition or whatever we're supposed to be calling it these days. Plus, a load more extra benefits that... Well. She'd never have had access to without me intervening for her."

"Why? Why wouldn't she have got them?"

"Turns out that she's got a bob or two tucked away in various savings accounts. Even though she lives like Stag of the Dump. And I've always believed even if you do have a few grand above the cut-off point for benefits. Well. It's nobody's business. You should be entitled to everything that scroungers who've never saved a penny in their life manage to get out of the system."

"Right."

"Yeah. So, I made a few phone-calls. Pulled a few strings. Got her the kind of support package that even Pointless couldn't get."

"Right."

"The works. Your Aston Martin DBS in personal care, too."

Only Shaun could use some poncey car as a metaphor for having your arse wiped by an overworked and underpaid day care nurse. But I didn't comment on this. He went on to tell me that he'd managed to persuade her to 'give it a go' and that it was better than moving her into a home which the Vim-sprinkled social worker had been angling for.

"Okay."

"Right." I gave my watch a purposeful glance. "So why are you telling me this?"

Shaun looked taken aback.

"Because – well. I mean, sure, she's got a bit of dementia and that but... she doesn't want to go in a home."

"No. She doesn't."

"And... I know that you're being sarky about her not being some 'project' of yours, but I... I thought you cared about her. You know – you helped her out on your day off and all of that."

"I do. Of course I care about what happens to her. I care about what happens to anyone."

"So...?"

"So what?" I glanced behind him. The hall was bristling with people by now. "I mean, do you want me to give you a medal 'cause you actually *did* something? Something that should be part and parcel of your job description anyway?"

"Jesus, Stan - visiting batty old ladies and getting paperwork filled in for them isn't exactly part and parcel of my job these days!"

"Yeah. Because you've got way more important things to do. Like... sorting out backhanders with major supermarket chains so that they can build crappy shops over what used to be our libraries. That's way more up your street, isn't it? In your so-called Communities and Leisure department..."

He bristled. "Christ. I thought you might be pleased. That you might give a shit."

I was tempted to provoke him further but something stopped me. His words had definitely had an effect on me, even though I was trying to disguise it. Yes, Shaun Elliot had actually taken the time out to do something personal. For someone else. For a human being who also happened to be old, confused and who also had an unattractive and pongy personal incontinence problem.

So, I backed down.

"No. No. I do – give a shit. Sorry. It's just that I'm... a bit stressed. Yeah – that's good news. That's great." In response, he warded me off with the sneer of a smile.

"Yeah, well. This isn't me trying to impress Rachael Russell, Saint of All Things Womanly and Destitute, you know. I just thought that I had to stick up for her. The social worker got Kath Casey on her side and they were banking on shoving her into residential. Kath's exact words were 'Well, Shaun, I've never held any truck with listening to the opinions of elderly people who have mental health issues. When you get to that sort of stage in life, you've effectively resigned your right to express thoughts on what you think is best for you."

"She said that? Bloody hellfire. It's a shame Miss Simpson is so frail these days. A few years ago, I bet she would have eaten the likes of Kath Casey for breakfast."

"Yeah," Shaun gave a tiny smile. "And actually," he held my gaze, "I think that Miss Simpson's got a bit of a soft spot for me." I grinned and added; "That'll be the dementia."

"Anyway," he said. "I'm glad that we're still on okay terms, Stan. I know that you would never have done that stuff... mentioning things. To Jess. That's not your style."

His eyes flicked to the left – down the corridor, checking that no-one was looking in our direction and then his hand moved up, towards me. Reaching to touch my hair. All of my previous bravado seemed to dissipate. It was a staccato moment. I wavered; unsure how to react.

And then a familiar voice came floating down the corridor.

"Hey hey hey! Found you at last!"

I was startled to see a very familiar form. But one that was completely out of place at Sisters' Space. It was our Vicky; heading towards us at an impressive pace on her crutches. I took a step away from Shaun and in just a few seconds more, she had reached us. She pecked me on the cheek. I asked her why she wasn't in London.

"Changed my mind at the eleventh hour. Managed to get a lift up north with some bloke. In this incredible Mercedes Benz. I called Mum and Dad when we were just past Birmingham and sprang it on them. So, it looks like I'm going to be staying in Stalybridge for the week. Dad was all 'Patricia! The Queen of Bloody Sheba is on the phone and has just announced her arrival!'"

Her eyes danced. But then turned to chips of ice as she looked over at Shaun, acknowledging his presence at last.

"Hello, Shaun."

"Vicky. Long-time no see. Been up to your usual tricks? Skiing with millionaires?"

Vicky had only met Shaun the once, many moons ago when I had been under the mistaken impression that he and I would one day have a normal, out-in-the-open relationship. I had introduced him to her - at some tea rooms or another in Bramhall. They hadn't taken to each other. Vicky sniffed and checked her nails. As lickety-split as ever.

"Not quite so glamorous, I'm afraid," she commented. "Falling down the stairs whilst minding Lydia. I'm not used to kiddy-based chaos. And you're not either, are you?" She tipped her chin at him, her handsome face hardening; "But I believe that your family status quo has changed recently. I heard you got married. How *is* your *wife?*"

A tremor of embarrassment skittered across my brow, but Shaun's reply was postponed indefinitely, because it turned out that Lydia had spotted Vicky's departure from the main hall. She came hurtling up the corridor after her auntie and threw herself against my legs, gabbling breathlessly;

"Mummy! Matthew is being really naughty! He stole a hot dog off a little girl and then wiped ketchup all over his coat. So Grandad told him off and Matthew tried to bite him! Seriously!"

She smirked with glee. Enjoying grassing her sibling up. And then she noticed who we were standing with.

"Oh. Hiya. I remember you. You're Shaun. What're you doing here?"

Shaun smiled and reached to pat her on the head. Lydia hadn't seen him since those few weeks after Adam's death. But she could clearly remember him. Popping around. Every now and then.

"Hi, Lydia. Jesus Christ, but you've grown! What a big girl you are now!"

Lydia pursed her lips. She disliked her hair being touched. And being patronised.

"Yes, well. You shouldn't use the Lord's name in vain. And yes - I might have grown up a little bit. Not that I want to. 'Cause adults are well-boring. But I bet that you haven't. Are you still an Emoshunnal Tree Tard?"

There was a stunned silence. Lydia took the opportunity to flounce off, back down the corridor.

"I have no idea where she got that from," I apologised to Shaun. He was still looking rather taken aback. I continued with;

"I mean it's quite an… *adult* expression, isn't it? She's probably been watching Hollyoaks without my permission or —"

Vicky started sniggering and muttered;

"And on that note, I'm off for a bacon butty. Too many pigs in one building. Some of them need to be made useful. And I'm not referring to the police force, by the way."

She made her way back to the hall, hopping after Lydia. I followed her, with Shaun behind me. He seemed to be chunnering something along the lines of;

"Family of shrews."

Back in the hall, Jade stalked her way over to me. She had trowelled on even more black and purple make-up than usual for the big day. She grabbed my arm and hissed;

"Oi – Rachael. Michael thingymajig has just arrived and he's askin' for you. I know that Shirley reckons he's handsome and ever-such-a-gent, but I still reckon that he's gay. You should see the twatty tank-top thing what he's wearing."

Michael was indeed sporting a dark green tank top. But I thought that it looked rather fetching. A nice contrast to Shaun's sharp-as-a-dart, bespoke Savile Row number. He was wearing it over a white shirt, with casual trousers. I wondered if he and Shaun had deliberately co-ordinated their outfits the day before. Nah. Probably not.

Trevor was standing directly behind Michael. I glanced around, attempting to look for the additional bodyguard that Michael said he had been forced to 'put up with' for today. It turned out that because this was an official ministerial appearance, the risk had been assessed as being greater than usual. Perhaps

Minder Number Two was hanging out with the special police officers who Michael had told me would be doing some low-key scouting for bombs that morning. Graham the Griper from the constituency office was also tailing the minister. He and I had previously met back in August, when Michael had first visited the Women's Centre. In his late fifties, his hair a tangle of steely-grey curls, Graham was heavily overweight and today he was sweating profusely. At least with all the noise in the background, I couldn't hear his usual moaning minnie performance. But to give him his dues, he worked hard at his job – which wasn't paid, after all. He nudged Michael that I had arrived. The minister's eyes met mine. He smiled widely, dimples a-dancing.

"Minister. Good to see you again," I said, sticking out my hand. "Thanks so much for staying in touch with us."

There was an impish glint in his eye;

"Rachael. Great to see you in the flesh again." And then he surprised me by keeping hold of my hand and planting a quick kiss on my cheek; murmuring in my ear; "Less of the clothes and more of the flesh next time…"

I tried not to smirk as I nodded over to our little makeshift stage and outlined the order of the day; explaining that there would be time for press interviews, once the event had ended.

"Perfectly sensible. Sounds good to me," said Michael.

A sudden 'Woah!' came from the side of the hall. I looked over to see that Matthew had fallen head first into the Lucky Dip barrel. Dad was too busy trying to win a bottle of whisky on the tombola to notice. Lydia and Grandma were trying to extract the kid. Good. At least it kept Liddy from noticing the arrival of Michael and Trevor.

Shaun and Councillor Casey emerged from the crowd, making their way towards us. Given the expression on her face, I half expected Casey to proffer a 'You May Kiss My Ring' gesture, rather than a handshake.

"Minister, we're most impressed that you could find time to come along to a such a small local event like this. Although I do have to say that it's a shame that your department hasn't made an effort so far to respond to the letter that the council sent to you. Several days ago now; in relation to our revenue funding shortfall."

I glanced at Michael. His brows were knitted - annoyed. Shaun towered over the Councillor and cocked his head to one side. A frosty atmosphere suspended itself above the three individuals. Casey, as political leader of the council commenced with most of the talking, but it was all snipes and jibes at the government. Still, I tried to remind myself that Michael knew that. He got the deal; it was just another day at work for him. When Councillor Casey finally decided to pause for breath, I suggested to the three of them that it was time for us to climb onto the makeshift stage. We stepped up to the platform together, tailed by Trevor.

"I'm afraid we don't have a microphone," I told them. "I tried to borrow one from your Partnerships Directorate. Who referred me to the Community Outreach Department. They took two weeks to get back to me and then put me onto the Council's Procurement and Entertainments Team. Who didn't get back to me until yesterday. And apparently, the only mic available was broken."

"Central government cutbacks again," said Shaun through wolfish teeth.

Michael pretended not to hear and rubbed his hands together.

"Not to worry. I'm used to shouting from the hustings. Enough of this reliance on technology. It'll be like the old days. And blimey – look at this lot now. You've got a great turnout today, Rachael. Good show!"

I caught Shaun rolling his eyes and mouthing 'good show' to himself. Then he lobbed a glance at me, but I refused to meet his gaze.

Michael was right – the hall was now packed with at least two hundred people. I noticed that Matthew had now been released from the barrel and was snorting and spitting sawdust at as many people as he could. There was a queue of at least another eighty folk outside, snaking around the building and waiting to be buzzed in. A couple of days before, I had met with a representative of the 'crowd control' section of the local police force so that we could plan the safest approach for the event. We had agreed that it would be dangerous to try and get a large group of people through the hall, down the corridor and into the much smaller space that housed the café and shop itself. So instead, we had opted for a 'gesture of opening' in the main hall.

I beckoned to Shirley and Andrea who were standing below us at the foot of the steps. One slow, shuffling step after another, they climbed up and onto the stage, laden with a large tray which housed a bulky object covered with a green velvet cloth. I noticed that Shirley's hands were trembling. This part of the day was certainly a big deal to her; the two of them had been working on some kind of a 'creation' for over a fortnight - their own idea and their own design apparently. I, however, had had been instructed to;

"Stay away from it – and from us, whilst we're working on it. It's a surprise for you, Rachael, as much as for anyone else."

And it damned well was. It turned out to be the most amazing replica of the women's centre, constructed entirely in different types and shades of chocolate. Our building – Medlock town centre's former primary school – had been recreated in exact miniature format. Every brick, every window, every tiny detail – even the redundant netball posts outside my office. Standing outside the building was a dinky chocolate family. A man. A smaller woman with a pony tail. Next to her had been sculptured a diminutive girl and an even tinier boy. It was incredible. And I was flooded with emotion. Because I had once told Shirley that the idea of the café and the chocolatiers had been suggested to me by Adam, just a few months before he was killed. Which was probably why she had wanted their creation to be an extra special surprise for me. She had deliberately put a family of four outside of the chocolate Sisters' Space. She could be a real soft bugger like that.

So, I dug my nails into the palm of my hand and I tried not to think of Adam. Not the time or the place to start getting all sentimental.

Interestingly, the arrival of the chocolate creation took the edge off the frosty atmosphere. Funny how chocolate can always bring people together, drooling with enthusiasm at the luscious brown stuff.

Michael told Andrea and Shirley; "Good God! You two are a pair of seriously talented women!"

As per usual, Andrea was too embarrassed to speak but Shirley provided an admirable response.

"Well. To be fair, it wasn't just us. We didn't grow the cocoa beans now, did we? The women farmers that we're linked with in Ghana did that bit of the job. So we shouldn't really forget their role in all of this."

Michael murmured his agreement and I was genuinely impressed with her take on things. But Shaun wasn't. He sighed with impatience and deliberately muttered, so that only I could hear him;

"*So* on message…"

I gave him a look of contempt. He threw back at me a 'What's the big deal?' grimace. I decided not to rise to the bait. Fair trade, concern for people on the other side of the world who he would never meet himself, clearly didn't matter to Shaun. No doubt because they didn't happen to pay Council Tax to Medlock. Perhaps I should just pity him for having developed this attitude. As opposed to wanting to knee him in the bollocks.

CHAPTER 27

It was time to get cracking. I clapped my hands together as loudly as I could, trying to attract the attention of a throng of noisy adults and shrieking children. No such luck. This really was where a microphone would have done the trick. I tried again, but the crowd continued to ignore the small, agitated looking lady hopping about on a crap stage. But just as I was about to turn to Shaun and ask him for a bit of help with the yelling, I felt a firm nudge against my shoulder. Someone pushed a bottle of whisky into my hands. It was my dad. He gave me a nod, curved his thumb and forefinger into a circle and stuck them into his mouth, producing one his finest Stalybridge Celtic 'football whistles.' I should have tried harder to master this as a kid but I had never even been able to do it, prompting my mother to once comment 'She whistles nearly as badly as she sings, doesn't she, Terry?'

But it did the trick. The crowd grew quiet and looked over to the stage. My dad winked at me.

He took the bottle back off me and hopped down and back into the crowd.

"Thanks. Thanks everyone for coming today. I'm afraid that I'm going to have to yell a bit though - as we don't have the funding for a microphone system."

"Here we go…" I heard Shaun mutter through clenched teeth.

I gave the audience a quick outline of the history of Sisters' Space and of our new enterprise; why Charlene's Chocolate Factory and Café honoured the name of Charlene Fullham - a young woman from Manchester who had been beaten to death by her partner – a man who had also torched their home, inadvertently killing their baby as well. It was hardly cheery stuff – but I wasn't going to lose the opportunity to get such an important message across. Then Shaun stepped forward and said a few words - mostly about how his local authority had helped to keep the centre going over the last few years. It was a shorter speech than I had anticipated, but I figured that from his perspective, the less said the better – given the fact that the council had recently taken the decision to pull the funding plug on us anyway.

And then it was Michael, who was charm-personified in his praise for the women's centre, but of course, he had to weave in the inevitable gloating about his own government's achievements. As Shirley and Andrea held the mini-chocolate Sisters' Space aloft, Michael officially declared the new enterprise open and the applause from the audience caused me to beam a big, goofy grin. A mixed bag of relief and sheer joy. And then I caught Shaun staring at me. I realised what I had been doing; twirling my cocoa bean pendant between my fingers. Shaun was looking intently at it. He knew that I didn't tend to wear much jewellery. So, I gently let the chain drop back into place and, instead, reached down to wriggle my wedding rings around. And around. Get the message, matey? His eyes moved back towards the crowd.

We climbed back off the stage and Shaun wandered off, whilst Michael posed with Casey for the photographs – taken courtesy of Jaz, Gill's current beau – a professional photographer who had offered her services for free today. People continued with their buying, their selling and their munching of hot dogs and we moved towards the cafe and chocolatiers, but our progress was hampered. A rodent-faced woman, who had ram-rodded herself into a tightly-tailored, hot pink business suit, was barring our way. She was in her late twenties and was quite attractive - in a gerbil-that-slaps-too-much-make-up-on, sort of way. Wielding a microphone, she was accompanied by a man clutching a TV camera to his shoulder. His equipment was emblazoned with a familiar logo - its trail of silver stars.

Hells Bloody Bells. How did they get in here?

"Hello, hello," Michael murmured. "Star News, so I see."

"Oh, God," I replied. "I can't believe the receptionists let them in! I'll bloody…"

"Well. Not to worry," he sighed. "I'll see them off," and then he turned away from me and towards the reporter.

"Hello. Not like *your* lot to venture so far up north. Have you run out of minor celebrities in London to dig the dirt on?"

The woman was all-hair, all-teeth and all-bones. And she must have been taking lessons from Councillor Casey because she winced a frighteningly similar fake smile at Michael;

"Erin Mayo from Star News, Minister."

"Ah, yes. And that means that you'll be from News of the Nation too, won't you, Erin? Aren't you the journalist who also moonlights as Simone Shaw's assistant when it comes to sniffing out…" Here he coughed politely and mimicked a deep American accent, uttering the newspaper's strapline; "'the stories that the public prioritise — '"

But Erin just jerked her head at the cameraman, signalling for him to commence with filming. And then she was off;

"Minister, you're here to open a new shop run by abused women. But it seems astonishing that in your speech, you made no mention of the fact that due to the overall fiscal mismanagement of *your government* – everything in this building here was all set to be closed down - only a few weeks ago! Surely your appearance here today marks the height of hypocrisy?"

Michael was caught off-guard. His eyes flicked over to mine. I turned to look at Shaun, who had reappeared at the side of Kath Casey. He was giving off his best I'm-as-bored-as-shite vibes as he attempted to ignore the intervention of the journalist. Instead, he was gazing across the heads of the crowd, towards some noisy situation that was developing at the back of the hall. Probably Matthew attacking the face painter because she wouldn't do a Spiderman logo on his bum or something. I seized the moment, stepping forward and in front of the camera;

"Mr Chiswick's office had no knowledge of the previous plans to cut funding from the centre. But as you can see from all the people here today – Sisters' Space is going from strength to strength. There's no story here for you. Other than a positive one."

Erin's eyes glazed over. Not interested in you, lady. She told her cameraman;

"We'll edit that out later," and then she dodged around me and thrust her microphone out again at Michael, continuing with;

"But Minister, this really is deceitful of you. Basking in the glory of today… when in reality, all of the poor women who use this centre – not to mention the staff as well – would have been out on their ears a few weeks ago, if it were up to your government…"

Clearly, News Of The Nation were still fishing for a big, bad news story on Michael Chiswick. I saw Councillor Casey shake her head and say something to Shaun. He flashed her a smile in return. Trevor moved forward now, planning to intervene as he put a meaty hand out towards Erin Mayo - warning her off. But I surprised myself, by moving in front of Michael again.

"Excuse me, but we didn't invite *your* media agency to today's event. And that's because we find the images of women that you use to sell your so-called 'news' – to be totally degrading. How you – as a female – can work for such a sordid and sexist so-called 'news' corporation is beyond me…"

She gave me a look of profound disgust and shot back;

"I'm not here to talk about what —"

"And," I continued. "Your determination to corner the minister here, is completely pointless. For your information – it's *central* government who are stumping up the cash for the social enterprise loan that Sisters' Space is now going to benefit from. So perhaps you should have done your research a little bit better before you…"

Michael interrupted me with a cursive snap;

"Yes, thank you for your help, Rachael, but I'm more than happy to speak for myself and for the government."

Colour crept into my cheeks and I caught the small shake of Shaun's head. A faint smile playing around the corner of his lips.

Bastard. This was just one big joke to him.

Michael's arms were folded and he was all ready to go head to head with Erin

Mayo and the camera, but before he could say anything more, there was a scuffle, a squeal and a;

"Oi! Watch it! You little git!"

And then a yelp from Erin Mayo. Sisters' Space's version of the cavalry had arrived as various people were rammed by a child's scooter. West and Mason were on the scene. Mason had deliberately elbowed Erin in the ribs (to be fair, it was hard to miss them) and West had stepped in front of the camera. Somehow Mason had managed to grab hold of the microphone, yanking it away from the journalist's spindly arm and yelling into it;

"Hey, coool! It's Star News! Are we LIVE? Are we? Are we friggin' LIVE then? Hey West – get your dick out and show it to the nation! Haha!"

West seemed to be as hyper as his brother – and was all set to take his older sibling's suggestion literally. He was already fumbling with his flies - desperate to oblige - when Dawn arrived, thin-lipped and pushing through the crowd, with Poppy-Rose thrown over one shoulder. She cracked West about the head with an open hand and then tried to do the same with Mason, who managed to duck in time.

"Little pair of shits!" she yelled. "After all the help, what Rachael's given us! An' here you are! Tryin' to ruin her TV appearance! Ungrateful little wankers!" She had another pop at Mason, who tried to shield himself from his mother's blows, as the rest of the crowd - eager for a chance to appear in front of the camera themselves - began to swell and to push towards us.

Shaun stepped up and tried to wrestle the microphone from Mason as the noise of the crowd ratcheted itself up another decibel; screeching and shouting from behind the cameraman. And then a deafening explosion blew the squirming circle of children, politicians, mothers and journalists apart.

The sound of gunfire ricocheted through the hall and we all hit the floor.

CHAPTER 28

A split second of silence.

And then a wave of screams; a stampede of people heading towards the back of the hall.

I lifted my head up but looked down again, fast - as I saw the flash of a gun - a man heading towards us. So, I stayed squirrelled on the floor, my nose squashed against the hall parquet. Dust in my nostrils and the tangy lemon scent of floor cleaner.

Another three blasts of gunshots. A man's voice shouting;

"No, you - get out! Get out! Get out! You! Get up off the floor - you, fuckhead, and get out! You too! You too! Go! Fucking GO!"

The scrambling and squeaking of shoes, of trainers against the floor. I lifted my head again; several pairs of feet were racing for the opening screen doors - the exit - at the back of the hall.

Get up and run too.

I twitched, about to stand up.

"No! No – you! Get down – bitch!"

A broad Mancunian accent.

"Stay down! Stay fucking down, you lot!"

And then came a quieter;

"Right. Yeah... Stay fuckin' still, all of you. Or you'll get it too."

Michael was on the floor next to me, wrapping one arm over my shoulders. The crook of his elbow was protecting my head, pinning it to the floor, even though I was trying to raise it - to look. To see. But he wouldn't let me. High-pitched howling drifted across the hall, from the left-hand side of us. Children. *I needed to see.*

"Just stay still. Don't move," Michael hissed into my ear. And then;

"It's okay, Rachael. The kids – your kids - they're not here. Just keep your head down." I felt him move, heard him call out;

"Alright. Alright. We're all down. Hold off… hold it off.'

Followed by the low moan of an adult, in pain. Then Michael again;

"Come on. It's okay. Just let us sit up – yes? No-one's going to do anything sudden. Can we all just… sit up slowly?"

A man's voice screamed back at him;

214

"No! No fucking way! You *all* stay on the fucking floor until I say! Get down! All of you! Stay down!"

A child sobbing.

Then Michael;

"Okay, fine. We'll stay down. Let's take it slowly."

There was no response to Michael's words this time. Just the sound of someone in pain, an eerie high-pitched whine. And there was a baby crying too. Escalating to full blown screaming.

I thought of the lime jelly that I had made last night. I had promised Matthew that he could have his favourite pudding for his tea today.

I thought of the fact that I hadn't paid the milkman. Again.

I thought of my bathroom cupboard. That we were probably down to our last toilet roll at home.

I thought of a cliff edge. Of Cape Point. A screech of tyres on that South African road. Hot tarmac and...

A motorbike.

A bike. Always a bike.

And then everything fell into place.

Vinnie Murray was playing with his accent, sucking on the;

"So ..."

That nasal, exaggerated twang. Vinnie sounded like a parody of all things Mancunian. A comedic attempt at cockiness. As though he had watched the Gallagher Brothers' Elocution Lesson on DVD once too often.

And there was the pad of soft-soled shoes, as he meandered about the bottom end of the hall. And then there was a grunt, a dull thud and his voice came from higher above us. He must have jumped onto the makeshift stage.

"So... Yeah. Who've we got 'ere then?"

No answer.

"Ha. Look at you lot. A right band of Merry Men, eh? And Merry Maids. Not as chipper as you all were a few minutes ago, though - eh?"

No one replied.

From outside came the sudden and shrill crescendo of police sirens. First one vehicle and then another. They were loud. But not loud enough to drown out Vinnie's words. He just ratcheted his voice up a notch or two.

"Well. Took that lot longer than I thought. Fuckin' slackers. But hey. Yeah – so... 'who's who' here? As-they-say."

No answer. He carried on;

"At number one we have... what's-er-name? Fat cunt. Or whoever she is, from the council. Hey. Looks like she caught a bullet or two there. Whoops. Sorry Council Laydee an' all of that...'

215

I jerked my head, trying to see what kind of a state Kath Casey was in, but Michael wouldn't let me.

"… and hey! Would you look at this? Fuckin' brilliant chocolate statue-fing what someone's made. Fuckin' amazing, that! Let's 'ave a bit…" He tailed off.

"Mmmf. Wow! That's good stuff, that is. Proper sticks to the roof of your mouth and that. I'll save some for the kids. Hey. Vinnie's high on the *sugar now* as well as… the old… So. What now? Oh yeah. Next, it's you lot, innit? My lot. My three. Who *no one's* gonna have."

A vicious edge to his voice.

"…Who *no one's* gonna take from me. Yeah-that's-right. Meaning - *you!* Their fuckin' slag of a so-called Mother! Our Dawny-girl. Dawn Hibbert - also present and correct in the old school hall. Tick!"

There was a stifled giggle at the back of his throat. Of course, I'd seen Vinnie all loop the loop before. And Dawn had said that as well as the slow motion enjoyed from heroin, Vinnie was also partial to cranking up his act big-time with a bit of bad crack. Add a gun to the latter and I couldn't deny that Vinnie was turning out to be one scary mo'fo.

"And who's…? Ah yeah. Here's that lanky bastard who's always in the newspapers banging on about car parks or whatever. Nice haircut, mate. And…"

The squeak of rubber on the hall floor as he jumped back off the stage.

"Let's bring this chocolate thing down here for my kids. Hee-yar… Not gotta share it with no other kiddies neither. All to yourselves. Hey… I'm Vinnie The Great Provider, me, I am."

He moved towards the bouncy castle. "But… ah shit. The castle's going down. Never mind lads. We'll eat the choc-o-lat and then head for Blackpool Pleasure Beach or summat. Better than this shit-hole they call Manchester. Always wanted to live over that way, anyways."

There was a pause and then came the over-exaggerated sound of Vinnie tutting.

"Uh-oh. Who's next? We've got some slapper from the telly. Some journalist for Star News. Fuckin' *hate* journalists, me, I do! But, ha. Maybe she'll do a feature on me next, eh? *What drove this man to kill?* Ha. Ha ha."

More chuckling to himself. But followed by a return to the aggressive edge - as though his teeth were clenched.

"Who drove me? Who drove me-to-fucking-kill? Well - she did. Dawn. Fuckin' slag of the century over there. An' who *taught* me to kill? Fuckin' army did, of course. Queen's Lancs regiment… an' then The Rifles. To be precise. But you never appreciate what they teach you until you've left… do ya?"

A pause for a minute.

"Did you hear that lads?" He called over to where the children must be lying. "You don't appreciate summat until it's gone. Till you've not got it no more. Did

216

you get that? West…? Mace?"

As well as the baby, I could hear sobbing from another child. Vinnie snapped;

"Fuckin' pussies. You don't deserve no fuckin' chocolate."

There was another squeal from one of his shoes as he whirled around quickly and boomed;

"So! Trained killer in your midst, my friends. Don't be taking the piss, okay?"

His voice was suddenly drowned out by the nasal projections of a megaphone from outside;

"The premises are surrounded by armed police. In the interests of your own safety and that of the members of the public inside, we request that you put down your weapons and move to the front exit of the building – with your hands raised above your head."

It was as though he hadn't heard a word. And then more steps. Coming closer now.

"An' next. We've got the bitch what runs this place. Getting' Dawnie her nice new house, far away from Vinnie. Yeah – you're a bad bitch – you are. One baaaad, bad bitch…"

Me. He means me.

Adrenalin was coursing down my spine, turning my legs to fire. I wanted to move, but Michael was applying even more pressure, pushing me down harder and not allowing me any room to shift position.

Poppy-Rose's screaming was escalating, along with the wailing of one of her brothers. It was West.

Vinnie interrupted himself and screamed;

"*Dawn!* Fucksake! Just shut the fuckin' kid up, won't you?"

I heard her.

"Shush, Popsy, shusssshhh. It's okay, shushhh."

A pause.

"And now finally. We've got our Reverend here. Your Very Right Reverend Minister himself." Vinnie's previous chuckle had turned into an all-out barking laugh.

"Hey – you lot! Can you believe that when I first met him… when I was first told that he was a Minister – I thought he was like, your vicar sort? Ha. Un-bel-iev-able. Thick-as-pigshit-Vinnie. Or what?"

But in a split second the laughter had stopped.

"But yeah yeah. He's alright, our Minister. Done his time in The Forces and - see! Bad bitch from Sisterhood United or whatever they're called is getting a nice bit of protection from the man in charge. So at least he's got some balls on him. Though he never called me back about me carburettors like his people said he would. Bit out of order, that."

My legs were trembling. It was impossible to keep them still. I had felt this

217

before; after a rather traumatic birth experience, courtesy of Matthew. So, I knew that it was just the shock of the situation, the body going overdrive into flight or fight. But even so.

Get a grip.

Your kids are okay. This is all that matters.

And they've lost their dad already. They don't need their mother going AWOL.

So, get a great, big, fat bloody grip on it.

I tried to swallow and semi-coughed. But my throat was dry, tickly. I attempted to generate some saliva, but I ended up gulping down air instead. It hurt, but I tried to stifle any more attempts at coughing. Michael's shirt sleeve was covering most of my eye but I could still see the trail of debris across the hall. An abandoned stuffed toy, a discarded handbag, hot dogs, drink cartons and the rest of the items dumped by a panicking crowd. Outside of Sisters' Space the police sirens stopped for a second, to allow the man with the megaphone to reiterate his previous words. As the final sentence died away, Michael tried again. A muffled call out to Vinnie.

"Shall we just get the kids out of here first, Vinnie? That'd be easier on everyone."

"No fuckin' way." With a flatness to it. "My kids are staying with me from now on."

There was another pause and then he carried on;

"But, cheers. Least you remembered my name."

From anyone else that might have been construed as sarcasm. But the tone of his voice told me that it wasn't. Sounded pathetically grateful. And then I heard Shaun's gruff tones from several feet away, nearer to the hall windows;

"Look – let me… let me and just *him* - get up at least? We won't do anything daft. We just need to get this here lady to a hospital."

Shaun sounded okay at any rate. Unharmed. Michael's voice directly tagged onto Shaun's;

"Yes. She really needs some help. The two of us can get her out of the hall so…"

"You're not fuckin' going anywhere!" Vinnie's bellowed.

We all stayed silent. Apart from Poppy-Rose. Vinnie again;

"Rucksack, Dawn! She's doing my fuckin' 'ed in!"

I heard Dawn murmuring again. Michael tried;

"Look, Vinnie. You don't want to be faced with an innocent – a civilian death - on your hands, do you?"

I clocked this one. An unusual turn of phrase to use.

No response from Vinnie. Michael continued;

"If we get her out now, all the better for you."

A low whistle.

"Funny guy. Do you think they're gonna let me off with a charge of *friendly fire* or something? Like... maybe I meant to hit the stupid bitch. Like, who the fuck is she to me? Why should I give a fuck if she dies? Some scumbag politician. No offence to you, like, mate."

A slow reply from Michael;

"None taken... I think,"

"Cause for me – it's the local politicians who are the real bastards. In it for themselves. Milkin' their backhanders and all of that. At least you and your poncey lot down in Westminster or wherever - make proper decisions. Like armies and – fightin' dictators and the war against terror all of that..."

Again, he wasn't being sarcastic.

And this was the longest and most eloquent speech that I had ever heard from Vinnie.

I felt Michael move, his arm slowly removing itself from the back of my head. He was trying to sit up.

"Stay fuckin' put!" Vinnie yelled.

But Michael didn't do as he was told. Inch by inch he was moving, creeping away from me. He spoke quietly; trying to reassure Vinnie.

"Just sitting up slowly."

Vinnie shrieked, his voice squeaking;

"What? What the fuck? Get down, I said!"

Michael's voice was louder now. Purposeful.

"Look. I'm going to sit up slowly and I'm going to keep my hands in the air. We need to get this woman out of the building. Me and the other guy here... we'll carry her to the front door. There are ambulances out there for her."

Now that Michael had moved his arm away from me, I took the opportunity to turn my head and to take in the scene. Shaun was lying next to Councillor Casey. She was face down and blood was curling out from underneath her. A crimson puddle pooling around her left-hand side. Legs crooked. One stiletto on. One stiletto off. I thought of Diddle Diddle Dumpling. Of Adam whingeing on and on about that sort of thing. He hated reading nursery rhymes to the kids.

I still couldn't move my head the other way. I didn't want to attract Vinnie's attention. In the short silence, I could hear a strange, snake-like hissing. My brain felt scrambled. It took me several seconds to realise that the sound was coming from the bouncy castle, some ten yards away from me. Hit by a bullet.

Vinnie still hadn't responded to Michael.

"So, let's just get the casualty out of here. Otherwise it's going to look really bad for you. And once we've got her out of the hall, we'll come back and you can tell us what it is we... I – can maybe help you out with?"

219

I half expected to hear Vinnie's laugh again. But instead, he spat out an impatient;

"Fuckin' whatever. Whatever. Just be quick. Watchin' you both."

Michael stood up, issued a 'Come on!' at Shaun and then scurried over, taking the Councillor's legs. Shaun followed his movements, rising to his feet and then doing his best to support her head and shoulders as both men lifted her up. Kath Casey was silent. I figured that she must have lost consciousness. And then, like a leaking shopping bag - a sudden gush of blood splattered all over the floor. More sobs came from my left where Dawn and the kids were. West must have seen it.

I inched myself up, propping myself onto one arm. Vinnie was distracted now - watching the progress of Shaun and Michael, so at last I could see the man himself. He was kitted out in combats along with a wife beater vest - the irony of which would no doubt have been lost on him. The guy was all lean-muscle, sinews and dripping sweat, just as he had been during our first meeting on Brindleford; presumably the effect of drugs – as opposed to early onset menopause.

It was November and Vinnie had ventured out in just a vest and without a coat. I wondered where he must have put his combat jacket. I couldn't imagine that he would have left it on our coat stand in the reception. He didn't seem the type.

I nearly smiled at myself. Thinking like a mother.

And Vinnie was actually holding two guns – not just the one. I couldn't have even attempted a guess what sort they were. Even the mention of guns had always left a sour taste in my mouth. But regardless– there he was with his two babies. Man's murder-machines. One pointing at Michael and Shaun and the other swinging lazily by his side. All casual like.

His feet were bedecked in the same Gangsta-slipper trainer-type things that he had been wearing outside Lancaster House, back in September. I remembered noting then, what a stupid and dangerous choice of footwear the guy had chosen to try and ride a motorcycle with. Thinking like a wife.

He meandered out of my sight, leaving me with a clear view of the hall. Michael and Shaun were halfway towards the exit and Vinnie was still out of my line of vision, slightly behind me and directly at the foot of the stage. So, I jumped as he suddenly yelled;

"Right! Just fuckin' leave her outside of the doors. Then you come back. Don't make a run for it. No heroes, thanks! Or I shoot this lot. Starting with scumbag journalist, here."

Erin Mayo began to cry. But then shrieked as Vinnie kicked her.

"Shut the fuck up! Bitch!"

Usually it only took me a few seconds to flounce my way down the hall on one of my more purposeful missions in the workplace. But the slow shuffle of the two men with Councillor Casey up the length of the room was seeming to take forever and a day. A garish trail of blood followed behind them. When Michael and Shaun finally reached the open concertina doors, I saw them move past the reception desk and towards the entrance where Renee the Rottweiler had received a drenching only a week before. They struggled with the main outside door. Michael was trying to keep Casey's head upright and steady whilst doing his best to push the door open with his backside.

No go.

I spoke up; more of a croak really.

"It's a door release system. Someone must press the red button on the wall so the mechanism releases itself. They need a free hand but…"

"Oh, for fucksake! Stupid fuckin' arsehole shits!" Vinnie spat. It was the same tone of exasperation that I adopt when Lydia is trying to do her homework and claims that the two times tables are still too difficult for her. Although Vinnie was a bit more free and easy with the profanities, than I tend to be with Lydia. He turned on his heel, heading up the hall to open the door for them.

As soon as I heard his footsteps stalking away from us, I whipped my head over to the left to where Dawn and the kids were lying. I ignored the small Hibbert-Murray family gathering - and instead, fixed my stare on the interview room; the first room off the corridor from the hall. It was part of the wing that led towards the kitchen and to my office. And its door was ajar. Bev had locked most of the internal doors, but not this one it seemed. I glanced back at Vinnie. He was now approaching the end of the hall and was tucking one of the guns into the back of his trousers. As he reached Shaun and Michael, he stuck out his hand to smack the red button.

I could hear the blood, pounding, pumping in my head.

And then all previous paralysis and fear suddenly drained away from me.

I was up.

Half running, half stumbling towards the interview room, growling a "Come on! Come on!" at Dawn. She saw what I was doing and she yelped at the kids;

"Go – friggin' GO!"

And then she was scrambling herself, trying to get up, with Poppy-Rose clenched in her arms. The boys and I raced into the interview room. But Vinnie was pelting back down the hall, roaring as he charged his way towards us. He threw himself at Dawn, knocking her off her feet as I was about to slam the door shut. The baby fell from her grasp and the little girl's howl yanked me back into the hall. Vinnie was trying to punch Dawn in the face as she lay in a foetal curl, trying to protect herself with her hands clutched over her head.

I grabbed Poppy-Rose and tucked her under my arm like a rugby ball – she was so much lighter than my own chubby-boy Matthew had ever been at that age – and I hurtled back into the interview room before Vinnie had the wit about him to realise what was happening. I kicked the door shut, twisted the deadlock across and parcelled the child into Mason's arms. Seconds later, Vinnie's body impacted against it. And then again. And again.

The whole room reverberated with the thud of his torso against the door.

"Bitch! Fuckin' cunt! I'll fuckin' kill you! Give me my fuckin' kids back!"

CHAPTER 29

West clutched at his older sibling, fingers gripping the nylon of his brother's Man City shirt. Vinnie was repeatedly slamming his shoulder into the door. The baby screamed. Both boys looked at me - wondering if this new state of affairs was preferable to that of remaining in the hall.

But the door held. So, Vinnie punched it. And then he cursed in pain. I turned my attention away from the door and towards the boys. They were not looking their best. West's tawny skin was almost translucent, his lips drained of colour. Mason's usually pallid complexion was flushed, furiously red. Poppy-Rose's face was a mess of snot and tears. Her tiny pink tracksuit was soaked in blood – Councillor Casey's I presumed – which she must have landed in when Dawn had dropped her onto the floor, because she seemed to have no obvious injuries of her own. But the kid was hysterical; it was "Mumma, Mumma, Mumma" - over and over.

I scuttled backwards, pulling all three of them into the far left-hand corner. I was banking on the fact that Vinnie wouldn't be so stupid as to try and fire his gun at the lock or through the door, for fear of hitting the children. But then - on the other hand - concern for the safety of his own kids hadn't stopped him earlier on when he had decided to embark on a shooting spree in a community centre. Perhaps even he had the sense to realise that the doors in this building were nearly all hard-arsed, stainless steel security doors. Not worth the risk of a bullet bounce-back.

I shuffled on my knees towards the red door with the green EXIT sign and tried the handle. Locked. It wasn't supposed to be locked from the inside?

Bloody Bev. I had told her to keep the fire exit routes unlocked. But this one was locked. And the internal door she was supposed to have locked had turned out to be unlocked. Bloody, bloody typical of my luck. Still. At least we were out of the hall now. And at least it felt that we were closer to the emergency vehicles outside. The intermittent burps of the sirens and the distant shouting of the police, the soldiers and whoever, were pathetically reassuring.

"What're we gonna do now, Rebecca?" – a trembled whisper from Mason.

"I'm called 'Rachael' – remember? Well, I… I thought we could maybe leave the building by this door here." I scurried back to them again and gabbled;

"Normally it's here as an extra escape route for someone who's using this room. But it's been locked today. So, we can't get out. Still, we're much safer in here than in the hall. So, you three just stay right here in the corner. Okay?'

I didn't want to frighten the kids further by adding that this was because Vinnie might try and shoot through the door.

"So yes… Just do whatever I tell you to. The police will be here any minute and will sort things out."

"But Vinnie 'ates the pigs…"

West added; "Yeah. If the pigs arrive, Dad'll get even more freaked…"

"Look," I said. "Don't worry about that, just…"

But I was interrupted by more shouting and screaming coming from the hall. Vinnie and Dawn; the sounds of an unequal match.

I tried to talk over the noise, to prattle on about the police and us all getting out safely and how I had seen an ice-cream van outside in the park earlier, but the attention of all three of the children couldn't be swayed. Each one of them was staring at the locked door. I wondered how many times they had had to witness this kind of thing - to see the fights and the beatings - never mind just hearing the noises of the brutality going on downstairs, or in the next room. Mason was doing his best to cuddle his little sister closer, but she began again. Inconsolable hysteria - reaching her arms out towards the locked door.

I scanned the place desperately, looking for something to distract them. The interview room was a small space, designed to give women some privacy to talk with caseworkers. There were three armchairs, a table with a box of tissues and, in the corner next to us, there was a storage cupboard containing a second-hand music system and a few toys that used to belong to Lydia and Matthew. I suddenly remembered that recently - after a member of staff had experienced a particularly stressful session in the room, when a screeching toddler had refused to leave his mum and to play in our crèche for half an hour – I had devised a cunning solution to such future problems. Several bags of lollipops had been purchased from one of Medlock's many cheap-as-chips shops and had been stashed in the cupboard. I had never signed up to the anti-sugar brigade when it came to parental desperation.

More yelling and shrieking. And now we could hear Michael's voice. Shaun's, too – back in the hall. I skittered across to the cupboard, wrenched it open and dragged a large packet of lollipops back with me. Plus, a couple of toys for Poppy-Rose; a pink Peppa Pig pretend-phone and a Hot Wheelz car.

I unwrapped the little girl's lollipop for her and let West and Mason concentrate on opening their own. Mason was looking at me as if I was a bit of a moron – doling out the sweets and trinkets whilst Vinnie was kicking the crap out of their mother only yards away – but he still managed to follow the actions of his siblings and stuffed the day-glow treat into his mouth. West asked me;

"Hey - can I have two of 'em? I like the blue ones best."

"You can have as many as you bloody well like. Just stay in the corner there - and do as you're told."

And then the effects of the sugar must also have brightened the mood of Mason, although his words were somewhat muffled by the lollipop as he pointed at the Peppa Pig plastic phone and said;

"Oooh, Poppy-Rose – you've got a nice pink iPhone 7 there! Is that your old one then, Rebecca? Well cool."

"It's Rachael…" I said slowly, ignoring the sarcasm. Mason must have inherited the gene from Dawn.

And then I remembered something else. The spy hole. There was a two-way viewer - for employee protection. It was there to let members of staff outside the interview room check that everything was okay inside, because there was always a risk that some women might lose the plot with us - start acting in a threatening manner. I was hoping that Vinnie wouldn't have the wherewithal to notice it - to look inside at us. And the spyhole also worked the other way round - so that someone on the inside of the room could view outside of the room and into the hall.

I moved over to the door and squatted next to it, motioning for the three children to stay in the corner. The lollipops were performing their magic, and both the sweet stuff and the sucking motion had induced at least some element of calm. Despite his flippant words, however, Mason's limbs were all of a-jiggle. I could see that he was desperate to do something. Dawn had mentioned to me before that Mason was not a child who liked to feel powerless in any given situation.

I moved the metal flap that covered the spy hole upwards and away from the glass. Dawn and Vinnie were just ten feet away from the door of the interview room. Vinnie's face was streaked with blood, so it looked like Dawn must have put up a good fight. But now she was all curled up on the floor again - her legs moving just a fraction. Vinnie looked to have reached breaking point. He was standing to one side of her, pointing the gun at her head and shouting;

"I'LL FUCKIN' KILL YOU! YOU FUCKIN' WHORE!"

And then;

"YOU FUCKIN', FUCKIN' CUNT!"

I wished that I had had the foresight to have switched the damned music system on, when I had spotted it stashed in the cupboard. Anything to muffle the malice pouring forth. Even Simply Red's 'Stars', purchased for the interview room from The Greyhound Rescue charity shop, would have been preferable to this.

And now we had the man with the megaphone churning out;

"Please release any other members of the public. We would also like to speak with you. You can call '999' and our operators will immediately connect you to us, so that we can talk to you about your situation."

I rubbed my forehead hard. Trying to think, think, think. If only I hadn't let bossy britches Bev do her security drill thing with the building - locking up every escape route available to us.

I turned back, glaring at the exit door which would have – should have - taken us straight out and into the little park next to our building. I contemplated getting the two boys to help me to kick at the exit door, but I had spent plenty of time as a housing officer - watching policemen built like brick shithouses struggling to boot down doors that already had the mortise lock closed on them. And when we had undergone our renovations a few years back, I had made sure that they were all top-notch, tough stuff. This one wasn't going to budge.

I looked back through the spy hole. The bouncy castle was finally giving up the ghost, about to fold in on itself. Four tacky turrets a-wavering and a-teetering. Michael and Shaun had been standing five or six feet away from Vinnie and Dawn. But then, all of a sudden, Michael took a step towards Vinnie – hands up and trying to pacify him. Quick as a flash, the other man swung round with the gun and pointed it at him, screaming;

"I SAID! I SAID - DON'T FUCKIN' MOVE!"

I flinched, but Michael didn't duck or look particularly anxious. And he didn't step back, either. He simply carried on talking. Quietly. I could only catch the words, "take the edge," "let me," and "in time." Shaun's hands were turned palm upwards, hanging by his sides. I had never seen him take such a stance; such a gesture of appeasement before. I wasn't sure that I liked it. It didn't fit, somehow.

A small movement came from behind Michael and Shaun. One that both were unaware of. The skin on my scalp tingled as I saw Erin Mayo inching her arm along - ever so slowly - into the pocket of her suit. The glint of a mobile phone, as she slowly withdrew it.

"*No, no – you stupid, stupid…*" I muttered, my jaw clenched. West's voice wobbled;

"Who? What's happening?"

"Nothing. Don't worry. Just stay there."

Erin raised her arm little by little. The brainless, tabloid-story obsessed woman was such a stupid div that she was trying to film what was unfolding before her. Meanwhile, as Vinnie was about to respond to something that Michael was saying to him, Dawn suddenly came to life again. She jerked her leg outwards at Vinnie, trying to kick him off balance as he stood over her. To be sure, it was a pretty half-hearted effort on her part, but that made no difference to him. He brought the barrel of the gun down on her head - hard. My stomach rolled over. I covered my mouth and had to look away.

Now Michael was shouting;

"Vinnie! Reasonable force. This is NOT reasonable force. You can stop this now! Let me help you! You've got mitigating circumstances… mitigating circumstances - going on here!"

Michael's words seemed discordant. Out of setting. But then I realised that he was trying to use military or perhaps even legal jargon, attempting every trick in the book - to stop Vinnie from smashing Dawn's skull in. I looked back again. Vinnie had paused - narrowing his eyes at Michael - his drug-addled brain trying to decode the message. But as his attention moved away from Dawn, he must have caught the wavering movement of Erin's arm from behind Michael and Shaun.

The gun swept upwards in an arc towards the reporter.

The slam of another gunshot echoed around the building.

Poppy-Rose began to sob again. I stared frantically through the spy hole, trying see if I could make out what was happening. Bodies seemed to have merged into one black tangle.

Shaun was lying on the floor.

Oh, God. God, no.

He was holding his palms upwards again, towards Vinnie. Don't fire. Blood on his hands. Blood seeping from his chest, making a dark stain against his oh-so-crisply-ironed-by-Jess-shirt. I couldn't see Erin now, because she was lying behind Shaun. But I could hear her;

"I've been shot! I've been shot!"

"Serves you fuckin' right, you stupid, fuckin' journalist bitch!' Vinnie raged.

He was holding the gun flat, shaking it towards her, Gangsta-style. And then there was a crack and then a crunch as he stamped twice on her phone, with his crap footwear.

"STAY STILL ALL OF YOU! OR YOU'RE ALL FUCKIN' DEAD!"

Dawn had already stopped moving, without the formal instructions.

Then the megaphone guy;

"If you do not release all further members of the public, we will have no choice other than to force entry to the building."

Michael was half-crouching on the floor, beside Shaun. Staring hard at Vinnie, taking his time - as a voice piped up, from behind me;

"Can I see?"

It was Mason. He had finished the remnants of his lollipop, but was keeping the little white stick at the crook of his mouth. Pushing Poppy-Rose into his brother's arms, he had moved over next to me and was now trying to look over my shoulder and through the spyhole.

"No, you bloody well can't! Get back in the corner!"

It came out harsher than I had intended it to. Because I couldn't afford to be distracted. I couldn't tear my eyes away from Shaun. And for some reason I seemed to be holding my breath.

Shaun was trying to sit up. His face was grey. His shirt was already an ugly shade of cherry red. My fingers walked their way up towards the deadlock on the door. Gripping it.

The first attempts at flirtation suddenly galloped across my mind; those double entendres occurring between us during that terrifically dull First Aid course in Manchester. And now – here and now - every cell in my body was yearning to recall whatever the hell it was we had both learned back then. I pinched the deadlock, fingers trembling with the urge to fling it back, to peg it over to the arrogant tosser. To screech at him to lie down flat, to slow his heart rate down, to stave off the blood loss. To get his legs propped up in the air - and all of that.

But Michael was there. Michael could help Shaun. Surely?

Michael, however, was still talking to Vinnie.

And Vinnie was unresponsive. Staring at the mess that he had made of Dawn. Perversely fascinated.

Poppy-Rose had finished her lollipop. She was back to her previous state, sobbing for her mother and wiping the little white stick into her hair. Mason and West were quiet again. They seemed to have given up on trying to comfort their sister, so I turned away from the door and crawled on my knees over to her;

"Shush, baby," I said, taking her in my arms. She snuggled into my chest, perhaps relieved to receive some adult comfort. As her thin arm fastened around my neck, something fell out of the pocket of her tracksuit top, clinking onto the floor.

"What's this?"

I picked it up, looking at the boys. But I knew damned well what it was. A starfish-shaped keyring which Lydia had given to me; "You can have this. I don't want it. Because I've only ever seen dead starfish in real life. They make me feel sad." Yes, a key fob that contained a very familiar set of jangly things.

I was met with silence. So, I repeated the question.

"Er… some keys?" West answered, all innocence. His brother punched him in the arm. Hard.

"You're a bleedin' klepto! Whatsamatter with you?"

"Shut it, yer dick."

Mason smacked his little brother around the head now and growled;

"You've got to pack it in, West! Nickin' everythin'! You can't thieve from this place! Rebecca and that lot are helpin' Mum out!'

The incongruity of his mother lying in a pool of blood in the very building that was supposed to be helping her out was not lost on me.

But West bit back;

"I didn't nick 'em 'cause I wanted 'owt from 'ere! That woman with the red, frizzy hair were pissin' me off when she was going round lockin' all of the rooms. She said she'd break me legs if I ran into her again on the scooter. So, I just nicked 'em out of Frizz 'Ed's coat pocket to get 'er in trouble with Rebecca!

See?" He looked at me and I just stared back at him, all incredulous. He carried on, trying to defend his actions;

"An' anyway. What's there to nick in this place? Some lollipops an' a shit music system? You can only play those CD things on it – Like, well-last century! It's bobbins, it is."

Fantastic. He'd been casing the joint. But I held my hand to my lips, shushing them. I would deal with Klepto-Kid later, but right now I needed to…

There was a sudden slam – a crash - against the door. All four of us jumped in unison, instinctively moving backwards and as far as we could, back into the corner of the room again. Vinnie must have heard the children's voices - reminding him of their presence.

"YOU LET ME AT MY FUCKIN' KIDS, YER BITCH! OR I'LL SHOOT EVERY SINGLE FUCKIN' BASTARD IN THIS HALL!"

But it seemed that the Gods of Fortune - or of pilfering little kids with anti-social behavioural tendencies - were at last on my side and the four of us no longer needed to be held as hostages to Vinnie's warped logic. I scampered the couple of yards to the external exit, flipped the key around in the lock and rammed the door open with my shoulder. The chilly November air was a very welcome slap in the face as the children scrambled out into sharp, early afternoon sunlight. A large group of firemen and police officers were standing about one hundred yards away from us on the narrow road that led up to the side of the hill, behind a bright yellow plastic barrier that had been erected and which ran along the perimeter of the park. From the other side of the building I heard megaphone-man again; the same message as previously.

"Run!" I told the boys.

They followed my orders, Mason jiggling his sister along on his hip.

I didn't go with them myself and I didn't wait around to see what the reaction of the police might be. Perhaps I should have done. But they would no doubt want to stall me, to ask me questions. And I didn't have the time for any of that.

An invisible cord was pulling me back.

I sprinted away from the protection outside and back into my workplace, dashing into the interview room. And after making sure that Vinnie had stopped slamming himself against the door, I moved up against the spy hole. And then I shouted;

"Vinnie! The kids are outside now - being looked after. So, it's up to you now! If you stop all of this… the courts will let you have a chance of seeing them again."

I was bluffing of course. I was pretty sure that no judge or jury in the land would be stupid enough to let Vinnie get within a mile of his children for a good few years after this little incident. But from what I had seen of the guy previously, and from his performance today, Vinnie had already proven himself to have a spectacularly low IQ and he wouldn't realise this - although, to be fair, the drugs and drink might be to blame for some of his depleted intelligence and the more murderous tendencies.

No response. It was as though he hadn't heard me at all.

He was now back at the side of Dawn again, standing over her. But I noticed that his posture had changed – his shoulders were slightly slumped. He turned round to look at Michael, who was still semi-squatting, one hand on the parquet to give him balance. In terms of Shaun – I could only see his legs, because Michael was blocking most of my view of him. But I could hear the occasional whimper coming from Erin Mayo.

"That's right, Vinnie," Michael said, looking up at him and nodding. "The courts would look pretty favourably on you, if you just let everyone go now. Why not call it a day?"

Vinnie stuck his bottom lip out as he moved the gun from one palm to another and fiddled with it, like a small boy with a vaguely interesting new toy. Then he cocked his head to one side and threw his head back, bursting out with;

"Bullshit!" the voice echoing around the hall. "Look at the state of her!"

He gestured to Dawn, whose face, arms, shoulders – her entire torso – was steeped in blood. "Yeah – right. I mean - the pigs'll take one look at her and go for me. Big time." He slapped the gun from one hand to another as he moved his eyes to the ceiling, contemplating his fate. I almost wanted to laugh – his posture, his facial expressions were so melodramatic. Macbeth of Medlock.

"And there's no way – no fuckin' way - that I'm going back to Ashworth. Never!"

Ashworth.

At first, I thought that he was referring to some army battalion – some military corps that I had never heard of. But then the penny dropped. Ashworth. A high-security psychiatric hospital, located over in Merseyside, used as an alternative to prison for men who have committed a crime but who also happen to be extremely mentally disturbed. In our previous conversations, Dawn had alluded to the fact that Vinnie had clocked himself up a criminal record 'for a thing or two.' But she had never mentioned Ashworth to me. She had told me once that he had spent a lot of time 'over near Liverpool'. But perhaps she didn't even know herself, that Vinnie had been at the damned place.

But Michael was onto this, straight away.

"Now, Vinnie. Hang on a minute, fella. If you've already served time at Ashworth, then that puts a different perspective on things. That is, if you let everyone go right now… I'm serious. You've got a good chance of getting off - with PTSD."

"Yer what?" Vinnie jerked his head back and grimaced. No comprendi, Monsieur.

"You must have heard of it... Post-Traumatic Stress Disorder. You know?"

I caught the spark that suddenly gleamed in Vinnie's eyes. It was accompanied by another pout. But he dropped the gun back down by his side;

"Whaddya mean... exactly?"

Michael moved slowly, from the crouching position, to a standing one and for once, Vinnie didn't tell him to get back onto the floor.

"Look – I was there too... Remember?"

"What? At Ashworth?" said Vinnie, his eyebrows knotted. He stroked the barrel of the gun with a finger.

"No," Michael shook his head. "I mean – in active combat. Afghan. All over. Northern Ireland too, long before that. I do remember you telling me that you'd been in The Rifles out in Bosnia. So, I realise what happened to your mates, of course I do. I know what you saw – went through – over there. You were just a boy soldier, Vinnie. And I've seen plenty of that kind of thing myself. So, I totally understand how the pressure can make you... feel like you're... going to crack up.'

Vinnie nodded. His answer came quietly, as if he were even surprising himself, with the reply.

"Some serious shit —"

"Exactly," said Michael. "Look. So, believe me. I get this. I get this more than ninety-nine per cent of the population ever could. And now that you've realised that I'm a different kind of minister to the kind of chap that you originally took me to be..."

Vinnie interrupted Michael's words with a strange barking noise. He sounded like a sea lion; it was hysterical laughter and it took him a few moments to stop. Then he wiped his eyes and pinched the bridge of his nose, shaking his head and looking over to where Shaun was lying.

"Hey – Big Dick. I still can't believe all of that. Can you? I mean... can you believe that I thought *he* was a vicar? Man of the cloth!"

And then I heard Shaun's voice responding. My pulse went into overdrive. His tones were watery, were weak - but he was playing along;

"Nah, mate - easy mistake to make. I actually thought he was a nun..."

Shaun had made a joke. Albeit a shit one. But he was still managing to talk.

Vinnie laughed. Michael was chuckling now too. But it wasn't a real Michael-laugh, it was more forced, more mechanical. He carried on with;

"And, don't forget, Vinnie, that I'm a cabinet minister. I've got the ear of the Prime Minister himself. We happen to be good... good pals. And he'll believe me. I can tell him about the PTSD; how it drove you to feeling utterly helpless. How... how you didn't know how else to cope with the situation."

No reply from Vinnie again. His head was down as he stared at the gun.

"So, let me help you get out of this mess... I'm probably one of the few people who can. I know what you've been up against. I can lend a hand. I promise you. Vinnie."

Suddenly Vinnie's whole demeanour altered. The change in his posture was so marked that even Michael seemed taken aback; I noticed a slight flinch of his eyes, perhaps steeling himself for another moment of Vinnie-instigated aggression. But rather than attacking anyone, Vinnie now raised both hands out to his side and began to grin, flashing gold-flecked teeth.

"Okay – you got me, Mr not-a-vicar-what-soever! You can pardon me sins and all of that. Let's throw the towel in … Enough's enough."

He looked over to where Shaun was again and asked him;

"What's he like? Eh? This ministerial guy!"

"My hero," came Shaun's faint tones. Sarky sod.

"Yeah. Let's pro-ceed then," said Vinnie. He was trying to adopt a refined accent, mimicking Michael's; "Therefore, I shall accept your int-teres-ting offer. Sounds maahvhallous."

So, Vinnie put the gun back into the side of his waistband. The final gesture of surrender. I licked my lips. They were bone dry. I wondered how the hell Michael had managed to…

And then I nearly jumped out of my skin. Someone poked me in the shoulder. But rather than the police (who I had been half-expecting to steal into the interview room at any moment) it turned out to be Mason.

"What are you doing back here?" I hissed. "You're supposed to be outside - until we can get your mum out! Go on! Bugger off! Do as you're told!"

"I just need to…" he began. But then he jerked his head towards the open exit door where every few seconds came the staccato blurp of a police car's siren.

"S'alright, Rebecca. The police are comin' in now anyways. But they said they need to ask you somethin' first. So's you need to go and talk to them. They said it were dead important."

He jerked his blonde buzzcut towards the exit. Baby-blue, eager eyes.

"They said go and get that Rebecca out, 'cause we need 'er 'elp. C'mon!"

Looking back, I should have seen through that little story straight away. It was hardly likely that the police would send an eleven-year-old boy back into close proximity with a hostage situation. But Mason had caught me off-guard. Vinnie seemed to be on a climbdown and my nerves, my logical brain was jumbled. And Shaun – well Shaun was still alive. Plus, Mason had delivered the trump card; tell Rachael Russell that someone needs her help. So, I stood up and turned to go, moving over to the exit with a grumpy throwaway comment;

"Okay. But, Mason - can you at least try and remember that I'm not called 'Rebecca?' It's really rude to keep calling someone by the wrong name when they've been told so many times…"

Then I realised. Mason wasn't following me.

My head snapped round as I saw him flipping over the deadlock, throwing the interview room door open and racing back into the hall.

I legged it after him - without any thought of guns or borderline-insane ex-soldiers or whether this was the stupidest thing that I had ever done in my life - and in a split second we were back in the hall. Mason ran towards Vinnie, his arms outstretched. Vinnie, caught by surprise, nearly lost his balance as Mason hurtled towards him. I stopped, frozen. Wondering what Vinnie's reaction would be on my own return to the hall and feeling utterly confused. What the hell was Mason doing? Why had he run to hug Vinnie, rather than to see what condition his mother was in?

And then there was another flash of action, as Michael lunged at Vinnie. Vinnie had been knocked off-kilter by Mason's embrace and Michael was seizing the opportunity. The two men dropped to the floor, Michael seemed to be trying to both restrain Vinnie and attempting to seize the gun from him. It was a blur of fists, elbows, knees, tank-tops and dodgy footwear. Mason dived on top of them both – and now it was three males wrestling along the hall floor in a free-for-all – with Mason inadvertently being kicked away by Michael. Struggling, shouts, expletives - and screams from Erin Mayo

And then the gun went off.

I hit the floor once more, landing on top of Shaun's legs.

The seconds ticked by.

CHAPTER 30

And then came an eerie calm as I lay against Shaun.

There were no more sounds of fighting. No more anything. I glanced up at him. His face was bleached white and his nostrils were pinched. A rasp came from his throat. My hair was wet with his blood.

'Shaun?' I whispered, touching an always be-stubbled cheek. 'How bad does it…?'

His eyes were locked onto mine, but he didn't reply. His pupils were dilated and then his gaze broke contact, moving over to the scene behind us. Like he was trying to drink in the horror of the scene. It was the same expression that he had had on his face when we had watched the Twin Tower footage together. Perhaps the very same how-does-this-compute countenance that a certain little boy had adopted some forty-odd years ago, amidst the detritus of the Birmingham pub bombings.

Vinnie was cocooned. He lay nestled in a tangle of pink, punctured bouncy castle. Soaking in a shallow bath of blood; legs buckled and twisted beneath him. A couple of yards away lay the squished remnants of what had once been the chocolate sculpture.

I was less than ten feet from him, but I could see that he was already dead. His eyes were fixed, staring towards the end of the hall. Perhaps I should have run to him, should have attempted to dredge up the remnants from one of those archaic first aid training courses, should have carried out some out-of-date version of CPR. But I didn't. As far as I was concerned, the guy was gone. His blood flowed in wide crimson ribbons along the rivets of the plastic. And then two of the yellow and pink stripy turrets collapsed inwards, flopping onto his body.

Done and dusted.

I stood up – I had to steady myself after a bit of a wobble – and took in the macabre scene. It was as though a massive pink, faux-Disney spider had opted to take out Vinnie in a final act of giant arachno-vengeance.

Michael was a few yards away, with Mason and Dawn. At first I had to do a double take. I thought that the boy was covered in brown paint. But it was just chocolate. Chocolate in his hair, smeared down his face, and there were great lumps of it all over his t-shirt. He must have landed on top of the Sisters' Space sculpture. He was crying as he stroked his mother's hair. His tongue kept flicking out the sides of his mouth; unconsciously searching for more chocolate-flavoured salty tears.

Michael told him;

"Your mum's still breathing. But we need to get her to the hospital fast. Stay right here with her and talk to her. I'll be back in a minute."

He ran out of the hall and I moved to crouch down again with Shaun. The wound was much higher up on the right hand of his chest than I thought it had been – it was more towards his shoulder. I was hardly an expert on this kind of thing but I hoped that this might be a positive sign. He had been trying to stem the blood flow with his hand and his jacket sleeve, but he hadn't been able to do much and the blood was still flowing freely. I looked around, grabbed a coat that had been dumped by a panicking member of the public and pressed it firmly under Shaun's jacket where the wound seemed to be. He grimaced;

"God, that hurts! Getting me back, are you?'

"What for?" I pressed a bit harder and he jumped;

"Fuck - ow! Yeah, for all those years of. Whatever. With me."

I considered those black on black eyes of his. Freaky alien-eyes, I used to call them. The pupils were more dilated than they were usually, so I decided not to get into a conversation and instead just shrugged, giving him a grim smile. He coughed and winced again. I looked around. Mason was cradling his mother's head, trying to reassure her. Erin hadn't moved, but she was still face down and was sobbing;

"I've been hit! I've been hit!"

Shaun managed to croak over at her;

"For God's sake woman, you bloody haven't."

"I have! There's blood – everywhere!'

"That's mine, you daft cow. Jesus Christ…"

The effort of talking caused him to cough. I told him to lie still and to shut his gob. I grabbed the lucky dip tub from the nearby stall and emptied out the sawdust and the crappy prizes and then dragged it over to Shaun, propping his feet up on it. Then I moved back to Mason and to Dawn.

Not one to feel the cold, Dawn had been wearing a skimpy, little top. She had a huge gash across her chest and along one of her arms from where Vinnie had repeatedly hit her with the barrel of the gun and where she had been trying to protect her head. But it was her face that horrified me the most; a sickening swirl of dried, clotted and fresh blood. It had pooled into her eyes, lending the macabre look of a death's head mask. Mason was rocking to-and-fro – keening - a quiet howl of anguish ("Mum, no - don't… Please!")

But at last we heard a stampede of feet, the jabber of voices. A dozen uniforms plunged into the hall; armed police wearing bullet-proof vests, along with paramedics who divided themselves between Vinnie, Dawn and Shaun. Michael was with them, heading straight for Dawn as he described to the professionals what had happened to her.

Erin Mayo was shrieking;

"Over here! Over here! Don't forget about me! He tried to shoot me – I'm think I'm bleeding too!"

She's bleeding annoying, I thought.

It took less than a minute for someone to throw a sheet over the mess that now remained of Vinnie. I let my gaze linger there for only a second and then my attention was straight back to Shaun, where a male paramedic had asked him his name and was quickly assessing his injuries, telling me;

"You did all the right things for him, love. Especially given the circumstances. Right. Come on, Shaun, lad. Let's get you straight to A & E, quick smart, and do some proper patching up. I think you're gonna be alright, mate." Two other ambulance men began to lift him gingerly onto a stretcher. They joked that he would be too big to fit onto it.

I took a deep breath. The relief flushed through my veins and it was reflected back at me from Shaun's eyes. Because surely, you're going to be okay, if the paramedics say so? If they're having a bit of banter with you?

Another paramedic was kneeling next to Erin Mayo;

"It's not your blood, love. It looks like it belongs to your big pal here. What happened?"

"I don't know," she whined. "Well, he… he was going to shoot me and then this other guy here sort of moved in front of me."

"Right. So, it looks like he tried to protect you – and he got hit instead of you?"

"Maybe… No – I - Yes, maybe."

I looked at Shaun. Sweat glistened on his upper lip. I raised my eyebrows. Did you?

"Maybe," he mouthed back.

And then a hand clenched my shoulder, followed by;

"How do."

It turned out to be Detective Inspector David Garratt. We had worked together on many occasions over the years; usually liaising over the more serious cases of domestic violence that occurred in Medlock and across Manchester.

"Dave."

"Bloody hell, Rachael! Don't you think that you see enough of the action and violence during your usual working week? Do you really have to spend your weekends in a hostage situation as well? I mean… Some people…"

I smiled at him. Sans humour. He nodded at the blood-covered hall.

"I mean… Jesus, Mary and Joseph. So, were you present throughout? What the hell went down here?"

I nodded. "Yeah. I was. But it was all so... so mad. It got really confusing towards the end and... hang on a minute. Shaun?" I called over to his stretcher, which was now following Dawn's hurried exit out of the hall, "Shaun, did you see what happened exactly? After I fell on top of you?"

"She fell on top of you?" one of the paramedics joked. "Lucky you. You didn't tell us about that – you little tinker! Best not mention it to your wife either, heh heh."

Shaun just laughed feebly.

"No. Enough of that," DI Garratt put his hand up, halting the conversation. "No offence," he called over to Shaun, who he also knew from our former days of social housing, drug dealers and evictions on various Manchester housing estates, "but you both know the procedures - the deal. Keep it schtum for now, if you don't mind."

I apologised. He brushed it off with;

"No problem, flower. You're usually seeing it from the other side of the fence, as it were. Now. I've got to have a quick once-over of me laddo here," he nodded towards the sheet, cradled in the latex pond of blood. "And then I'll be back with you, pronto."

Michael had moved away from a group of police officers and other official looking people and was now striding towards me. Trevor was by his side and another man too - the same beefy build as Trevor and Brian, but wearing a checked shirt and jeans. I recognised Ross - the 'blend into the crowd' bodyguard for today. Both men looked grim and Ross couldn't seem to stop shaking his head. Michael reached me and put both arms round me. The gesture – given the number of people surrounding us - took me by surprise. He asked me if I was alright and I nodded - enjoying the now familiar scent of the nook of his neck - but uncomfortable with such intimacy in front of others. Perhaps he could sense this, as he moved away again, hastily;

"Now don't hug me too tightly – I'm pretty sure I've cracked a couple of ribs. Done that several times before," I glanced at his face; he had several gashes on his cheek.

"Oh. You've broken a tooth!'"

"Ha. Politics. Risky business."

One of the paramedics was soon on his tail and began a quick assessment. I shook my head when they asked me if I had sustained any injuries myself. I was close to saying something a bit glib - about the only damage for me being a half-trashed workplace and an overspend on my salary budget thanks to the inevitable overtime for Jules the cleaner - but for once, the words wouldn't come.

DI Garratt and his companion threw the sheet back over Vinnie's body and strode over to us. Dave, yet again, was all very polite but firm.

"Ever so sorry, Mr Chiswick - but I'd prefer it if you two don't speak to each other until everyone involved on the scene has been interviewed. I'm sure that you'll understand that we all have to follow procedures correctly."

Michael tried to joke;

"Even government ministers?"

DI Garratt shot back;

"Especially government ministers —"

"Surely we can at least have a few moments together to —"

"I'd really prefer it if you didn't, sir. You know how these things can pan out if we don't..."

Michael acquiesced and the DI nodded to two of his colleagues, telling me that the pair would escort me to the station. That he would need to interview Michael first and then it would be my turn. I was filled with a sudden rush of indignation, so I shook my head.

"Actually, Dave. Do you know what? I'm not happy with this. It's like... we're the guilty ones here. And not Vinnie. He's the one who..."

"Come on, Rachael. You know it's not like that. This is just the usual procedure. The way it..."

I dug my heels in.

"No. I'm not going anywhere until I've seen my children. My parents. My... oh my God!" I suddenly remembered. "My sister - Vicky! How the hell did she get out of the hall in time – without getting hurt? She's on crutches. I mean - they were *all* here."

The DI sighed and shook his head.

"Look, Rachael - they're all fine. Everyone who got out of the hall is fine – no problems whatsoever. They'll all be a bit shaken of course, but they're fine." He stuck his hand in the air, beckoning a young female police officer over;

"Jenny, love. Can you go back outside and locate Rachael Russell's family? Let them know that she's okay and no injuries or anything and that she'll be back home in a few hours." The woman nodded briskly and headed back out of the building.

I frowned at him. Still feeling the need to warn him.

"Right. Well. So long as this interview thing is quick. I've got to get back to my kids, they're bound to be..."

He cut me off and gesticulated with a;

"Ta-dah!" pretending to give me a fanfare; "Ah yes! Your kids. I've already had the pleasure of encountering your children. Your little boy was involved with an incident outside, involving a runaway fire engine. A rather large, twelve-tonne, bright red vehicle being driven by children... that very nearly ran me over in fact. And so, what with all of the fun of that... I can totally reassure you that your own offspring hardly even noticed that you were stuck in here with the likes of Rambo. So, as I said. Don't worry about them."

This all sounded so ridiculous, that I knew instantly that it was highly plausible. Only Matthew could have become involved with 'a fire engine incident'. So, I reluctantly headed out of the building, accompanied by two police officers as we followed Michael and Dave Garratt. Michael looked over his shoulder towards me, gave me a reassuring smile and winked, mouthing;

"Call you later."

The DI and two other senior detectives interviewed Michael first. It took them less than thirty minutes; I had expected it to last longer. I made good use of the time, washing my hands and face in the ladies' room. I could scrub Shaun's blood off my skin at any rate, even if my hair was still matted with it. I watched the pinky pigmented water swirl down the plughole. And then it was my turn to be led into a stuffy, little windowless room. It was unusual for more senior members of the police force like DI Garratt to carry out interviews and I realised that all of this was probably because of Michael's involvement; that there would be issues of national security to consider. My interviewers seemed to find it quite useful that I had watched most of the events through the spyhole, but I felt frustrated that I couldn't tell them exactly what had happened after I landed on top of Shaun. They didn't linger for too long on that aspect of the incident – how the siege was ended. But I knew that it would be important to them. Half way through the interview, when they let me nip to the loo and the recorder was turned off, the DI had told me;

"Can't fault your security in that building, Rachael. You actually make the station here look pretty shitty in comparison. So, don't you be blaming yourself for some nutter who manages to get inside with a gun."

This made me feel slightly less anxious that I – we – had done something wrong at the centre. But I knew that there would still be a lot of issues for the police to unpick. At the end of the interview, when the tape recorder had been switched off again, I stood up to leave them, but then thought of something;

"I do have one question for you lot actually. How on earth did Mason - an eleven-year-old lad - manage to get past you and back into the building? I got the three of the kids outside - specifically for the police to protect them."

The DI looked at the other two officers. Too much eye contact. They were deciding whether to tell me something or not. The older man finally said;

"That incident with the fire engine that I mentioned to you before. Well. It momentarily distracted some of the officers, so that the lad – Mason - was able to run past the barriers and back into the building."

No. No bloody way.

Go Home, Rachael. Don't think about this one right now.

A police squad car took me back to my parents' home. My own car was still stuck outside of Sisters' Space because handbag, car keys and phone had all been locked away in my desk drawer on Bev's advice. And the place was still crawling with coppers so I was told that everything would have to remain there until the forensic team had completed their no-doubt long and laborious examinations.

Dark thoughts swirled around my head as we drove back to Stalybridge. Apart from the fact that my workplace had suddenly become the scene for an armed siege and death - my own children had been on the scene. Vinnie - who had seen me as one of the interfering bitches that was trying to get Dawn away from him – wouldn't have been aware that my own family were present at the launch.

But what if he had? What if he had picked up on the fact that at the last minute, three generations of my lot had trucked up to the event?

I sat in the back of the police car, picking at my nails. Wiggling my wedding rings up and down. Maybe Adam had been right, after all.

It was a Thursday evening. I was heavily pregnant with Matthew. Adam was stomping up and down in our kitchen. He was furious; fuming. Full of the Effs. That afternoon there had been an incident at Sisters' Space. My car had been vandalised by the partner of a service-user. Adam rarely lost his temper and this wasn't anything to do with the car-damage, he said. Which was true, because I had a battered old Renault Clio at the time and it was due to hit the scrapyard anyway. But for some reason, this particular incident had really gotten to him.

"I mean, look at you – you're due to give birth in a few weeks, for God's sake! And you're doing a job like this? With a load of psycho blokes hanging around! Why can't you go and get a job in policy again? Work for the council, even!"

"It's safe at Sisters' Space, Adam. You know how much time I've spent on choosing the best security features. Come on."

"I'm not talking about them getting IN - I'm talking about what happens OUTSIDE! Like in your car park. Like some sicko nutter following you to Tesco's or summat. Like someone finding out where you live and seeing that you've got little kids and…"

"Oh, don't be such a drama queen, Adam!"

I went on to say that if he had wanted a-stay-at-home-and-mop-the-bathroom-floor-once-a-week-or-something-weird-like-that sort of wife then he had bloody well married the wrong woman. And in response to that, he grabbed his coat, got into his car and headed for the KFC in Huddersfield. Because it was nearly tea time and because he knew that it was the surest way to naff me off. Afterwards, when we had both apologised to each other and I had made him remove the empty cartons from his car, because they would stay there for at least four months otherwise, he had said;

"But it's not just about us anymore, is it, Rach? Everything we do… could potentially have an impact on our kids. That's why I finally agreed, when you wanted me to get rid of the bike. I mean, I love the fact that you're helping other mad cows like you - sort their own lives

out. I think that it's great that our two will have a mum that has a job that really does make a difference for people who're living some sort of God-awful existence. And yeah – you can call me sentimental if you like - but I can also overlook the fact that you're crap on the housework."

"Cheers for that, you sexist tosser."

"My pleasure. Yeah, I can overlook that bit, 'cause I happen to think that you're a brilliant mum. And I just don't want some dickhead wife-beater doing you in before you get to see your own kids growing up!"

"Yeah, well. Your own profession - exposes you to nothing more dangerous than dropping the odd bit of computer hardware onto your toes. Painful, perhaps… but I don't think that you can ever really understand why I do what I do. I mean - you don't exactly get an adrenalin rush with the old 'Oh, what if my internet browser won't open today' sort of problem at work now, do you?"

"Ah, Rach. That's just it. Some of us don't need the buzz of danger in the workplace. You should be keeping your craving for thrills and spills out of your nine to five, I say. Anyway."

"Anyway."

"Yeah, anyway. I'm off to wipe Lydia's bum. She's been sat on the loo for ten minutes shouting for one of us."

"Goodo. It's your turn anyway."

He turned round and gave me that beautiful toothy, crooked smile of his;

"Love ya, Rach. But think about what I just said, won't you?"

I feigned a Scarlett O'Hara southern-belle and touched the back of my hand to my forehead;

"Oh Rhett! Rhett! Where will I go? Whatever would I do without you?"

I heard the laughter and the 'Quite frankly my dear, I don't give a damn,' as he headed up the stairs in order to extract his daughter's arse from the porcelain. Meanwhile, I rubbed my distended belly as child number two attempted a spot of stage-diving onto my bladder.

And didn't all of this just seem like the most pathetic irony now? We had done all that we could to minimise the risks in our lives - and to keep an eye on the future. We had done the serious, grown-up conversations, planned for the pensions, installed a burglar alarm and even baby-proofed my dad's allotment shed.

But neither of us had ever dreamed that it would be something as daft, as spur of the moment, as Adam's hankering after a bit of one-off biking on his holidays - that would wrench our little family apart.

I remembered how that conversation had ended. Adam's voice had drifted down the stairs;

"And anyway, Rachael. You promised me way more sex if I got rid of the bike."

Followed by Liddy's high pitched tones;

"What's Waymosecks? He can't have none. He's not washed his hands, after wiping my bum."

CHAPTER 31

I smudged away tears as the squad car pulled up outside my parents' home. I had spoken to my mother over the phone, just before the police interview had taken place, so the necessary familial reassurances of my safety had already occurred. My parents had ferried the children back to their terrace in Stalybridge and were expecting me to stay the night with them.

As soon as I was through the front door, Lydia threw herself at me, employing her best am-dram use of language;

"Mother! We all thought that you were dead!"

But then she pushed me away, screwing her nose up;

"The state your hair's in! Did you try and dye it brown?"

I made a quick exit for a hot shower. I scrubbed long and hard at my scalp and then at every inch of my body. Wanting to get rid of the stench of injury and death. Shaun's blood was swirling away in rosy rivulets. And right now, I still didn't have a clue as to how badly injured he was.

I contemplated Jess. Who had told her about Shaun? Where had she been when she got the phone call? Perhaps she had been chanting an extra mass for the soul of Saint Jerome of Abergavenny, or some other transparently fake religious entity. Or maybe she was half way through running a marathon in Edinburgh for Bengali asylum-seeking iguanas.

For a second or two, I thought about calling her – 'a concerned colleague of your husband' – but then I realised that I didn't have their home phone number. That she would probably be at the hospital anyway. And that it would be the wrong motive for calling her - more of a perverse desire to hear her voice for the first time, as opposed to the genuine concern for her well-being. I wondered who would break the news about Shaun, to his other nearest and dearest - to Ozzy the Cat. Perhaps the poor, little pussycat might be so traumatised about what had happened to his father figure that it would put him off his fishy treats that evening.

I started sniggering to myself – but it soon descended into more of a maniacal cackle. And then I began to sob. But the self-pity moment was quickly averted by the sound of my mum's voice outside the bathroom door;

"I've left you some fresh clothes on the bed. I'd put them away to give you them on your birthday but now's as good a time as any. And it's not like you can fit into any of mine. Not since you were fourteen. You've always had hips from your dad's side of the family."

In the spare bedroom, she had laid out a pair of silver tracksuit bottoms and a matching t-shirt. The t-shirt instructed the reader to 'Dance Till You're Dizzy!' This was perhaps the most inappropriate early birthday present that she had ever presented me with. Because I definitely did not do the running-thing, never mind *any* form of dancing. I topped off the ensemble with one of my dad's fleeces. In solidarity with my father; 'She hates fleeces, your ma. I wear them as much as possible.'

Back downstairs, the kids had been parked out of earshot and in front of the TV. So, armed with a strong cup of tea I provided my parents with a basic outline of what had occurred inside the building. My dad listened - head cocked to one side - and then nodded slowly;

"Well. Personally speaking, I've always thought that Michael Chiswick was a bit of a willy-woofter —"

"Terry!" my mum chipped in, "That sounds rather too homophobic for my liking."

Dad continued; "Hang on, Pat, I was just going to say – but whether he's a bit of a poofter or a posh slimy git or whatever. I was going to say… that after today – I'll give the fella his dues. I stand corrected. He sounds alright. And it's not often I say that sort of thing."

My mother shook her head, irritated;

"No. Very generous of you. And anyway, as for me - I couldn't give a monkey's about what his sexual orientation is and whatever Michael Chiswick gets up to in his own bedroom…"

God, how clueless can you two be? But I'm rather glad about that, Mum. As the two of us have been shagging like a pair of sex-starved dirty dingos these last few weeks.

"Although I've never been too sure of his politics, quite frankly – he's got that big, cheesy smile thing going on there - so I can't help but think of Tony Blair when I look at him."

Cheers, Mum. Why not go the whole hog and says he reminds you of Bernard Manning? Put me off sex with him for life, why don't you?

I wanted to distract them from Michael's involvement, so I asked my mum to tell me what had been going on outside of the centre, whilst we were all still trapped inside.

"Well, we weren't in the building when it all went crazy. We'd decided to take them outside for a run around in the park. Matthew had started spitting at old ladies again and I hate it when he does that. So, we were at the swings when we heard what I suppose must have been the first shots being fired. Everyone came screaming and running out of the building. Your dad wanted to get back to the place to find you. But there were so many people… just running out of there. They were lucky they weren't trampled to death."

A baleful look from Dad;

"I did try, love. I really did. It was all just a complete…"

"I know, Dad. Don't be daft."

Mum wandered over to the kettle and flicked it on again, shaking her head.

"And of course, there were already a few coppers about the place – because of your VIP sorts. So, they were at the front door instantly - wouldn't let anyone back in. And… oh. That was the scariest bit. Not knowing whether you'd got out or whether you were still in there. Or that something worse had... I feel like I've aged fifty years in the last few hours, I really do."

Dad suddenly brightened. "You'd be doing bloody well there, Pat. You'd be a hundred and seventeen years old. Damned good innings, that."

"Oh, shut up, Terry."

She went on to outline the scenes outside;

"Police cars, sirens. Everyone standing around and fretting. Some woman from your workplace said that you'd been at the far end of the hall when the gun was fired - that you were probably still inside. So, I started thinking the worst. Well, you would, wouldn't you? But of course, having the children around meant that we had no choice other than to concentrate on them. And well, with your two – neither of them are good at being ignored, are they? Although you'd think that with living with you they'd be alright with… Anyway. Matthew was very giddy. He was quite taken with the excitement of all the police cars and the firemen. All of that."

She brought a fresh pot of tea over to us, along with the biscuit barrel. Dad prised it open, snaffling a handful of bourbon creams for himself, telling me;

"Yes. The fire engine. I took the kids over to see it. I think the driver must have felt a bit sorry for us because we said that you were still inside the building. So, they let Matthew climb up and have a nosey. And then your ma called me away for a minute because she was trying to tell one of the policemen what you were wearing - but she couldn't remember. Brain like a bloody sieve! Can't even remember what she's wearing herself, half of the time…"

Mum did the Shut-Up Terry thing with her eyes. He ignored her.

"… Anyway, the next thing we know, all hell was breaking loose, because it seemed that Matthew had been fiddling with the handbrake. And of course, we all know that he's a proper strapping little lad and all of that…"

Mum sniffed and pushed the biscuit barrel away from her.

"I'm actually worried that he's going to be obese one of these days, Rachael. The way he troughs his food."

Dad seized the barrel and helped himself to four custard creams.

"But there's no way that a kiddy like Matthew could have taken the handbrake off. I mean – come on! The leverage that you'd need to release that kind of thing! We're talking some serious traction for an HGV of that size! So, I'm betting that they didn't have the damned handbrake on properly in the first place. Doesn't make sense."

Lydia interrupted us. The sound of the biscuit barrel opening had momentarily lured her away from the telly. She helped herself to three Foxes Gingernut Creams as she complained;

"I don't know why everyone's talking about Matthew. He didn't make the fire engine move. He's just a silly baby. He couldn't even reach the steering wheel properly. It wasn't him."

I asked;

"So, what happened then, sweetie?"

She reached for a fourth biscuit, surprised that the adults were too interested in the conversation to prevent her from engaging in a biscuit-a-thon. Pocketing it, she casually remarked;

"Oh, it was all to do with that lad. The big boy. With the yellow hair. The naughty one with the flashing scooter. He'd just arrived with his brother and their little baby sister near the fire engine. The police were talking to them. And when Grandad went to tell Grandma about what clothes you had on, the fireman got talking to this woman with humongous boobs. He was leaning out of the window and smiling at her."

"Right."

"And then when the police were looking at the baby to check she hadn't been hurt, the big boy just ran over to the fire engine to us. And he hopped up onto the seat next to our Matthew. At first I thought he was covered in poo – but when I said, 'Eew – is that poo?', he said 'No, stupid, it's chocolate, get out of the way'. He was very rude actually! He pushed right in front of me - even though I was waiting for my turn to go inside the fire engine very nicely, thank you very much! But as usual – Matthew Patthew was hogging everything and being ratty and bratty…"

I nudged her back to the story;

"So, he went in front of you?"

"Yeah! He climbed up next to Matthew and he went; 'Help me pull this' and they pulled that handle thingy up and then - he jumped out again fast. And he nearly knocked me over. And then the fire engine started rolling – with our Matthew still in it! It was dead funny. But maybe a bit scary too," she admitted.

"Good thing the fireman had quick reflexes and stopped it in time, eh?" my dad commented.

"Exactly," I added. "Was Matthew okay? Was he upset?"

Dad shook his head.

"Was he buggery. He threw a right paddy with the fireman when he managed to stop it… before the damned thing ran any of the policemen over. The gob on that kid! I tried to drag him out of the cab by his legs – and then his trousers came off. So, he was shrieking and holding onto the steering wheel, in just his t-shirt and underpants."

Lydia chewed her biscuit - gob open as usual - and chipped in with;

"And then Grandad had a right row with some fat, orange lady who had a name badge what said 'Dee.' She was telling Matthew off for screaming. So, Grandad told her not to shout at his grandson. And then she called Grandad a bald old coon."

My dad shook his head.

"She said *coot*, Lydia. And I think you're confusing the word 'coon' with the word 'coot.' A coon is..."

"A word we should never really use anymore!" added my mother helpfully.

But I had switched off. No longer listening to Lydia prattling on. Things were making a bit more sense now. Mason had clearly employed a distraction technique so that he would have enough time to run back down the hill towards the centre and to get back inside the building. Without any adults stopping him.

Lydia meandered back to the living room. Mum said;

"And you should call Vicky. She knows you're okay. But I'm not best pleased with her. She was meant to be staying here tonight, but she's decided to stay in some hotel in Manchester instead. Met some fella."

My dad coughed. With purpose. Mother stood up and moved over to the vegetable rack. She prodded the potatoes and then began to pick out the ones that had started sprouting and were looking a bit too much like whiskery old men.

"What?" I spat - all incredulous. "She met a man? When? Today? Whilst all of this was happening at the centre?"

Mum began to pop the maggot-like roots out of the potatoes, using the edge of her fingernail. A significant twinge of disapproval flickering across her face;

"Well, she says that they've been seeing each other for a few weeks now. And she was all very evasive, when we met her outside your centre-place this morning. She said that this 'friend' from London had given her a lift up north – and had dropped her off there. But as it turned out - he was at your little event too! We even ended up meeting him in the park - just after it all started going hell for leather inside. Apparently - he carried her out of the building. Just picked her up and ran out with her. And it's a good job too - she would have been stuck in there otherwise, what with that pot on her leg."

Mum stamped on the pedal of the litter bin and plopped the white pile of rejected potato offspring into it. She turned to open the fridge.

"So yes. Whilst I can't say that I approve of Vicky dashing off to a hotel with him rather than staying here – because I'd already gone to the effort of making up the camp bed for her and put the brighter light-bulbs in for her like she prefers. Yes, well. Rescuing her like that... He can't be a bad egg."

"Aye," said Dad. "Bit bigger than your average egg though. More like an ostrich egg. Bloody massive bugger. And he's black."

Mum's head appeared from round the corner of the fridge door.

"And just why would you mention that, Terry? What does it matter - what colour his skin is?"

Dad got all defensive.

"It doesn't! Bloody hell, Patricia – don't start accusing me of racialism now or whatever! I just believe in describing people... how they look. Like your friend, Beryl – I'll say she's 'pig ugly' 'cause she is! And the bloke who works in the post office with the dodgy eye, I'd just say..."

I cut in.

"What's he called?"

"No idea," Dad answered. "I'm only ever asking him for stamps, or giving him your ma's bloody parcels for her Avon returns."

"No – not him. Vicky's fella, I mean."

Mum slammed the fridge door and yanked open the freezer.

"Trevor's his name." she said. "That's him. Pierced ear. But nice teeth. It'll have to be sausages, then. Can't have chicken, two nights running."

I choked on my biscuit, coughing biscuit crumbs and saliva all over the embroidered tablecloth. The linen was promptly swapped for a fresh one and it finally dawned on me that Vicky's taxi trip in the ministerial car was far less about extreme generosity on Michael's part and much more about the Vicky and Trevor factor.

Rotten sods – and Michael too. For not telling me earlier.

As if on cue, the telephone rang. It was the lady herself, calling from her hotel in Manchester. I took myself off to the hallway to speak to her. She demanded a blow-by-blow account of what had happened, telling me;

"Jesus, Rachael! I'm so glad that I only deal with microchips on a day to day basis - as opposed to society's down and outs. But have you spoken with Michael yet? I've not let on to Mum and Dad about you and him —"

"Yeah. You're good at keeping relationships top secret, aren't you? So perhaps you could ask Trevor for Michael's number. Because my phone is still at Sisters' Space and I've no idea how to get hold of him at the cottage."

But Vicky didn't miss a beat. She proceeded to tell me that;

"Yes, after everything that you've gone through today, I thought that it'd be best if I got out of everyone's way. Let you have the room at Mum and Dad's for tonight. Plus, it's nice being in the Malmaison of course. So ... Trev?" Her voice moved away from the phone, "What's Michael's number?"

There was a pause for a few seconds and then she carried on with;

"Oh, Rach – Trevor's telling me that the BBC is saying... that another person

247

who was admitted to hospital – a woman – has died from her injuries. Oh, that's awful! You'd best go and check it out, yeah? We're off to grab something from Chinatown in a minute. We're both ravenous, and it's weird, 'cause I've actually been digesting Chinese food a lot better these days..."

I zoned out. Dawn. My mind began to race with the thought of Dawn. Of Dawn dying. Of her children – who would break the news to them? So many horrible, indiscriminate and freakish incidents that had occurred in my life in the space of just a few short hours. And yet here was my sister wittering on about the Yang Sing, banquets for two and her increasing and remarkable ability to be able to tolerate monosodium glutamate. So, I got a bit snippy with her;

"Well, as unimportant as your personal life actually is to me, Vicky – in comparison to what happened in my workplace today – thanks – yeah, *thanks, Sis* – for making sure that I was the last person to know about your latest romantic liaison. Cheers for not telling me about the fact that you've been hanging around with the Special Protection branch - even more so than Michael does. And yes - whilst I go and find out whether any more of my friends or colleagues were killed today – please don't forget to call me back and let me know whether you and Trevor plumped for the Peking duck, or for the beef chow mein in the end..."

But Vicky was not one for being quick to take offence. Hide of a rhino.

"Sorry, Rachael. Life has been... a bit unusual I suppose. It all... it all just began when Trevor kept popping round to the flat to see if I was okay. He knew that I don't have family in London. It was very sweet of him. And whilst at first we just talked armoured vehicles and latest technology in one-to-one security and protection..."

"Jeez —"

"Well. It progressed quite quickly. And I didn't want to mention it on the phone to you - I thought it would be better to talk about it face to face. What with the Michael-Factor and everything. But he's – Michael's - really cool about it. In fact, he's the one that said it was best to tell you in person. Ha. Heh heh. I think that he's getting to know you pretty well, eh?"

"Hmph. Maybe. Maybe not. And look. I need to go —"

"Well, either way – I'm hoping that he'll do right by Trevor."

"What do you mean?"

"Well, both of them – Trev and Ross, too. Ross was doing the covert surveillance stuff. And they both could get into serious shit over this. Questions will have to be asked as to why Trevor didn't stay by Michael's side for the long haul. Why he carried Lady with Duff Leg out of the hall instead."

"Oh. God, yeah..."

"Yes. It's all a bit worrying. And... also - Shaun. Trevor said that this 'Shaun character' actually got shot. Jesus – I mean... is he okay?"

"I don't know, Vicky. Dunno. But I do need to go and find out. So, will you just get off the phone and go and order your dim sum, or whatever?"

A few minutes later and, with Michael's phone number discreetly scribbled on the back of my hand, I was upstairs, watching the TV in my parents' bedroom. The siege was headline news on every TV station. The version from the BBC declared;

"The dramatic gun siege that took place today in Greater Manchester, involving a senior cabinet minister, has ended in the death of two people. Michael Chiswick, Minister for Communities and Local Government, was attending a local event in the Medlock area of Greater Manchester when he and several adults and children were taken hostage by a gunman. The siege ended with the death of the gunman. And we have just heard that a second person involved in the hostage situation – a female in her early 60s – has died as a result of her injuries…"

"Oh, thank God!" I spluttered out loud, shaking my fifth mug of tea so that some of it slopped onto my mother's side of the bedspread. "Thank God, it wasn't Dawn!"

So, I was swamped with relief. But it was then tempered with guilt. Because I had never liked Councillor Casey. I had always thought her to be a po-faced, old bag. But I wouldn't have wished her any harm – well; certainly, not that level of harm. I gulped the tea down and plonked the cup on the bedside table, hugging my knees to my chest as I cradled myself on my parents' bed. Lydia's voice travelled up the staircase, shrieking with delight;

"Hey, Matthew! We're getting sausage and mash for our tea! Yeah – again! And then ice cream Mars Bars for afters! It's great when there's a disaster! They just feed you whatever you want!"

And then I heard Matthew yell back;

"Cool! Let's make another one happen!"

No doubt Lydia would be writing in her 'What I Did This Weekend' news report for school on Monday morning something along the lines of, 'This weekend I was nearly made a Norphan!!!!! And then I ate so much junk food!!!!!! That I threw up all over the second tablecloth!!!!'

The news coverage on the BBC was 'live'. The images moved to the front of the Manchester Royal Infirmary. A hospital spokesman was standing on the front steps of the red-bricked building as he confirmed the death of Kathleen Casey to waiting journalists. He went on to say that;

"… another woman - aged twenty-five - is in a critical condition. She is in intensive care and is in a coma. We also have a forty-four-year-old male with gunshot wounds who is in a stable but serious condition. And a twenty-nine-year-old female who has just been discharged."

'Stable but serious'. What did that mean exactly? I wanted to call the hospital to find out how badly injured Shaun was, but I realised that it would probably be pointless right now; the world and his wife would be calling them for more information.

Then the broadcast went 'Live to Downing Street' where a government spokesman had just begun to give a statement to the media. It was Alex The Twat. Bet he was chuffed to bits with my involvement in the entire horror-fiasco.

"I can confirm that today, Michael Chiswick, Minister for Communities and Local Government - received minor injuries in the siege that occurred at the Sisters' Space Women's Centre in Medlock, Manchester and where two people tragically lost their lives. The Prime Minister would like to express his shock and horror at what occurred today – on a day that was intended to be nothing more than a happy community celebration. He extends his utmost sympathies to all the families of those involved and would like to assure the public that there will be a thorough police investigation into the incident. He has spoken at length to Michael Chiswick, who has also provided the police with a full statement of his experience. The Prime Minister would also like to emphasise that the situation was an isolated incident, initiated by a single individual and that there are absolutely no terrorist connections or affiliated threats to national security."

Alex was doing his best to look all maudlin, all caring and concerned; little shrugs of his shoulders, a faux-weary spin doctor-esque rub of the almost-albino eyes. But I knew damned well that he didn't give a shit about the people involved. The journalists then asked who the gunman was. Alex replied; "He was a local man and already known to the police. They will be releasing further details in relation to his identity as soon as possible."

Finally, the media asked about Michael's injuries;

"He was very fortunate – he only sustained a cracked rib and several cuts and bruises." And then nodding at the camera he added, "And that's what you get for screwing around with common- as-shite biffers from up north."

Oh, okay then. The last sentence was a product of my overactive imagination and paranoid delusions.

I shuddered, switched off the tosspot's wheedling voice and vanquished his ugly mug from my parents' TV. I picked up the phone at the side of the bed and dialled Michael's number. He answered just after a few rings, telling me that he had just been about to call Trevor and ask Vicky for a landline number to reach me. He asked if he could drive over from Mottram - to my parents' place.

"No. That'd be too much for my folks in the one day," I explained.

Instead, Michael offered;

"Well, why don't you come here instead? I do need to talk to you… about everything. And I can't really do that over the phone. Obvious reasons. Is there any way that you could swing an escape route for tonight...? Stay over?"

I mused. Perhaps.

Use the Best Friend Blag.

Kate had called my parents after hearing about Shotgun City At The Women's Centre and she had already told my mother that if I needed a bit of space that night, I could kip at hers.

I trotted back downstairs. And explained what I planned to do. My mother was snipping skin between the defrosted sausages. She plonked them on top of the grill pan and nodded in agreement.

"Whatever's best for you love, after the day that you've had."

She made it sound like we had attended a Teddy Bear's Picnic at Stalybridge's Stamford Park, which had somehow resulted in Lydia being stung by a wasp and Matthew wetting his pants due to excess Fruit Shoot consumption.

"That's fine with us. Your dad can run you over to Kate's, what with your car still being at the centre and all of that. It'll only take him ten minutes to get to her place in Greenfield, won't it, Terry?"

Oh Crap. No. Not part of the plan. Tit's n' Balls.

"Terry? Terry? Where are...?"

Mum shoved the sausages under the grill and stalked away, into the lounge.

"Terry-Bloody-Stanley!"

Mum hardly ever used what she considered to be 'bad language', so when she did default to her own, odd perceived version of a profanity – you knew that she was really pissed off.

Dad was nestled in his favourite armchair. He appeared to be halfway through a bottle of red wine. Mother was all-one hand on hip and the other changing the remote control - she didn't let dad watch too many nature documentaries; "They make him a bit too frisky for my liking."

"I don't believe it! Terry Stanley! It's only six o'clock!"

"Bleedin' stressful day, Patricia – what with this lot!" nodding towards me and the children who were scowling at Grandad because he had switched 'Garfield Goes Grunge' off. "No offence, love."

I smiled. Saved by the bottle.

"Oh, none taken. I'll get a taxi. Call you tomorrow about getting the kids back off you."

For practically the first time ever, I thanked The Lord that far too many women of my mother's generation had never learned to drive and I borrowed some overnight toiletry and cosmetic gubbins off her – make-up and toiletries.

"Won't Kate be able to lend you that kind of thing?" she asked. I lied again, telling her that Kate had recently developed a terrible allergic reaction to anything other than organic hemp-based products.

"Maybe she's got thrush," Mum offered. "I've always thought that those jeans she wears are far too tight for a woman of her age. And size. I mean, she's got twin boys. She should be thinking of them – not of how her backside appears to men. None of you are getting any younger, you know…"

I picked up the phone and dialled the number for a taxi. As fast as I could.

CHAPTER 32

Fifteen minutes later and I was at Michael's cottage in Mottram.

He didn't look too bad; just a smear of lime-yellow bruising above his eyebrows and under one of his eyes - plus the cuts on his cheek which already seemed to be healing nicely. And the chipped tooth. I told him that it made him look rather charming; "Quite rakish, actually."

"Depressing, isn't it?" came the reply. "I've only had this constituency seat for three years and already I'm beginning to look like a true Manc. What with the scars on the face and the broken teeth."

"Look on the bright side," I said. "Perhaps that'll help you swing an even better majority come the next election. More people might vote for you if you look less like a southern wuss."

"Good point. Anyway. How's you?"

"I've had worse. Worse days I mean."

"I know."

Once the front door was closed, we held each other for a long time. And then we went to bed. It was very slow, very tender stuff (Michael's cracked ribs not lending themselves too well to unbridled passion). After that, it was time to feed the other appetites. Michael ordered in a take away. Only then - as we lazed on his living room floor, chomping down on Mr Chow's finest, inspired by Vicky's food preferences for the evening - did he tell me what the rest of his day had been like; nearly two hours on the phone discussing the situation.

"Certainly not the kind of conversation that I thought that I would ever have with the Prime Minister – 'Sorry, PM, that I couldn't reply to your email about the election of the new party chairperson – was locked in armed combat with a psychotic wife-beater.'"

And then we talked about the siege. I told him that I had seen most of the events through the spyhole and that I had managed to get the kids outside, to get them to the police. But that the only part of the whole event that still seemed a bit fuzzy to me, was how the situation ended – after I had fallen on top of Shaun. He tried to help me to fill the gaps;

"First off. Did you realise that Vinnie had two guns?"

"I did actually. But don't ask me what bloody make and model they were. Which you no doubt were aware of – straight away."

253

Michael grinned and helped himself to more egg fried rice;

"Glocks. Would hardly have been my weapon of choice. But anyway. Whilst he was hitting Dawn with one of the guns, he had the other one tucked down the back of his trousers. Which," he reached over and grabbed a spring roll, "was a very stupid thing to do. Especially considering his army raining. So, one can't help but suspect from his actions that Vinnie was either a pretty poor soldier - or that all the drugs had interfered with his capacity for making sound judgements. Illegal drugs or otherwise, I mean. You heard him mention Ashworth?"

I nodded.

"Yes. I caught that one. Bit of a conversation stopper."

"I'll say," Michael agreed, in between chewing. "So… we had quite a few tactical errors there on the part of Vinnie. Him putting the gun into his waistband. Him leaving the hall in order to help us with opening the doors - which we were faking a struggle with by the way —"

"Really?"

"Of course," he smiled. "We were deliberately hamming that bit of things up. I said to… our mutual friend from Medlock Council… that I hoped that you might be able to think of a way of getting you - or the kids - out of the place if we delayed things enough. And you rose to the challenge beautifully. Clever girl."

I chose to ignore his reference to me as being a 'girl'. About to hit forty is hardly indicative of being a mere slip of a lass. Normally I would have ticked him off for coming across like a patronising git. But after today - well, it was nice to be praised, after all.

"But overall," he continued, "it seems to me that Vinnie's biggest error was that he didn't really have a strategy. He made no demands of anyone, did he? He didn't ask anything of Dawn. He didn't refer to a specific incident or issue. Just this vague 'no one's taking my kids away from me' stuff. It was only when you got the children into the side room that he started ranting on about that one again. I'm guessing," he stopped for a few seconds to scoop up some black bean sauce, "that he must have been bottling up his anger. And that shortly after learning about the launch day – he decided to turn up armed. And that if Dawn was there – which in all likelihood she would be - he would have a go at scaring her. More than he even usually did."

I screwed my face up.

"Hmm. That's probably true. But for me, the crazy thing is… that I've been getting so het up about persuading Dawn to sort out an injunction against him. And now I can't help but think that, well… That it wouldn't have made a blind bit of difference. He would still have done what he did, if that was the way that his mental health – his mind - was going. And yeah - the Ashworth thing. I don't think that Dawn even knew about that."

"Who knows? But anyway. All I had to do was to pick up on the signs that he was displaying. To look for gaps in his thinking; to try and exploit them. The old military head here," he tapped his bruised forehead, "always tends to dictate the way I view situations…"

I looked towards the ceiling and gave an exasperated sigh.

"Yes, Field Marshal Montgomery. Spiffing stuff, old chap. Do carry on."

He tried to poke me in the ribs and I threatened to do it back to his own injured set, so instead he continued with;

"Right, so you would have seen through your spyhole that in the last part of the siege, we were making pretty good progress."

"Apart from Shaun getting shot, because of that imbecilic journalist."

He swallowed another mouthful of food, "Apart from that. But we managed to get past that point. Vinnie surrendering. And for me, the next step was this – to get those guns off him quick-smart. Because you can never be sure… until you're back in control of the arms."

"So, you were going to ask him to hand them to you?"

"Precisely. But then the kid comes flying into the room and comes running towards us." He paused and added more prawn crackers to his food mountain.

"And, Rachael - that's where Vinnie really came unstuck. He can't have been one of the best thinkers in the army. You know… when he and I were tinkering with his bike that time on Brindleford? He told me quite a bit about the combat he had experienced. Bosnia in 1996 with The Anvil. Funnily enough, I was there too at that point. And Northern Ireland. And later action; Iraq and Afghanistan. I mean – I had already realised that he must only have been about eighteen when he was involved in The Anvil."

"Yes, I heard you saying that to him. 'Boy soldier' – didn't you say? Is that the term that the army use for kids as cannon fodder then?"

He grinned. Getting used to my sarcastic snipes at the military by now.

"Yup. We use it to refer to the lads aged eighteen and under. So, it's no wonder he ended up a bit of a basket case – having been there, done that. But the fact is this; a half-decent soldier would have been wary of anyone running towards them during a combat situation."

I hadn't a clue what this Anvil stuff was all about. No doubt some Horror of War that men liked to sit and ruminate about. But now wasn't the time to get into it.

"What?" I asked. "A child running towards you? Of course, you might lose your focus. Especially if… it's your own child."

Michael shook his head.

"Doesn't matter. If you're carrying a weapon - you should never, ever forget that fact. And doubly so in the middle of combat. But Vinnie didn't remember. And he didn't have the wit to anticipate that Mason might be coming back – to end the siege himself. No-one ever suspects a child. That's why your Al-Qaeda and your Islamic State are more than happy to recruit children as suicide bombers."

"So, you think that Mason actually ran back into the hall to end things?"

Michael frowned and cleared the remnants from his plate.

"Yes. And he's clearly a clever child. He must have realised that he was more capable of distracting his father – perhaps even of halting the siege – than the adults were. It's just sad... No. It's utterly tragic, that he hadn't seen that only seconds earlier we had managed to persuade Vinnie to back down, already."

I noticed that Michael had used the term 'we'. I thought that it was exceedingly generous of him.

"Well, please just spell out what actually happened for me. Because I couldn't see properly from where I was."

"Ah, yes. Busily occupied between the legs of your ex-lover."

I pulled a face at him and asked;

"So, Mason ran at Vinnie, giving you the opportunity to try and wrestle the gun off him? And... you ended up shooting Vinnie?"

He breathed out heavily. He had finished most of his plate now and tinkered with the remnants.

"Yes. And no."

"What do you mean?"

Another sigh.

"Vinnie had two guns, like I said. I saw straight away that Mason wasn't trying to hug Vinnie in the normal fashion. The boy's hand went straight to the back of Vinnie's waistband."

"He was trying to get the gun?"

"Yes. Which is why I wanted to get hold of both guns as soon as possible. Hence me jumping at Vinnie."

"And so... Vinnie got shot... in the whole struggle for a gun. He got shot, by you."

"By both of us," he said softly.

"Both...?" I pushed my plate away.

"I tried... I aimed at his legs though. To take him down quickly. Not that firing at anyone, anywhere, on the body is 'safe'. No such thing. But yes – I went for the legs. In the forces, I was a bit of a crack shot. An area of expertise, I suppose."

"Oh."

"But you've never seemed to like talking about that kind of thing, Rachael."

"What kind of thing?"

"Conflict situations. War."

"Oh, yeah. Yeah, I hate war and all of that. And I hate anything to do with military... but never mind. Carry on."

"So, I haven't really spoken about it before, with you. The details of my previous career, as it were. But it can't have been all that bad, as it did get us out of a bad situation today. But anyway - back to your question. Yes, we both shot him. Mason didn't know any better. Other than go for the 'Blam, Blam!' approach. He aimed straight at Vinnie's chest – exactly at the same time that I fired. He shot him dead. Straight off, Rachael. Straight off."

"Oh, my God. He didn't. Really?"

He nodded.

We were both quiet for a minute. Then Michael added;

"I checked Vinnie's body straight away. I was going to try and do some resus... But I've seen that kind of injury before. Too many times. You just sort of know... it's fatal. There was no point. Absolutely no point. Yes, I had hit him... exactly as I had intended to. Just above the knee. Enough to have floored him. But Mason was just... blindly wanting to end the siege. By waving one of his dad's guns about."

"Mmm," I added, shaking my head. My skull felt sore, achy - full of jumbled thoughts. I took another glug of wine and the confusion began to ease; settling into more of a pattern. "No. I'm not sure that I agree with you on that. I think that Mason's motives might have been a bit more calculated."

Michael stared at me.

"How so?"

"Well. Mason didn't go to Vinnie's body. Didn't check it out. He went straight back over to Dawn. And think about it... the kid has been witness to violence in his own home from a very young age. And I know for a fact that every other film or TV series he tends to get exposed to are completely inappropriate; eighteen certification stuff. And West also gets to watch the same kind of thing. Brenda – the warden - at Lancaster House had to ban both from watching various sicko films whilst they stayed there. So, Mason had a diet of violence and aggression whether at home - or in his leisure time."

Michael was quiet. Considering this. I continued;

"But also – I would put my money on it that he didn't have a good relationship with Vinnie. The army service meant that he was away from home for most of the time. Plus, Ashworth, too. The guy was rarely near Brindleford for several years. Dawn told me that he played virtually no role in their lives. Father in name only. Or when it suited him".

"Hmmm —"

"Also – and most importantly of all. Mason isn't Vinnie's son. The other two children – West and Poppy-Rose - are. But Dawn and Vinnie met when she already had a two-year-old – Mason... and..."

I paused. Michael looked at me. "Go on."

"During quite a few of her conversations with us at the centre, Dawn said that a lot of their rows were about Mason. Vinnie's jealousy; about Mason's real father – whoever he was. Apparently, Vinnie often complained that he was trying to do his best by Mason, but that the kid caused problems."

Michael swayed his head and then slapped his forehead. Grimaced as the pain from the bruise kicked in.

"Of course. How stupid of me. The kid is blonde! Freckles. Blue eyes. The other two are clearly mixed race. Like Vinnie. How on earth did I miss that?" I laughed at him.

"Well, there aren't exactly hard and fast rules for the appearance of kids with mixed parentage," I smiled. "So, don't beat yourself up too much about that"

Michael's brow was crumpled, deep in thought.

"So, if Vinnie wasn't Mason's natural father. And if Vinnie viewed the child as … a cuckoo in the nest… and if Mason had indeed experienced all of this violence from Vinnie over the years. Well… it would be quite understandable that a young lad might…"

"… Might want to do more to liberate his mother. Might want to do more than just ending a siege."

"You know, you're quite a clever gi…"

I narrowed my eyes at him before he could finish the sentence. He got my drift.

He stood up, wincing with the pain of his injury. We began to gather up plates and containers and to transport them back to the kitchen. He mused;

"Well, all of this will no doubt be unravelled by the police. And they'll have to interview Shaun Elliot and that dreadful Erin woman, of course."

As we dumped the cartons into the bin and began to wash the plates, I told Michael about the fire engine incident. He shook his head and then grimaced again.

"Ouch. Shouldn't laugh. But your children, eh? You couldn't make it up."

"I know. But that also bothers me. What Lydia said about the way that Mason behaved in the fire engine. I can only think that he must have orchestrated it – as a bit of a 'distraction'."

He was about to reply but then his mobile rang and he glimpsed the number, mouthing 'Downing Street' at me. A call important enough to jilt me for a little while. He moved to the next room to speak more privately and the occasional word drifted down the corridor. But in comparison to our previous, rather easy-going chat over the meal, the tone of his voice had changed completely. He now sounded more than a little bit animated – more stressed - and was on the phone for twenty minutes more - giving me time to wash up, dry up, put everything away and peruse a copy of the Radio Times from several months ago. Finally, he returned to the room.

"The PM and Alex the Twat etcetera etcetera. They've been tossing ideas about - in relation to damage limitation after today's events. I need to talk to you about all of that side of things."

I was tempted to provide an off-hand comment regarding the row that we had had several weeks ago – would Alex the Twat perhaps want Lydia to take the blame for an armed siege and deaths via mortal gunshot wounds? Would cheesy religious accessories play a part in it all? But I managed to rein it in.

Michael took out his packet of cigarettes and flicked his head towards the back door. I followed him. He lit one and took a long drag on it.

"Right. It's this. Do we go public with me – a cabinet minister – being named as having shot Vinnie dead? Or do we go with what actually happened; the truth of it. That Mason shot Vinnie. Whether he meant to do it deliberately, or not."

"Why would you *not* tell the truth?"

Michael shrugged and blew out a line of smoke;

"Just my thinking. Spare the child. Spare the family the knowledge…"

"Oh, come on Michael. You won't spare him anything. You said that he was a smart kid! Right, so… say that he didn't mean to kill Vinnie, or didn't realise that it was his gun that actually caused his death; so even if you could convince him of that – what's to stop him at the age of sixteen – or someone else - getting hold of the autopsy report, the inquest files and finding out for himself?"

"True."

"And anyway. It's looking far more likely that he did it on purpose, isn't it? So… he'll know that you're lying. And one day it'll all come out in the wash - when he tells one of his mates about it or something. Not good for anyone. Not in the long run."

He didn't say anything. I remarked;

"But then you're a politician. You're probably thinking more about the short run, aren't you? Election results. Polls and jockeying for position."

Michael shook his head and stared determinedly out of the window. It was pitch black outside, but clear and cold. We could see tiny pricks of light – constellations – in the night sky.

"I'm sorry, Michael. I didn't mean that to sound… critical of you…" I tried again. "I actually think that it's very admirable, that you feel that Mason should be protected. But it would be pointless. You wouldn't be doing anyone any favours. And I also think that you'd be taking a big and very silly risk in terms of your own career."

He rubbed one of his eyes with the heel of his palm. Looking exhausted.

"Well. You're right. Of course. But that's also something else that I need to talk to you about. All of this… my involvement in the shooting today. It might dredge up stuff from the past."

"Yeah?"

"Yes. Things that only the PM and his closest know about. Things that we've managed to keep out of the public eye so far. Some of the more perceptive… the more tenacious hacks might put two and two together and come up with the right number."

"The right number… being?"

"Being… Oh hell. Meaning that I suppose it's also about time that I got honest with you."

The grandfather clock chimed the hour. Followed seconds later by a cuckoo clock in the hallway. I made a mental note to myself to try and find out how much the damned things cost. Lydia had been asking for a 'proper old-fashioned cuckoo clock – just like in Chitty Chitty Bang Bang,' for over three years now. Perhaps the Aldi in the centre of Huddersfield had a cheaper version and I could…

"Hello?" Michael waved his hand at me. "Did you hear what I just said? About me, not having been completely straight with you - with regards to… the truth."

I shrugged and shivered slightly. Smothered in my dad's XL spruce-shaded fleece. Why did Dad always insist on wearing various shades of green? Was it so that he could camouflage himself down at the allotment when Mum came looking for him? Or perhaps he was, in fact, a reincarnation of one of Robin Hood's Merry Men. I had noticed previously that he seemed to possess an irrational hatred for Kevin Costner. Only the other week he had informed Lydia that under no circumstances could she ever watch 'that crap American actor' and his version of the legend under Terry Stanley's roof, and that Errol Flynn's 'Robin' would only ever be allowed to…

"Rachael? Are you alright?"

"Sorry," I rubbed the tip of my nose. "I have this habit of… uuhhm… moving on to think about other things. When – when people are about to confess… that they've been lying to me."

"No. That's not it at all. I haven't been lying to you. Please don't think that."

I stared at him. Well spill the sodding beans then.

"Look. When I've mentioned to you in the past. Before. About me serving in the military. I wasn't just any old soldier. If that doesn't sound too… high and mighty. I was in the SAS. Quite senior. Covert ops. So, you can imagine why this isn't something that I tend to divulge in everyday conversation."

"'Everyday' meaning me?"

"No. Not at all. Come on. Just imagine what —"

He put his hand on my forearm.

"Right," I said.

Things that I had wondered about Michael over the last few weeks – conversational gaps that he hadn't attempted to fill. Even the scarring on his back. Perhaps these aspects contributed towards all of this; this small bit of the jigsaw puzzle that seemed to have been missing.

His eyes were serious. Weighing up my response.

So, this man, the nice, affable, un-child-friendly Michael wasn't all that he had led me to believe. No. He was an international man of sodding-bloody-mystery.

And I could laugh and joke and make sarky remarks about it until the cows came home. But the fact of the matter was this; that here was yet another man in my life who made a habit out of deceit, secrets and of screwing people over. And I had had enough – more than enough - of the fannying around in darkened car parks and of the lying. Of putting my own life on hold to accommodate the whims and the wants of the male species.

He must have felt my body stiffen because he moved his arm away from me.

"And, so. You don't have an opinion other than 'right' - on this matter? That's not like you, Rachael."

"Well, I do actually. But what can I say? You're a grown man. You were when you first joined… the forces or whatever you call it. You make your own decisions in life."

"I'd like to know what you think. I suppose it's a bit of a…"

"Does it matter what I think? That you earned a salary by going round and killing people? Even if you hadn't been in the SAS – if you hadn't misled me to believe that you were just Joe Plebby Soldier – well. Let's face it. That's all the army is anyway. That's what it's all about, ultimately."

"Rachael, please try and put your prejudices aside for a minute."

"Oh, frigging hell, Michael!" I snapped. "You could have maybe mentioned this to me a little bit earlier! You know my beliefs on this kind of thing by now. I mean – you know what my job involves. You know the kind of people that I'm working with. The whole point of Sisters' Space is that we're all about anti-violence. We're all about trying to look for peaceful resolutions to conflict." He interrupted me with;

"And yes. That's all very nice and something to aspire to and I agree with that, of course. But the fact of the matter is this - that in the real world, there are people like Vinnie out there. And worse. There are people like Vinnie out there who are far more intelligent than he is… was. People who are much more ruthless. And so – for the greater good – we need to be able to react to that effectively."

"Oh, please. Don't start off on an ideological ramble about Pacifism versus Just War… I simply thought that…"

He began to scratch the back of his neck in frustration. I stood up and moved away from him and directed my attention out of the kitchen window. At the view across the rolling hills.

"You thought - what?"

"That we've been seeing each other for a few weeks now. Been sleeping together. So, I kind of hoped that you could have – would have – at least told me what you used to do. For a living. I mean, I wouldn't be pissed off if you used to be a trapeze artist. Or a pig farmer. But… everyone and his dog knows what the SAS get up to."

Michael shook his head and muttered;

"Yes, give the general public a bit of exposure to Andy McNab's books and the like and they think that they know everything about it."

"Well, I've never read an Andy McNab book in my life, so I couldn't possibly comment. But anyway. Don't you think that I'm entitled to feel a bit shocked? Appalled? Annoyed?"

The slight hitch of his shoulders;

"Oh, Rachael, please. Be fair. You knew that I served in the army. Did you really need the detail of what I did? Have I asked you for the exact minutiae of your past? Things that maybe you're not particularly proud of. That leave a bitter taste in your mouth?"

I interrupted him with a toss of my head.

"Oh yes. I've got plenty of things in my life that I'm not proud about, but hand on heart I can tell you that I haven't murdered any Rag Heads or Johnny Foreigners in the last thirty-odd years!"

We both fell silent now. Michael tried again.

"Look. Please. Listen to me. All of a sudden – because of this knowledge – I can understand that you might think that I'm a different person to the one that you've been getting to know. That I'm some sort of … of Mr Hard Man SAS Guy."

"Ha!"

I didn't expand on the 'Ha', however. Because an image of Ross Kemp suddenly sprang to mind and I wasn't going to admit to Michael that I'd always had a secret thing for ol' bug eyes. He carried on;

"… But I'm not. I'm still me. And the SAS me? That was a *Me* of some years ago now. Rachael, please do remember that I was young when I joined up. Fresh out of Oxford. For me, it was the dream career. I've always had a bit of a strategic head. Like to calculate risk. I was a lot fitter and packed a lot more muscle back then. It made perfect sense at the time. And isn't one's career – isn't one's life – a journey? Aren't we allowed to change the direction that we always thought that we were heading in?"

I proffered a limp shrug and toyed with a plastic clothes peg that happened to be lying next to the sink. I wondered whether I should do 'a Matthew' and put it on my nose in order to side-track the grown-up from wittering on at me too much. I decided against it and tossed it back onto the side of the sink. All resigned, like. He put one hand on my right shoulder and then placed his other on the left. Squeezed them gently.

"I'd really like you to try and understand, Rachael. To understand why I made certain choices in my life. And why – yes – why I'm no longer doing that kind of job."

The ice was melting now. So, I asked;

"You mean you want me to understand things like... why – how - you ended up with those scars on your back?"

"Yes. It was just a job back then. But one day I realised that it wasn't a good way to be living my life. Longer term. And that perhaps it wasn't helping me to develop the kind of thinking about life... the kind of philosophy that I wanted to cling to, in my old age. And nor was it helping my fellow human beings. On a grand scale, I mean. Me living – and working like that."

"Right. So, don't tell me. You left the SAS, went on a Buddhist enlightenment retreat... and thought that mainstream politics would be the true pathway to karmic fulfilment, then? Jeez. I've heard of some odd and hopeless spiritual paths in my time but..." I started sniggering.

His mouth twitched but he was still trying to be serious.

"Come on. Don't laugh. You were very kind not to laugh at me when I showed great ignorance of your little old ladies - your Miss Simpsons - sitting in urine-soaked armchairs for months on end. It was just a job. For me – at that time in my life. But not now."

He looked me in the eyes and it struck me. He had only known me for a few weeks and already he knew how to disarm me from one of my frenzied sulks or rages. Just hug the woman. Try a joke. Listen to her. Appeal to her social conscience.

The Git.

And then when he realised that he was finally getting through to me, he kissed me hard on the mouth and said;

"Okay?"

"Okay," I mumbled and kissed him back. Harder than Mr Big SAS man was anticipating.

After a few seconds, we broke away from each other and Michael turned to drain the contents of his beer bottle.

"Right. So maybe I do owe you a bit of an apology for holding off until now – about telling you the actual truth of what I used to do for a living."

"Yes. And your apology will only be graciously accepted if you agree to not talking any more twaddle about trying to cover up the fact of what Mason actually did."

"Fair enough." He bent to kiss my nose. I added;

"And maybe I should apologise to you too. Because I've only just realised that I haven't told you how bloody amazing you were in there. In the hall, today. Really, impressive… God. I hate to use the word 'courageous' as it smacks of everything that I feel – politically and socially - in this society that we value wrongly and…"

He was rolling his eyes now. Doing the 'blah blah blah' thing. I thumped him on the arm.

"Oh alright, Michael. You had courage. Shitloads of it! Wow! Zowee! And all of that."

He smirked. "You didn't do too badly yourself. For a girl." I cuffed his ear and he dodged me. "My, for a woman of non-violence, you're really not helping your cause. And anyway…" he said as he placed the empty bottle onto the draining board. "Even your old buddy Shaun Elliot showed a bit of courage out there. And I've just heard that he's doing alright, actually. Nothing to worry about on his side of things. He'll patch up nicely."

He was hovering, waiting to see my reaction. So, I smiled a brief, non-committal grin.

"Oh. That's good – that's really good. I did try and call the hospital myself – but couldn't get through. That's a relief."

"Yes," agreed Michael. He looked away and continued with. "Certainly is. He was quite the big, plucky fella. I've seen trained men go to pieces in less of a situation. He even jumped in front of that silly tart Erin Mayo. Quick reflexes. Brave stuff. And quite changed my opinion of him actually."

"Really?"

"No. The man's a dick."

And on that note, we went to bed.

CHAPTER 33

In the morning, over toast and marmalade (me) and six shredded wheat (Michael) we talked about Trevor and Ross and their absence from the hall. They had been ordered to take time off until the Met Police's Special Protection branch had investigated why and how Michael had been separated from them. Both were shaken by the events and had apologised to Michael. He said;

"I actually don't blame either of them. As you saw – it was utter chaos in the hall when Vinnie started firing."

But Michael knew that Trevor's actions would not be viewed with such sympathy by the powers that be. And apparently, the same level of scrutiny would be directed at Ross – both men were faced with the very real risk of having the accusations of 'neglect of duties' levelled at them. Even though they both could have been killed if they had stayed in the hall.

"It's crazy," I told him. "Having to investigate their actions. Because if they had tried to intervene… Surely that would have been much more dangerous for everyone? I mean, you can save your own bacon. Quite obviously."

"Special Protection wouldn't see it like that," he said, shaking his head, "because – come on - most cabinet ministers would have been totally helpless in such a situation. Orders are orders."

So, even though Ross had managed to yank dozens of the less-startled and more-curious by-standers out of the hall and even though he was first on the scene to assist Councillor Casey once she had been put outside the exit doors, the overriding concern of Special Protection would be that both men may have acted in direct contravention to what they were supposed to be doing. In short, Michael told me – it wasn't their job to be helping Joe and Josephine Public.

I got angry.

"Well then. It sounds like a shit job to me. Even if they are on a good whack."

My irritation was curbed by his next statement – that he could come in for criticism himself – as it would be on record with Special Protection that Vicky had travelled up to Manchester, in the ministerial car with them. He wondered aloud whether some might see it as him encouraging Trevor to become distracted, from his job.

"Oh, bloody hellfire. Really?"

"Yes, but I think that I've got a good story. Well, an alternative spin on things."

Michael told me that after the formal interview with the police, the DI let slip that there had been 'a bit of a kerfuffle' at the entrance to the building where Ross had been stationed. That Erin Mayo and her camera guy had been trying to get in and that the receptionists tried to turn them away, informing them that press were not allowed inside. But clearly, the journalists got through anyway. Apparently, the police seemed to be thinking along the lines that thanks to all the argy-bargy, Vinnie must have sneaked past the receptionists.

"See where I'm going with this, Rachael?"

"Yeah. Both Sandra and Cerys know what Vinnie looks like. They would never have allowed him access. So, yeah. All of that sounds a bit more acceptable than Ross neglecting his duties. Yes, nice one. Let's blame the press!"

"And furthermore - do you remember when Mason and his brother were shrieking about being on the TV?"

I nodded and Michael reminded me that the crowd had suddenly surged forward to try and get their own mugs on the telly. He told me that for a few seconds, he and Trevor were separated from each other and that if Trevor had tried to get back to the minister's side he would have been directly in Vinnie's firing line. And whilst it was Trevor's job to assess risk and to protect senior politicians;

"It isn't about him taking a bullet for us. So, as it was, Trevor took the next viable option - which was to get vulnerable people – i.e. your sister – out of the hall. As fast as he could. Anyway, that's what I'll be saying to Special Protection and at any inquiry."

I was impressed and told him so. He shrugged the praise off with;

"Thank you, but there's no need for thanks. It's what I do for a living. I make things sound more impressive than they actually are."

With breakfast now being completed, Michael proposed to try and impress me again. But as we stood up to leave the table and to return to the bedroom, his mobile rang. He took the call. Lots of "uh-huh," and "I see" and then he hung up, explaining;

"Marvin," with a sigh. "Alex the Twat has been onto him. Marv and the boys want me back in London, pronto. Bit of a tête-àtête about spinning a good story. Making the most of everything."

I did propose that Number Ten get with the twenty-first Century and discuss such matters via Skype or Facetime or whatever. But apparently, this sort of thing was no-go. Michael in the flesh was all that they would settle for.

"Which is a shame, as I was planning on staying up here for a few days. There's only another week before recess ends and the House sits again. Thing is as well… Medlock police said that I might be needed for further enquiries."

"Right."

"But… it can't be helped. The police up here will just have to send someone down to London to grill me further if they need to. And I'm sure as dammit that

Graham the Griper won't be dragging me out to any constituency fêtes today, as originally planned. The poor chap nearly had a heart attack yesterday. It's going to take him ages to recover from all the excitement. The biggest thrill that he's ever been exposed to before, in the world of local politics, was when a bag of icing sugar burst all over his new suit at the sugar factory tour in Droylsden."

I nodded.

"So, I'd better head back to the Big Smoke."

I nodded.

I understood. Of course I did. And yet.

He finally realised.

"Oh, Rachael. Here I go again… we'd planned to try and spend some time together this week before the bloody recess is over. Just the two of us. And now it's all gone tits-up. Oh, Christ. I'm sorry."

I shook my head.

"No. I'm the one who should be apologising. Me getting you to support us lot at the Women's Centre has ended up with things getting so crazy. So, messed up for you."

He pulled me towards him. Brushed toast crumbs from my lips.

"Don't be ridiculous. But yes, let's try and think about all of this positively. It might be more helpful – for everything – if we both tried to lie-low for a few days. Away from each other, I mean. Because you can just imagine the story the press would cook up if they get a whiff of the two of us being an item."

So yes, it all made sense. Perfectly logical. And therefore, I tried my best to shrug off the irrational emotions. To do the Michael Thing. To act all cerebrally-driven, rather than operating on emotional impulse. To stop being a wuss. But as we said our farewells to each other just an hour later, I couldn't help but hear an echo; a reverberation, a hangover from the past and a dangerous reminder. That someone whom I was far too keen on, wanted their involvement with me to be kept contained. A secret.

Shades of Shaun.

So, it was a swift farewell from a minister on his mission down south. And it was an even more hurried bon voyage to my parents. I gathered my offspring with rapid speed as I thanked my folks and quickly bundled the twosome into the car.

On the drive back home I chewed over the fact that yet again, the fallout of my life - and more precisely my workplace - would be resulting in headlines for Michael. But right here and right now, I was surprising myself. I didn't really care too much about all of that. Perhaps after the Brindleford biker situation and after the Jesus badge fiasco, I was becoming hardened to the calamities that my little family seemed to be inflicting on Michael's political life.

267

And maybe I should also be looking at it another way. Rather than feeling sorry for Michael (correction – rather than feeling *guilty*) about the Russell Familial Effect, perhaps I should be viewing it from another paradigm. What if the Right Honourable Michael Chiswick happened to be the dodgy ingredient in my life? The element responsible for hurtling the various crises in my general direction.

I asked myself what Adam's thoughts on the matter would have been. No doubt something along the lines of "Well, Rachael, the bloke's got a decent bike. So, he'll not be a bad 'un."

Something that he had once said about Shaun.

After a cheap and quick Sunday lunch - baked beans on Ryvita as we had run out of bread - the doorbell chimed. Detective Inspector Dave Garratt and another man were standing outside my home, pretending that they were not examining the number of empty wine bottles in the recycling box.

"Yes, I know' said the DI. "I'm like a bad penny. Rachael - meet Detective Les Forsyth. We decided to pootle on over here to see you, rather than drag you back to Medlock on your day off."

"Nice little Sunday afternoon drive actually," commented the other man. He was tall and skinny in his navy rainmac, and he sported tiny wire-rimmed spectacles. All very 1990s.

"Yep," added Dave. "Gorgeous up on the moors there. Can see why you defected from the Lancashire side to live on the border. Can almost forgive you for being Yorkshire these days."

I did my best to smile warmly, but my heart was flipping like a fish gasping for air. I ushered two nosey children away from the door and into the lounge, shoving some Disney-tosh on to distract them. I tried to appear relaxed, to act the genial hostess. But it's always unnerving; having the police visit you at your own home, only twenty-four hours after you've been held hostage in a workplace siege with accompanying dead body count. I sat the pair of them down in the kitchen with a cup of tea and a plate of Lydia's favourite Party Ring biscuits and the DI told me that Dawn had regained consciousness and kicked the coma into touch. Cue relief all round. And me offering a silent prayer to the God of Hard-Arsed Mancunian Women. I asked about her kids.

The DI gulped a mouthful of tea.

"With their grandmother. And yes, the children. Well, that's why we're here really. Mason Hibbert to be more precise. We interviewed him this morning. Yesterday the doc's ended up giving him a sedative - after what he went through. So, it was a very gentle interview of course – the kid being only eleven."

I nibbled a biscuit. I noticed that Les Forsyth was dunking his Party Rings into his tea. Big baby.

The DI carried on, more of a musing this time;

"So, Rachael, well - we've known each other for quite a few years, haven't we? And normally I wouldn't be relaying this kind of information to another witness involved. Not so soon, anyway. But I wanted to gather a bit of background on the lad. And you're the obvious person to ask."

"Fine. Ask away."

Here the DI coughed and made eye contact with the other detective. A smidgen of embarrassment seemed to be hovering over the table.

"You told us, Rachael, that you didn't see who fired what gun. But given that... given that... your er – you seem to be quite friendly with Mr Chiswick, shall we say... given that..."

"Oh, for God's sake, Dave! This is me, remember? Don't beat around the bush."

Les grinned, eyes cast down into his mug of tea where a Party Ring had fallen foul of too-long a dunk. Dave harrumphed again.

"Righteo. Given that you two are good pals. I imagine that by now you know what *did* actually occur in the hall?"

"You mean that Mason fired the fatal shot – rather than Michael? Yes. I do know that. Now."

Then he informed me that Mason's version of events had chimed exactly with what Michael had told the police about the gunshots. And the autopsy had already been carried out on the body – confirming the same; Mason had fired the shot that had killed Vinnie. He went on to ask whether I found this fact to be surprising, or not. I paused before answering. Wanting to play fair by Mason, but also mindful of the fact that I had no idea whether the detectives were privy to information in relation to Michael's own former gun-wielding career. If I blurted out "Yes, it's certainly quite startling – but what really surprises me is that Michael turned out to be a crack shot and hostage negotiator for the SAS! Wow! I mean - how spectacular is that?" it might not go down too well with Michael, if he was still not wanting his cover to be blown. So instead I said;

"Well... in that any child shot an adult. Yes, that does surprise me. But given Mason's background... given ..."

DI Dave finished my sentence off for me.

"You mean, given that the kid grew up with an ex-con - a violent bastard as his father-figure– a man who was in and out of Ashworth – given that the kid was born and bred on the shittiest housing estate in Manchester... along with having a mother who would probably never get shortlisted for the Parent Of The Year award? Given that —"

"I don't really know, Dave. About Mason. I couldn't tell you much about his personality, really..."

But again, my mind wandered back to the day when I had first met the three children at the hostel. I told them about Mason and West - their eyes glued to the TV screen; Scarface. Both clearly knowing the entire dialogue off by heart. That Dawn seemed to be pretty free and easy about the viewing habits of her eight and eleven-year-old boys. That most of their conversation seemed to be a little bit too peppered with references to violent films. But that at the end of the day, tens of thousands of kids get to watch films like that. And they don't turn around and deliberately shoot someone.

I moved to a kitchen drawer to fetch a teaspoon for Les. I could tell that he was wanting to scoop out the sludgy biscuit and enjoy the gloop. He seemed the type.

Les smiled gratefully and I continued;

"What I think might have been more important factors in all of this, could have been that the kids - the boys – had exposure to guns. When I first met them, I remember them talking about Vinnie having a 'Glock.' It took me a second to figure that one out. I'm not exactly a big fan of weaponry myself."

"So, I see," murmured Les, as he eyeballed the 1970s CND poster on my kitchen wall.

I told them that it seemed to me - that the biggest element in what happened might well be the fact that Vinnie wasn't Mason's real dad. And that the lad had been witness to countless beatings of his mother over the years; that he must have been feeling totally defenceless and utterly ineffective – when faced with a bastard like Vinnie, kicking his mum about every few days. And then suddenly there he was, trapped in that little side room with me and his siblings – and to the four of us crouching there, it had very much been looking like - and sounding like - Vinnie had killed their mother.

"So, maybe," I offered. "It isn't too surprising that he wanted to get back into the hall, to throw Vinnie off his guard. To have a try at shooting him."

"Hum. I tend to agree." The DI considered this, stroking his chin. "And when we interviewed Mason he did display a disturbingly good knowledge of gun technology… of terminology."

Les took his seventh Party Ring (Lydia would be hopping mad to find an empty packet later) and chipped in;

"Sorry though, Rachael – but I do think you're being a bit generous here. And not just with the biscuits."

"How do you mean?"

He bit into it, crunching the pink, marbled icing.

"A lot of people will look at it like that, of course. Be thinking about Mason, saying 'Poor kid – what he must have gone through! Who can blame him for shooting that bastard and wanting to protect his mum?' But let's go back to the fire engine incident."

"Oh yes. I needed to tell you about that. It wasn't my two. Lydia told me that it was Mason who caused the damned thing to start rolling away! And…"

Les took his glasses off and started wiping them with a handkerchief;

"Well, it livened up a not-so-dull-already day. That was for sure. Nearly running DI Garratt over here… along with several other of our finest members of the force."

The DI nodded and muttered to himself,

"That reminds me. The wife keeps nagging. Must get the wills sorted."

Les pointed his spectacles at me and continued,

"Well – yes, your daughter was right about all of that. Mason admitted that he wanted to get the police out of the way so that he could get back into the building. And that he tried to enlist the help of the kid in the fire engine – your little lad - to do it. For me… that is a *big* cause for concern. He wasn't bothered about putting the lives of others at risk. See?"

We were all quiet for a moment.

"You're right," I said. "And I think that – if you haven't already done this – that the police should be asking social services to carry out a full psychological assessment of Mason. And of West too."

Dave nodded. "Good one. Be handy for the IPCC too. Covering ourselves. The inevitable inquiry,"

"Woah," I said. "Why on earth is an inquiry needed?"

"Chief Constable wants it all nipping in the bud, before someone accuses the force of putting innocent members of the public at risk. There's already been consternation over whether there were misunderstandings between Mr Chiswick's security team and our lot. Allegations that between us, we didn't communicate effectively beforehand."

"Ah, I see."

Les offered, with a sigh;

"Yes, transparency is the order of the day at our place. So, that was another reason as to why we wanted to get ourselves over here, pronto - to check out a few things with you – before we have the IPCC lot crawling all over our offices. We needed to check out all lines of enquiry."

"We know, of course," said the DI. "We know, of course – a little bit of the background to the er… 'relationships' involved. That Mr Chiswick met Vinnie Murray previously. When he was on Brindleford… erm assisting an elderly lady. In the company of erm, you… And then Dawn Hibbert and her lot arrived at the hostel. And you all ended up helping her and her family. With photographs er… later appearing in the national press of…"

I fixed him with a steely glare. Daring him to accuse me of being The Blonde In the Photographs. He took the hint and continued with;

"So… do you think that Vinnie turned up at Sisters' Space to try and threaten you? *You* personally, I mean. For helping Dawn out? For assisting her to get away from him?"

I pursed my lip before I answered decisively, with a "No."

"What makes you so sure, Rachael?"

"Because when we were all lying on the floor – he definitely knew who I was. But he didn't single me out for anything. His anger was directed at Dawn. Sure – he had a go at the journalist and clearly, he didn't feel any remorse for shooting Kath Casey. But he wasn't interested in me. Called me an 'interfering bitch' or something or other. But that was as far as it went."

"Right. So, any further thoughts on why he chose the launch day – of your chocolate shop thing – to turn up like the O.K. Corral?"

I shrugged.

"The only thing I can think of, is that he got wind of the fact that Michael Chiswick was going to be there. After their first little encounter - when he mistook Michael for a vicar – Vinnie soon realised who he really was, after the photos in the papers. Maybe he wanted to re-establish a connection with him. Celeb culture stuff going on there? There were a few things that he said that made me think that he had … respect for Michael. Probably the 'all lads together in the army' thing going on for him. And he even turned up to Sisters' Space the other day, asking for Michael's number so he could talk to him about his carburettor problems." Dave shook his head in disbelief at me. I carried on, "But either way, if your lot had taken a bit more of an interest in the kind of things that Vinnie was doing to Dawn - then maybe it wouldn't have ended up like…"

The DI held his hands up;

"Now, now, Rachael, love –you know how bloody difficult it is. Did she ever get an injunction out against him I mean? No. And sure - the guy had done time in Ashworth for some pretty serious stuff that I won't go into now. But at the end of the day. If a woman doesn't report it – what can we do? It's like the…"

I interrupted him.

"Okay. Alright. Let's not go there right now. We've both been around the block enough times on this one. Let's save it for another day."

And no matter how much I could try and accuse the police of neglecting their duties with regards to women being beaten by their partners, no matter how crap the current legal system was for a woman wanting to flee from domestic violence, it still rankled deeply with me; it pissed me off good and proper - that even if I had managed to get Dawn to enact an injunction against Vinnie - the whole damned disaster would probably have happened anyway.

'Cause life can be like that.

Both detectives stood up, ready to leave. Les snaffled the last Party Ring (greedy-guts) and I walked them to the front door. As they strolled down to their car, the DI turned round to me and said;

"And just so that you're aware, Rachael, it's best for you to be prepared for having to answer yet more questions before the whole thing has had a line drawn under it. The IPCC are buggers for going over stuff a million times."

"Yup."

"But whatever, I'll be keeping any… unnecessary information about your personal life out of the picture … so far as I can."

Les was pretending not to listen and, instead, was examining the wrought iron work on my garden gate. Polite chap. Dave gave me a wink as he opened the driver-side door;

"And actually… I do hope that things work out with your minister bloke. He's alright. And that's more than I can say for the rest of his lot. Bunch of tossers."

I smirked, almost feeling obliged to try and stick up for 'Michael's lot' but I wasn't really a party-political animal these days. Dave and I went back a long way, so I didn't think twice about calling out to him;

"Oh, forget about the politics, Dave. I'm just with him for the sex!"

But I hadn't banked on my next-door neighbour putting her milk bottles out on her front doorstep at that particular moment in time. Poor old Mrs Finnigan very nearly had a nasty accident.

After the boys in blue had departed over Holme Moss, I carried on with allowing the children to engage in back-to-back viewing of kiddy films. Hell, all normal rules and modicums of behaviour had flown out of the window this weekend, after all. I decided to check the telephone answering machine. My home landline had barely stopped ringing since we had arrived back, but as per usual, what with running around after the children, I hadn't bothered to answer it. It turned out that there were a dozen or so messages left by various newspapers – all of them wanting an exclusive interview with me, thanks to my credentials as manager of Sisters' Space and Gun Hostage Lady. And then there were plenty more from friends who were worried about me, along with the inevitable distressed call from Adam's parents, who my mother had eventually been able to reassure. The penultimate message came from Jake Bamber;

"Rach! I just saw some footage of you on the TV – you were leaving the centre with the police! So, you must be okay! Ooh... stop shouting at yourself, Jakey… remember the hangover. Got the worst hangover of my life! Again. But oh, dear Lord, Rachael! The things you get involved with! Anyway. You were looking quite glamorous considering. New frock? I do hope that you've washed your hair though by now. It was looking a bit icky. So… call me. I need to know why the hell all of this happened. Although working class alienation theory will no doubt be at the root of it all."

Bless him. Daft swine.

But the last message caused me to take a sharp breath, to sit down. It was Big Jim. Adam's best mate. Jim who had been on the back of the bike with Adam and had been with him in the last few minutes of his life. Jim who still blamed himself for Adam's death. His voice was muffled, was cracking with;

"Thank Christ, oh thank Christ, Rachael - that you're alright!"

I allowed a trickle of a tear, over that one.

And then I spent half an hour catching up on the TV coverage of the previous day's events. The media focussed on statements from Downing Street, from various police personnel and from Shaun's boss, the Chief Executive of Medlock Council. Roger Dawson stood on the steps of the Town Hall as he answered the press' questions. He expressed his 'profound shock and distress' at the death of Kathleen Casey, who he described as a 'woman of integrity, drive and compassion'. Which wasn't exactly how I remembered her, but there you go. He explained that Medlock Council had been supporting the Sisters' Space service financially, outlined the reasons behind the day's celebrations and emphasised that Shaun Elliot was expected to make a full recovery. He went on to say that he couldn't answer any questions in relation to the gunman and when pressed by reporters to comment as to why the siege might have taken place, he replied;

"Well, I'm afraid that your guess is as good as mine at this early stage. But we have to remember that centres like this will always attract women who are involved in abusive relationships with unstable men".

I was gobsmacked. And then I was incandescent. He might as well have said that the women's centre had been deliberately breeding a pack of women who 'bring it on themselves'. Yep – sieges, guns, hostages and real-life death. We're up for it, ain't we sisters?

Shaun had been wrong after all. Roger was not as thick as pigshit. He was simply a total and utter dick.

Thinking about Shaun again, I called Manchester Royal Infirmary, to see if I could find out anything further about his condition, but the phone seemed to be constantly engaged. I decided to try later.

Turning back to the TV, I flipped from the BBC and over to the twenty-four-hour news channel. I was more than a little bit taken aback to see Dee's chunky form on the screen. Yes – our very own Dee; wildcard extraordinaire. On my parents' telly, the day before, I had caught a flash of her being interviewed outside the centre by the TV stations. Dee had been more than happy to find her fifteen minutes of fame; she was someone who couldn't care less about her anonymity and who wasn't worried about her violent partner seeing her mug plastered up there on the plasma - given that he was safely behind bars, after all. And today it looked as though the national media were trying to milk the last dregs of yesterday's news, tracking down the previous day's interviewees who lived on the estate closest to Sisters' Space. The coverage was 'Live' and Dee was slouching back up her front garden path, accompanied by three of her children. They had just been to the supermarket, if the number of carrier bags were anything to go by, and a male reporter called to her from over the dilapidated wooden fence;

"Denise - the police haven't yet identified the identity of the gunman. So – following your interview with us yesterday - could you tell us who it was? Was it one of the partners of the women who use the centre?"

She didn't even bother to look around as she unlocked the front door. Just swung her arm behind her and gave them the finger - already fed up with the media hoo-hah by the looks of it. Or perhaps she did feel a smidgen of loyalty towards Dawn and the kids after all – because let's face it, anyone who had anything to do with Sisters' Space would know who the gunman had been by now. Either way, she wasn't the only person wanting to get rid of the journalists because there was a sudden yell from one of her kids, sounding something like;

"Piss off - you scumbags!"

And something that looked suspiciously like an open can of lager hurtled itself towards the camera. The 'Live' footage disappeared into a black fuzz. Nice.

I switched the TV off and went to see what my own children were up to.

CHAPTER 34

Monday morning. But not my usual start to the week. I was still car-less and so my dad had offered to drive over from theirs at six AM to help us out;

"Rachael, there's not many people I'd do that Saddleworth moor drive in the dark for, but these things can't be helped when you've bred accident-prone children like you and our Vicky turned out to be. Plus of course, there's that smashing bacon butty van on the Greenfield Road on the way over here. So, I had a little stop-off on the way. But don't tell your ma. I'm sick of her whinging on about my cholesterol."

We deposited the children even earlier than the norm at the child-care and half an hour later my dad had dropped me off at Sisters' Space in Medlock;

"There's that award-winning pork pie shop just off the ring-road on the way back. Don't tell your ma, though."

And in many ways, Monday morning at Sisters' Space was proving to be very different. Bev, Jade and Gemma had turned up early to help clear away the mess left after Saturday's events, which meant that Jules the cleaner wasn't half as po-faced as I had expected her to be, after encountering the state of the place, what with all of the rubbish left behind by the panicking crowd. Some of the police's crime scene tape remained outside the building and the hall itself was still completely out of bounds – with the yellow tape criss-crossed across the door and the obligatory policeman on duty. I jerked my head towards him;

"Has he been here all weekend?"

Jade nodded. "Yeah, well - outside. Marsha locked up on Saturday night after they had to do all of that forensics shit. They've had police shifts outside here the last twenty-four hours, so he's only just got inside now. Poor bloke – he were freezing! So's I just brewed up for him. He said the rest of the cops will be here in half an hour to be doing some more checking; to be talking to the people who were 'ere. Just keep 'em away from Dee though won't you, Rachael? You know how she hates the pigs. An' now she hates the journos too —"

"Ah yes. I saw her family's little performance on TV yesterday."

Bev chimed in;

"Yeah. Feelin' a bit persecuted by the media – like she's Angelina Jolie or summat. Daft bint. Right, well, anyways. I'll do reception until Sandra trucks up. Oh… and I gotta tell you, Rach. I've been frettin' all weekend. Was gonna call you. But I didn't have your number."

"Fretting about what?"

"Keys. Remember me takin' yours off you and lockin' all the internal doors?

Well. I can't bloody find 'em anywhere. Swear to God they were in me pocket. Our Gaz says I'm gettin' early onset dementia."

"Oh. Don't worry, Bev. I've got them. Sort of found them. Not your fault."

"Yeah? Wow! How did that 'appen?"

"That's one for another day I think."

"Right. Well anyway. Gill just called before - to say she'll be a bit late as she got stuck on the Princess Parkway. So's I told her whichever gay member of the Royal Family that she's been havin' a sticky-shag with at this time in the mornin' is none of my business…"

Whilst Bev took up her post on reception, the other two women followed me to my office, providing me with snippets of further information and random gossip; "Bugsie Bradshaw says that Vinnie went mental 'cause Dawn told him that Poppy-Rose weren't his. But I'm not havin' that. That little girl's a dead ringer for her arsehole of a dad," and "Face painter woman says that one of Dawn's kids nicked a tenner from her cash box – but that she won't be doin' nowt about it, 'cause the lad's probably been traumatised for life now. An' a juvenile record for petty theft won't really be helpin' matters," and "speakin' of money, Rach – we thought we'd left all the cash inside, when we legged it out of the hall. But guess what? That Marmaduke Magician bloke produced the entire takings of both the tombola AND the lucky dip from his top hat - when we were all stood outside in the park. Guys a fuckin' conjurin' genius!"

I unlocked my desk drawer and grabbed my handbag, telling them;

"I've got to go out and clear up a few things this morning. You okay to hold the fort until Gill arrives?"

"No worries, Rach" said Jade "But just so yer know… once the police an' forensics say it's okay for us to go back into the hall again. Well. Jules is sayin' that she won't go anywhere near it. Says it's not in 'er contract, moppin' up blood from dead people. An' that if she'd wanted to be doin' that sort of stuff she would've gone an' worked for Medlock morgue. Or for Man City."

I nodded. Jules had always been a bit too jobsworth for my liking. But then again, she was probably right. Your average cleaner's pay wasn't enough to remunerate the scrubbing up of dried blood and guts. I fished out my mobile phone and jotted down the number of DI Garratt for them.

"Tell him that I asked you to call him. That we need to know when the police's deep cleaning team will arrive. Tell him we've got women and children needing to use the hall in the next few days. Of course, it might well be that the women… may not want to use the hall now. But that's not the point." Gemma took the piece of paper and looked at it;

"Think they will, Rach. Everyone what we've spoken to are, like – adamant about staying here at Sisters' Space. We're all feeling like… more solidarity than ever - against the patriarchy and against misogynistic behaviour."

"An' I mean, where else are we gonna go?" added Jade. "Where else can yer get shit biscuits an' get to watch the telly for nowt? I'm up in court next week for not havin' me TV licence."

They went off to make the phone call to the DI.

I slung my handbag over my shoulder and went out to the car. It was damned cold inside, so I started the engine and tried to generate a bit of heat. And then I began the task of checking my mobile. There were no less than thirty missed calls, twenty text messages and ten voicemails. Just as it had been with my home answering machine, it was more than a little bit disconcerting to hear the messages left by anxious friends. I sent a mass message to all my phone contacts that said;

> *By now you'll all know I'm fine. Any £ you can offer us at Sisters' Space wd b apprectd. We need it. Pls tell others*

Hell – why not turn a disaster into a generic and ongoing appeal for funding for an important charitable cause? Sir Bob Geldof had managed to get away with it, and he lacked both my charisma and affability. Although I must concede that he is a little bit better at ironing than I have ever been.

And now for the next challenge. Before work that morning, I had finally managed to speak to the nursing staff at Manchester Royal Infirmary and then it was;

"I'm sorry but we can only disclose the condition of a patient to close relatives."

Infuriating.

So I had given up the ghost on that one and decided instead to hop across town and to brave the hospital itself. I snuck my farty little car into what seemed to be the last available parking space - no doubt causing the fella in the big Eff-Off 4WD in front of me to jealously covet a 1000cc engine for the first time in his entire life - and once inside the main building I managed to track down the relevant wing and then the correct floor and ward. When I got to the security doors at the end of the corridor, I decided that I would brazen it out and claim the prized 'relative' status.

"I'm here to see Shaun Elliot," I told the person on the other end of the intercom. But the faceless lady didn't even ask who I was and I was immediately buzzed in. And then I waltzed right past two nurses who were otherwise occupied with looking befuddled about something on a computer screen. So, within a couple of seconds I had located the correct room.

Ah. The glories of our NHS.

As per usual, Shaun had ended up with the best deal going. This will be where they shove the VIPs, I thought. Or perhaps the trouble makers. It was a private room, but it had glass observation windows, which at that precise moment in time, I was very grateful for - because they prevented me from walking slap-bang into an encounter that I would not have particularly relished.

A willowy frame leaned over the end of Shaun's bed, smoothing out the sheets. She had dark russet hair, shaped into a neat, glossy bob and she wore a short, stylish raincoat with belt yanked around the waist, emphasising that oh-so-svelte figure. Funky, pillar-box red calf-length boots matched a shiny handbag which had been placed at the foot of the bed. Although we had never met, I recognised her straight away. Even though I had only ever seen a couple of images of her before.

The first photo that I had been exposed to had been courtesy of the internet; something or other in relation to her assisting with abused alpacas or replanting the rainforest or whatever it was that her top-notch job working for a large and much-celebrated NGO usually entailed. And yes, I *had* been unashamedly noseying about to see what she looked like. In the past, Shaun had never been the sort to have pictures of his loved ones in a wallet or as a screen-saver.

So, needs-must, I had figured, leading to me stumbling across the online photograph of her. And the other time – more recently - I had noticed a picture of her on Shaun's desk in his office at Medlock Town Hall. But perhaps the framed photo wasn't entirely Shaun's idea. Perhaps she had presented it to him as a Christmas present one year; 'For your desk, Shaun. It's me with Gurgles the Gorilla in Uganda. You always said that this was a cute photo of us both!' Or maybe I should just face facts; Shaun thought that his wife was a bit of a looker and wanted all and sundry to know about it.

Whatever. Damn Her. Because she had looked to have been attractive enough in that framed portrait, but everyone knows that the camera can lie for a one-off snapshot of your wife, that you don't mind the odd colleague seeing. But now, here she was in real-time, bearing more than a passing resemblance to Jackie Onassis – wide spaced dark, liquid eyes. Immaculately turned out. The woman possessed it; that alluring balance between style and the understated. And she topped it all off with that luminous halo blushing above her head. Or could the latter just be a product of my overactive imagination?

I moved back from the observation window, but I was unable to look away. Transfixed by the scene. This was something that I had never witnessed before. Not just Jess in 4D, but here was Shaun with His Wife. Be a dispassionate observer, I told myself. Don't let your emotions rule the roost. You're not the brazen type, not the sort of woman to storm into a room and to use it as a chance to unload years of bitterness and bile.

You're not the sort to slink into their presence and make pokey; suggestive remarks, stirring the pot.

And anyway. It was over long ago with Shaun, wasn't it? Eons, long gone. Yonks and donks ago as they say in Manchester. This little, private viewing should mean nothing to you.

But bollocks to all of that. Oh, how it smarted. Seeing her move - seeing Saint Jess walk and talk and adjust her knickers - because she thought that no-one was looking. It nipped at me one hundred times more than seeing a cute photo-of-her-with-orphaned-meerkat could ever do.

She finished off with the straightening of the NHS' bulk-buy bed linen and then moved up to concentrate on Shaun. She dropped a kiss onto his lips and rubbed his cheek. Kissed him again. And then I heard her soft voice, the hint of a Scouse burr;

"See you later then, sweetie. I'll bring you some pyjamas."

I had never thought that she might be a Scouser. Shaun had never mentioned this. Not that I've got anything against Scousers, you understand – but there's been nearly two centuries of a long-running feud between the more ignorant Mancunians and their Pudlian cousins. So, it does tend to colour the way one might think about those sickeningly ever-cheery sorts over there in the rival city. Even if you like to think that you're above all of that.

But then she moved towards the door, so I span round abruptly, pretending to read posters about MRSA and prostate cancer on the opposite side of the corridor. She clicked past me in those expensive-looking boots. I counted out sixty seconds. Then entered the room.

Shaun looked a lot better than I had expected. His colouring was almost back to the usual swarthy skin tone that fortune had bestowed upon him. There was only a bruised cheek and a stitch over one eyebrow. But judging by the bulk from under his hospital gown he was heavily bandaged. He had just started to open some cards that Jess had left with him, when he glanced up to see me. Surprise etched itself across his face. And then concern.

I sauntered up to the bed, arms folded. His eyes darted to the doorway.

"Don't worry," I jibed. "I saw her. I stayed back until she'd gone. Although these days there's hardly any reason for me not to meet her. Not like 'owt's been going on. But, still. Why would you want to change the habit of a lifetime, Shaun?"

A weak smile. Grateful, even.

"Nice to see you, Stan." He gestured to me to take a seat.

"So. Do you really wear pyjamas at home?" I grinned. "My, oh my, Shaun. What an image of domestic bliss I encountered just now."

I was quite enjoying this.

He screwed up his eyes and concentrated on the cards that he was opening. I let him fumble one-handed with them and on his third one, he did the Robert de Niro gurn and said;

"Well, Stan, got to say that you're looking a lot better than you were on Saturday. Your hair looked like you'd been dragged through a hedge backwards. Never seen you looking so rough."

"Cheers for that. But it was your blood that added to the overall roadkill-on-the-head effect. And it was a right bugger to wash it out, believe me. But never mind talking about aesthetics - get you! You've got to have over fifty-odd cards here."

Several large bowls of fruit and boxes of chocolates presided alongside a flurry of 'Get Well Soon' cards along the windowsill and on top of the crappy Formica unit next to his bed.

I suddenly realised that I hadn't brought anything with me. I apologised.

"Don't be stupid," he commented, yawning and thrusting his chin upwards - towards the fruit and cards and the various frivolities;

"Gesture politics. Bunch of hypocrites. Nearly all of this shite comes from people to do with work. The sorts who wouldn't exactly count themselves as my number one fans. In fact, half of them would've been quite happy if I'd ended up kicking the bucket on Saturday."

I sniffed and picked up a card from the bedside table. From Medlock Golf Club. 'Look forward to seeing you back on the Fairway soon!'

I shrugged.

"Oh, Shaun. So self-important. Even from your hospital bed, with a frigging gunshot wound. I mean, I hardly think that you register on most people's 'Top Ten of The Mildly Irritating Bastards That I Would Like to See Dead' list. Can't you simply accept that ninety-five per cent of folk are just... nice?"

I must have plucked at a rarely available heartstring, because his working arm jerked upwards towards me and he smiled, unexpectedly reaching over for my hand. My brain told my fingers to brush him away. But my instinct allowed him take it. His thumb began to rub up against my palm.

"Well, whatever you say, Stan. You always seem to think that you're the expert on humanity and interpersonal skills. But regardless of you being a know-it-all, I've got to say that I'm more than a bit glad that you're okay. I honestly thought... when we were coming back into the hall..."

He stopped for a moment and wiggled himself upwards in the bed, slightly short of breath.

"... When I saw you legging it into the other room with the kids. I thought that you'd have no chance. You're bloody mad, you are. I don't know anyone else mental enough to take that kind of risk."

He shut his eyes and gave his head a tiny shake. The room was so quiet that I could hear the number one – the sound of his stubble-cut – grating itself on the

281

back of the pillow. I dismissed the back-handed compliment and looked towards the window. The sky was ice-blue outside. It still wasn't quite winter yet, but it almost seemed like it was going to snow. His thumb had been stroking my palm in tiny, repetitive concentric motions. Now it stopped and began to sweep itself up and down. Up and down.

I moved my hand away, dipping it into my coat pocket and retrieving my phone. I pretended to check it as I commented;

"Bad about Councillor Casey, eh? Her poor family."

"Really bad. Bit of a shocker to us all. Gobsmacked at what happened to her. Can't get my head round it. Seriously bad. Bad stuff..."

Even Shaun was willing and able to feel the prickle of recoil and of horror – on that one. Or so it seemed.

"I mean…" he carried on, "I had this woman from that charity - Accident Aid - turn up here – just after nine AM this morning. She wanted to offer me counselling. Bleedin' counselling, for Christ's sake! Probably Roger, instructing Human Resources to wheel her out. He's a total and utter fuckwit. Knows I'm after his job once he retires. And he's obviously got an issue with that. God knows why."

I stood up a couple of cards that had fallen down on the table, but then realised that this was the kind of thing that Jess would do. So, I stopped. He carried on;

"I mean, I don't get why he might want me to have trauma-counselling or whatever they call it. He was never a big fan of Casey. I reckon he's just feeling threatened. Knows I'll be able to do his job standing on my head. Patronising me by sending some therapist along —"

"Or perhaps," I said, "It's not all about big boy game plans and strategies, Shaun. Perhaps, even a fuckwit like Roger might think that it could have been horrible for you to watch someone that you worked with, bleed to death in front of your own eyes."

Shaun seemed to catch my drift and looked away, towards the window and at the view stretching out towards leafy Cheshire, to all things successful and six-bedroom-detached. He bit his bottom lip. I wondered what he was thinking about. Perhaps an IRA bomb some forty-odd years ago. Of a little boy being orphaned in a split second. Of him developing an extra tough emotional shell in order to deal with the loss.

He was quiet for a minute. And then asked me how 'whatsername' was. I reached over to the jug at the side of his bed and poured him a glass of Vimto.

"Dawn's on the other side of the hospital here. Apparently, she's out of her coma now. But I don't know anything more than that. You saw… he very nearly killed her. Even without the help of bullets."

"I know. I've seen some shit on the estates in my time. But never anything like that."

I picked up a magazine that Jess had left on the chair next to the bed for him. It was 'Yorkshire Life,' and I wagged it at him;

"Did you know that Mason – Dawn's eldest - admitted that he shot Vinnie?"

This was news to Shaun.

"Blimey. He shot his own dad? Really? Shit. I was thinking that it must have been your Chiswick bloke that shot him. I couldn't exactly see much from where we were. But, God. His own dad?"

I nodded.

"But he wasn't his dad. His real dad, I mean. Vinnie was the father of the other two kids. But anyway. All the same."

Shaun looked me straight into the eyes. Unwaveringly. He held his gaze.

"Meladdo was alright though… Your minister pal. Not a bad job. Clearly made of the invincible stuff. Golden Boy. Luck of the Gods maybe…?"

I gave him a bleak smile;

"Yes, he does seem to be a bit like that, at the moment. Everything bouncing off him. But he assures me it's just a phase - that he gets enough of the crap the rest of the time."

Footsteps at the door announced the arrival of a male nurse - clipboard in hand, but instead of speaking to Shaun, he looked at me;

"Can I ask who you are? We don't have a note of your arrival at the nursing station."

I smiled. All friendly, like.

"That's because your colleagues were too busy gassing in order to pay me any attention."

He frowned. Annoyed at me for dobbing his medical chums in.

"Well, Mr Elliot is still under strict observation and we can only allow very close family members in to visit. So how might you be related?"

I grabbed hold of Shaun's hand.

"I *might* be his wife," I said. Smirking.

"But his wife just left…" the man looked befuddled. He stared at Shaun. "She, uhm. She asked us to do a double check on your meds… as you were mentioning the pain again."

I carried on gurning at the fella. I realised that I probably looked a bit manic. But right now, I was past caring about anything. The world had gone to hell in a handcart over the weekend and I was only an inch away from completely losing the plot.

Shaun was trying to let go of my hand. I wouldn't let him. His eyes wavered over to mine again. He was looking a tad bit unnerved. My nails dug into his skin.

"So… huhm," asked the nurse again. "Can I ask again, who you might…?"

I stopped smiling. I could feel my nostrils flare. Horsey Madam.

"I told you!" I snapped. "I *might* be his wife! A man can have more than one wife, you know! It's a cultural issue. An ethnic thing. I would have thought that someone who works for the NHS would have realised that it's quite offensive to challenge other people's traditions in terms of societal 'norms' – with regards to relationships."

I felt Shaun cringe. Ha. I jerked my chin towards the big lug in the hospital bed and heard my voice deliver a rather impressive baritone as I held the copy of 'Yorkshire Life' out to him.

"… And although he might *live in* Manchester – he's actually from Yorkshire. Yorkshire is a nation unto itself in terms of customs and unusual practices. I mean… have you never heard of places like Hebden Bridge? We do things a bit differently there. Surely you… know about Hebden Bridge?"

Shaun emitted a guttural groan. Until this point, he had been trying his best at a bit of bravado-male eye contact with the chap - which, to be honest – he had never been much cop at with his peer group anyway - and then he surrendered, coming out with;

"Look, mate – just give us ten minutes, alright? It's all a bit complicated."

The nurse gawped at me – lady with the freaky grin, refusing to let go of Shaun's fingers. He noted the other bloke's acquiescence and he finally got the picture. He scribbled something onto the patient's medical chart – probably something about upping the levels of morphine and tailing-off on the number of wives.

And then he left us to it.

CHAPTER 35

I let go of his hand. Feeling ever-so light headed. Bit of a giddy-kipper.

"Hey, Shaun. That's a first! First time *ever* that you've had to panic over being caught out for something that you *weren't* actually up to…" I walked to the window, taking in the skyline of the more marketable side of suburban Manchester.

"What the hell did you talk about… wives and that for? That was just stupid."

I chuckled and moved closer to the window. Nose touching the cool glass. Making puffs of steam as I exhaled.

"Yeah, well. You know me and authority. The minute they impose all of these ridiculous rules about relatives-only and visiting hours. It just gets my back up. And anyway, if people like me didn't fiddle around with the regulations – people like *you* would only have Jess as a visitor. Because your only other relative is Ozzy the Cat. And he'd be far too germy and furry to be allowed into the building."

"Cheers, Stan. Just rub it in, why don't you? We can't all have hordes of interfering barmy blood-relatives from Stalybridge marauding through our lives."

Fair enough. It wasn't his fault that both sets of his natural and adopted parents were dead. I might be getting better at tackling Shaun head-on these days, but I wasn't one for sticking the knife in and giving it a good twist. So, I changed the subject and asked when he expected to be back at work;

"I've been working this morning. Emails from my phone. Picking up stuff that Roger should have done. Jesus, yeah, it really is a pain that I won't have Casey batting for my side anymore."

One-track mind, or what?

"Yes. How very inconsiderate of her. Getting killed off before she could fix up the new chief executive's terms and conditions for you."

He seemed to take the point, as there was silence for a few seconds. And then he said;

"Actually, Stan. There is something that I need to tell you. I wasn't going to say anything, but… honesty being the best policy and all of that. And given the visit that I've already had from DI Dave and his pal… who tell me that there's going to be an IPCC investigation."

I turned away from the window and tapped my fingers against my elbows. He continued;

"The reporter involved in it all. Erin Mayo. She works as northern correspondent for News of the Nation too. Sort of an assistant to that big-shot celeb journalist - that Simone Shaw."

"Yeah, I know," I replied. "And I can't believe that they found out about the launch. I wouldn't have invited them over my dead body. 'Scuse the pun."

He just looked at me. Through me.

Penny dropping moment.

"Shaun? Shit. No way. No way! You mean to tell me … that *you* got them to come along to the event? Fed them some titbits! That *you* told them about Michael being a VIP guest there and did it to – what? Embarrass him?"

He shifted uncomfortably. Reached for his glass of Vimto. Said nothing.

"Well. You know, Stan. You know what was going on between our lot and the government. What *is* going on I mean. Over the budget cuts."

"Frigging hell, Shaun! So, this was all – your doing? You were the one who… yes, I remember now! You pissed off to the back of the hall when we were stood with Kath Casey for the photos… *You got them into the sodding building, didn't you?*"

"Yes. Your receptionist let them through when I instructed her to. And I'm not ashamed of that. I've got to look out for the best interests of my patch. And if your Mr Chiswick is playing silly buggers with us and cutting the revenue flow. Well. Why shouldn't we play the game the proper way? Invite his adversaries along to cause a bit of bother. Just stirring it. Nowt major!"

I was stewing. Steaming. I ranted. I raved for about five minutes and then ended it with;

"I can't believe that you'd stoop so low! Don't you see what you did? Because of all the hassle with getting Erin and her cameraman into the building - the police reckon this is how Vinnie sneaked in, behind them both!"

Shaun shrugged. Gifted at nonplussed dismissal. He even had the gall to blame the police and Michael Chiswick's team for not being 'competent enough' in their jobs.

He put the glass down and reached for a handful of grapes. Managed to toss two into his mouth.

"And actually," he chewed and swallowed, pointing a finger at me. "Don't be thinking that your man Chiswick's some great big hero. Easy for him to swan about all macho-like when he's wearing a bullet-proof vest. Some of us don't get issued with that kind of protection when we work for a local authority." He lobbed another grape into his mouth.

"… I was bloody lucky that the bullet wasn't just a couple of inches lower, the doctors said. And meanwhile, your fella knows damned well that he's padded up in comparison to us other muppets in the hall. Bet you never thought to check out whether his undies are Kevlar-laminated, did you?"

He removed a pip from his lips and pinged it onto the hospital floor.

No, though. I hadn't noticed a bullet-proof vest hanging about the boudoir on Saturday night. I had been more than a little bit preoccupied.

But his seeds of doubt had been duly sown, so I flared up again – this time with an added dose of defensiveness.

"Just *listen* to you, Shaun! *Look* at you! I came here today – wanting to see for myself that you're okay. Because I do give a shit about you. And fuck knows why, now that …"

I was simmering, my face was on fire. I turned round and stalked out of the room, hearing him calling after me;

"Hey – hold your horses, Stan!"

I strode past the nurses' station and yelled over my shoulder;

"Just fuck off, you fucking imbecile!"

There were no nurses at the desks right now and I was glad of this; no-one to see me shrieking obscenities down the passageway like some sort of Mancunian fishwife. But then the exit door into the main hospital corridor wouldn't open. So, I shouted a string of curses aimed at the inconvenience of security doors and the failings of the NHS in general and received a thumbs-up from a chap who had his leg in traction on one of the beds in another side room. I could hear Shaun still calling me from his hospital bed and then a buzzer sounded. Seconds later, the same male nurse scurried over to me and asked me to keep the noise down and to go back into the room to make 'peace with your husband, who seems rather agitated and is asking for you.'

So, I flounced back into the room, all-intent on giving Shaun a snarl and the one-fingered salute. But I saw that he was holding up his hand in a gesture of surrender. It unnerved me then – just as it did before in the hall on Saturday when faced with Vinnie and the gun.

"Just let me say this," he spoke quietly. "Have you not had a phone call this morning? Or an email?"

I clicked my tongue. I would give him the benefit of a few seconds. Nothing more.

"Yes. I've had a million. And I've hardly had a second to —"

"Well, as I said to you before – I've had a fair few phone calls myself this morning. And one of them – first thing after nine AM… was asking for me to provide a reference. For you."

I pushed the door back, closing it again. Nosey nurses now back at the station were trying to earwig the Hebden Bridge threesome family dispute.

"What the hell are you on about? I've not applied for any jobs. And even if I had. *You'd* be the last person I'd put down for a referee, anyway."

Shaun threw out a strikingly good impression of Lydia's 'God, Mum - you're thick' face at me.

"No. Get with the picture. Not a reference for you, personally. One for Sisters' Space. A reference for a funding bid. Some application that you made a bit back – one which ended up getting rejected. The Ellen Elevation Foundation or something."

"Yeah?" I remembered that. "The bastards said that our budget projections hadn't been robust enough. It's always the same these days; you can't even get it past their bloody desk officers. Kids aged about thirteen or something – making decisions - no experience of life – and your entire service is in the hands of some wet behind the ears, little brown-nosing…"

"Well, don't be dissing them now. Seems that you've been successful. Seems that they've reconsidered their original rejection of the women's centre. "

"What?"

I stopped my gob. And then my mouth dropped open. Guppy face. Shaun mirrored it with a broad smile.

"Yep. They called me. Wanted to run it past me. Whether I thought that Sisters' Space was fit for purpose enough. Did I approve of this grant that they've now decided that they want to furnish you with."

"Bloody hell. I mean… Really? Seriously? What…? How much would it be for? I can't even remember what I asked them for. It was ages ago."

I had been trying to clutch at so many funding-straws recently. Trying to keep so many different balls in the air that I had no idea what we had requested.

Shaun looked at his phone.

"Hang on. Hang on…they emailed me your original application form. It was for… yeah. It was for six hundred and fifty thousand. Over three years. Which they wanted to agree to."

"Shit. No way."

"Yes-way, Stan. And whilst you might not run as tight a ship as I would be doing if I was in your position, I wasn't going to begrudge you the dosh. I won't say anything negative. I mean – sure, I *did* say that you might want to sort out your 'let's have a little gun siege this weekend' tendencies but…"

I shook my head.

"But what about that… everything on Saturday. When they find out what happened to us?"

Shaun did the thicko-face again and then smiled secretively. I hated that expression of his. He looked at his phone again and tried to sit upright a bit more. Grimaced at the pain.

"Oh, come on. The entire country knows about it all. And that's the bizarre thing about it. Apparently, the siege is exactly the reason behind why they've changed their mind and want to fund you now. The Foundation's money comes from this mega-rich woman called Ellen – one of those founders who likes to get too involved in doling out the dosh."

"Yeah. Ellen Evelyn. She's pretty well known in the domestic violence campaigning circles."

"Well, I'd never heard of the old mare. Anyway. Turns out that she saw the news and remembered that she'd liked your application and that you'd only just fallen short of getting through. She actually called me up herself."

"Kidding!"

"Sadly not. Started telling me her life story and why she has a passion for campaigning against domestic abuse. I had to switch the TV on half-way through. She didn't half go on. Ex-husband from Tobago who used to make her stand naked in the gardens of her stately home whilst he fired a bow and arrow at her. God, it was boring - before she'd even got onto the bit about the pony and trap…"

But the rest of his words were lost on me. A heady concoction of shock and relief was pulsing through my veins. Now I wouldn't have to rely on the New Banks loan. Now I could finally focus on the centre itself, rather than spending all my time completing doomed funding applications. Now…

I turned back to Shaun as he spoke;

"And it must have helped - that this Ellen woman actually spoke to one of the 'victims' involved. I played up the old gunshot wound here. And then said that you desperately needed the money. That if anything can prevent this kind of stuff happening in the future – men being violent towards women in our male-dominated culture yah-di-yah - that it's the Sisters' Spaces of this world that can make all the difference. I'm not going to do the dirty on you for half a million, am I?"

The gobsmacked moment was over. Done and dusted with. I was now so elated that I clapped my hands together and did a little victory tap-dance. Shaun shook his head but was beaming at me.

"So, Stan. You don't have to rely on anyone now, do you? Not us lot at the council. Not Martyn Pointer and his little loan."

"Yeah. Not that you and Martyn ever had a schoolboy rivalry thing going on there…"

"He's the one with the problem. Like I always say – Short Man Syndrome."

Elation took over. I dashed over to his bed and grabbed his face in both hands, kissing him hard on the lips;

"You may be a total nobsack most of the time, but you're truly wonderful!" I exclaimed, kissing him again.

Just as Jess walked back into the room, singing out;

"Got halfway down Buxton Road, sweetie - and then I realised! I've forgotten…"

She stopped. A look of abject horror on her face.

"… Your dirty laundry."

For the second time in two days, my brain flashed into overdrive, causing me to act without thinking. Jess was standing there in the doorway, staring at us. Looking as if her entire world had suddenly come crashing down about her ears.

But I seized the day – and the wife - rushing towards her, grabbing her in a huge bear hug and gabbling at her;

"Your husband is the most wonderful man in the world! I hope that you realise how lucky you are!"

And then I gave her a huge kiss on the lips too. Followed by a shriek of;

"Got to go! I've got *so* many desperate women to cheer up!"

And with that, I dashed out of the room.

Later, over the phone, Shaun told me that any other woman in the world wouldn't have known how to have dealt with the situation so quickly, so effectively. But not me. Apparently, I am the best person ever - to have had an affair with - because my behaviour can be so ridiculous and "so off the wall' that I can convince most innocent bystanders that I have some sort of a serious mental problem.

"Perhaps I do," I shot back at him, "Because I got involved with the likes of you."

At any rate, Shaun told me that Jess had instantly believed my story, as presented to her – that her husband had truly saved the day. Which wasn't actually a story – it was the God's honest truth. Or at least, how I was feeling about things at that particular moment in time.

Shaun had added more convincing details for his wife; explaining to her that everyone at Medlock Council was aware that I had been 'on the edge' for some time – ever since Sisters' Space had been faced with the council axing our funding. And that the siege was looking to be the last straw, nudging poor Rachael Russell's sanity to finally crack. He had told Jess that he had asked me to come to the hospital, so that he could break the news to me about the grant that had just been awarded to the women's centre. That he had hoped that this would somehow prevent me from "going off the rails completely." But that after the way I had behaved in his hospital room, he was now going to have a discreet chat with Sisters' Space's chairperson with regards to the delicate issue of Rachael's mental health and wellbeing. I clearly a lady in need of a lot of help.

Jess bought his story one hundred per cent. She had heard my name in the past – mainly in relation to Adam's death. So, she already had me down for tea and sympathy; perhaps even a prayer or two or maybe the odd Hail Mary, at the time of the accident.

So, Shaun was all chipper about this. Didn't even have the grace to temper his words;

"Yeah. She thinks you're a right loonytune now. Feels right sorry for you."

"Cheers for that, Shaun."

After the unexpected encounter with Jess, I was feeling more than a tad bit shaky, but I managed to make it to the opposite side of the hospital, to the intensive care unit. I told the nurses on duty that I was one of Dawn's sisters, so I was permitted to spend a few minutes at her bedside. And it wasn't a complete fib – I mean, we're all sisters at Sisters' Space – aren't we?

Dawn looked ghastly – the parts of her upper body which were exposed and not wreathed in plaster were pockmarked with indigo-yellow bruises. I had to steel my reaction when I saw what Vinnie had done to her previously pretty face, because she was still virtually unrecognisable. The nursing staff told me that she had suffered a broken jaw, cheekbones, nose and even an eye socket. But according to them, she had already turned the all-important corner; she was conscious. And she immediately recognised my voice, heard me dropping my backside down on the plastic chair next to the bed. She managed to open one of her eyes wide, attempting a lopsided smile. A couple of her teeth had been knocked out too. She gestured at all the tubes that were weaving between her body and the various machines, and she rolled her eye at me, mouthing;

"Cah t wai t'geh ouh heh!"

I told her to take it easy, that I would check in on the kids who were staying with her mother. She nodded. I didn't want to assume that she already knew about Vinnie's death. She had been completely unconscious at the time that he had been killed. But she slurred to me;

"They tol' me. Bou' Vin."

I nodded. Her one-opened eye looked flat. Hard.

I tried to shake away the urge to talk – about everything that had happened. To talk away how she must be feeling. Or of how the rest of the family might be dealing with it all. And it certainly wasn't my place to tell her about her own son's involvement. That would have to come later, from the police. But I did ask;

"Have they pushed you for your statement yet?"

She tried to shake her head, saying;

"Lay-keh."

"Yes, later. Be firm on that one with the police, Dawn. Not until you can speak properly."

I held her hand and squeezed it. A muffled;

"Shtil owim furnappish".

I frowned and then suddenly realised who she was talking about. Michael – and the nappies that he had bought for Poppy-Rose when we had rescued her from yet another beating, that first time we had all me, over on Brindleford. I told her;

"Ha. You don't owe him anything. He can afford it, Dawn. Don't believe all the crap those politicians claim about not being paid enough!"

She smiled with her good eye. I carried on;

"You're a tough lady. They're going to fix you up properly. It won't take them long. You'll be back to normal before you know it."

She nodded, trying to smile. I continued;

"And there's going to be no more of this now. I know it was the worst possible way to end something. But you've got your own – new – life. And the kids to think of now. I promise that it's going to be nicer… bedlam in Dawn Hibbert's household now. Okay?"

She nodded again. I noticed a tear running out of the corner of her eye. I grabbed a tissue and wiped it away for her. And I did the same with my own eyes, as they appeared to be leaking too. Then Dawn tried to say something to me. I asked her to repeat herself.

"Ger y'own tissue. Muckeh buggah!"

CHAPTER 36

I had already had a quick scan at the Foundation's email on my phone whilst sitting in my car, but back at the centre I thudded down at my desk for a proper read of it on the laptop. It was just as Shaun had said. Six hundred and fifty thousand. On condition that I tinkered with the budget and updated it to include 'damage to the women's centre caused by violent attack.'

I duly tinkered. As I tarted about with the spreadsheet, my phone buzzed. It was Martyn Pointer. He also knew about the offer of the grant and he was sounding somewhat jaded. I couldn't tell whether he was being his usual un-emoting self, whether he was irritated by the fact that we had been offered over half a million and would no longer need the support of his social enterprise loan, or whether he had a cob-on because he still felt crappy because of the shingles. So, I said;

"Anyway, Martyn, you shouldn't be calling me. You're supposed to be ill."

"I am. I feel lousy. I'm calling you from my sickbed. Marianne's banished me to the spare room. But I'm still trying to keep my hand in with the emails."

What is it with these people and their all-consuming careers?

"So how did you hear the news about the funding?"

"Ah. Shaun Elliot managed to drop it into a cryptic little email from his P.A. Issuing her with commands from Manchester Royal Infirmary, no doubt."

"I'm so sorry, Martyn, I really didn't mean for this to happen."

"What on earth are you apologising for, Rachael?"

"Well. I thought that you might be pissed off after all the trouble that you've gone to. All of the work that you lot at New Banks did, getting us the bleeding loan…"

"Don't be silly. I'm delighted that you've been awarded this. It's really difficult to get any kind of grant these days – let alone something as big as this one! Much, much better for you than a loan – in the long run."

"God, I'm so frigging glad to hear you saying that! If I were in your position, I'd be well fucked-off as…"

Yet again I had to stomp on the verbal brakes far too late. What is it about me and cursing around Jehovah's Witnesses? I'm never like this around Muslims or Sikhs.

Martyn did his best to disregard my profanities.

"But as always, I'm not best pleased at the way Shaun Elliot goes about things. He couldn't resist dropping the news in on me, whilst he's meant to be on sick leave and whilst I'm out of the action with the shingles. I had really hoped that having a near-death experience might have shown him the error of his ways. You know, perhaps have turned him onto a different path."

I wanted to say 'Sorry, Martyn, but you won't be seeing Shaun Elliot down the Kingdom Hall anytime soon. Unless you have a new recruitment idea that involves offering sinners test drives of the latest Lexus model.' But instead I said;

"Sadly, not. Leopards. And spots."

"Hmm. Quite."

I hung up as I saw Bev storming into my office. The police's deep cleaning team had mopped up the worst of the mess in the hall and we were now allowed back into it. But Bev's face was like thunder.

"Don't be looking at me like that," I said. "Promise I'll be with you all in a just a minute, to help finish off with the clearing up."

She lobbed a plastic bag onto my desk. Curled her lip.

"What's that?" I asked.

"Brenda. Her what owns 'Brenda's Big Baps' round the corner. She's just been in. Made a load of butties up for us. Said they were on the house. 'Cause she felt awful for us all – said she can't get over what 'appened here on Saturday."

"Really? Oh, bless. That's so sweet!"

Bev shook her bushy barnet at me;

"Well, it would have been if there were 'owt that I fancied. I mean – it's like these days – even your scruffy sarnie shops like hers… think that doing your bog-standard cheese butty is beneath them."

"Well, I for one am grateful," I replied. "And it's come just in the nick time. I'm ruddy starving." Brenda had written on the paper bag 'warm chilli chicken'. I ripped it open and bit into the sandwich. "Lush," I said, smearing half of the concoction down my chin, "So you - with your boring cheese preferences - will just have to go hungry then, Miss Fussy Pants."

Bev tutted and turned on her heel. I was all ready to enjoy my second mouthful, until she called over her shoulder "Well, enjoy your menstruation on a muffin, then. You look like you've just wiped a used sanitary towel all over yer face."

At least some things at Sisters' Space would never change.

Ten minutes later and we were all busying ourselves in the – now - blood-and-bodily-fluids free Sisters' Space hall. Gemma trundled over to me as the final remnants of rubbish and stampede-deposited items were collected and catalogued for our lost property box. I recognised the child's scooter that she was dragging behind her.

The sight of this abandoned child's toy gave my heart a momentary squeeze. It was too symbolic of Mason - of his existential journey to date. From annoying little kid with relatively low life chances anyway, due to class and accident of birth - to a pre-pubescent killer. And all of this in the space of a few minutes, on a November Saturday afternoon at Medlock's Sisters' Space.

Gemma prodded me out of my melancholy, twisting the corner of her mouth as she tried to keep her voice low.

"I've just seen this scooter and wanted to get it into the lost property before Dee clocked it. Not being a grass, like, but there were a right nice – like, proper fake Prada handbag - what someone had dropped at the other end of the hall. Where Dee were supposed to be cleanin'. An' no one's seen it since."

I took it from her and asked her to rally the troops. I was calling a quick meeting of all the women who had turned up to help with the clean-up operations. Gill, Marsha and two other paid members of staff had arrived - as was normal for that time on a Monday. But in addition to the employees of Sisters' Space, today we had far more women than usual, milling about the centre. Maybe Gemma had been right about the sense of solidarity, of loyalty at this place.

Although perhaps not, in terms of all the service users. Before Gemma had showed me the scooter, I had already noted that rather magpie-esque gleam in Dee's eye. I had seen her cast a quick scout about; to see if anyone was looking - and had witnessed her stuffing some unidentifiable object or another down the elasticated front of her jeggings.

Eighteen women squashed themselves into our small meeting room. I thanked them for their help in cleaning up the place, informed them how Dawn was doing – and then finally moved on to providing them with the news about the funding. Until that point, the collective body language had been pretty wretched. Slouches, folded arms, hunched shoulders, the odd sigh and the irritating twiddling of piercings (Jade). But when I spilled the beans, the combined reaction was like I had doled out speed to them; plenty of whoops, Gill punching the air and Dee giving it;

"Bleedin' hell. Who'd a-thought it? You get people killed and then someone gives you more than half a million. Who else finks that Rachael must work for the Mafia, eh?"

After Bev had told her to shut the fuck up and Gill had managed to prevent Dee from answering Bev back with a Glasgow Kiss, the questions began to flow. Even though I had anticipated that the announcement might have taken the edge off our collective dejection, dampened down the doom, gloom and the despair – I really had not expected such jubilation and positivity. The overwhelming consensus was this; that Sisters' Space should Carry On As Was. That it would be crazy not to open the café and the shop the next day. That it would be sending out all the wrong signals if we stayed closed. I was even more surprised when

Kirsty, oh-so-painfully shy Kirsty, piped up with;

"Why don't we make the most out of all of those rubber-neckers hanging around outside? You know – the journalists and that… who're wanting to have a nosey at where The Medlock Massacre took place. Can't believe that they're calling it that!"

Bev glowered. "Bloody tabloids. Bloody massacre? All that happened was some bastard who deserved it ended up getting' shot. And some crappy local politician who no-one liked much anyway… met her maker a bit sooner than she were bankin' on."

Gill winced.

"Jeez, Bev. That's a bit harsh. And I mean… what about Dawn?"

Bev was unrepentant. "True. Shit stuff for Dawn. Big time. But even that's got a good side. She's finally gotten rid of that fucker, Vinnie Murray."

"Anyway," said Shirley, primly "Whatever people think about comeuppance, I think that Kirsty's right. There's about a dozen people palming around outside. I bet they'd like a decent brew. And – yes - every cloud does have a silver lining - think of all the free PR that we've had. Half of Britain knows about Charlene's Chocolate Factory and Café now."

Jade took up the idea with gusto, "Yeah! They must be freezin' their tits off outside. Come on. Let's make money out of the sicko bastards!"

I wasn't sure of the ethics behind it all, or whether indeed the idea of sipping cappuccinos amidst a recent murder scene would appeal to the average shopper in Medlock. But what was life without risk? Why play the victim? Why not start to act like the social enterprise we were trying to become? Beat the capitalists at their own game.

Our meeting was interrupted by the arrival of Dawn's mother. I nipped outside, to hand Mason's scooter over to her, to tell her about my visit to see her daughter and ask her thoughts about us opening the café and shop. She pursed coral pink-painted lips and commented;

"Well, Dawn would agree with you all. Get the frig on with it, that's what she'd say. If that fucker hadn't mashed her in, like he did."

Her mum had left the three grandchildren with a friend, saying that she had felt that it would be too traumatic to bring the kids back to the centre. Although I did notice that she was decked up to the nines in her bling and that her young squeeze - 'Giovanni' - was sitting outside in his BMW. Apparently, they were off to the cinema at Salford Docks and then heading for dinner at the Brewer's Quay.

I asked her how Mason was;

"Dunno really," she said. "He's never been one for sayin' much, has our Mason. They're givin' him counsellin'. Social services or whoever. He won't tell me nothin' of what happened on Saturday, so apart from what the telly's said - I've no idea. Other than, that fucker is dead. An' fuckin' good riddance too - is what I say. One of these days it would have been me shootin' the bastard, for the way that he always treated our Dawn."

"Well, I can understand you feeling like that," I replied. "Course I can. But… he was still the kids' father, wasn't' he? West and Poppy-Rose, I mean."

Her eyes flashed contempt.

"He were never a fuckin' father to no-one. World's a better place without that fucker."

I wondered whether her hatred for Vinnie would be less vehement if she – when she – learned that her grandson had pulled the trigger.

No. Probably not.

With only half an hour to go before I needed to leave and collect my own children, my mobile rang. It was Michael on his 'unknown' number again; I was beginning to recognise the digits from the SIM card that he used. I answered with a laugh;

"Hey… is that my man of international mystery?"

"Ah yes. Something like that. How have things been today – you and your lot at Sisters' Space?"

I gave him a cursory outline of the day's events. His voice stiffened when I mentioned the visit to see Shaun. And then I had to hold the phone away from my ear when I told him that Shaun had admitted responsibility for the appearance of Simone Shaw's media cronies.

I agreed with him that he had behaved like a, "total and utter first-class shit," but told him that Shaun had redeemed himself somewhat in my eyes – thanks to his support for the new grant. Michael sounded jubilant at the news and told me;

"Really and truly, Rachael – it's so thoroughly well-deserved. For all of you. But all the same – you simply mustn't go giving Shaun Elliot any of the credit for this. I mean - did he spend weeks of his own time, writing the funding application for you?"

"Well… no."

"And didn't he have plans to close Sisters' Space down only a few weeks ago?"

"Er yes… but his take on it was that it was all the fault of your government and your austerity cuts."

"Well, of course it would be. But let's get this straight. Cut to the chase. All that he's done, is to tell a very nice group of people – who seem to be quite determined to give you nearly half a million anyway – that Rachael Russell and Sisters' Space aren't complete incompetent idiots."

"Well… yes. I guess —"

"And so, there's no two ways about it, Rachael. The man is a brilliant manipulator. A master of his own small-fry in Medlock and Mancunian political games. Someone as smart as you – falling for that sort of rubbish? He does nothing at all to help the survival of your women's centre – no – he actually tries to make life more difficult for you – and doubly difficult for me – and yet you still want to thank him."

"I didn't say that… I said…"

"Alright, then. You said that he's redeemed himself somewhat. Which quite frankly, Rachael - is utter codswallop."

I was silent for a moment, drinking it all in. Michael was right. Was absolutely right. But there was one element that he had not included in his analysis.

The Shaun and Rachael factor. The unseen thread that always seemed to snake its way back into my life, no matter how many years had passed. Or how many times I had felt sure that I had sworn myself off any level of involvement with him 'this time'.

And then Michael said, "But anyway. Let's change the subject. I've also got some interesting news myself. I've just come out of a meeting with the PM and Deputy PM. Alex The Twat and Max have been doing a sterling job of spinning the events of Saturday into a 'Bold and Brave Minister' story for me. PM's green with envy, actually. I can tell."

"Big head."

"And the latest is all very confidential of course. So, keep this under wraps. There's a bit of a cabinet reshuffle coming up. PM wants me to swap portfolios. With Spencer Greaves."

"Isn't he the health minister?"

"No, silly. That's Bob Porteus. Honestly, you've really taken your eye off the ball with cabinet positions, haven't you?"

"I do try to keep abreast of it all, Michael, but Scooby Doo monopolises my TV at home. And at work, I'm a little bit too busy dealing with women who've had seven shades of shit kicked out of them."

"I'm sure. But anyway. It's the defence post! Ministry of Defence. So, what do you think of that then? Rather up my street, don't you think?"

Although I wanted to leap into a gushing, congratulatory verbal repost, all that my mind could conjure up was an image of Lydia. Of my eldest seizing a water pistol from a naked Matthew in the paddling pool last summer;

"Matthew Russell – we hate guns in this house! And if you ever join the army, both me and Mummy will kill you! You'll be as dead as a dormouse!"

But I managed to provide him with a verbal pat on the back. His voice softened;

"Do you really mean that? I mean, the words that we had the other night when you heard about my past military exploits… you were clearly *not* too enamoured with that side of things. So, I've got to say that I *have* been wondering whether me becoming Secretary of State for Defence… would be very problematic for you."

Gee no, Michael. How could it possibly bother me? A person who – until recently, when I couldn't afford the direct debit any longer – happened to be a card-carrying member of CND. How could I possibly not be delighted to be dating the man in the government who I always used to refer to as 'Dr Death?'

I lied. And reassured him. I mean, after all, he was a good man – now in a bad job, for sure – but, hey. Better than Shaun being given the post, I thought.

"So, all this stuff about needing to keep your career in the SAS under wraps," I said. "Won't that get a bit blown out of the water? Now that you'll be tampering with Trident and you'll have bigger fish to fry than funding streams for old folk's homes. I mean, the media are going to go over your CV in painstaking detail. They're going to find out exactly what you did in the military."

"True. It seems rather pointless to try and pretend otherwise, these days."

"Plus, I never really understood why it needed to remain secret about your previous stuff with the SAS. I mean, there's already precedents in government. Paddy Ashdown was also the Milk Tray man, wasn't he?"

Michael laughed and answered;

"True. But Paddy was more of your light-touch brigade. I'd – we'd – rather that the public don't know of the very specific kind of operations that I was involved with."

"Like?"

"Oh, that's a chat for another day," he rushed on. "But I'm really looking forward to a new post. And I've been thinking. I'm going to set up a new working group – to create some sort of an early-warning system for cases like Vinnie. Get them the help that they need, with issues such as PTSD. Before they end up cracking."

I sighed.

"Sorry, Michael – but my sympathies might run a little bit thin on that side of things. Your time might be better spent on trying to figure out why such psychotic freaks are attracted to the army in the first place. Maybe you can start with yourself."

"Oh, most amusing. But seriously. I'm glad that you're okay about it. Because it actually makes things easier for both of us now."

He paused and then continued;

"Here at the Ministry – at Communities, I mean - we've got a few new posts coming up. Created as a direct response to what happened on Saturday. Three new advisors on Domestic Violence and The Family. We all feel that the government hasn't been taking the issue as seriously as it should have been."

"Well, that's true enough."

"And, Rachael it was suggested – given your previous background as an advisor to Whitehall – and what you do now. And deal with - so well. That one of the jobs – a Tsar's role in effect – might have your name on it."

I was stunned.

And then I was cynical.

"Are you taking the piss? If so – that's not very funny."

"No. Not at all."

"Right," I did my best not to sound sarcastic; "So… are you offering me a job?"

"No. I'm not offering it to you. I'm about to move government departments, remember? And anyway. It wasn't me as such who flagged you up. It was actually the PM who suggested your name, to begin with."

I brayed like a donkey.

"You have got to be kidding! Oh now; don't tell me. Another one of his publicity stunts. Or is the use of my name, of association with Sisters' Space, another way of him going about with his damage reduction techniques?"

Michael dismissed me;

"No. He got a few people to ask around about you. Apparently. This was even before he asked me what I thought of 'this Rachael girl doing the job.' You do happen to have a good reputation from your previous work with government, you know!"

My head was buzzing. My heart was giving Skippy the Bush Kangaroo a run for his money. But I still couldn't seem to stop my gob from trotting out;

"Huh. Like the 'girl' bit. Charming."

"Oh, he doesn't mean to be offensive. Of the old school, the PM is. So why don't you just go… well, go… and think about it. We can talk over the details later tonight. Or on Friday when I come back up north."

"But, Michael, we're – on a roll with the café and Chocolatiers now. And this new funding that we've just been granted… I couldn't possibly consider…"

"Of course you can, Rachael. There are plenty of other good women who can run Sisters' Space. No one is indispensable. I told the PM and the civil servants that I thought you'd be excellent. Don't you want to change things for women at the very centre of things? Get your teeth into the bigger picture? Like you did previously – but with far more power to be able to influence things?"

"Of course, but I'm… And wouldn't this be a London-based post?"

"Well, yes. But the salary is a bloody good one. Fixed term contract of two years. You could talk 'secondment' with Sisters' Space or something. And I'm sure that you and Lydia and Matthew could bunk up with me until you find a place… or decide to stay indefinitely… or something."

To this, the only words that I could manage to dredge up were;

"But Michael, I hate London. I really do. I hate all cities. But especially London."

Straight back at me;

"Ah yes. But you don't hate me, do you? I think that you have a propensity to not-hate me. As I do to you… to not-hate you."

My brain felt like treacle. My thought processes; the speed of neuron-transmitter thingies had suddenly been afflicted with sludge in the works. He wheeled on, cheerfully;

"Come on, Rachael. This is a once-in-a-lifetime opportunity. A job that'll get you fixing up a botched system for all your oppressed women, everywhere. The offer of me and my home. Access to some fantastic schooling for the children. Appallingly bad musicals on tap for Lydia. Horseguard Parade for Matthew. And a high-speed rail link back up north, anytime you feel like seeing the folks."

"You're really —"

"Plus – your sister is here already."

"Oh, God. This is all just too big, Michael."

"Look. I have to go now. Promise me that you'll think about it. Yes?"

I promised him. I blew him a London Luvvie 'Mwah' down the phone and then I hung up and stared across at the scrubby and faded playground equipment opposite my office. The yellow police cordon tape was flapping a farewell in the wind.

Swings and roundabouts.

A man who had stuck his neck out for me, both professionally and personally. Who thought that I possessed enough talent and ability to help women across the country; as opposed to just propping up those living on my home turf.

A man who felt a healthy disregard for anything under the age of sixteen and yet who was willing to fling open his very un-Marmite besmeared Bloomsbury front door.

A man who hadn't exactly told me that he loved me yet. But who – to all intents and purposes – was acting more and more like a love-struck big Jessie. As my dad would have said.

Swings and roundabouts.

There was a knock at the door. Kirsty tiptoed in, carrying an enormous bunch of red and yellow roses.

"For you – lucky thing! I've never, ever had flowers bought for me. Ever." But she didn't sound jealous or jaded. Just pleased for me. She shot me a quick smile and then left the room.

I opened the card. It said;

'Stan. You know I don't do the L-word. But after this weekend, I will. Blame the morphine, maybe. Whatever. Love always. S.

PS – did you ask him about the vest...?'

A man who knows every trick in the book.

Or rather, two men – who both seem to be pretty savvy at doing that kind of thing.

And a third fella – no longer operating in this stratosphere; father of my children - who would no doubt be egging me on to embrace the risk and the sheer edginess of all of this.

Time to play the blokes at their own game.

To hell with the northern prejudices for once.

We're off to London. Me n' Mine.

74863384R00187

Made in the USA
Columbia, SC
11 August 2017